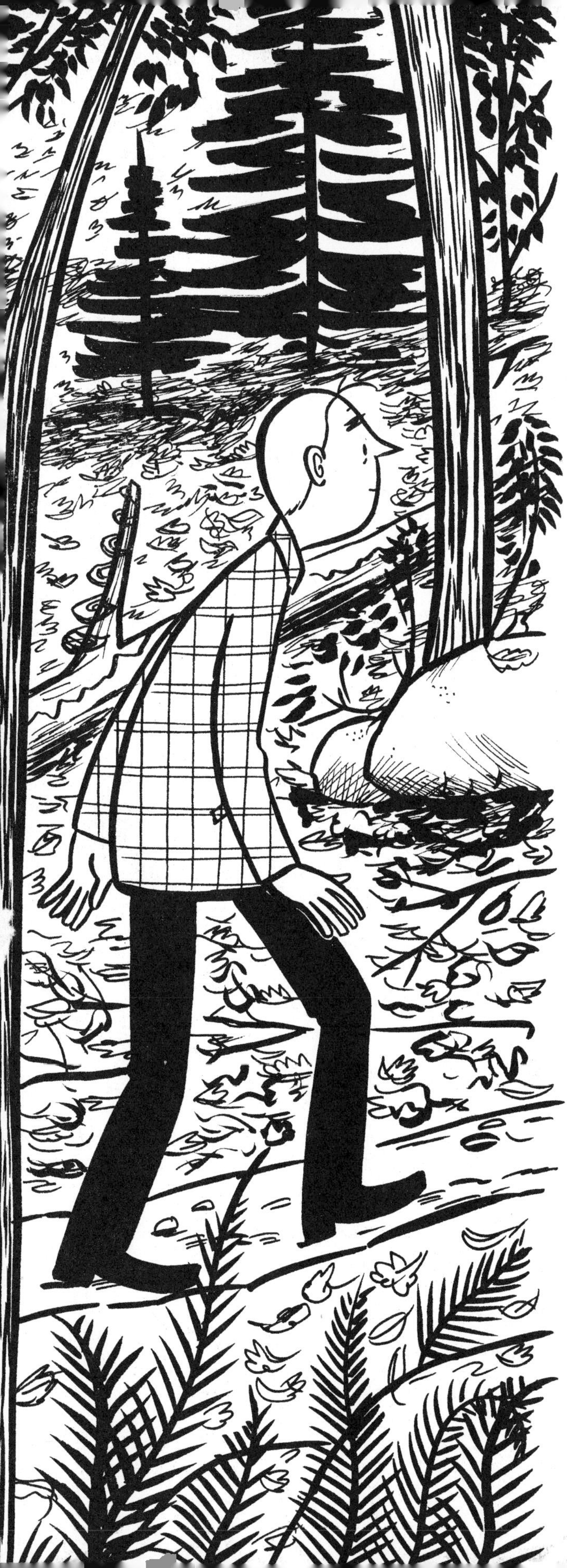

The song of Roland

To Louisette

You live your life as if it's real,
A thousand kisses deep.

— Leonard Cohen

The Song of Roland
© Michel Rabagliati, 2012

Originally published as *Paul à Québec* by Les Éditions de la Pastèque, 2009

Translation by Helge Dascher. With special thanks to Dag Dascher.
Thanks also to Kate Battle, Karen Houle and Steve Louis.

Editorial assistance by Rupert Bottenberg
Production assistance by Tracy Hurren
BDANG logo by Billy Mavreas
BDANG Imprint edited by Andy Brown

Library and Archives Canada Cataloguing in Publication

Rabagliati, Michel

　　The song of Roland / Michel Rabagliati.

Translation of: Paul à Québec.

ISBN 978-1-894994-61-3

　　1. Graphic novels.　I. Title.

PN6734.P38595R3213 2012　　　　741.5'971　　　C2012-900450-2

First English Edition
Printed by Gauvin Press in Gatineau, Quebec, Canada

MIX
Paper from
responsible sources
FSC
www.fsc.org   FSC® C100212

Conundrum press acknowledges the financial support of the Canada Council for the Arts and the Government of
Canada through the Canada Book Fund toward its publishing activities.

We acknowledge the financial support of the Government of Canada, through the National Translation Program for
Book Publishing, for our translation activities.

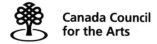

Canada Council　Conseil des Arts
for the Arts　　du Canada

Michel Rabagliati

The song of Roland

Conundrum

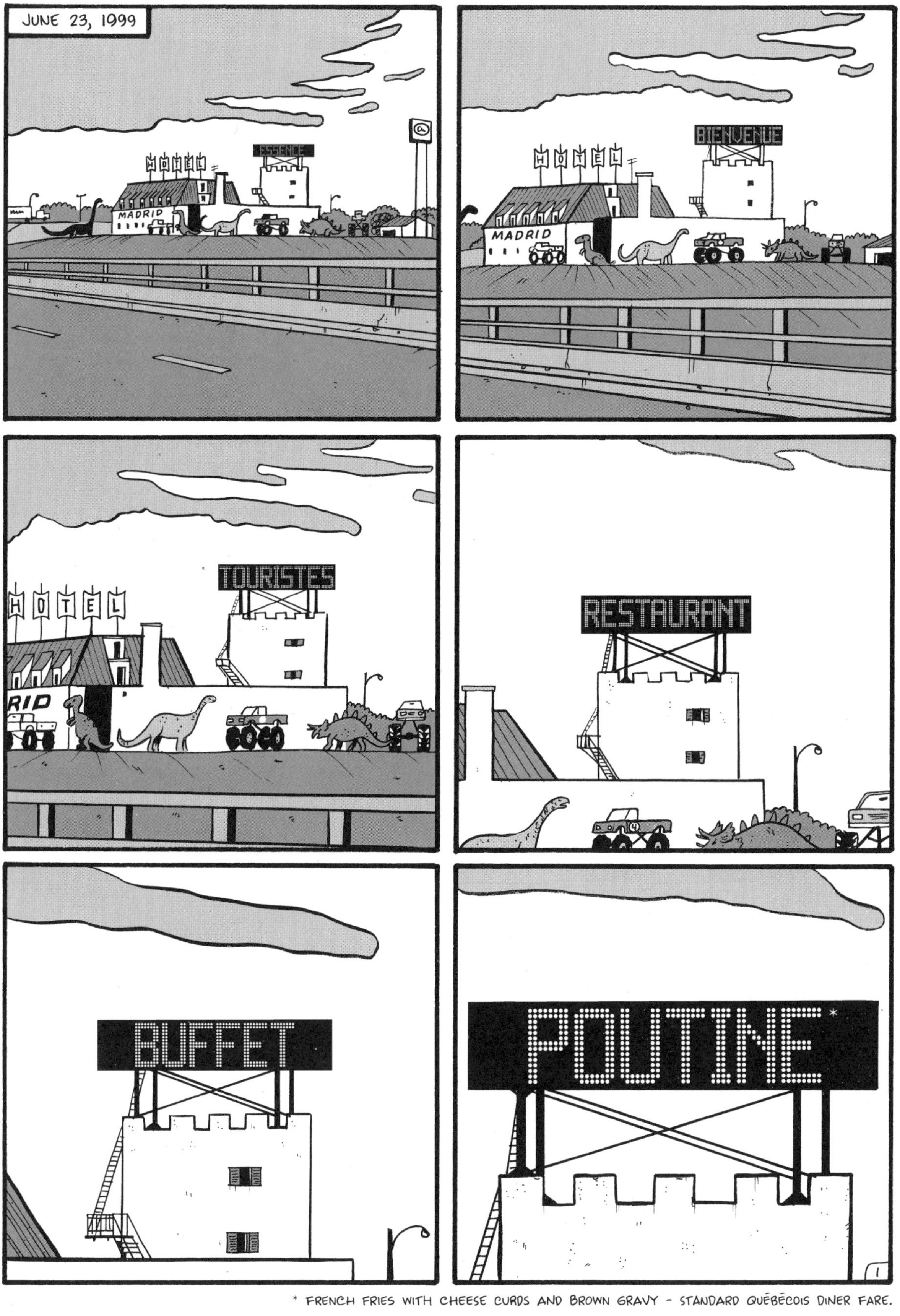
JUNE 23, 1999
HOTEL
ESSENCE
MADRID
BIENVENUE
HOTEL
MADRID
HOTEL
TOURISTES
RID
RESTAURANT
BUFFET
POUTINE*

* FRENCH FRIES WITH CHEESE CURDS AND BROWN GRAVY - STANDARD QUÉBÉCOIS DINER FARE.

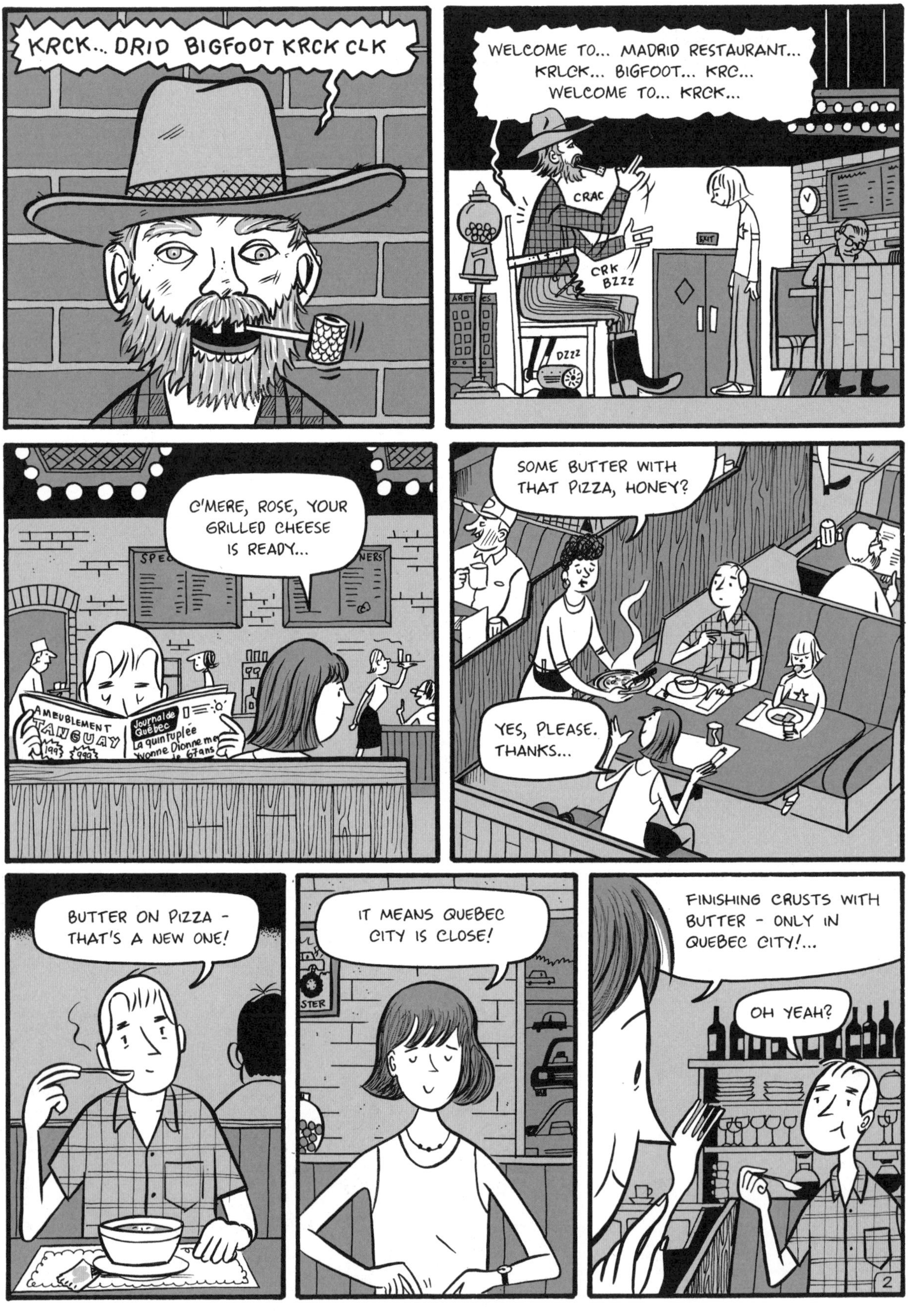
KRCK... DRID BIGFOOT KRCK CLK
WELCOME TO... MADRID RESTAURANT... KRLCK... BIGFOOT... KRC... WELCOME TO... KRCK...
CRAC
CRK BZZZ
DZZZ
EXIT
C'MERE, ROSE, YOUR GRILLED CHEESE IS READY...
AMEUBLEMENT TANGUAY
Journal de Québec
La quintuplée Yvonne Dionne me... 67 ans
SOME BUTTER WITH THAT PIZZA, HONEY?
YES, PLEASE. THANKS...
BUTTER ON PIZZA - THAT'S A NEW ONE!
IT MEANS QUEBEC CITY IS CLOSE!
FINISHING CRUSTS WITH BUTTER - ONLY IN QUEBEC CITY!...
OH YEAH?
2

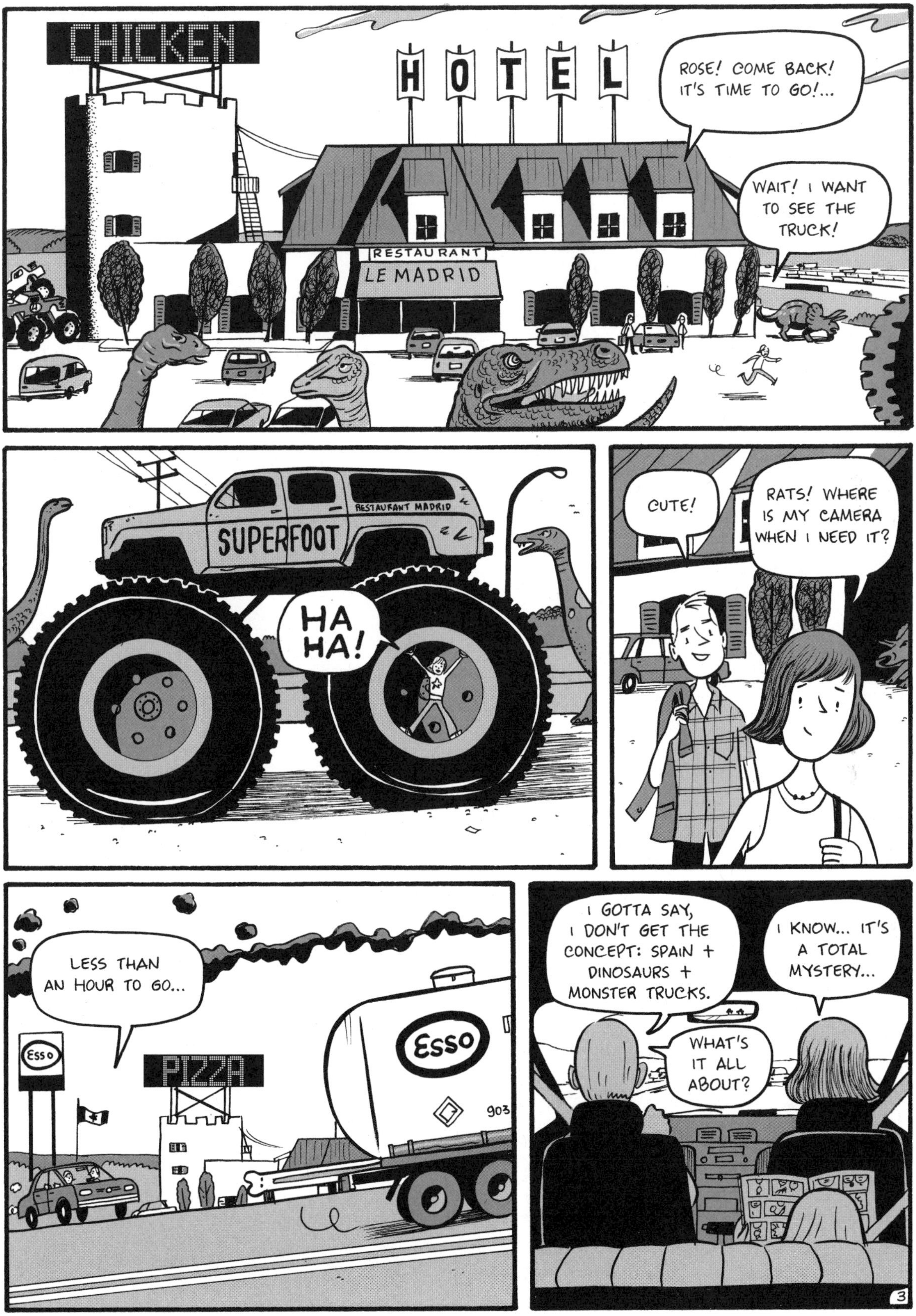
CHICKEN
HOTEL
ROSE! COME BACK! IT'S TIME TO GO!...
WAIT! I WANT TO SEE THE TRUCK!
RESTAURANT
LE MADRID
RESTAURANT MADRID
SUPERFOOT
HA HA!
CUTE!
RATS! WHERE IS MY CAMERA WHEN I NEED IT?
LESS THAN AN HOUR TO GO...
Esso
PIZZA
Esso
903
I GOTTA SAY, I DON'T GET THE CONCEPT: SPAIN + DINOSAURS + MONSTER TRUCKS.
I KNOW... IT'S A TOTAL MYSTERY...
WHAT'S IT ALL ABOUT?
3

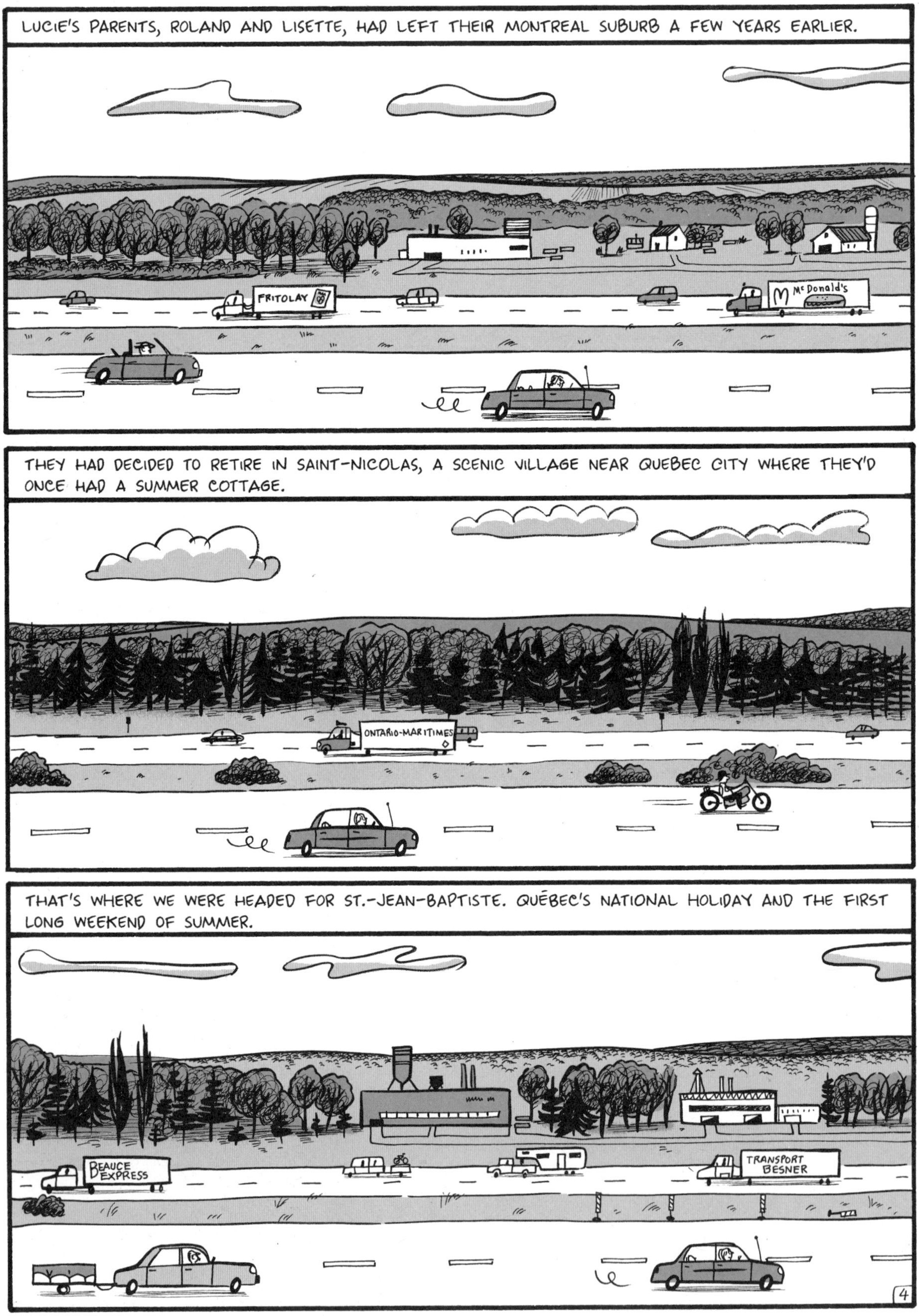
LUCIE'S PARENTS, ROLAND AND LISETTE, HAD LEFT THEIR MONTREAL SUBURB A FEW YEARS EARLIER.
FRITOLAY
McDonald's
THEY HAD DECIDED TO RETIRE IN SAINT-NICOLAS, A SCENIC VILLAGE NEAR QUEBEC CITY WHERE THEY'D ONCE HAD A SUMMER COTTAGE.
ONTARIO-MARITIMES
THAT'S WHERE WE WERE HEADED FOR ST.-JEAN-BAPTISTE. QUÉBEC'S NATIONAL HOLIDAY AND THE FIRST LONG WEEKEND OF SUMMER.
BEAUCE EXPRESS
TRANSPORT BESNER
4

HUOT
1250
BOUCHERIE
FILET MIGNON
EVERYBODY'S ALREADY HERE!
VIVE LE QUÉBEC LIBRE!*
LET'S GO, QUÉBEC!
YES SIR! YOU SAID IT!
HA HA!
MOM, DON'T YELL!
HELLO, KIDS!
WOU HOU!
ROSE!
LOULOU!
HERE THEY ARE!
5

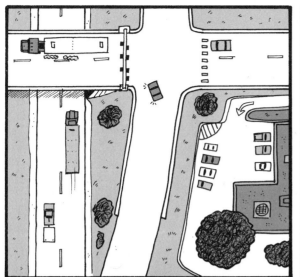

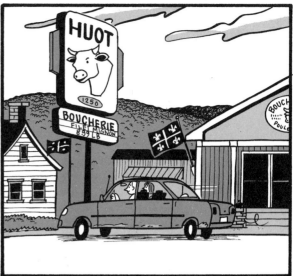

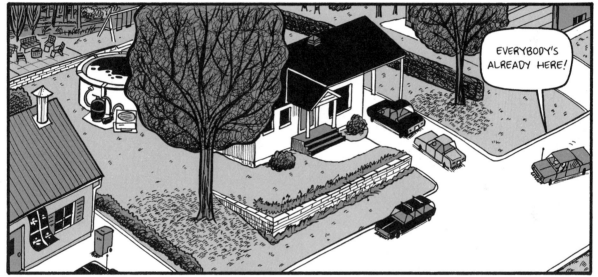

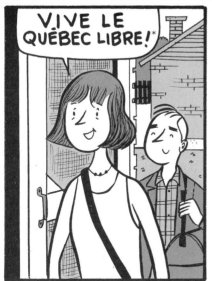

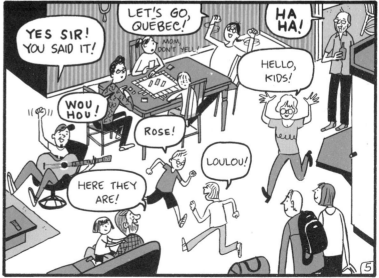

* "LONG LIVE FREE QUÉBEC!" CONTROVERSIAL DECLARATION OF SUPPORT FOR QUÉBEC SOVEREIGNTY MADE BY FRENCH PRESIDENT CHARLES DE GAULLE IN MONTREAL IN 1967.

My father-in-law calls all his kids "rabbits" and his grandkids "li'l rabbits." Here's how the rabbit hutch breaks down:

SUZANNE RABBIT #1	LUCIE RABBIT #2	MONIQUE RABBIT #3
LOUIS-PHILIPPE LI'L RABBIT #3 — MATHILDE LI'L RABBIT #5	ROSE LI'L RABBIT #4 — JUDITH LI'L RABBIT #1	MYLÈNE LI'L RABBIT #2

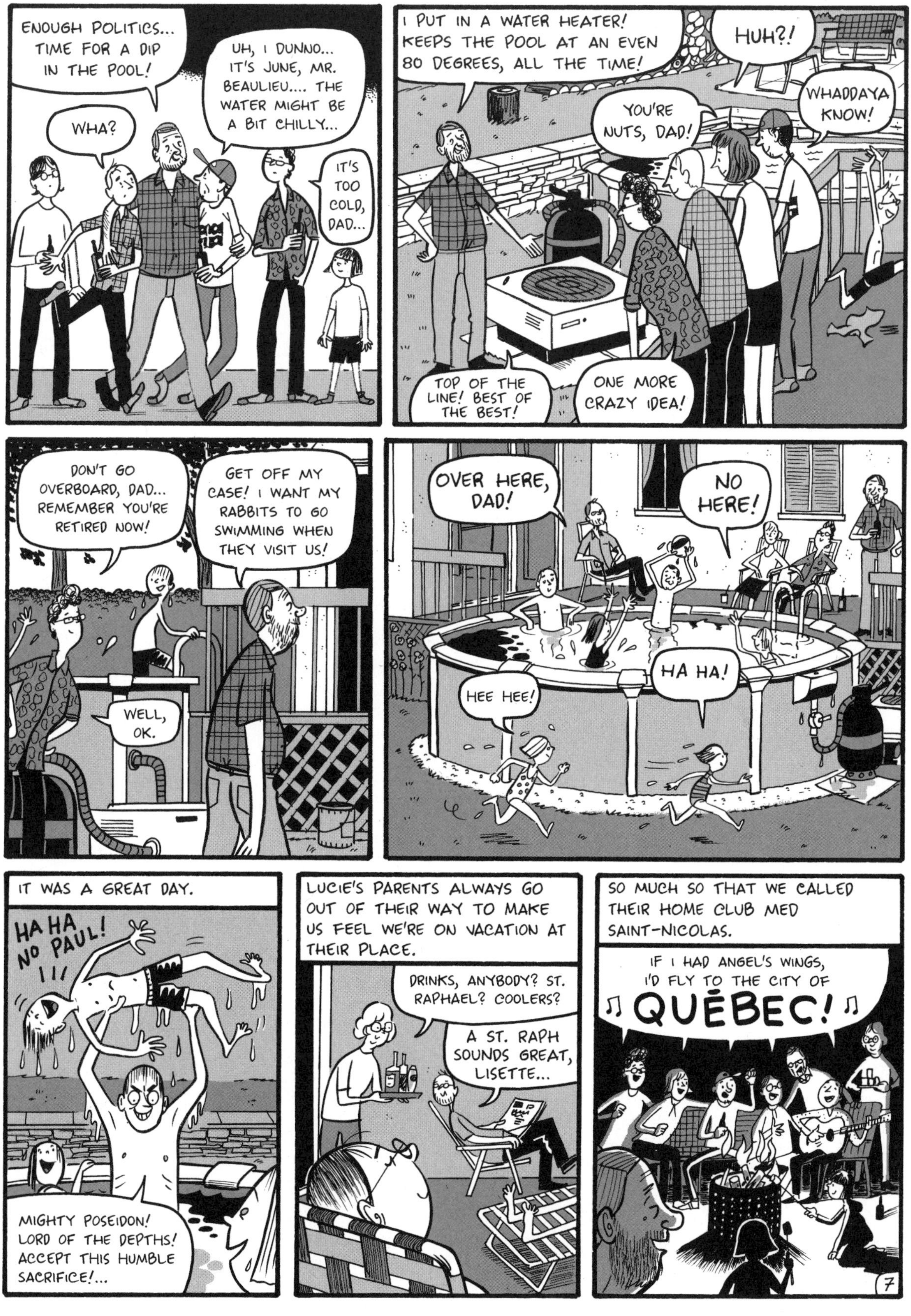
ENOUGH POLITICS... TIME FOR A DIP IN THE POOL!
UH, I DUNNO... IT'S JUNE, MR. BEAULIEU.... THE WATER MIGHT BE A BIT CHILLY...
WHA?
IT'S TOO COLD, DAD...
I PUT IN A WATER HEATER! KEEPS THE POOL AT AN EVEN 80 DEGREES, ALL THE TIME!
HUH?!
YOU'RE NUTS, DAD!
WHADDAYA KNOW!
TOP OF THE LINE! BEST OF THE BEST!
ONE MORE CRAZY IDEA!
DON'T GO OVERBOARD, DAD... REMEMBER YOU'RE RETIRED NOW!
GET OFF MY CASE! I WANT MY RABBITS TO GO SWIMMING WHEN THEY VISIT US!
WELL, OK.
OVER HERE, DAD!
NO HERE!
HA HA!
HEE HEE!
IT WAS A GREAT DAY.
HA HA NO PAUL!
MIGHTY POSEIDON! LORD OF THE DEPTHS! ACCEPT THIS HUMBLE SACRIFICE!...
LUCIE'S PARENTS ALWAYS GO OUT OF THEIR WAY TO MAKE US FEEL WE'RE ON VACATION AT THEIR PLACE.
DRINKS, ANYBODY? ST. RAPHAEL? COOLERS?
A ST. RAPH SOUNDS GREAT, LISETTE...
SO MUCH SO THAT WE CALLED THEIR HOME CLUB MED SAINT-NICOLAS.
IF I HAD ANGEL'S WINGS, I'D FLY TO THE CITY OF ♫ QUÉBEC! ♫
7

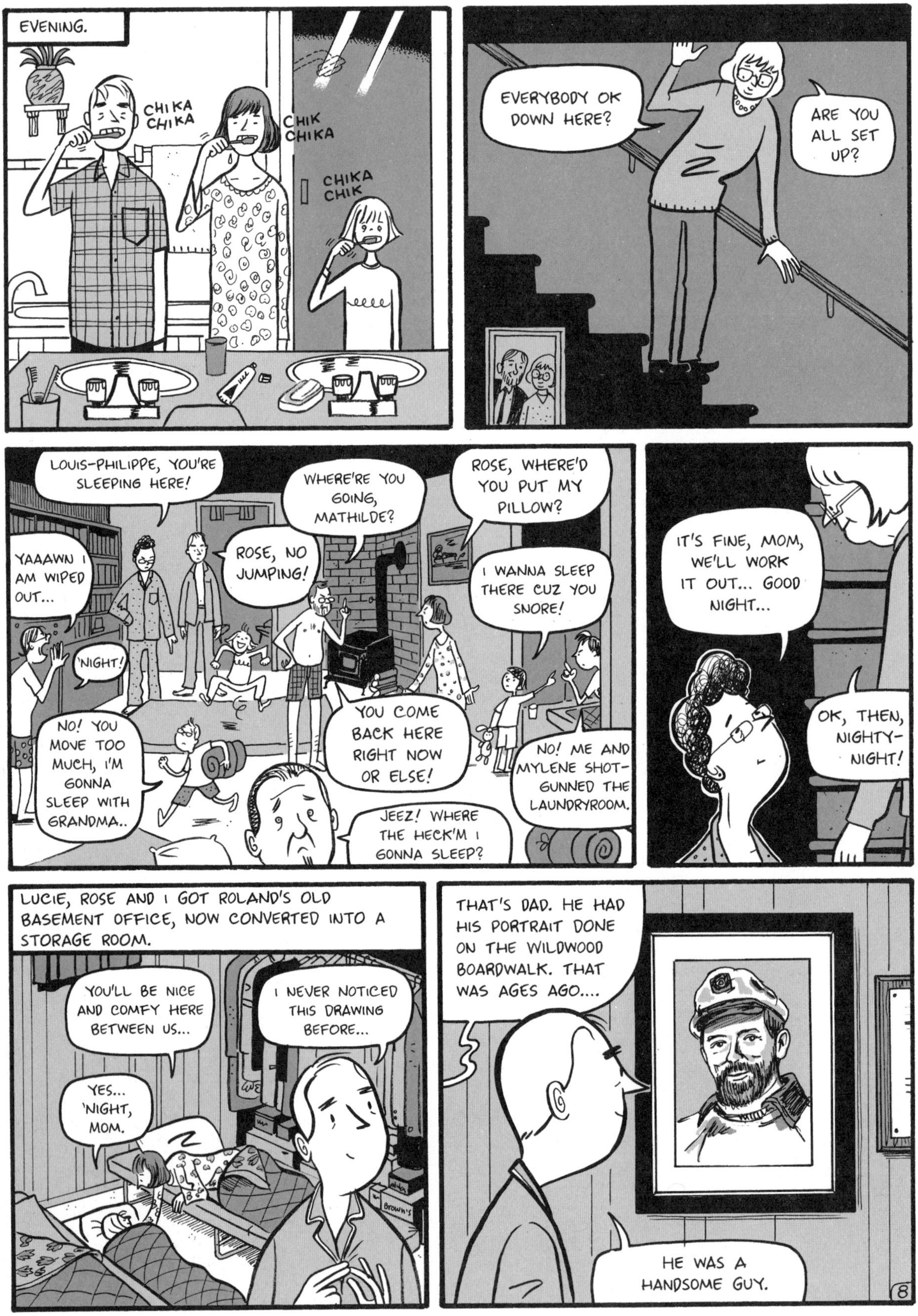
EVENING.
CHIKA CHIKA
CHIK CHIKA
CHIKA CHIK
EVERYBODY OK DOWN HERE?
ARE YOU ALL SET UP?
LOUIS-PHILIPPE, YOU'RE SLEEPING HERE!
YAAAWN I AM WIPED OUT...
'NIGHT!
NO! YOU MOVE TOO MUCH, I'M GONNA SLEEP WITH GRANDMA..
ROSE, NO JUMPING!
WHERE'RE YOU GOING, MATHILDE?
YOU COME BACK HERE RIGHT NOW OR ELSE!
ROSE, WHERE'D YOU PUT MY PILLOW?
I WANNA SLEEP THERE CUZ YOU SNORE!
NO! ME AND MYLENE SHOT-GUNNED THE LAUNDRYROOM.
JEEZ! WHERE THE HECK'M I GONNA SLEEP?
IT'S FINE, MOM, WE'LL WORK IT OUT... GOOD NIGHT...
OK, THEN, NIGHTY-NIGHT!
LUCIE, ROSE AND I GOT ROLAND'S OLD BASEMENT OFFICE, NOW CONVERTED INTO A STORAGE ROOM.
YOU'LL BE NICE AND COMFY HERE BETWEEN US...
YES... 'NIGHT, MOM.
I NEVER NOTICED THIS DRAWING BEFORE...
THAT'S DAD. HE HAD HIS PORTRAIT DONE ON THE WILDWOOD BOARDWALK. THAT WAS AGES AGO....
HE WAS A HANDSOME GUY.
8

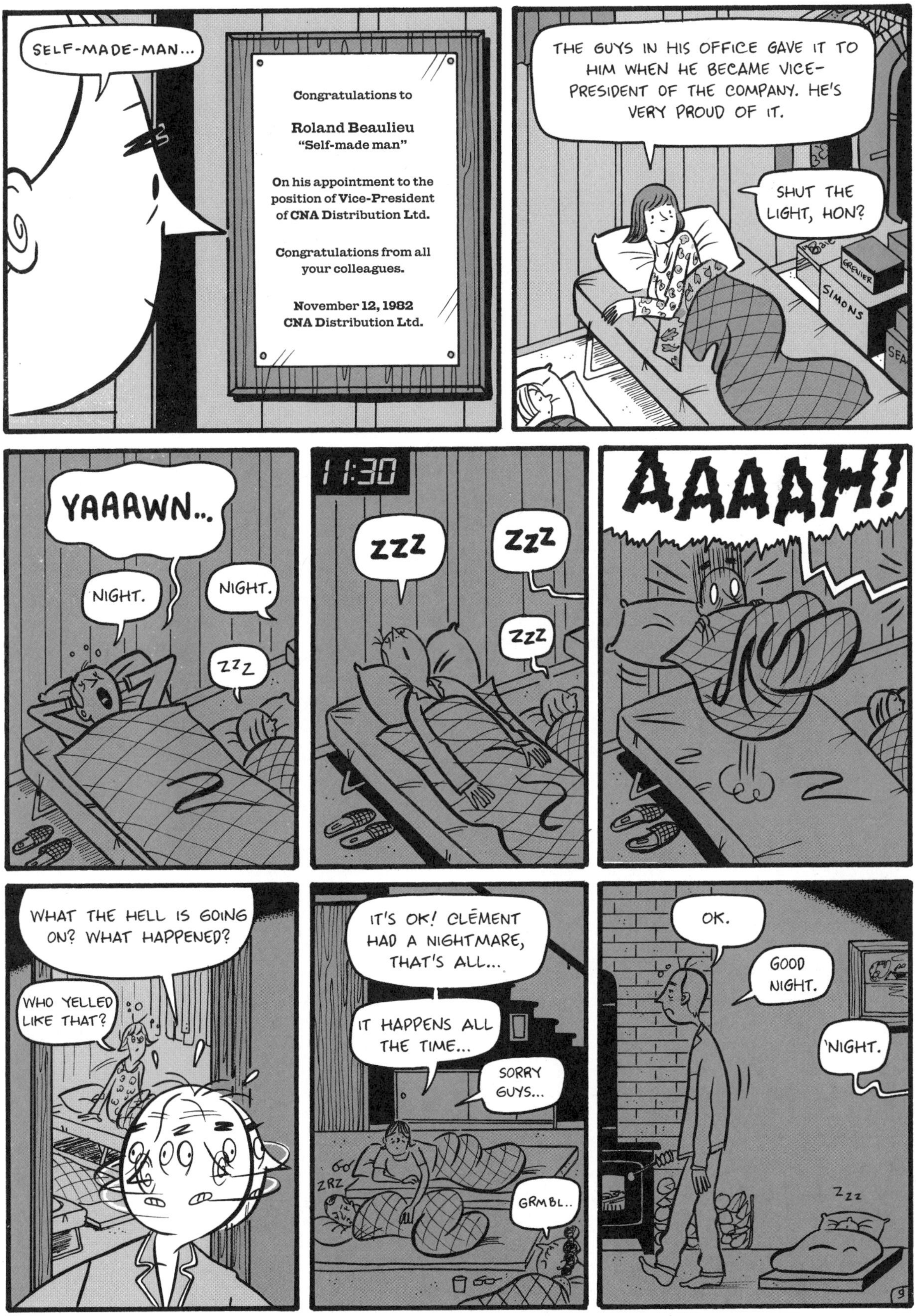
SELF-MADE-MAN...
Congratulations to
Roland Beaulieu
"Self-made man"
On his appointment to the position of Vice-President of CNA Distribution Ltd.
Congratulations from all your colleagues.
November 12, 1982
CNA Distribution Ltd.
THE GUYS IN HIS OFFICE GAVE IT TO HIM WHEN HE BECAME VICE-PRESIDENT OF THE COMPANY. HE'S VERY PROUD OF IT.
SHUT THE LIGHT, HON?
GRENIER
SIMONS
YAAAWN...
NIGHT.
NIGHT.
ZZZ
11:30
ZZZ
ZZZ
ZZZ
AAAAH!
WHAT THE HELL IS GOING ON? WHAT HAPPENED?
WHO YELLED LIKE THAT?
IT'S OK! CLÉMENT HAD A NIGHTMARE, THAT'S ALL...
IT HAPPENS ALL THE TIME...
SORRY GUYS...
ZRZ
GRMBL..
OK.
GOOD NIGHT.
'NIGHT.
ZZZ

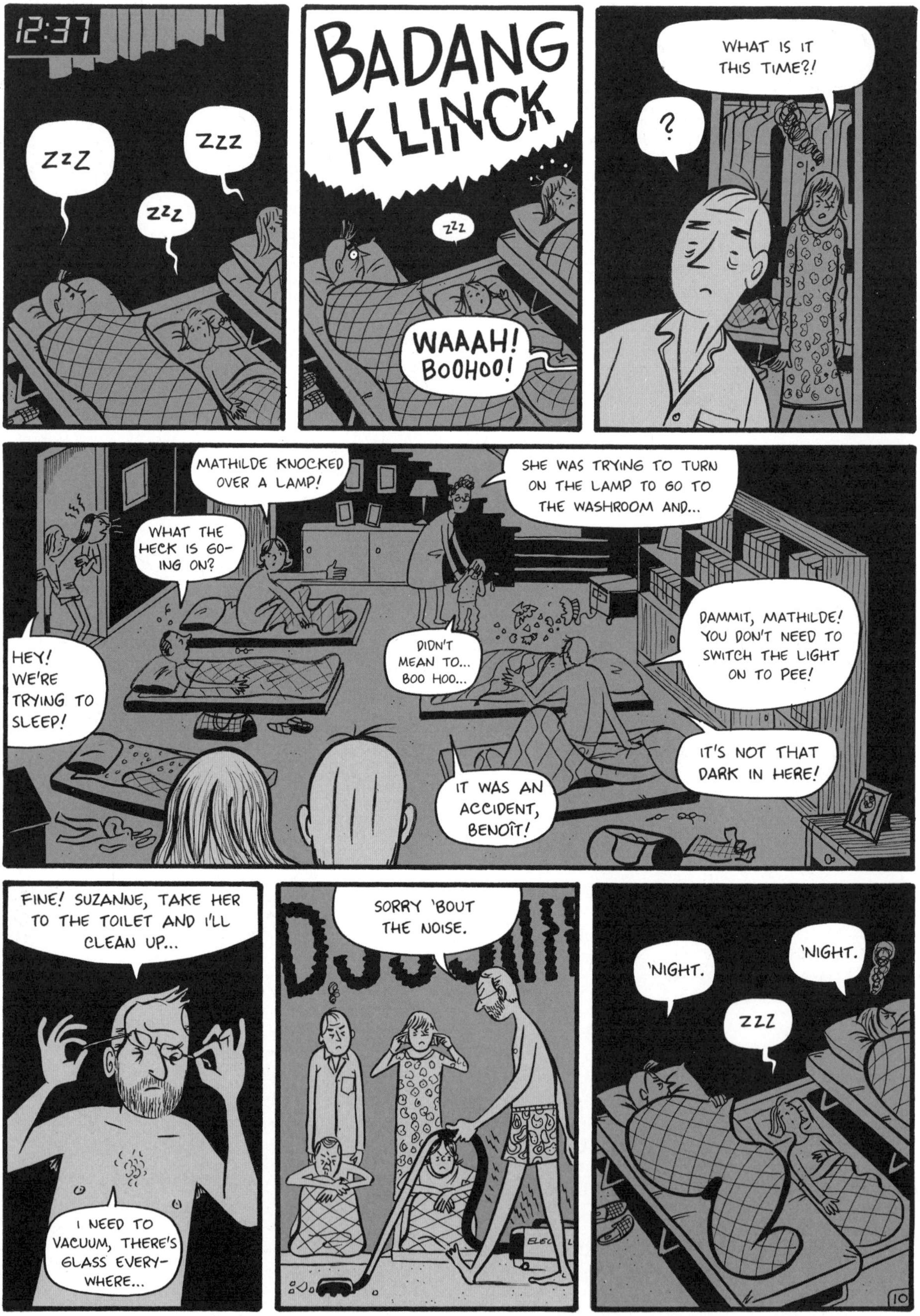
12:37
ZZZ
ZZZ
ZZZ
BADANG KLINCK
ZZZ
WAAAH! BOOHOO!
?
WHAT IS IT THIS TIME?!
MATHILDE KNOCKED OVER A LAMP!
SHE WAS TRYING TO TURN ON THE LAMP TO GO TO THE WASHROOM AND...
WHAT THE HECK IS GO-ING ON?
HEY! WE'RE TRYING TO SLEEP!
DIDN'T MEAN TO... BOO HOO...
DAMMIT, MATHILDE! YOU DON'T NEED TO SWITCH THE LIGHT ON TO PEE!
IT'S NOT THAT DARK IN HERE!
IT WAS AN ACCIDENT, BENOÎT!
FINE! SUZANNE, TAKE HER TO THE TOILET AND I'LL CLEAN UP...
I NEED TO VACUUM, THERE'S GLASS EVERY-WHERE...
SORRY 'BOUT THE NOISE.
'NIGHT.
'NIGHT.
ZZZ
10

2:45

Zzz

Rzzz

zz

WIIRJJJJ

zz

@!!# &?⁂%@!
CAN'T A PERSON GET SOME SLEEP HERE?!?

WII

SHUT IT OFF, DAD!

WHAT DO YOU THINK I'M TRYING TO DO, HUH?

WIIRJJJ

AQUAPURE 2000

WHAT THE HECK IS THAT THING?

A WATER PURIFIER! YOUR FATHER PUT IT IN A FEW WEEKS AGO...

@✳!

CLICK CLICK CLICK

CAN'T YOU SHUT IT DOWN?

I'M PRESSING THE OFF BUT-TON! NOTHING'S HAPPENING!!!

PULL OUT THE PLUG, WE'LL RECONNECT IT TOMORROW!

GOOD IDEA!

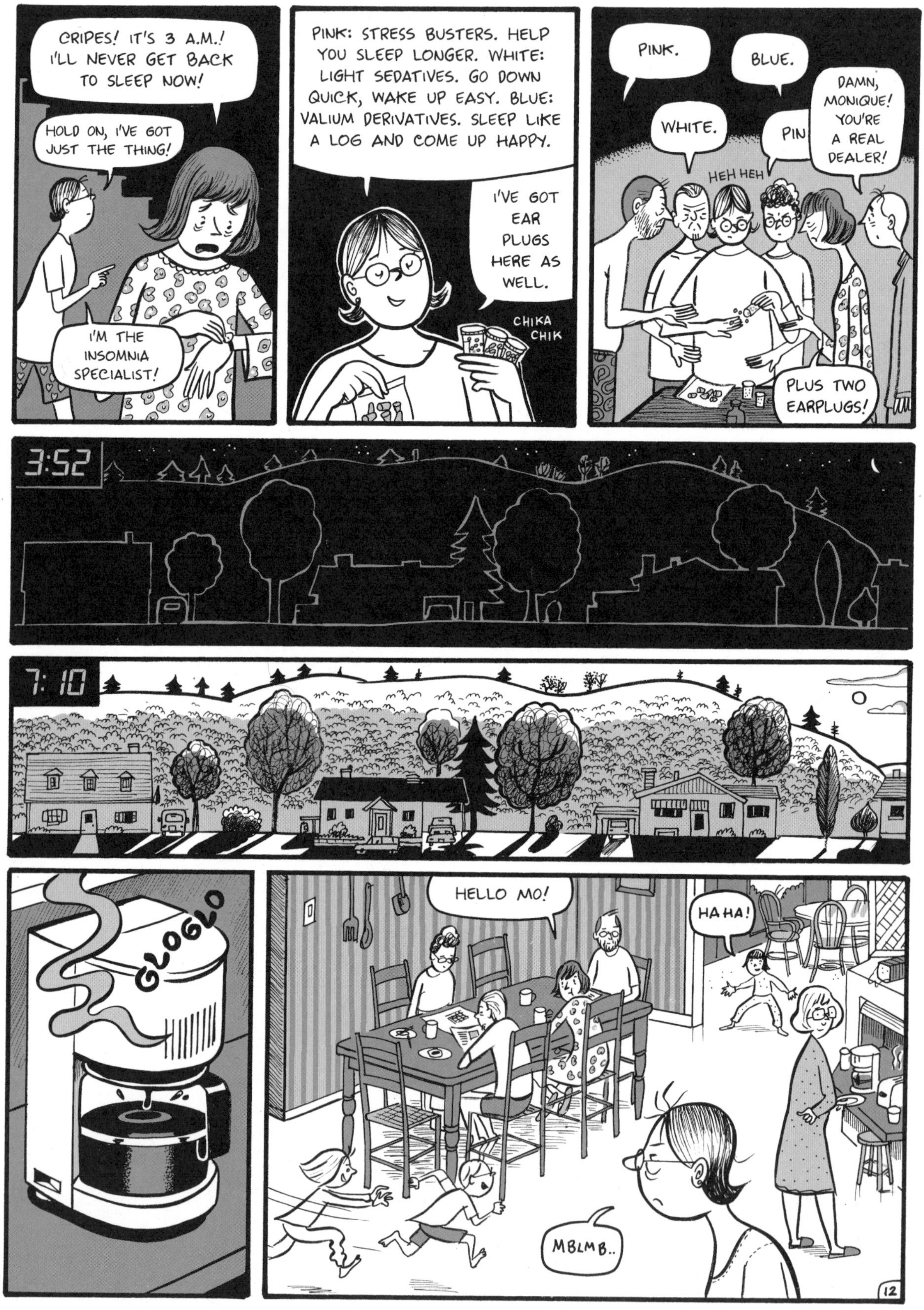
CRIPES! IT'S 3 A.M.! I'LL NEVER GET BACK TO SLEEP NOW!
HOLD ON, I'VE GOT JUST THE THING!
I'M THE INSOMNIA SPECIALIST!
PINK: STRESS BUSTERS. HELP YOU SLEEP LONGER. WHITE: LIGHT SEDATIVES. GO DOWN QUICK, WAKE UP EASY. BLUE: VALIUM DERIVATIVES. SLEEP LIKE A LOG AND COME UP HAPPY.
I'VE GOT EAR PLUGS HERE AS WELL.
CHIKA CHIK
PINK.
BLUE.
WHITE.
PIN
DAMN, MONIQUE! YOU'RE A REAL DEALER!
HEH HEH
PLUS TWO EARPLUGS!
3:52
7:10
GLOGLO
HELLO MO!
HA HA!
MBLMB..
12

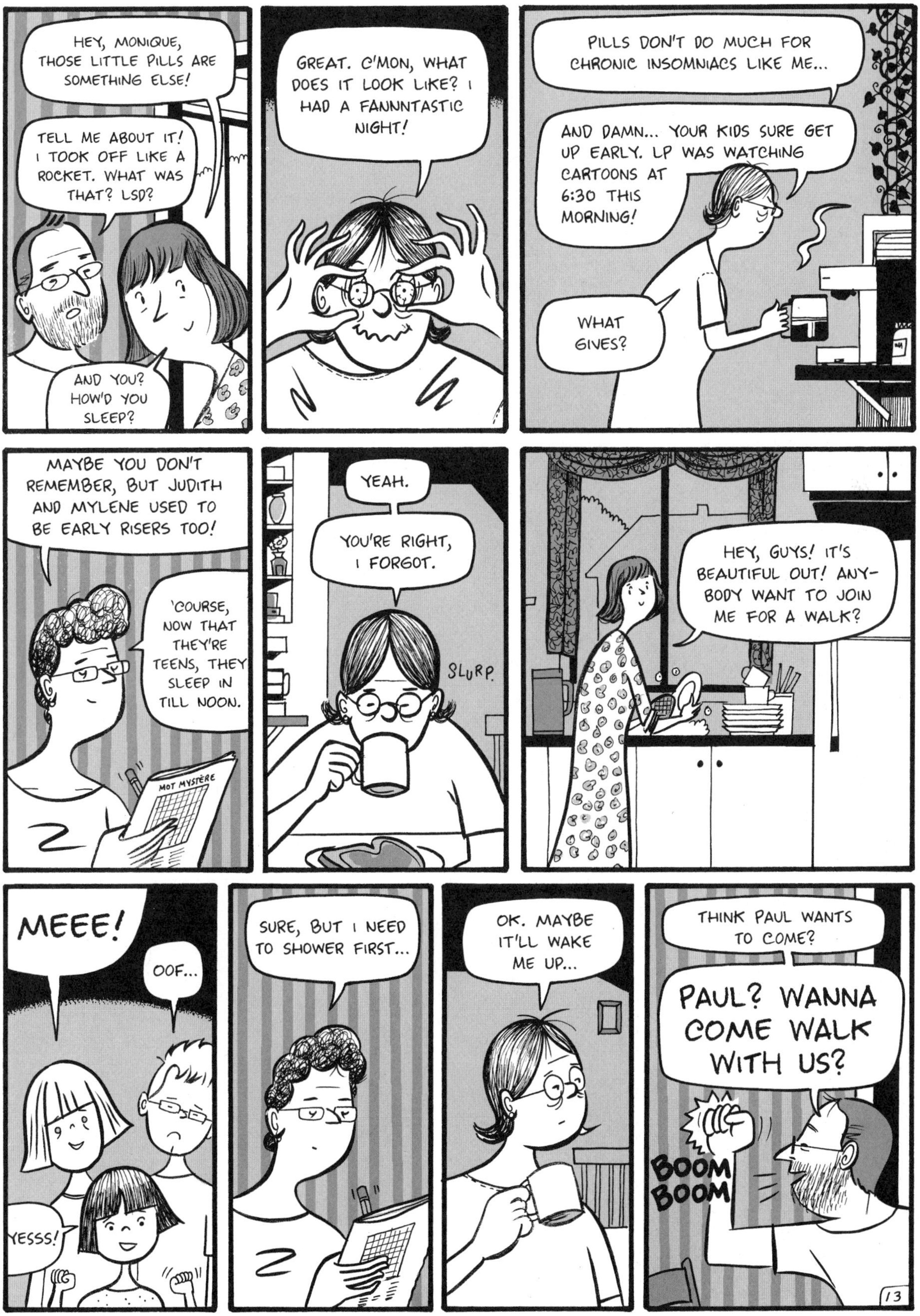
HEY, MONIQUE, THOSE LITTLE PILLS ARE SOMETHING ELSE!
TELL ME ABOUT IT! I TOOK OFF LIKE A ROCKET. WHAT WAS THAT? LSD?
AND YOU? HOW'D YOU SLEEP?
GREAT. C'MON, WHAT DOES IT LOOK LIKE? I HAD A FANNNTASTIC NIGHT!
PILLS DON'T DO MUCH FOR CHRONIC INSOMNIACS LIKE ME...
AND DAMN... YOUR KIDS SURE GET UP EARLY. LP WAS WATCHING CARTOONS AT 6:30 THIS MORNING!
WHAT GIVES?
MAYBE YOU DON'T REMEMBER, BUT JUDITH AND MYLENE USED TO BE EARLY RISERS TOO!
'COURSE, NOW THAT THEY'RE TEENS, THEY SLEEP IN TILL NOON.
MOT MYSTÈRE
YEAH.
YOU'RE RIGHT, I FORGOT.
SLURP
HEY, GUYS! IT'S BEAUTIFUL OUT! ANYBODY WANT TO JOIN ME FOR A WALK?
MEEE!
OOF...
YESSS!
SURE, BUT I NEED TO SHOWER FIRST...
OK. MAYBE IT'LL WAKE ME UP...
THINK PAUL WANTS TO COME?
PAUL? WANNA COME WALK WITH US?
BOOM BOOM
13

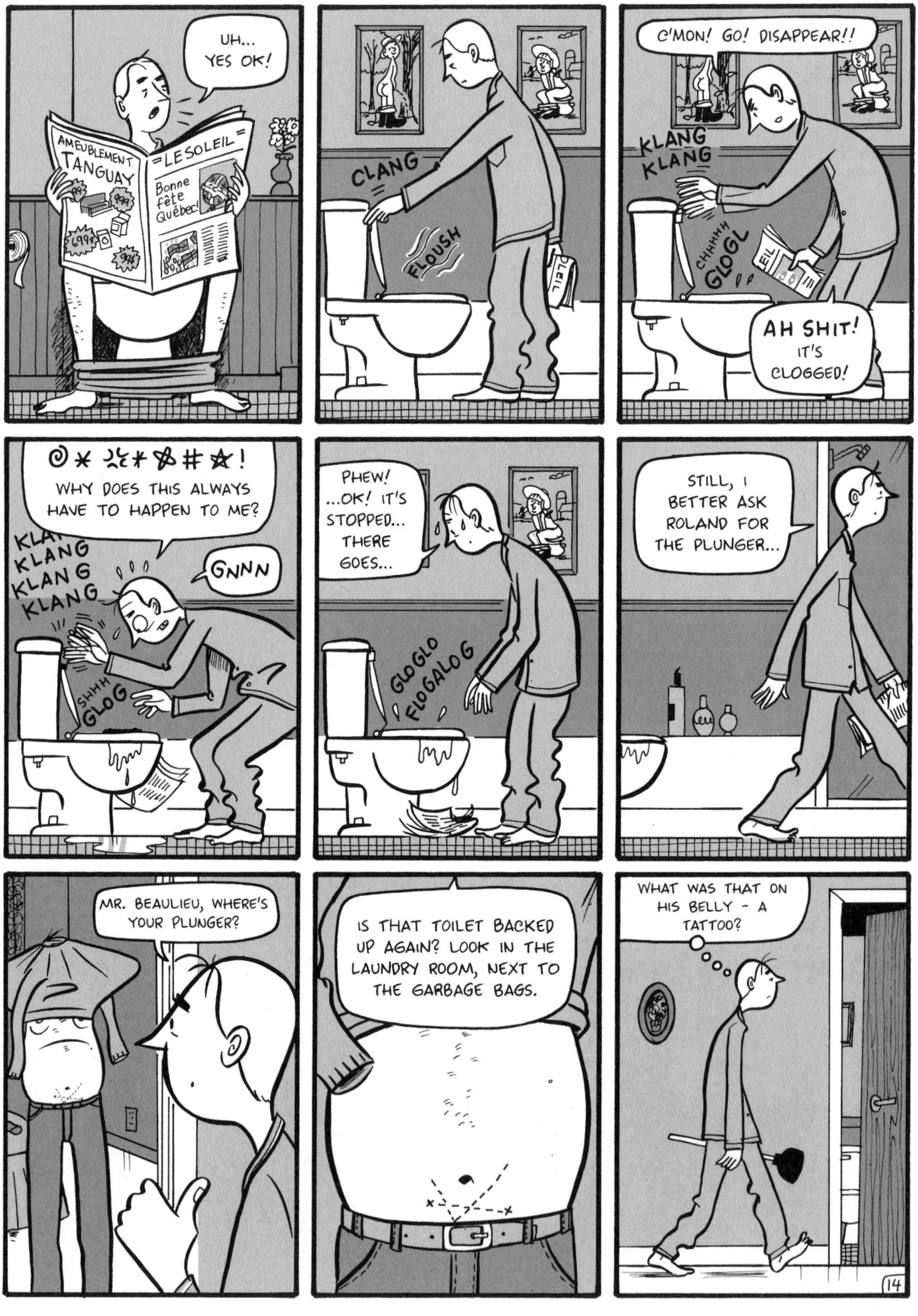
UH... YES OK!
AMEUBLEMENT TANGUAY
LE SOLEIL
Bonne fête Québec!
CLANG
FLOUSH
C'MON! GO! DISAPPEAR!!
KLANG KLANG
CHHHHH GLOGL
AH SHIT! IT'S CLOGGED!
WHY DOES THIS ALWAYS HAVE TO HAPPEN TO ME?
KLANG KLANG KLANG
GNNN
SHHH GLOG
PHEW! ...OK! IT'S STOPPED... THERE GOES...
GLOGLO FLOGALOG
STILL, I BETTER ASK ROLAND FOR THE PLUNGER...
MR. BEAULIEU, WHERE'S YOUR PLUNGER?
IS THAT TOILET BACKED UP AGAIN? LOOK IN THE LAUNDRY ROOM, NEXT TO THE GARBAGE BAGS.
WHAT WAS THAT ON HIS BELLY - A TATTOO?
14

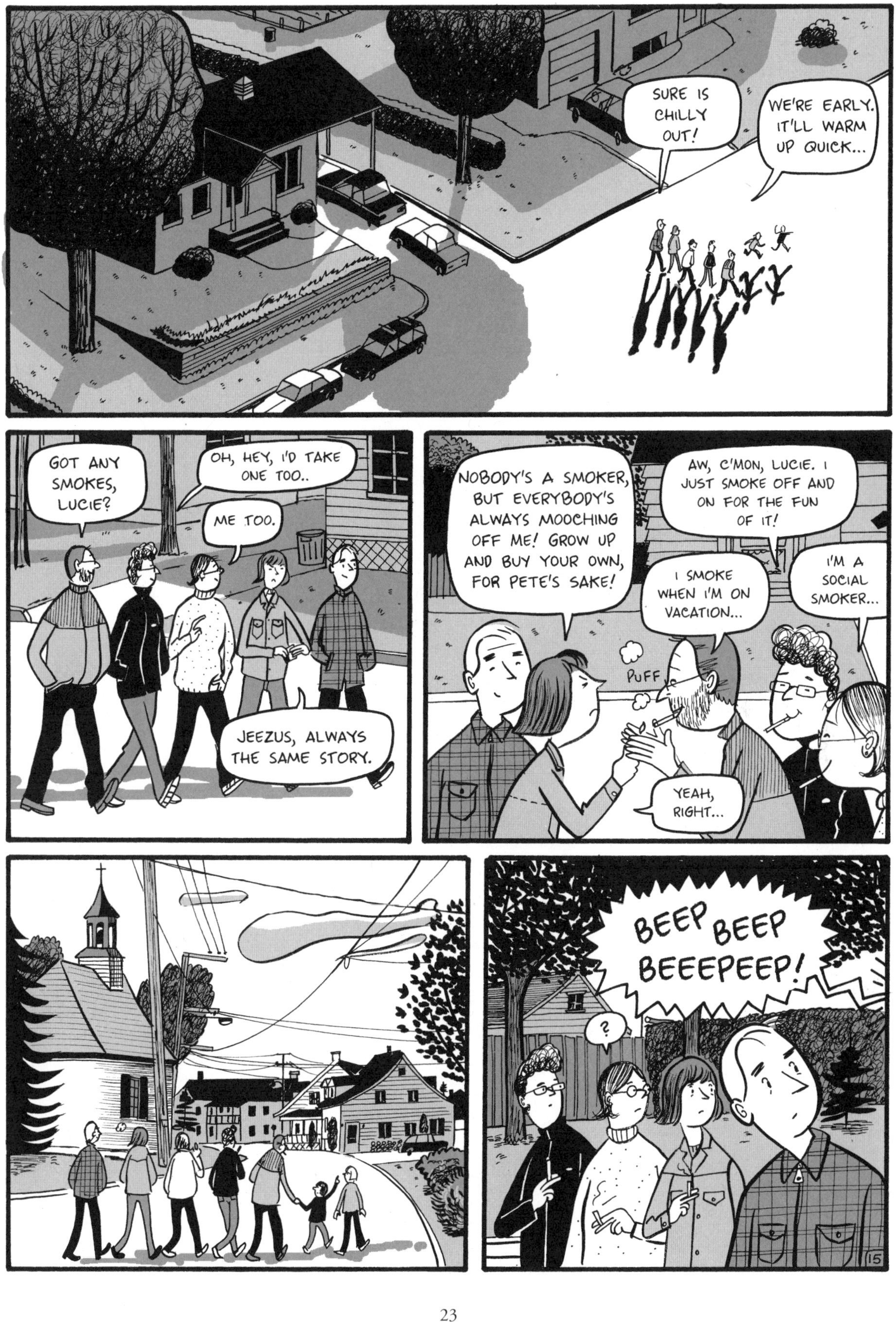
SURE IS CHILLY OUT!
WE'RE EARLY. IT'LL WARM UP QUICK...
GOT ANY SMOKES, LUCIE?
OH, HEY, I'D TAKE ONE TOO..
ME TOO.
JEEZUS, ALWAYS THE SAME STORY.
NOBODY'S A SMOKER, BUT EVERYBODY'S ALWAYS MOOCHING OFF ME! GROW UP AND BUY YOUR OWN, FOR PETE'S SAKE!
AW, C'MON, LUCIE. I JUST SMOKE OFF AND ON FOR THE FUN OF IT!
I SMOKE WHEN I'M ON VACATION...
I'M A SOCIAL SMOKER...
PUFF
YEAH, RIGHT...
BEEP BEEP BEEEPEEP!
?
15

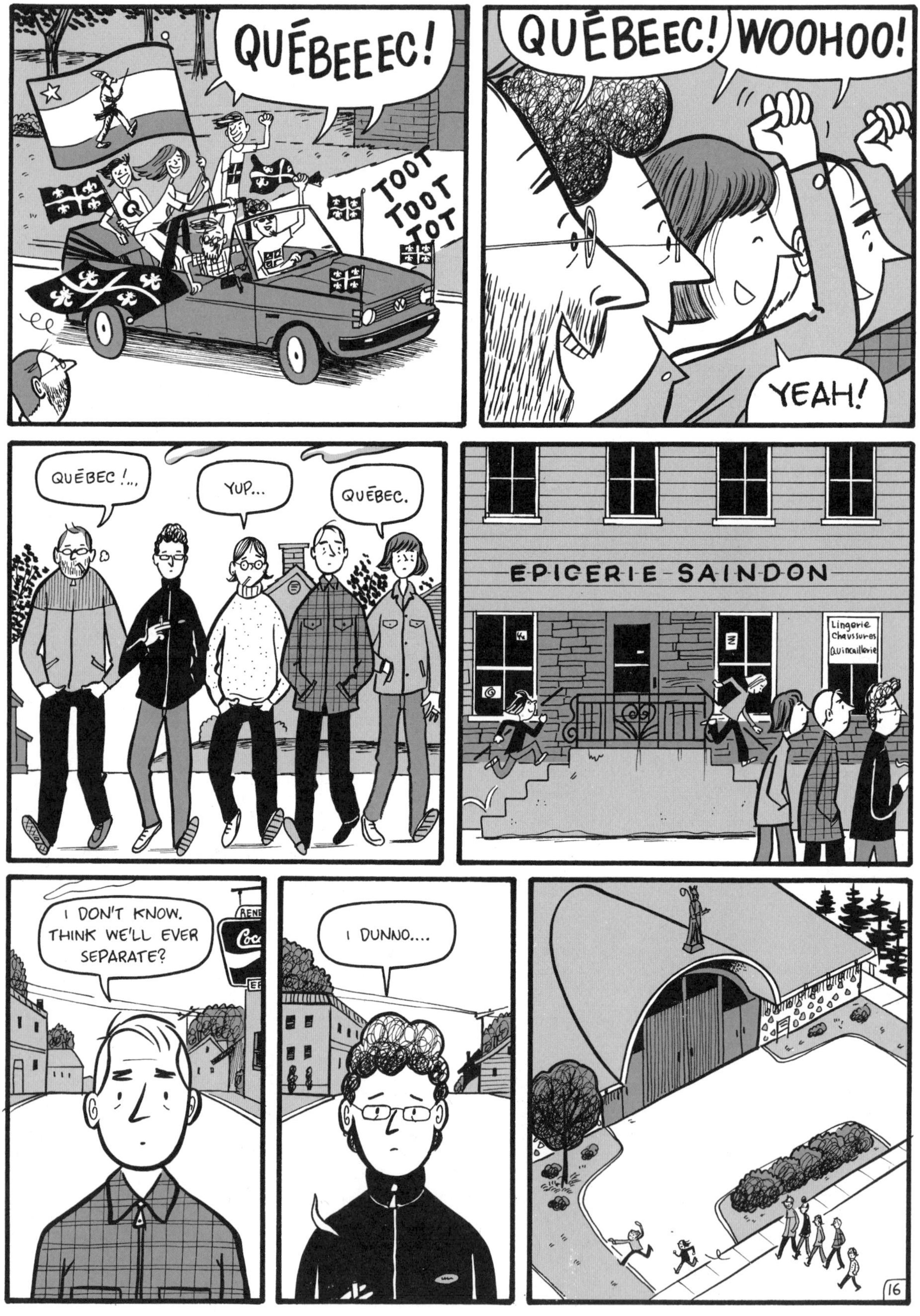
QUÉBEEEC!
TOOT TOOT TOT
QUÉBEEC!
WOOHOO!
YEAH!
QUÉBEC!...
YUP...
QUÉBEC.
EPICERIE SAINDON
Lingerie
Chaussures
Quincaillerie
I DON'T KNOW. THINK WE'LL EVER SEPARATE?
I DUNNO....
16

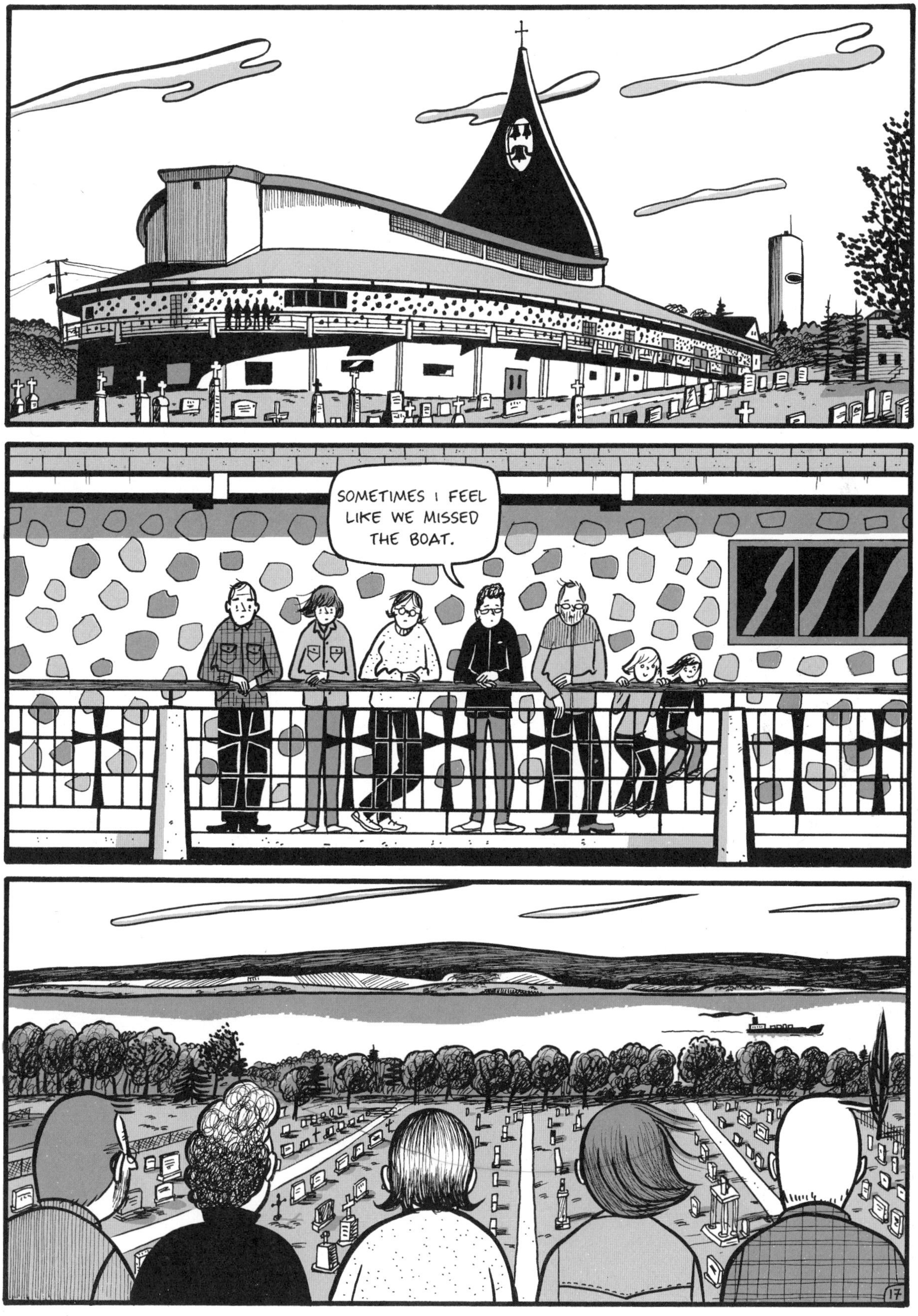
SOMETIMES I FEEL LIKE WE MISSED THE BOAT.
17

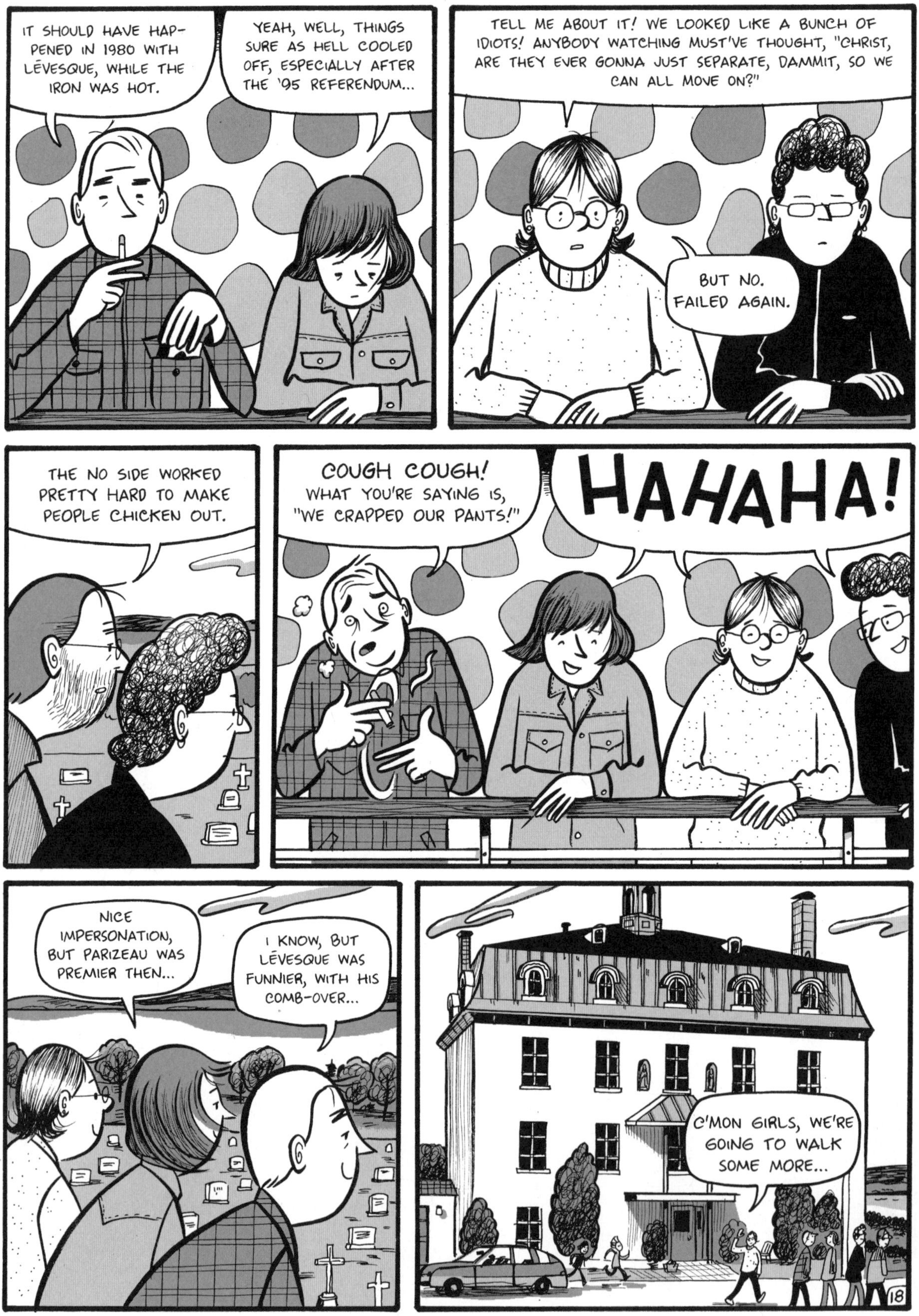
IT SHOULD HAVE HAPPENED IN 1980 WITH LÉVESQUE, WHILE THE IRON WAS HOT.
YEAH, WELL, THINGS SURE AS HELL COOLED OFF, ESPECIALLY AFTER THE '95 REFERENDUM...
TELL ME ABOUT IT! WE LOOKED LIKE A BUNCH OF IDIOTS! ANYBODY WATCHING MUST'VE THOUGHT, "CHRIST, ARE THEY EVER GONNA JUST SEPARATE, DAMMIT, SO WE CAN ALL MOVE ON?"
BUT NO. FAILED AGAIN.
THE NO SIDE WORKED PRETTY HARD TO MAKE PEOPLE CHICKEN OUT.
COUGH COUGH! WHAT YOU'RE SAYING IS, "WE CRAPPED OUR PANTS!"
HAHAHA!
NICE IMPERSONATION, BUT PARIZEAU WAS PREMIER THEN...
I KNOW, BUT LÉVESQUE WAS FUNNIER, WITH HIS COMB-OVER...
C'MON GIRLS, WE'RE GOING TO WALK SOME MORE...
18

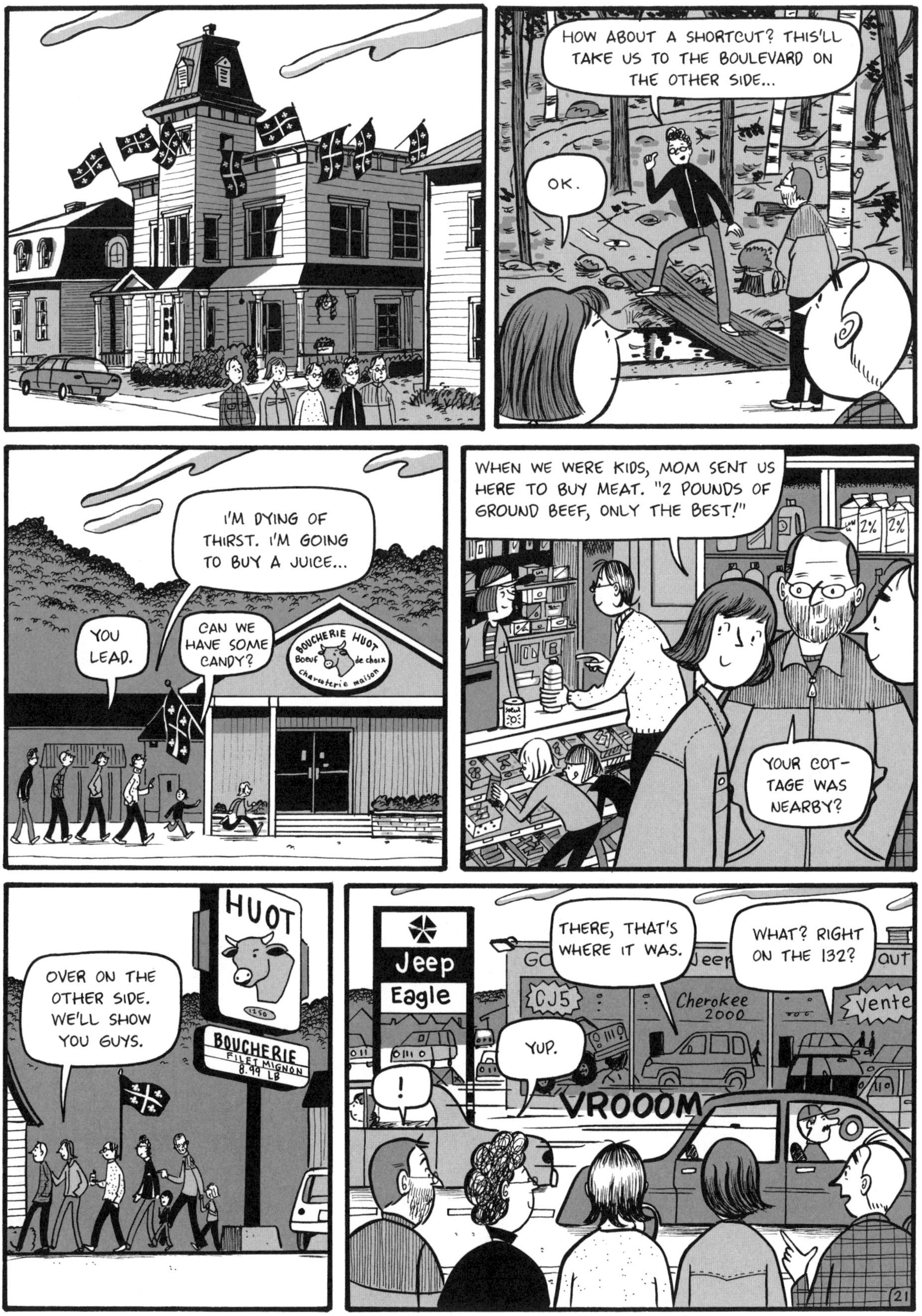

HOW ABOUT A SHORTCUT? THIS'LL TAKE US TO THE BOULEVARD ON THE OTHER SIDE...
OK.
I'M DYING OF THIRST. I'M GOING TO BUY A JUICE...
YOU LEAD.
CAN WE HAVE SOME CANDY?
BOUCHERIE HUOT
Boeuf de choix
Charcuterie maison
WHEN WE WERE KIDS, MOM SENT US HERE TO BUY MEAT. "2 POUNDS OF GROUND BEEF, ONLY THE BEST!"
2%
2%
YOUR COT-TAGE WAS NEARBY?
HUOT
1250
BOUCHERIE
FILET MIGNON
8.99 LB
OVER ON THE OTHER SIDE. WE'LL SHOW YOU GUYS.
Jeep
Eagle
CJ5
Cherokee 2000
Vente
THERE, THAT'S WHERE IT WAS.
WHAT? RIGHT ON THE 132?
YUP.
!
VROOOM
21

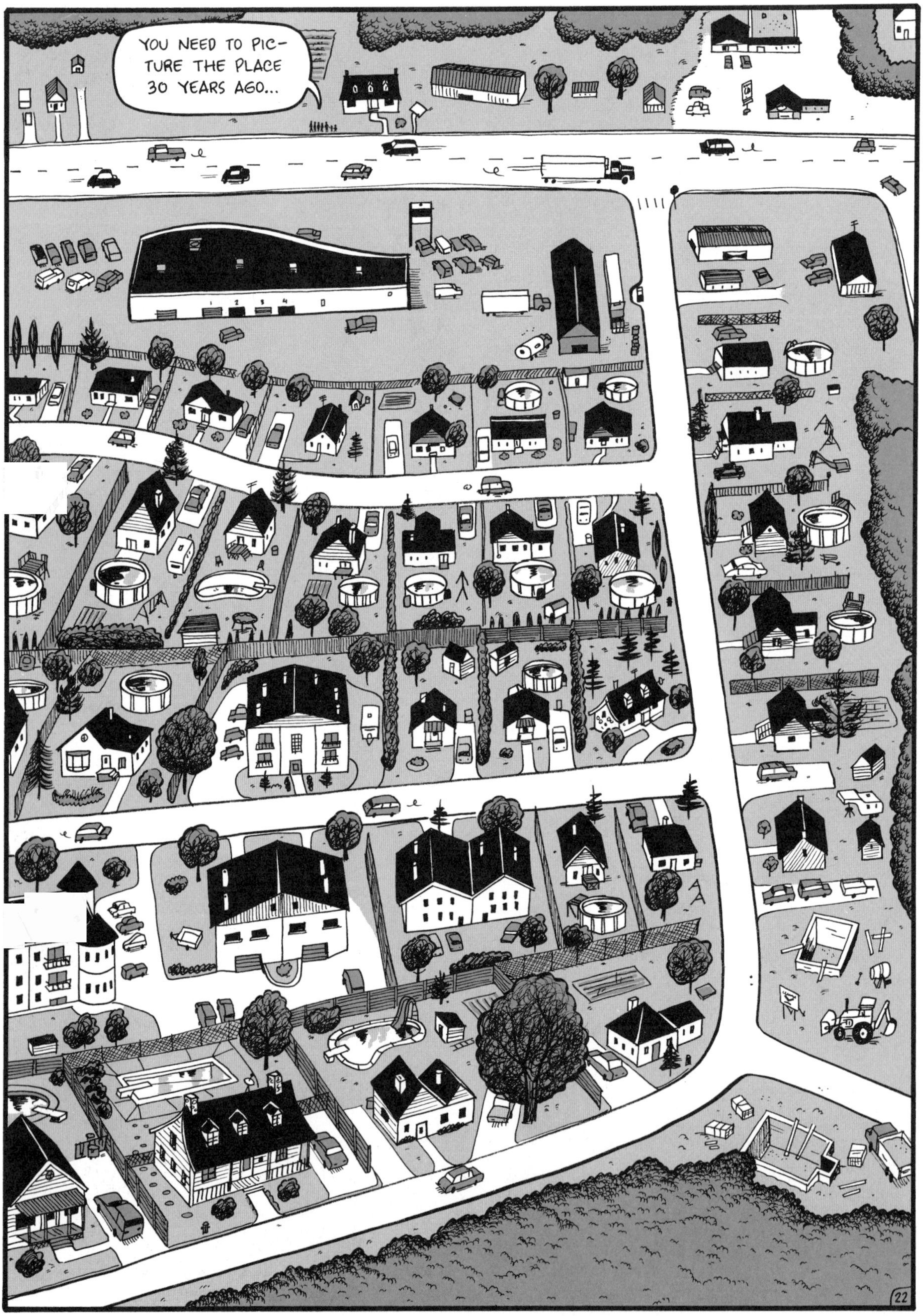
YOU NEED TO PIC-TURE THE PLACE 30 YEARS AGO...

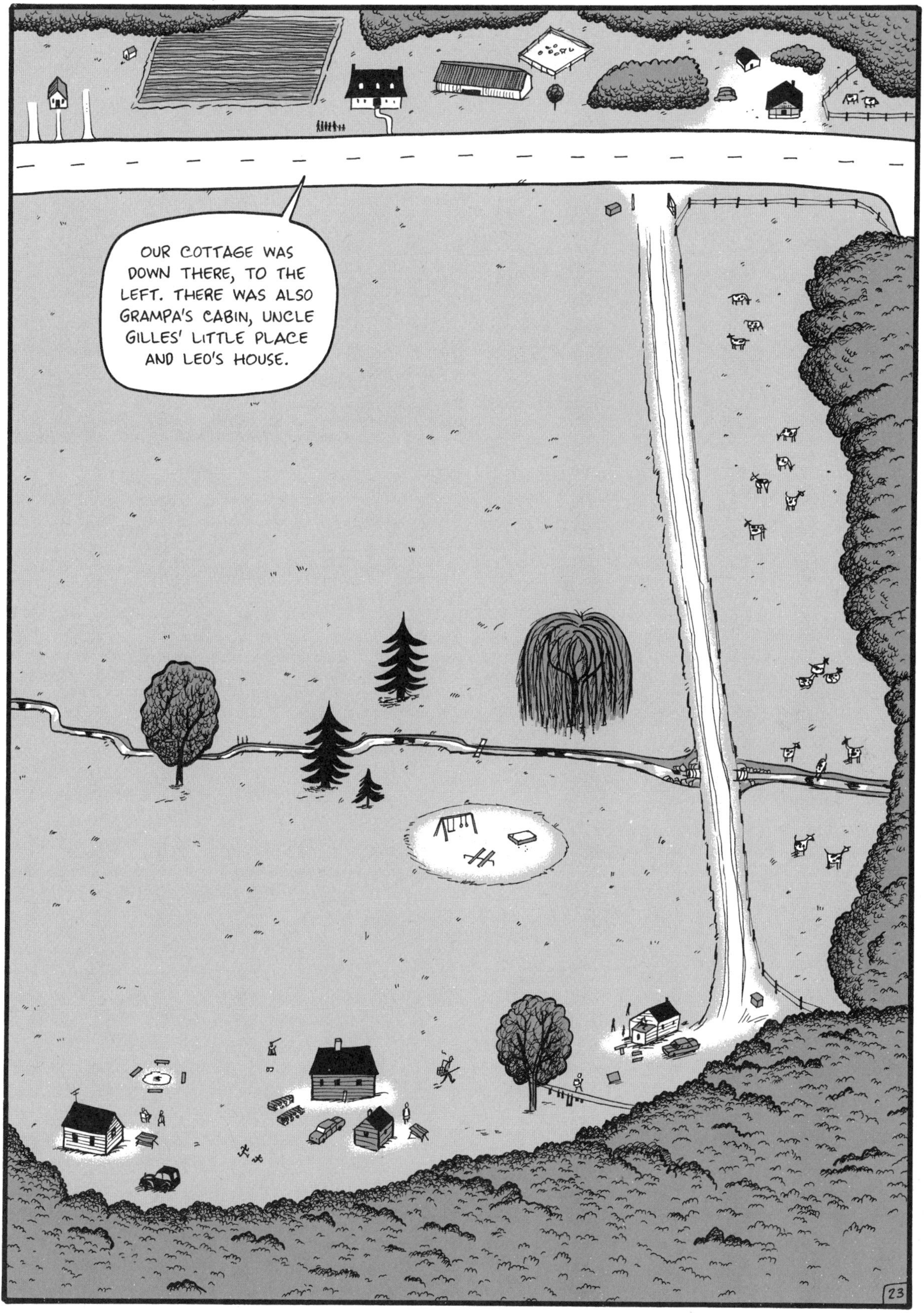
OUR COTTAGE WAS DOWN THERE, TO THE LEFT. THERE WAS ALSO GRAMPA'S CABIN, UNCLE GILLES' LITTLE PLACE AND LEO'S HOUSE.
23

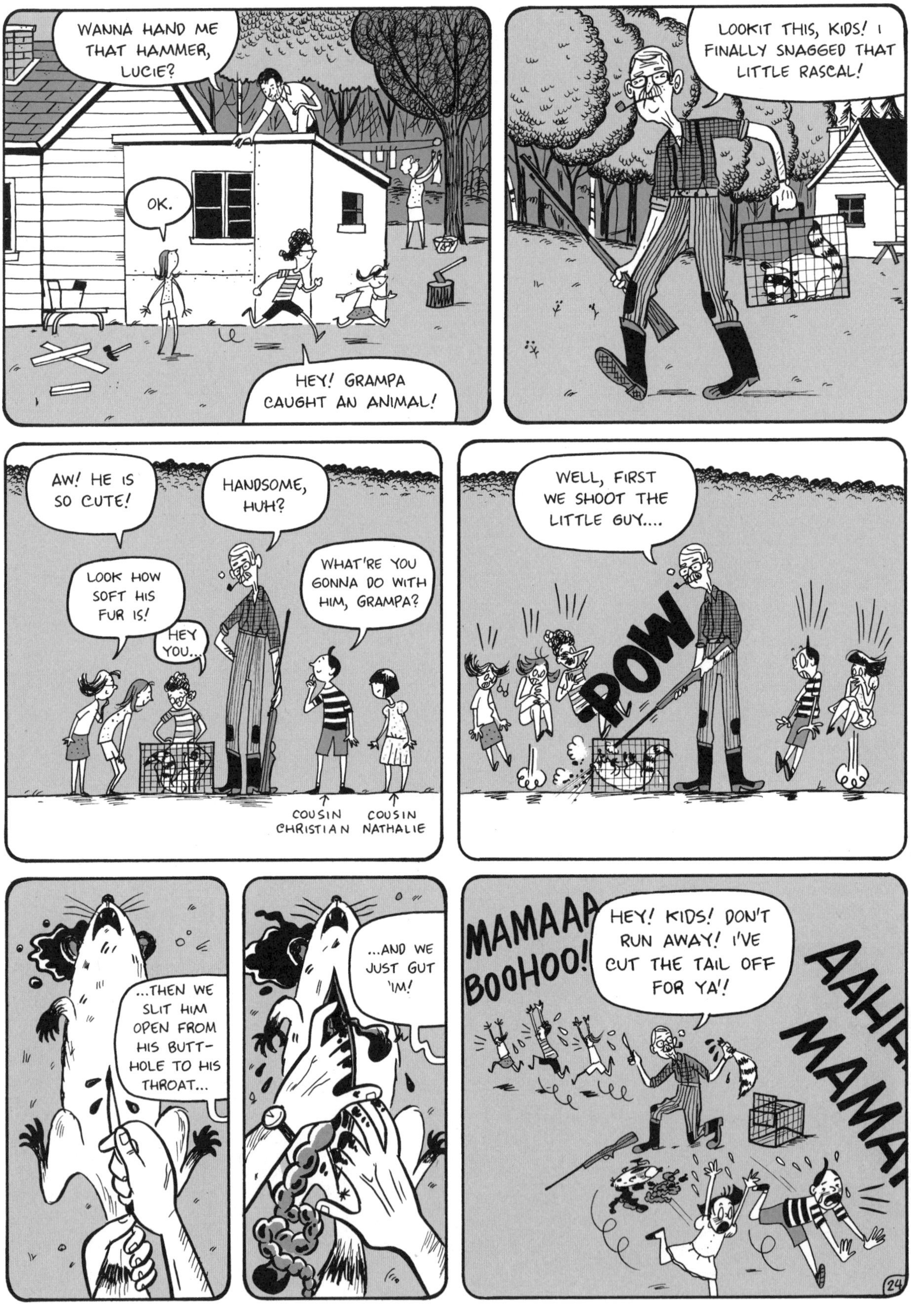
WANNA HAND ME THAT HAMMER, LUCIE?
OK.
HEY! GRAMPA CAUGHT AN ANIMAL!
LOOKIT THIS, KIDS! I FINALLY SNAGGED THAT LITTLE RASCAL!
AW! HE IS SO CUTE!
HANDSOME, HUH?
LOOK HOW SOFT HIS FUR IS!
HEY YOU...
WHAT'RE YOU GONNA DO WITH HIM, GRAMPA?
COUSIN CHRISTIAN
COUSIN NATHALIE
WELL, FIRST WE SHOOT THE LITTLE GUY....
POW
...THEN WE SLIT HIM OPEN FROM HIS BUTT-HOLE TO HIS THROAT...
...AND WE JUST GUT 'IM!
MAMAAA
BOOHOO!
HEY! KIDS! DON'T RUN AWAY! I'VE CUT THE TAIL OFF FOR YA'!
AAHH, MAMA!
24

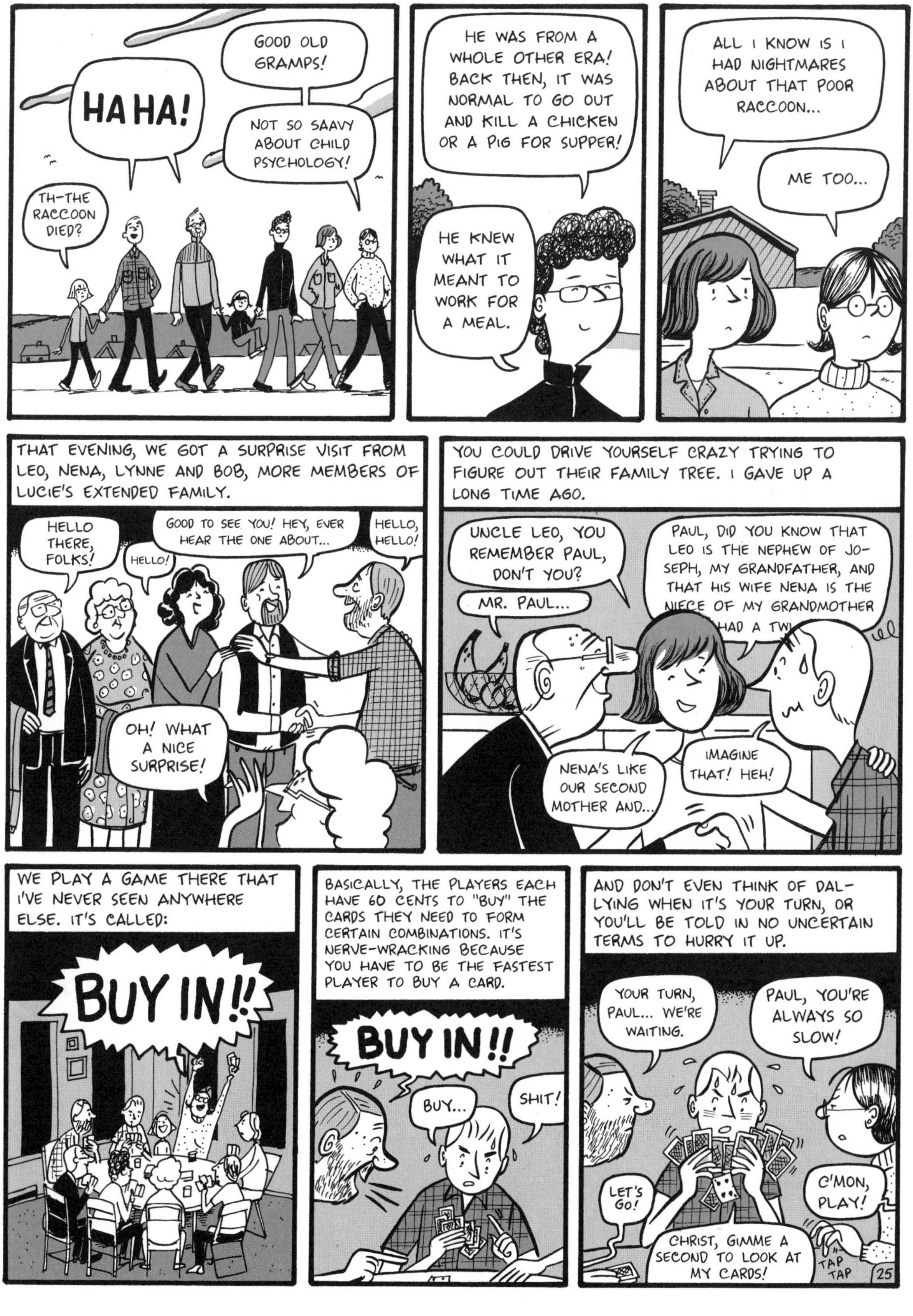
TH-THE RACCOON DIED?
HA HA!
GOOD OLD GRAMPS!
NOT SO SAAVY ABOUT CHILD PSYCHOLOGY!
HE WAS FROM A WHOLE OTHER ERA! BACK THEN, IT WAS NORMAL TO GO OUT AND KILL A CHICKEN OR A PIG FOR SUPPER!
HE KNEW WHAT IT MEANT TO WORK FOR A MEAL.
ALL I KNOW IS I HAD NIGHTMARES ABOUT THAT POOR RACCOON...
ME TOO...
THAT EVENING, WE GOT A SURPRISE VISIT FROM LEO, NENA, LYNNE AND BOB, MORE MEMBERS OF LUCIE'S EXTENDED FAMILY.
HELLO THERE, FOLKS!
HELLO!
GOOD TO SEE YOU! HEY, EVER HEAR THE ONE ABOUT...
HELLO, HELLO!
OH! WHAT A NICE SURPRISE!
YOU COULD DRIVE YOURSELF CRAZY TRYING TO FIGURE OUT THEIR FAMILY TREE. I GAVE UP A LONG TIME AGO.
UNCLE LEO, YOU REMEMBER PAUL, DON'T YOU?
MR. PAUL...
PAUL, DID YOU KNOW THAT LEO IS THE NEPHEW OF JO-SEPH, MY GRANDFATHER, AND THAT HIS WIFE NENA IS THE NIECE OF MY GRANDMOTHER
HAD A TW
NENA'S LIKE OUR SECOND MOTHER AND...
IMAGINE THAT! HEH!
WE PLAY A GAME THERE THAT I'VE NEVER SEEN ANYWHERE ELSE. IT'S CALLED:
BUY IN!!
BASICALLY, THE PLAYERS EACH HAVE 60 CENTS TO "BUY" THE CARDS THEY NEED TO FORM CERTAIN COMBINATIONS. IT'S NERVE-WRACKING BECAUSE YOU HAVE TO BE THE FASTEST PLAYER TO BUY A CARD.
BUY IN!!
BUY...
SHIT!
AND DON'T EVEN THINK OF DAL-LYING WHEN IT'S YOUR TURN, OR YOU'LL BE TOLD IN NO UNCERTAIN TERMS TO HURRY IT UP.
YOUR TURN, PAUL... WE'RE WAITING.
PAUL, YOU'RE ALWAYS SO SLOW!
LET'S GO!
C'MON, PLAY!
CHRIST, GIMME A SECOND TO LOOK AT MY CARDS!
TAP TAP
25

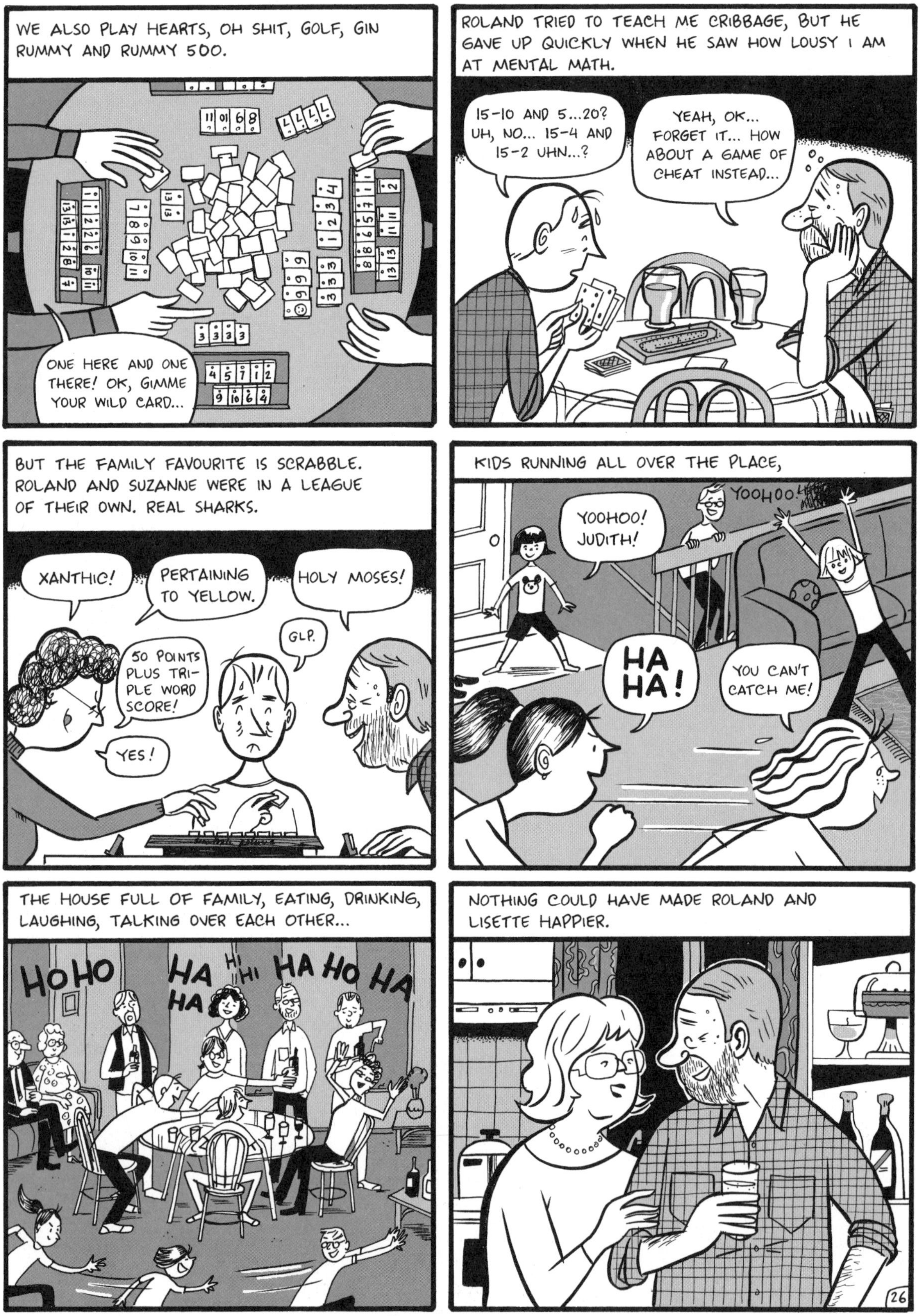
WE ALSO PLAY HEARTS, OH SHIT, GOLF, GIN RUMMY AND RUMMY 500.
ONE HERE AND ONE THERE! OK, GIMME YOUR WILD CARD...
ROLAND TRIED TO TEACH ME CRIBBAGE, BUT HE GAVE UP QUICKLY WHEN HE SAW HOW LOUSY I AM AT MENTAL MATH.
15-10 AND 5...20? UH, NO... 15-4 AND 15-2 UHN...?
YEAH, OK... FORGET IT... HOW ABOUT A GAME OF CHEAT INSTEAD...
BUT THE FAMILY FAVOURITE IS SCRABBLE. ROLAND AND SUZANNE WERE IN A LEAGUE OF THEIR OWN. REAL SHARKS.
XANTHIC!
PERTAINING TO YELLOW.
HOLY MOSES!
GLP.
50 POINTS PLUS TRIPLE WORD SCORE!
YES!
KIDS RUNNING ALL OVER THE PLACE,
YOOHOO!
YOOHOO! JUDITH!
HA HA!
YOU CAN'T CATCH ME!
THE HOUSE FULL OF FAMILY, EATING, DRINKING, LAUGHING, TALKING OVER EACH OTHER...
HO HO
HA HA
HI HI
HA HO HA
NOTHING COULD HAVE MADE ROLAND AND LISETTE HAPPIER.
26

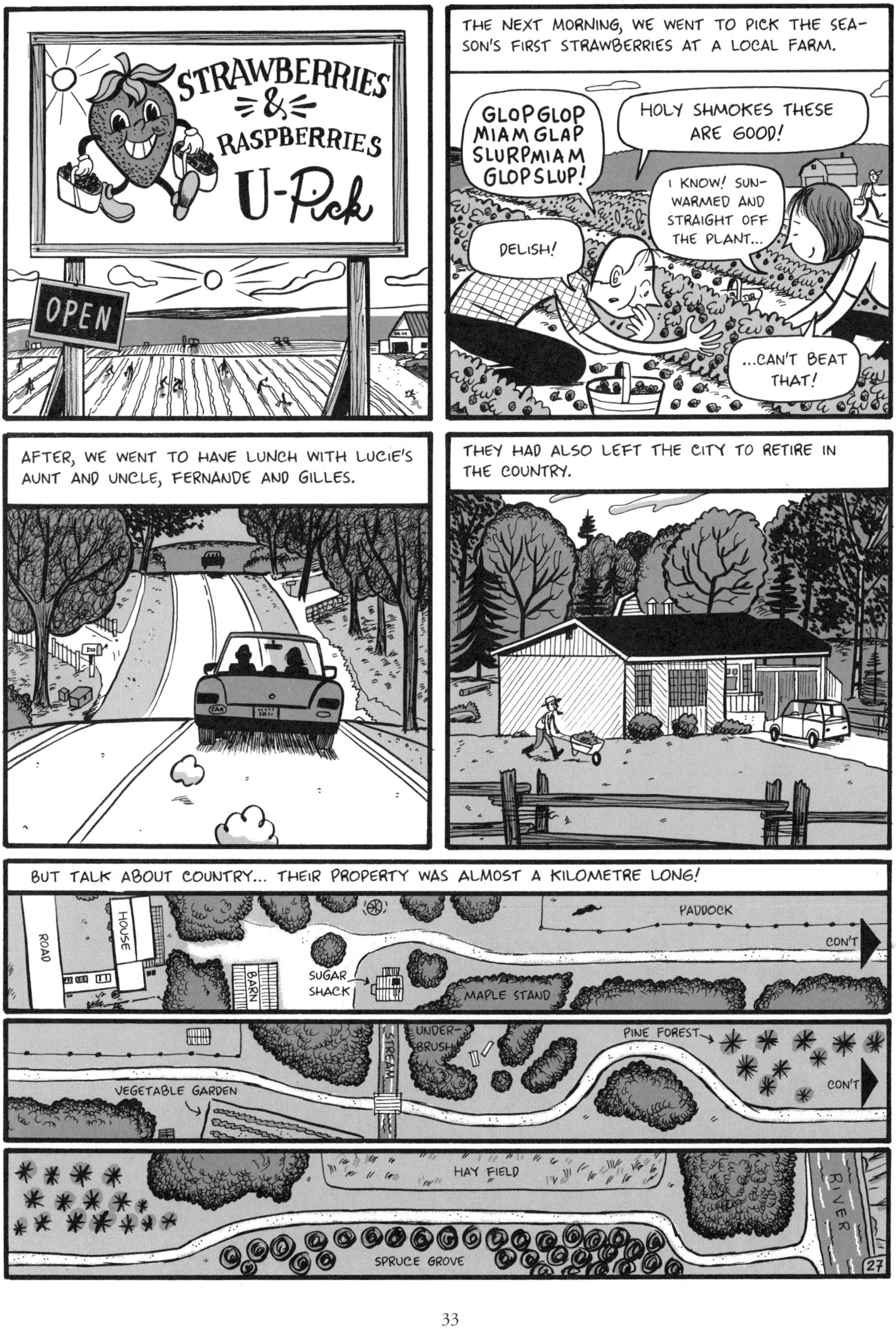
STRAWBERRIES & RASPBERRIES U-Pick
OPEN
THE NEXT MORNING, WE WENT TO PICK THE SEASON'S FIRST STRAWBERRIES AT A LOCAL FARM.
GLOPGLOP MIAMGLAP SLURPMIAM GLOPSLUP!
HOLY SHMOKES THESE ARE GOOD!
DELISH!
I KNOW! SUN-WARMED AND STRAIGHT OFF THE PLANT...
...CAN'T BEAT THAT!
AFTER, WE WENT TO HAVE LUNCH WITH LUCIE'S AUNT AND UNCLE, FERNANDE AND GILLES.
THEY HAD ALSO LEFT THE CITY TO RETIRE IN THE COUNTRY.
BUT TALK ABOUT COUNTRY... THEIR PROPERTY WAS ALMOST A KILOMETRE LONG!
ROAD
HOUSE
BARN
SUGAR SHACK
MAPLE STAND
PADDOCK
CON'T
VEGETABLE GARDEN
STREAM
UNDER-BRUSH
PINE FOREST
CON'T
HAY FIELD
SPRUCE GROVE
RIVER
27

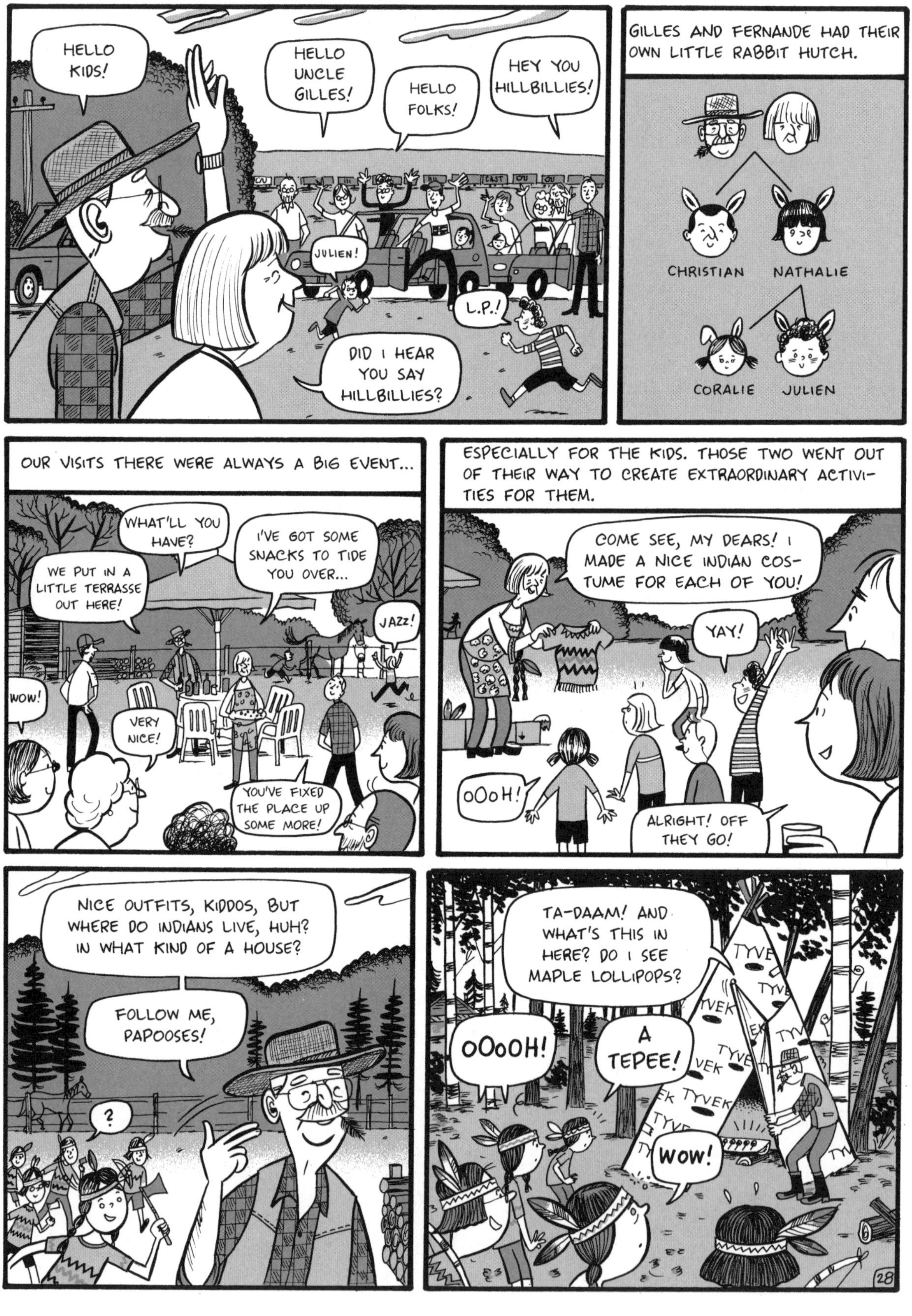
HELLO KIDS!
HELLO UNCLE GILLES!
HELLO FOLKS!
HEY YOU HILLBILLIES!
JULIEN!
L.P.!
DID I HEAR YOU SAY HILLBILLIES?
GILLES AND FERNANDE HAD THEIR OWN LITTLE RABBIT HUTCH.
CHRISTIAN
NATHALIE
CORALIE
JULIEN
OUR VISITS THERE WERE ALWAYS A BIG EVENT...
WHAT'LL YOU HAVE?
I'VE GOT SOME SNACKS TO TIDE YOU OVER...
WE PUT IN A LITTLE TERRASSE OUT HERE!
JAZZ!
WOW!
VERY NICE!
YOU'VE FIXED THE PLACE UP SOME MORE!
ESPECIALLY FOR THE KIDS. THOSE TWO WENT OUT OF THEIR WAY TO CREATE EXTRAORDINARY ACTIVITIES FOR THEM.
COME SEE, MY DEARS! I MADE A NICE INDIAN COSTUME FOR EACH OF YOU!
YAY!
OOoH!
ALRIGHT! OFF THEY GO!
NICE OUTFITS, KIDDOS, BUT WHERE DO INDIANS LIVE, HUH? IN WHAT KIND OF A HOUSE?
FOLLOW ME, PAPOOSES!
?
TA-DAAM! AND WHAT'S THIS IN HERE? DO I SEE MAPLE LOLLIPOPS?
OOoOH!
A TEPEE!
WOW!
28

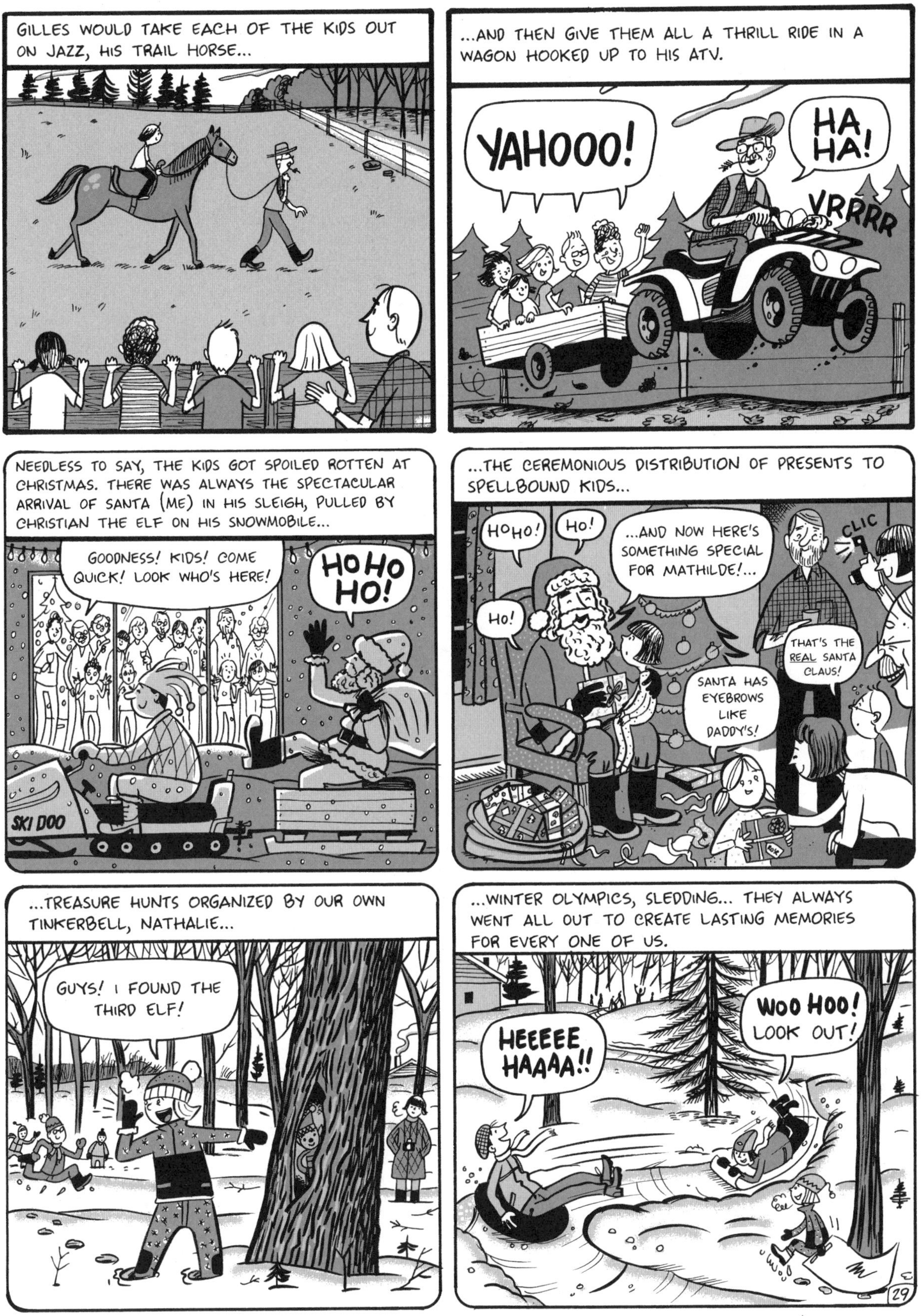
GILLES WOULD TAKE EACH OF THE KIDS OUT ON JAZZ, HIS TRAIL HORSE...
...AND THEN GIVE THEM ALL A THRILL RIDE IN A WAGON HOOKED UP TO HIS ATV.
YAHOOO!
HA HA!
VRRRR
NEEDLESS TO SAY, THE KIDS GOT SPOILED ROTTEN AT CHRISTMAS. THERE WAS ALWAYS THE SPECTACULAR ARRIVAL OF SANTA (ME) IN HIS SLEIGH, PULLED BY CHRISTIAN THE ELF ON HIS SNOWMOBILE...
GOODNESS! KIDS! COME QUICK! LOOK WHO'S HERE!
HO HO HO!
SKI DOO
...THE CEREMONIOUS DISTRIBUTION OF PRESENTS TO SPELLBOUND KIDS...
HOHO!
HO!
HO!
...AND NOW HERE'S SOMETHING SPECIAL FOR MATHILDE!...
CLIC
THAT'S THE REAL SANTA CLAUS!
SANTA HAS EYEBROWS LIKE DADDY'S!
...TREASURE HUNTS ORGANIZED BY OUR OWN TINKERBELL, NATHALIE...
GUYS! I FOUND THE THIRD ELF!
...WINTER OLYMPICS, SLEDDING... THEY ALWAYS WENT ALL OUT TO CREATE LASTING MEMORIES FOR EVERY ONE OF US.
HEEEEE HAAAA!!
WOO HOO! LOOK OUT!
29

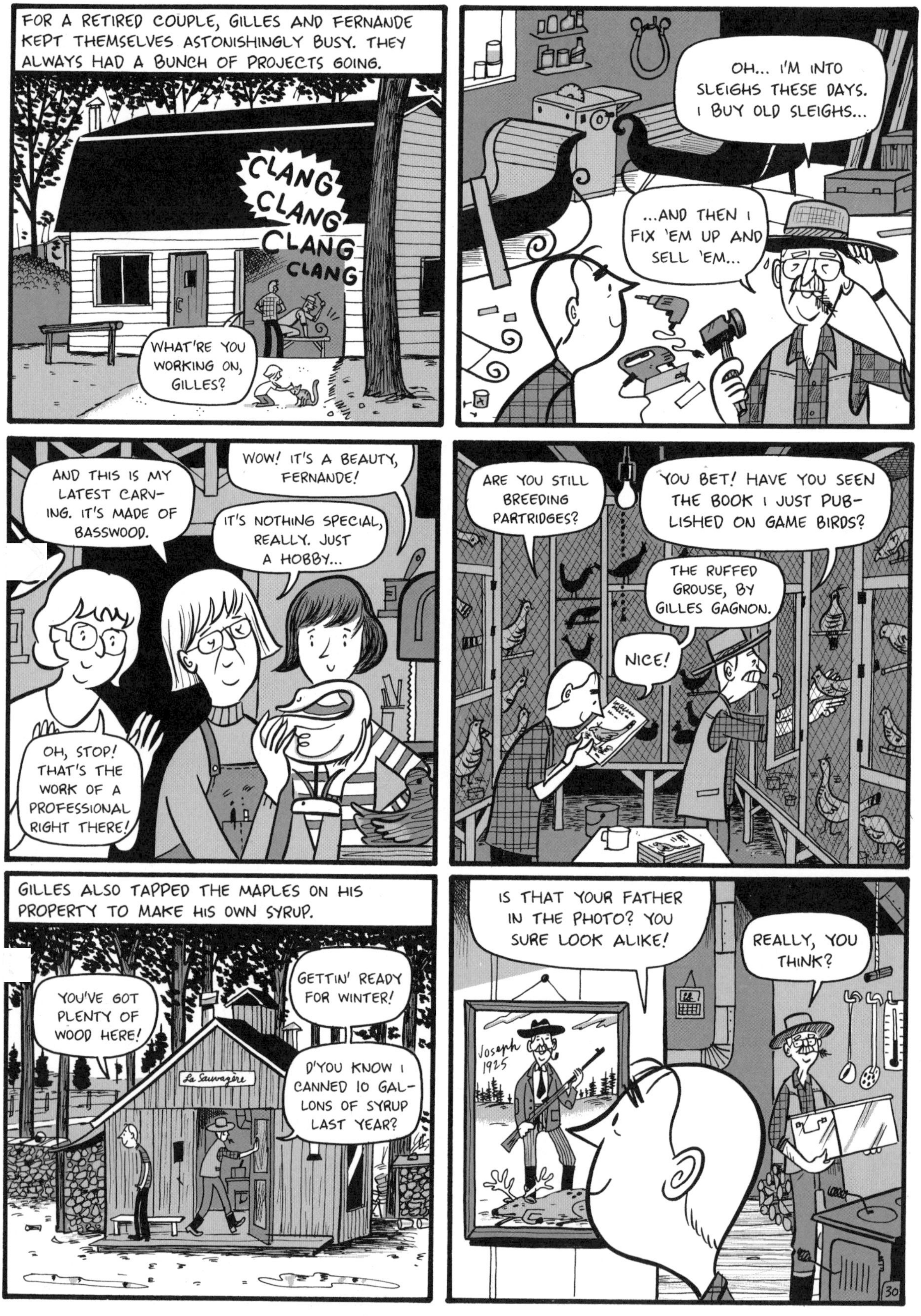
FOR A RETIRED COUPLE, GILLES AND FERNANDE KEPT THEMSELVES ASTONISHINGLY BUSY. THEY ALWAYS HAD A BUNCH OF PROJECTS GOING.
CLANG CLANG CLANG CLANG
WHAT'RE YOU WORKING ON, GILLES?
OH... I'M INTO SLEIGHS THESE DAYS. I BUY OLD SLEIGHS...
...AND THEN I FIX 'EM UP AND SELL 'EM...
AND THIS IS MY LATEST CARVING. IT'S MADE OF BASSWOOD.
WOW! IT'S A BEAUTY, FERNANDE!
IT'S NOTHING SPECIAL, REALLY. JUST A HOBBY...
OH, STOP! THAT'S THE WORK OF A PROFESSIONAL RIGHT THERE!
ARE YOU STILL BREEDING PARTRIDGES?
YOU BET! HAVE YOU SEEN THE BOOK I JUST PUBLISHED ON GAME BIRDS?
THE RUFFED GROUSE, BY GILLES GAGNON.
NICE!
GILLES ALSO TAPPED THE MAPLES ON HIS PROPERTY TO MAKE HIS OWN SYRUP.
YOU'VE GOT PLENTY OF WOOD HERE!
GETTIN' READY FOR WINTER!
D'YOU KNOW I CANNED 10 GALLONS OF SYRUP LAST YEAR?
La Sauvagère
IS THAT YOUR FATHER IN THE PHOTO? YOU SURE LOOK ALIKE!
REALLY, YOU THINK?
Joseph 1925
30

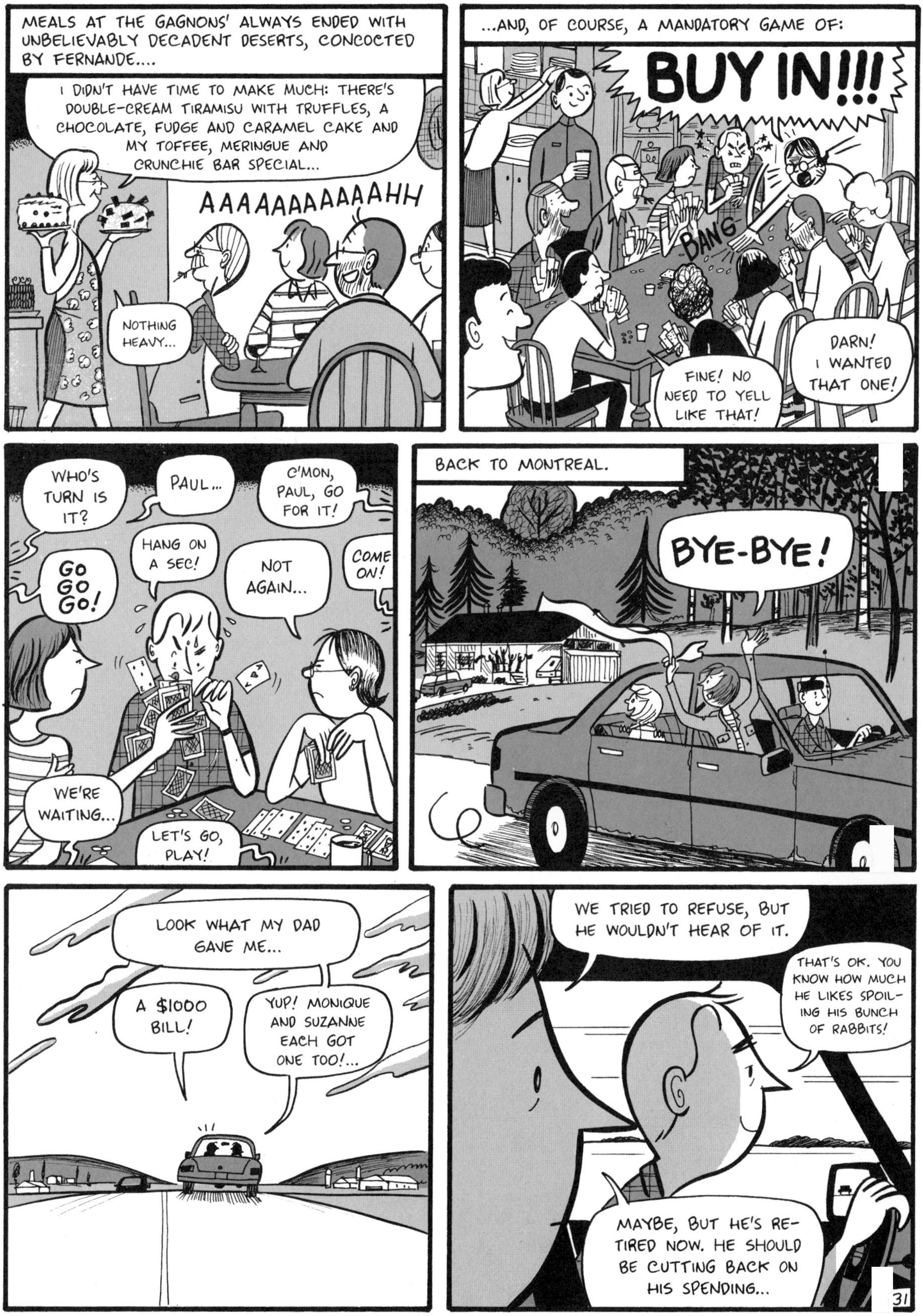
MEALS AT THE GAGNONS' ALWAYS ENDED WITH UNBELIEVABLY DECADENT DESERTS, CONCOCTED BY FERNANDE....
I DIDN'T HAVE TIME TO MAKE MUCH: THERE'S DOUBLE-CREAM TIRAMISU WITH TRUFFLES, A CHOCOLATE, FUDGE AND CARAMEL CAKE AND MY TOFFEE, MERINGUE AND CRUNCHIE BAR SPECIAL...
AAAAAAAAAAAHH
NOTHING HEAVY...
...AND, OF COURSE, A MANDATORY GAME OF:
BUY IN!!!!
BANG
FINE! NO NEED TO YELL LIKE THAT!
DARN! I WANTED THAT ONE!
WHO'S TURN IS IT?
PAUL...
C'MON, PAUL, GO FOR IT!
GO GO GO!
HANG ON A SEC!
NOT AGAIN...
COME ON!
WE'RE WAITING...
LET'S GO, PLAY!
BACK TO MONTREAL.
BYE-BYE!
LOOK WHAT MY DAD GAVE ME...
A $1000 BILL!
YUP! MONIQUE AND SUZANNE EACH GOT ONE TOO!...
WE TRIED TO REFUSE, BUT HE WOULDN'T HEAR OF IT.
THAT'S OK. YOU KNOW HOW MUCH HE LIKES SPOILING HIS BUNCH OF RABBITS!
MAYBE, BUT HE'S RETIRED NOW. HE SHOULD BE CUTTING BACK ON HIS SPENDING...
31

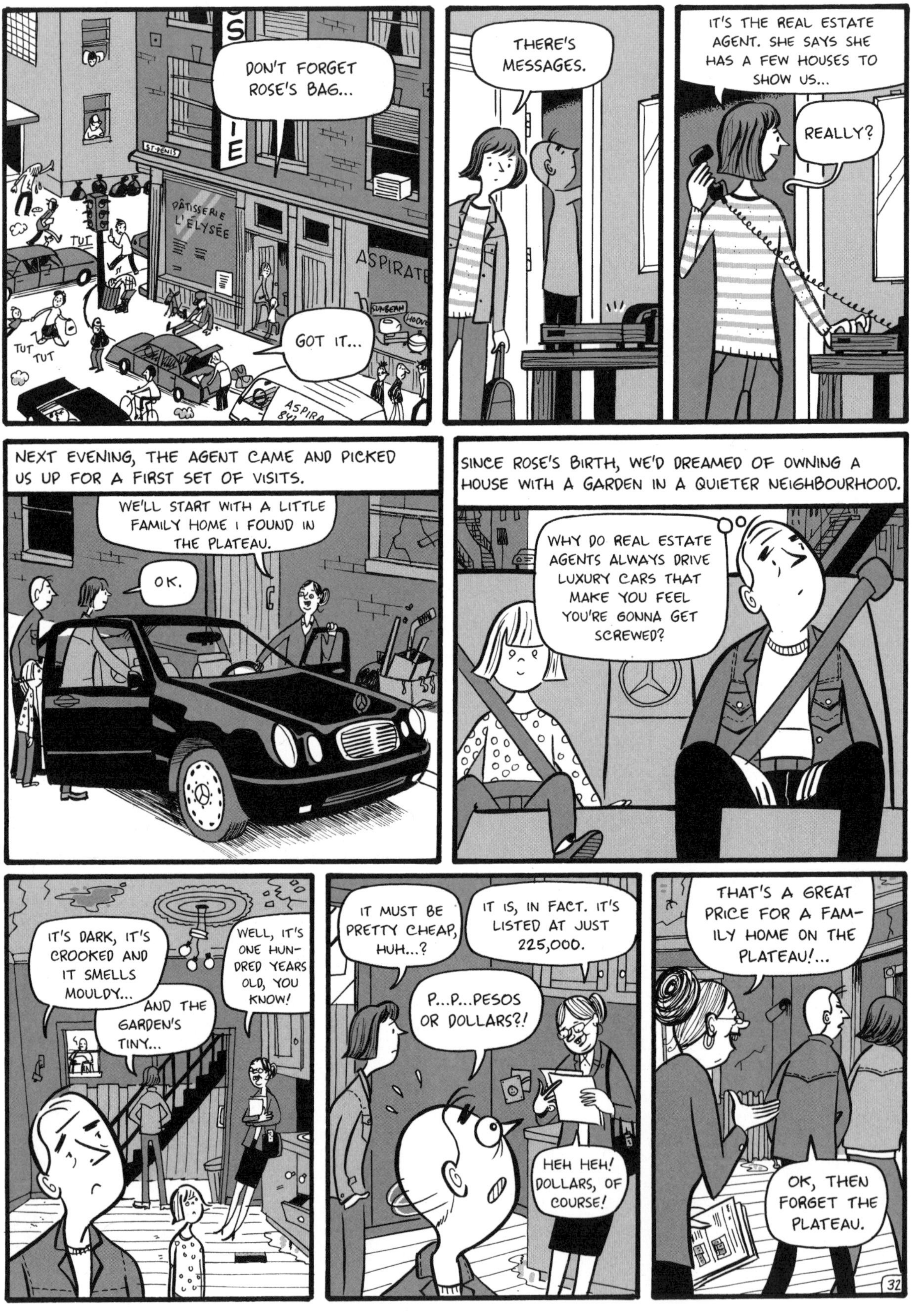
DON'T FORGET ROSE'S BAG...
ST-DENIS
PÂTISSERIE L'ÉLYSÉE
ASPIRATE
SUNBEAM
TUT
TUT TUT
GOT IT...
THERE'S MESSAGES.
IT'S THE REAL ESTATE AGENT. SHE SAYS SHE HAS A FEW HOUSES TO SHOW US...
REALLY?
NEXT EVENING, THE AGENT CAME AND PICKED US UP FOR A FIRST SET OF VISITS.
WE'LL START WITH A LITTLE FAMILY HOME I FOUND IN THE PLATEAU.
OK.
SINCE ROSE'S BIRTH, WE'D DREAMED OF OWNING A HOUSE WITH A GARDEN IN A QUIETER NEIGHBOURHOOD.
WHY DO REAL ESTATE AGENTS ALWAYS DRIVE LUXURY CARS THAT MAKE YOU FEEL YOU'RE GONNA GET SCREWED?
IT'S DARK, IT'S CROOKED AND IT SMELLS MOULDY...
AND THE GARDEN'S TINY...
WELL, IT'S ONE HUNDRED YEARS OLD, YOU KNOW!
IT MUST BE PRETTY CHEAP, HUH...?
IT IS, IN FACT. IT'S LISTED AT JUST 225,000.
P...P...PESOS OR DOLLARS?!
HEH HEH! DOLLARS, OF COURSE!
THAT'S A GREAT PRICE FOR A FAMILY HOME ON THE PLATEAU!...
OK, THEN FORGET THE PLATEAU.
32

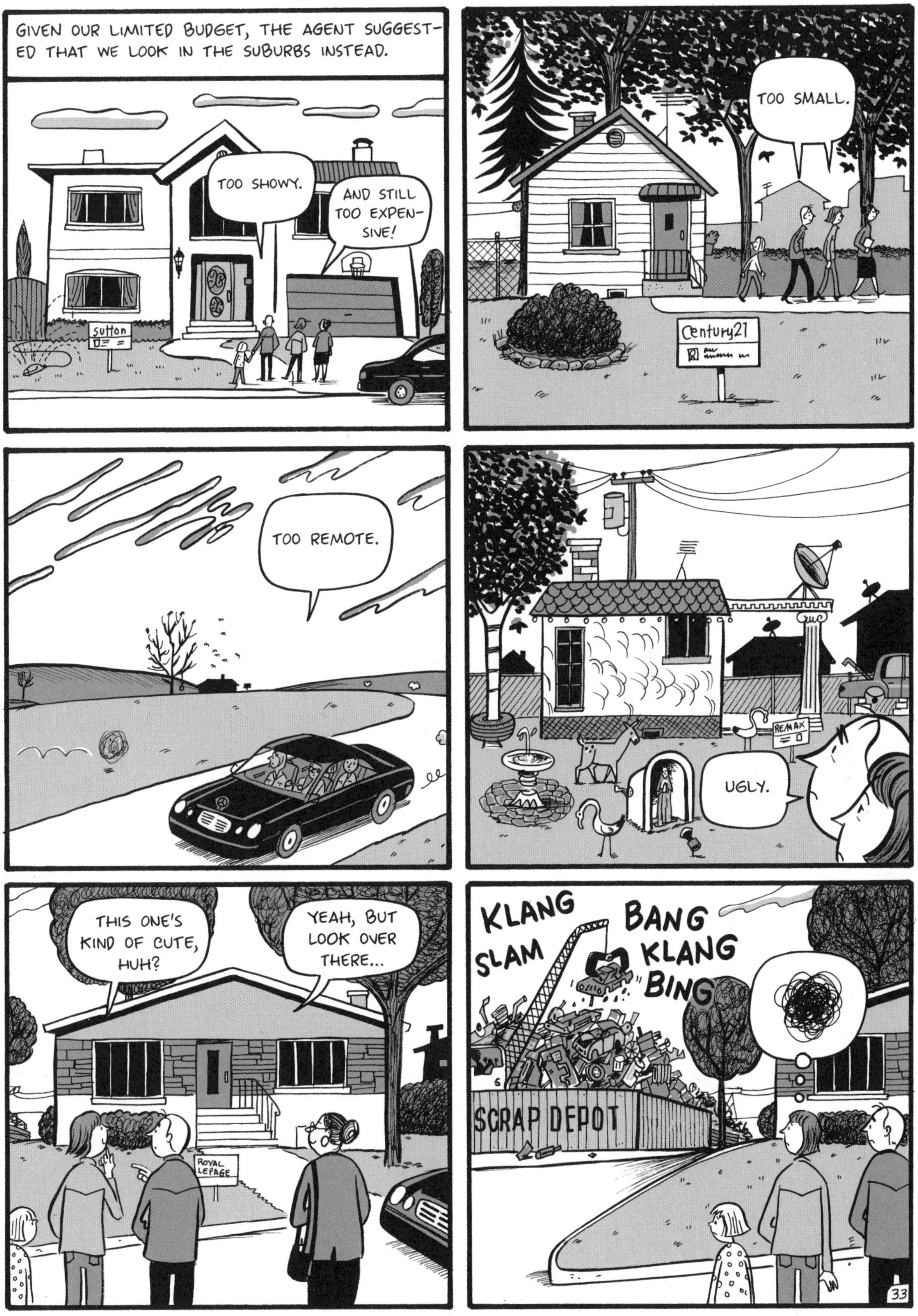
GIVEN OUR LIMITED BUDGET, THE AGENT SUGGESTED THAT WE LOOK IN THE SUBURBS INSTEAD.
sutton
TOO SHOWY.
AND STILL TOO EXPENSIVE!
TOO SMALL.
Century21
TOO REMOTE.
RE/MAX
UGLY.
THIS ONE'S KIND OF CUTE, HUH?
YEAH, BUT LOOK OVER THERE...
ROYAL LEPAGE
KLANG
SLAM
BANG
KLANG
BING
SCRAP DEPOT
33

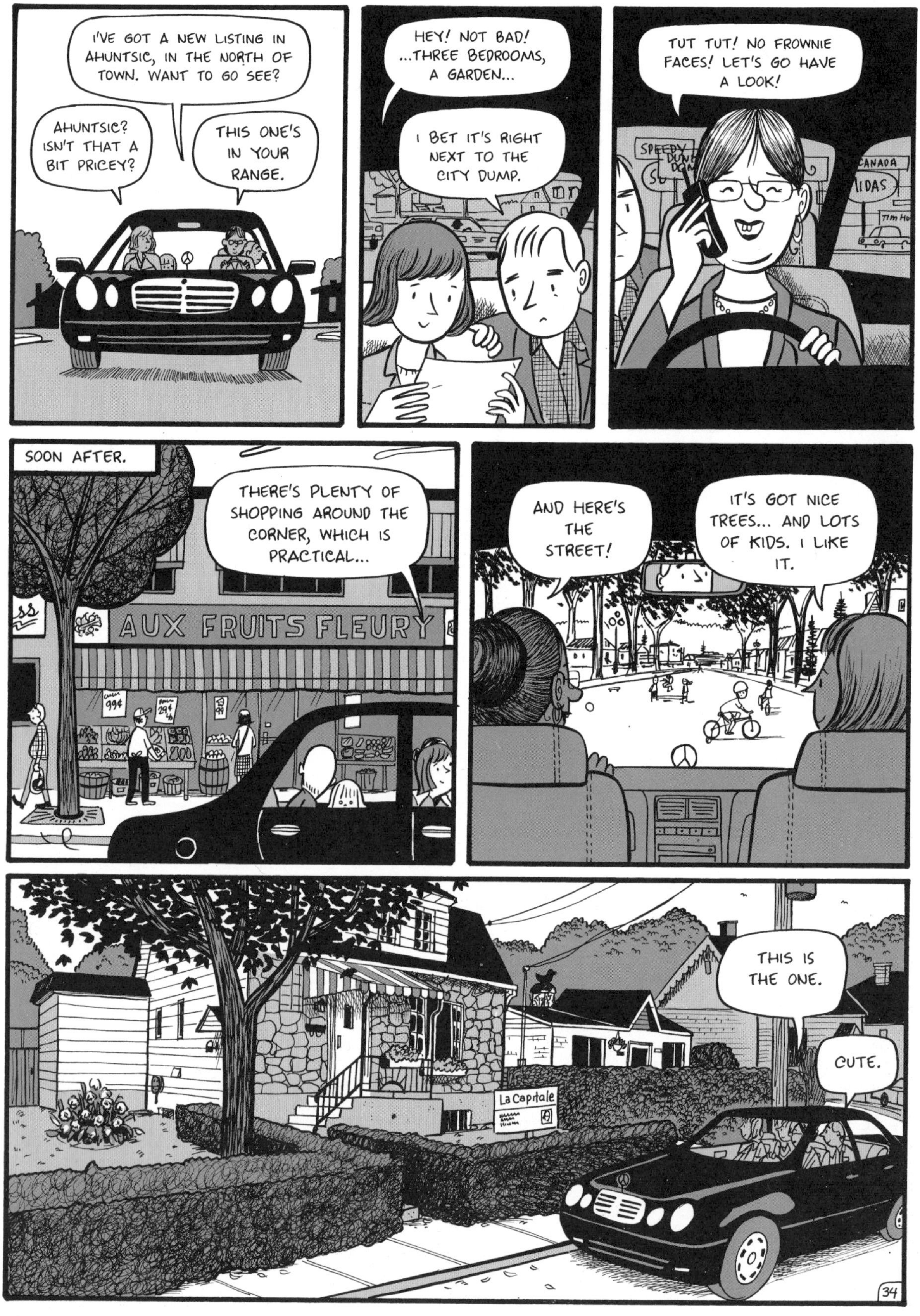
I'VE GOT A NEW LISTING IN AHUNTSIC, IN THE NORTH OF TOWN. WANT TO GO SEE?
AHUNTSIC? ISN'T THAT A BIT PRICEY?
THIS ONE'S IN YOUR RANGE.
HEY! NOT BAD! ...THREE BEDROOMS, A GARDEN...
I BET IT'S RIGHT NEXT TO THE CITY DUMP.
TUT TUT! NO FROWNIE FACES! LET'S GO HAVE A LOOK!
SOON AFTER.
THERE'S PLENTY OF SHOPPING AROUND THE CORNER, WHICH IS PRACTICAL...
AUX FRUITS FLEURY
AND HERE'S THE STREET!
IT'S GOT NICE TREES... AND LOTS OF KIDS. I LIKE IT.
THIS IS THE ONE.
CUTE.
La Capitale
34

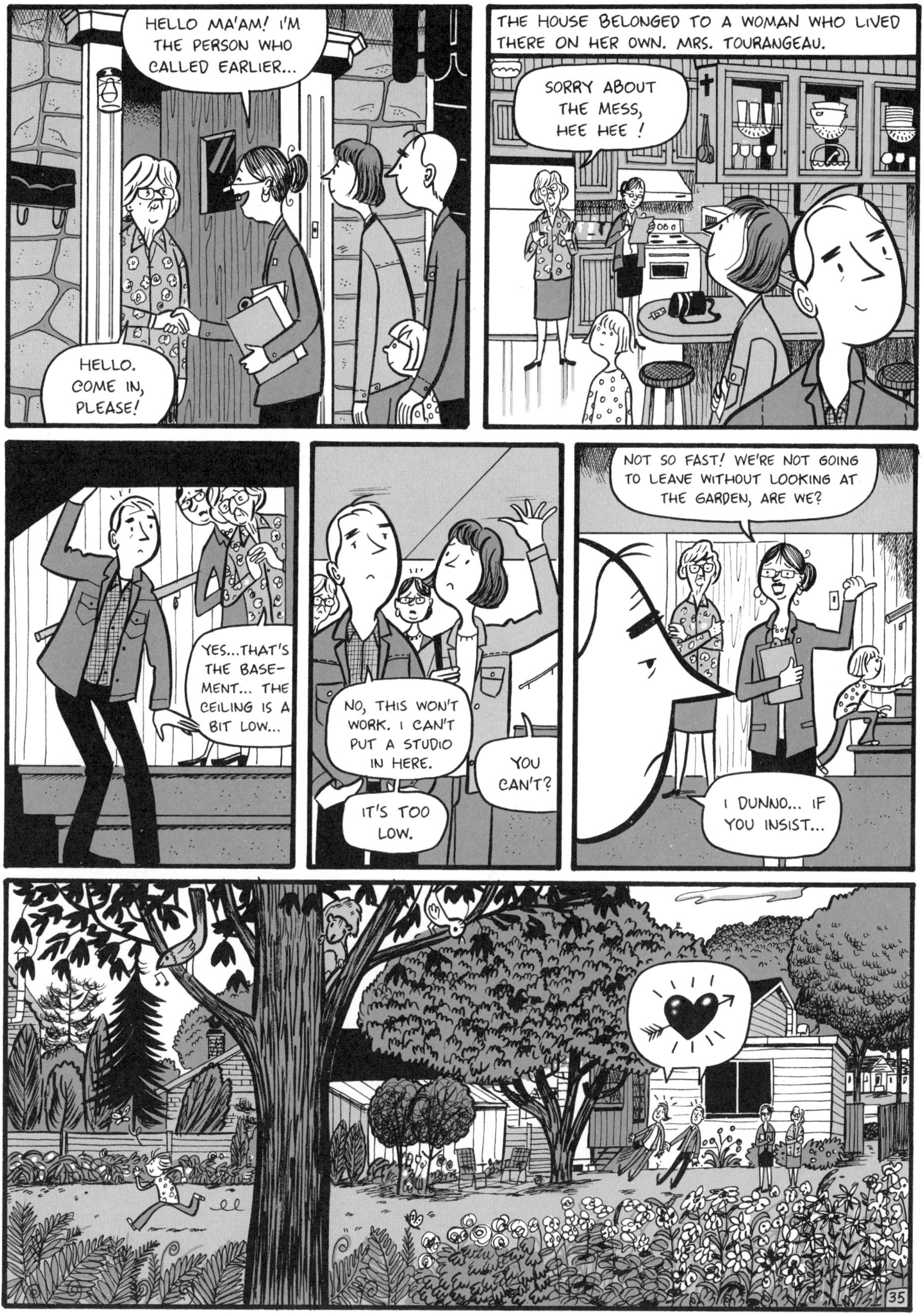
HELLO MA'AM! I'M THE PERSON WHO CALLED EARLIER...
HELLO. COME IN, PLEASE!
THE HOUSE BELONGED TO A WOMAN WHO LIVED THERE ON HER OWN. MRS. TOURANGEAU.
SORRY ABOUT THE MESS, HEE HEE!
YES...THAT'S THE BASE-MENT... THE CEILING IS A BIT LOW...
NO, THIS WON'T WORK. I CAN'T PUT A STUDIO IN HERE.
YOU CAN'T?
IT'S TOO LOW.
NOT SO FAST! WE'RE NOT GOING TO LEAVE WITHOUT LOOKING AT THE GARDEN, ARE WE?
I DUNNO... IF YOU INSIST...
35

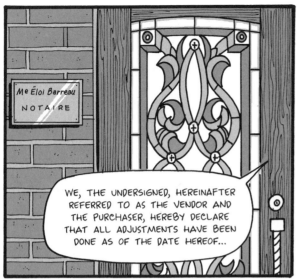

Me Éloi Barreau
NOTAIRE

WE, THE UNDERSIGNED, HEREINAFTER REFERRED TO AS THE VENDOR AND THE PURCHASER, HEREBY DECLARE THAT ALL ADJUSTMENTS HAVE BEEN DONE AS OF THE DATE HEREOF...

...IN ACCORDANCE WITH THE STATEMENTS PROVIDED, AT OUR MUTUAL SATISFACTION, ETC. ETC.

SIGN HERE.

AND HERE.

I HOPE YOUR FAMILY WILL BE HAPPY IN MY HOUSE.

YES! I'M SURE WE WILL, MRS. TOURANGEAU...

GOOD LUCK WITH YOUR MOVE AND ALL!...

UH... CAN WE DROP YOU OFF SOMEWHERE?

SNIFF... THANKS. MY NEPHEW IS PICKING ME UP....

GOOD BYE.

IT LOOKS LIKE SHE'S LESS HAPPY ABOUT THE SALE THAN WE ARE...

SHE TOLD ME SHE'S SPENT MOST OF HER LIFE IN THAT HOUSE. SHE NEVER MARRIED. SHE LIVED WITH HER PARENTS AND TOOK CARE OF THEM UNTIL THEY DIED. THAT'S TOUCHING, ISN'T IT?

I GUESS IT MUST BE BREAKING HER HEART TO SELL THE HOUSE...

36

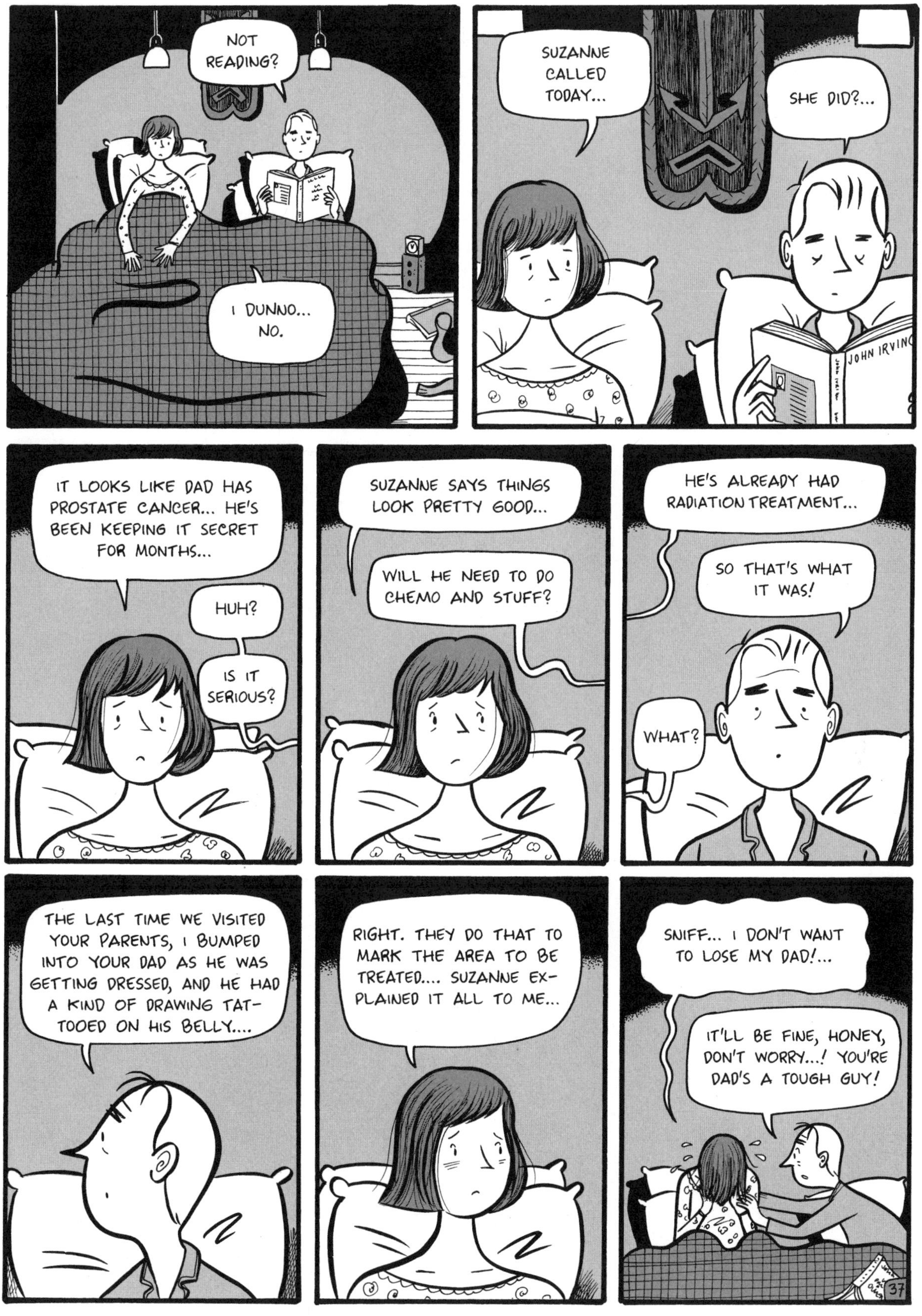
NOT READING?
I DUNNO... NO.
SUZANNE CALLED TODAY...
SHE DID?...
JOHN IRVIN
IT LOOKS LIKE DAD HAS PROSTATE CANCER... HE'S BEEN KEEPING IT SECRET FOR MONTHS...
HUH?
IS IT SERIOUS?
SUZANNE SAYS THINGS LOOK PRETTY GOOD...
WILL HE NEED TO DO CHEMO AND STUFF?
HE'S ALREADY HAD RADIATION TREATMENT...
WHAT?
SO THAT'S WHAT IT WAS!
THE LAST TIME WE VISITED YOUR PARENTS, I BUMPED INTO YOUR DAD AS HE WAS GETTING DRESSED, AND HE HAD A KIND OF DRAWING TAT-TOOED ON HIS BELLY....
RIGHT. THEY DO THAT TO MARK THE AREA TO BE TREATED.... SUZANNE EX-PLAINED IT ALL TO ME...
SNIFF... I DON'T WANT TO LOSE MY DAD!...
IT'LL BE FINE, HONEY, DON'T WORRY...! YOU'RE DAD'S A TOUGH GUY!
37

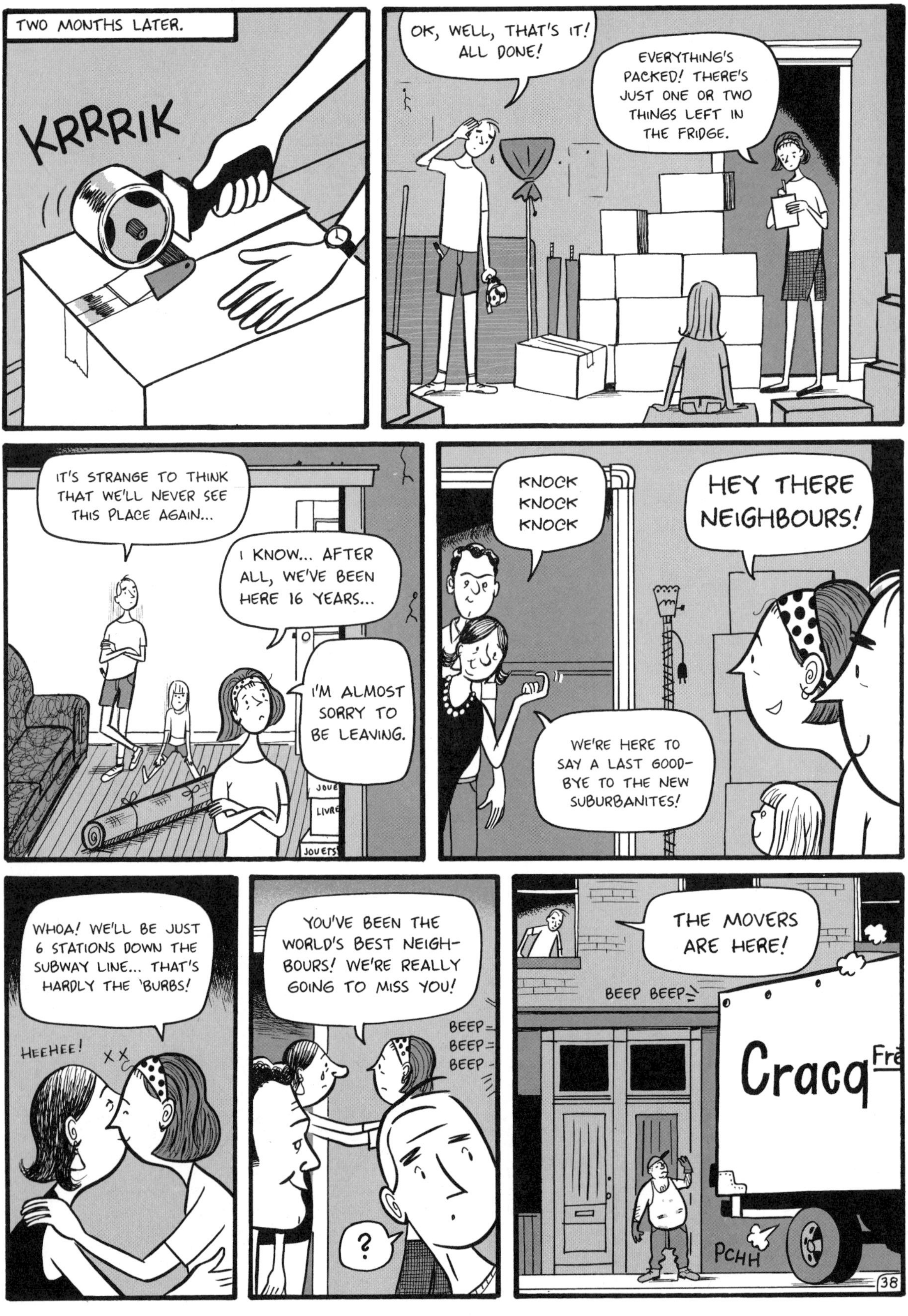
TWO MONTHS LATER.
KRRRIK
OK, WELL, THAT'S IT! ALL DONE!
EVERYTHING'S PACKED! THERE'S JUST ONE OR TWO THINGS LEFT IN THE FRIDGE.
IT'S STRANGE TO THINK THAT WE'LL NEVER SEE THIS PLACE AGAIN...
I KNOW... AFTER ALL, WE'VE BEEN HERE 16 YEARS...
I'M ALMOST SORRY TO BE LEAVING.
JOUETS
LIVRE
JOUETS
KNOCK KNOCK KNOCK
HEY THERE NEIGHBOURS!
WE'RE HERE TO SAY A LAST GOOD-BYE TO THE NEW SUBURBANITES!
WHOA! WE'LL BE JUST 6 STATIONS DOWN THE SUBWAY LINE... THAT'S HARDLY THE 'BURBS!
HEEHEE!
YOU'VE BEEN THE WORLD'S BEST NEIGH-BOURS! WE'RE REALLY GOING TO MISS YOU!
BEEP BEEP BEEP
?
THE MOVERS ARE HERE!
BEEP BEEP
Cracq Frè
PCHH
38

THREE HOURS LATER.

OH! THIS IS SO NICE! MRS. TOURANGEAU LEFT US A NOTE: "WELCOME TO YOUR NEW HOME! I PICKED A FEW APPLES FOR YOU SO THEY DON'T SPOIL. DON'T FORGET TO RESET THE CIRCUIT BREAKER FOR THE HOT WATER HEATER. IF YOU HAVE ANY QUESTIONS AT ALL, PLEASE FEEL FREE TO CALL ME." MUGUETTE TOURANGEAU.

THAT'S SWEET!

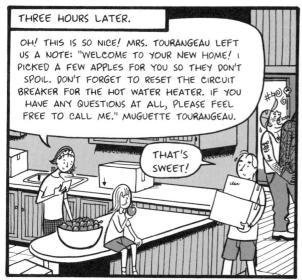

THE APPLE TREE WAS HEAVY WITH FRUIT AND BIRDS WERE CHIRPING. THE GARDEN WAS MORE BEAUTIFUL THAN WE REMEMBERED.

THIS IS OURS! CAN YOU BELIEVE IT?

I KNOW... IT'S CRAZY!

HOW ABOUT WE INVITE FRANCE, PETER AND THE GIRLS? WE CAN ORDER PIZZA AND HAVE A PICNIC OUT HERE TO CELEBRATE! SOUND GOOD?

COOL! GOOD IDEA!

YES-SS!

IT'LL BE OUR FIRST SUPPER HERE!

HELLO FRANCE, LUCIE HERE...

??? ?

HUH?

WHAT'S WRONG?

NO!

WHERE'S HE NOW?

DON'T WORRY, IT'LL BE OK!...

OK, WELL, LET US KNOW...

WHAT'S GOING ON?

BYE.

FRANCE AND PETER HAD A FIGHT.... PETER LEFT TO "THINK THINGS OVER"...

OH WELL, IT'S HARDLY THE FIRST TIME...

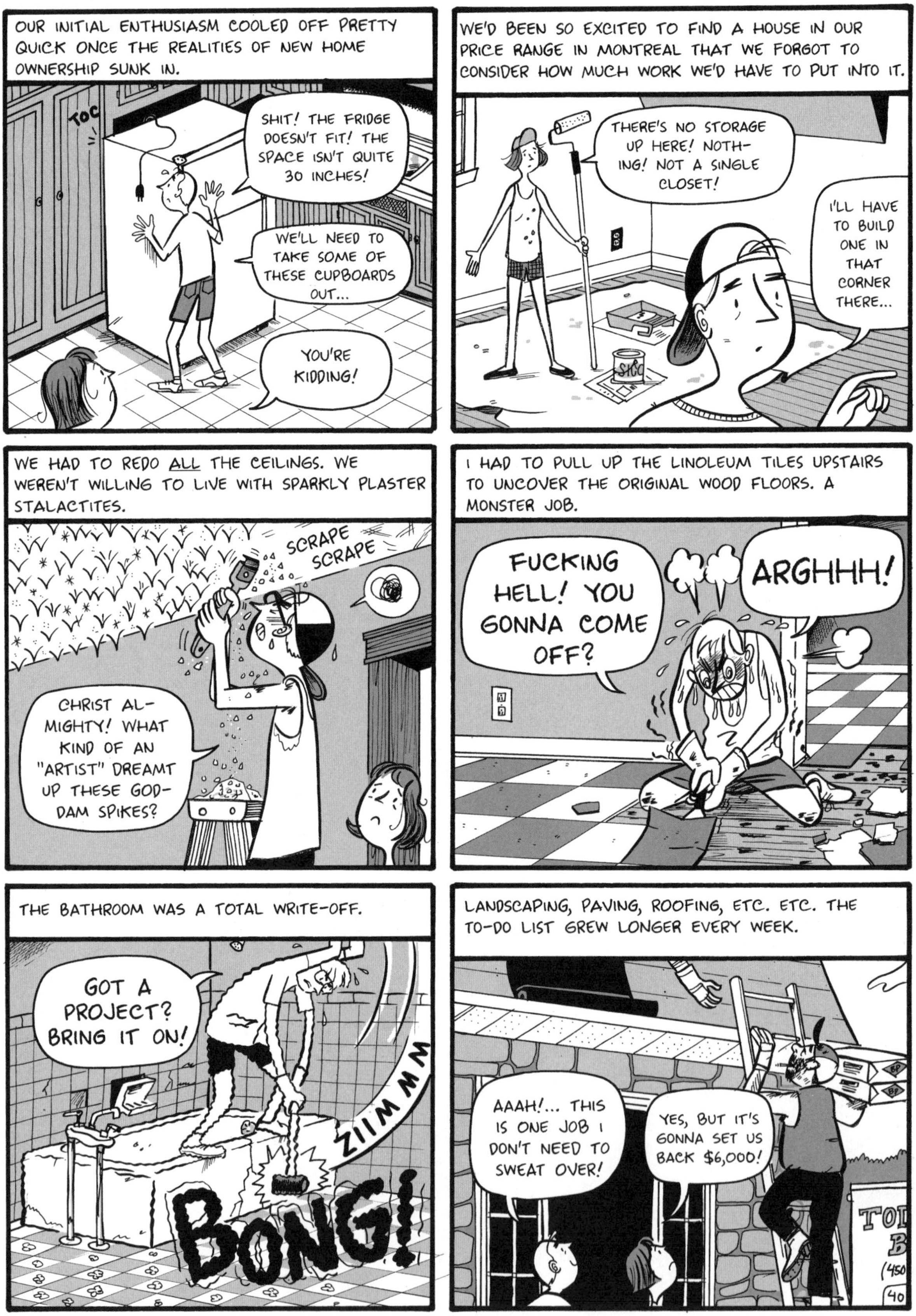
OUR INITIAL ENTHUSIASM COOLED OFF PRETTY QUICK ONCE THE REALITIES OF NEW HOME OWNERSHIP SUNK IN.
TOC
SHIT! THE FRIDGE DOESN'T FIT! THE SPACE ISN'T QUITE 30 INCHES!
WE'LL NEED TO TAKE SOME OF THESE CUPBOARDS OUT...
YOU'RE KIDDING!
WE'D BEEN SO EXCITED TO FIND A HOUSE IN OUR PRICE RANGE IN MONTREAL THAT WE FORGOT TO CONSIDER HOW MUCH WORK WE'D HAVE TO PUT INTO IT.
THERE'S NO STORAGE UP HERE! NOTHING! NOT A SINGLE CLOSET!
I'LL HAVE TO BUILD ONE IN THAT CORNER THERE...
WE HAD TO REDO ALL THE CEILINGS. WE WEREN'T WILLING TO LIVE WITH SPARKLY PLASTER STALACTITES.
SCRAPE SCRAPE
CHRIST ALMIGHTY! WHAT KIND OF AN "ARTIST" DREAMT UP THESE GOD-DAM SPIKES?
I HAD TO PULL UP THE LINOLEUM TILES UPSTAIRS TO UNCOVER THE ORIGINAL WOOD FLOORS. A MONSTER JOB.
FUCKING HELL! YOU GONNA COME OFF?
ARGHHH!
THE BATHROOM WAS A TOTAL WRITE-OFF.
GOT A PROJECT? BRING IT ON!
ZIIMMM
BONG!
LANDSCAPING, PAVING, ROOFING, ETC. ETC. THE TO-DO LIST GREW LONGER EVERY WEEK.
AAAH!... THIS IS ONE JOB I DON'T NEED TO SWEAT OVER!
YES, BUT IT'S GONNA SET US BACK $6,000!

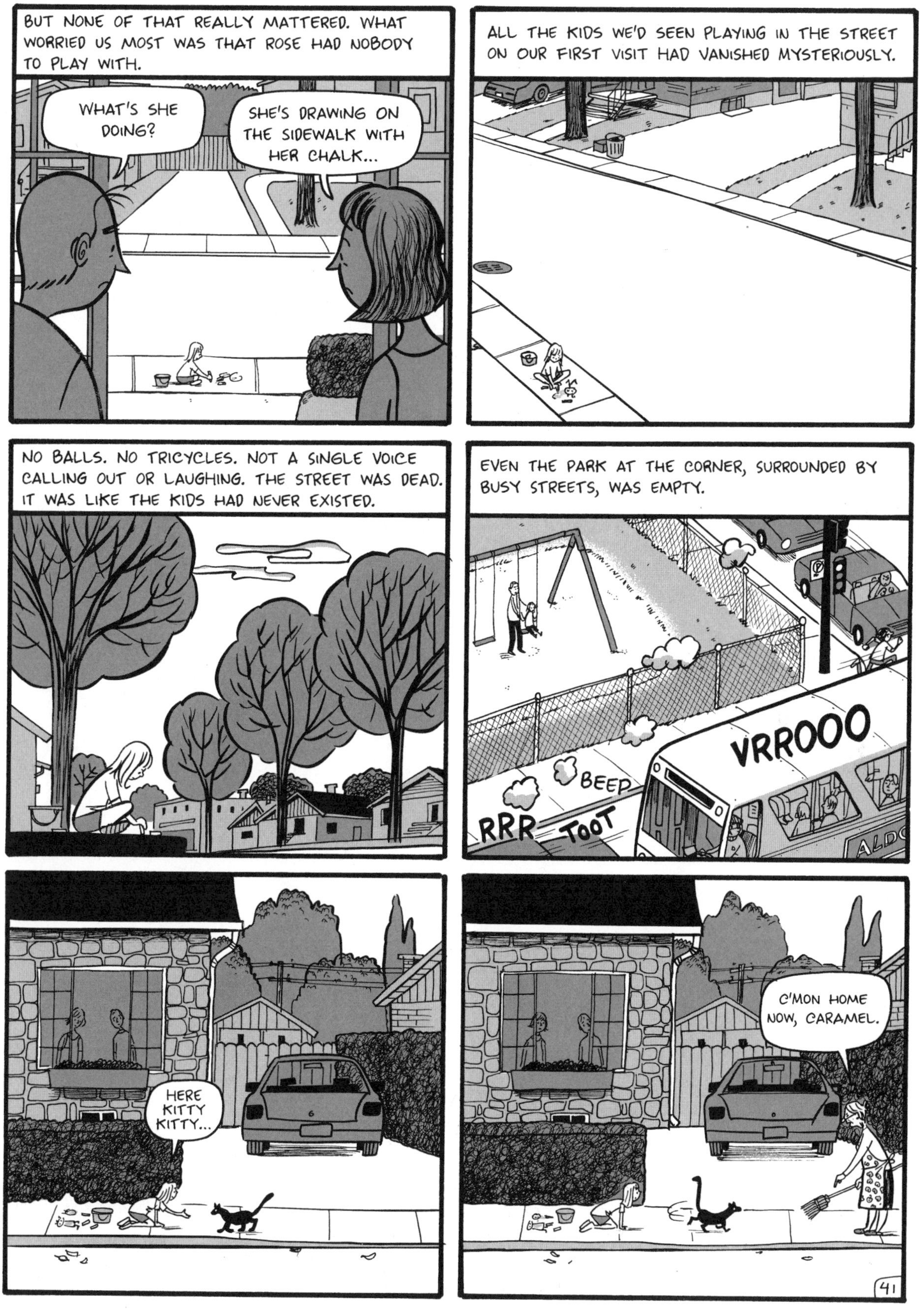
BUT NONE OF THAT REALLY MATTERED. WHAT WORRIED US MOST WAS THAT ROSE HAD NOBODY TO PLAY WITH.
WHAT'S SHE DOING?
SHE'S DRAWING ON THE SIDEWALK WITH HER CHALK...
ALL THE KIDS WE'D SEEN PLAYING IN THE STREET ON OUR FIRST VISIT HAD VANISHED MYSTERIOUSLY.
NO BALLS. NO TRICYCLES. NOT A SINGLE VOICE CALLING OUT OR LAUGHING. THE STREET WAS DEAD. IT WAS LIKE THE KIDS HAD NEVER EXISTED.
EVEN THE PARK AT THE CORNER, SURROUNDED BY BUSY STREETS, WAS EMPTY.
VRROOO
BEEP
RRR
TOOT
HERE KITTY KITTY...
C'MON HOME NOW, CARAMEL.
41

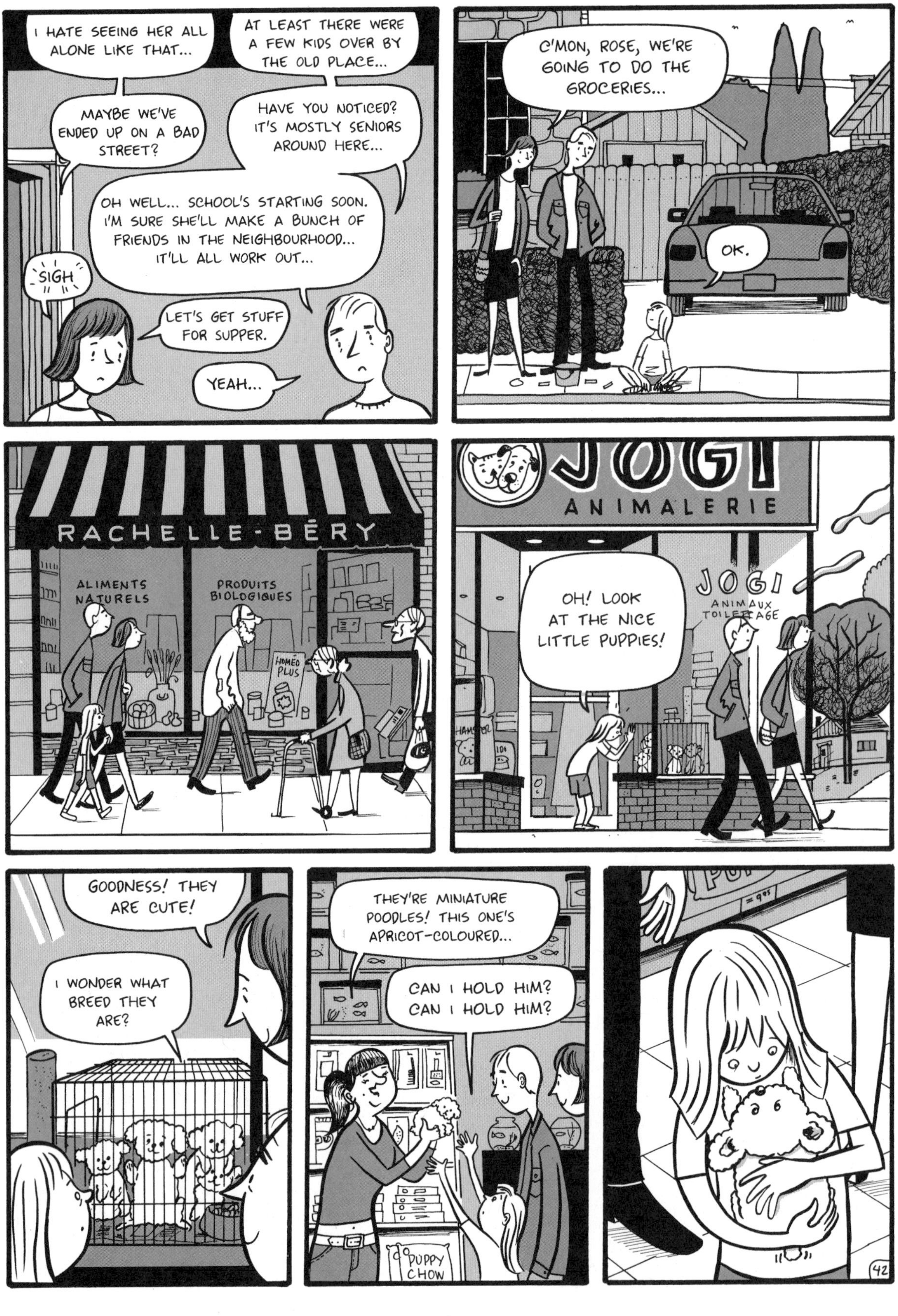
I HATE SEEING HER ALL ALONE LIKE THAT...
AT LEAST THERE WERE A FEW KIDS OVER BY THE OLD PLACE...
MAYBE WE'VE ENDED UP ON A BAD STREET?
HAVE YOU NOTICED? IT'S MOSTLY SENIORS AROUND HERE...
OH WELL... SCHOOL'S STARTING SOON. I'M SURE SHE'LL MAKE A BUNCH OF FRIENDS IN THE NEIGHBOURHOOD... IT'LL ALL WORK OUT...
SIGH
LET'S GET STUFF FOR SUPPER.
YEAH...
C'MON, ROSE, WE'RE GOING TO DO THE GROCERIES...
OK.
RACHELLE-BÉRY
ALIMENTS NATURELS
PRODUITS BIOLOGIQUES
HOMÉO PLUS
JOGI
ANIMALERIE
OH! LOOK AT THE NICE LITTLE PUPPIES!
JOGI
ANIMAUX TOILETTAGE
GOODNESS! THEY ARE CUTE!
I WONDER WHAT BREED THEY ARE?
THEY'RE MINIATURE POODLES! THIS ONE'S APRICOT-COLOURED...
CAN I HOLD HIM? CAN I HOLD HIM?
PUPPY CHOW
42

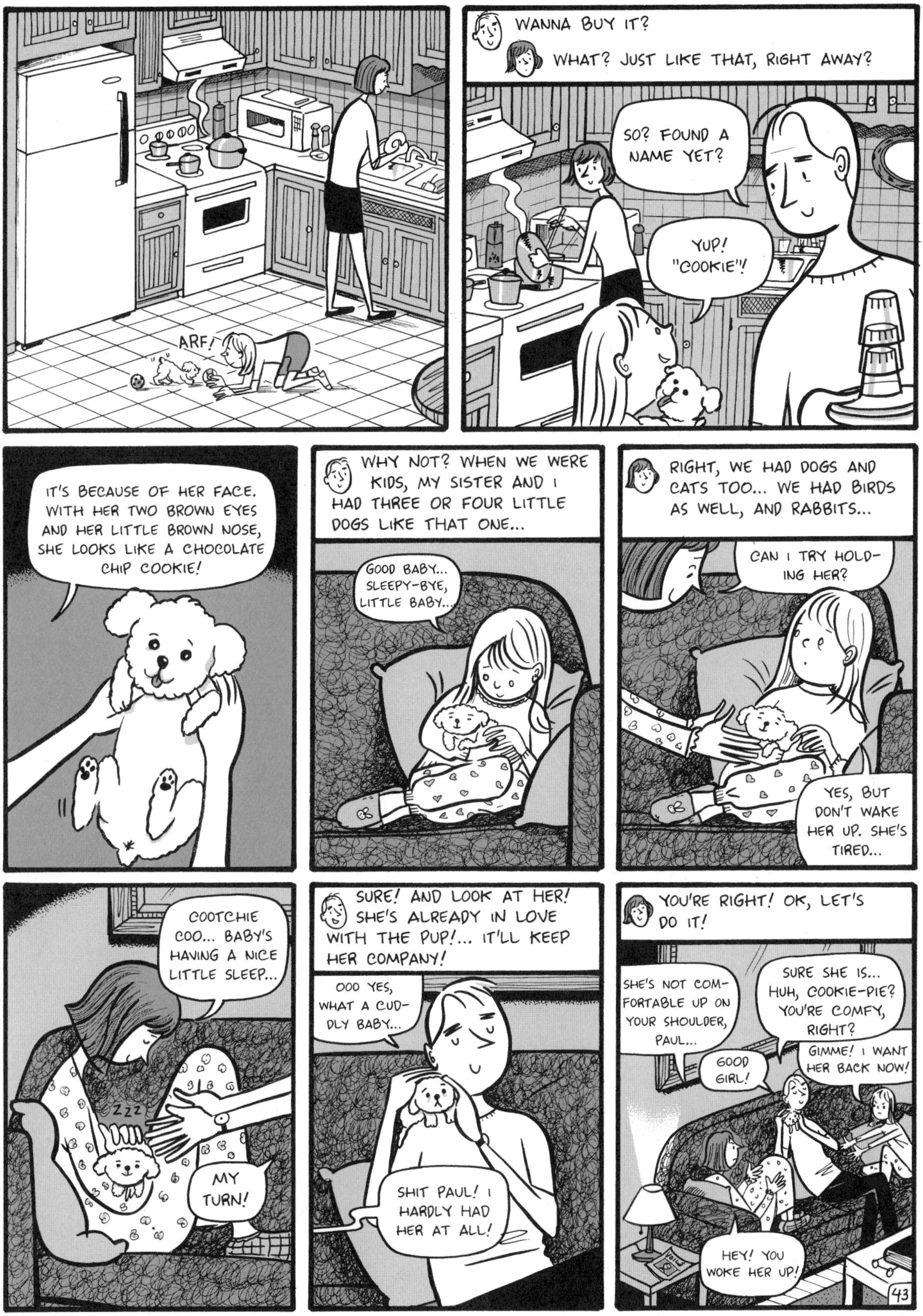
ARF!
WANNA BUY IT?
WHAT? JUST LIKE THAT, RIGHT AWAY?
SO? FOUND A NAME YET?
YUP! "COOKIE"!
IT'S BECAUSE OF HER FACE. WITH HER TWO BROWN EYES AND HER LITTLE BROWN NOSE, SHE LOOKS LIKE A CHOCOLATE CHIP COOKIE!
WHY NOT? WHEN WE WERE KIDS, MY SISTER AND I HAD THREE OR FOUR LITTLE DOGS LIKE THAT ONE...
GOOD BABY... SLEEPY-BYE, LITTLE BABY...
RIGHT, WE HAD DOGS AND CATS TOO... WE HAD BIRDS AS WELL, AND RABBITS...
CAN I TRY HOLDING HER?
YES, BUT DON'T WAKE HER UP. SHE'S TIRED...
COOTCHIE COO... BABY'S HAVING A NICE LITTLE SLEEP...
ZZZ
MY TURN!
SURE! AND LOOK AT HER! SHE'S ALREADY IN LOVE WITH THE PUP!... IT'LL KEEP HER COMPANY!
OOO YES, WHAT A CUDDLY BABY...
SHIT PAUL! I HARDLY HAD HER AT ALL!
YOU'RE RIGHT! OK, LET'S DO IT!
SHE'S NOT COMFORTABLE UP ON YOUR SHOULDER, PAUL...
SURE SHE IS... HUH, COOKIE-PIE? YOU'RE COMFY, RIGHT?
GOOD GIRL!
GIMME! I WANT HER BACK NOW!
HEY! YOU WOKE HER UP!
43

COOKIE WAS A REAL POOP MACHINE. ANYTIME SHE'D GET HER PAWS OUT THE DOOR, SHE'D CRANK OUT A NUGGET.

I'M SURE I SAW ONE OVER IN THIS CORNER...

*#◎!

FOR EASIER SCOOPING, WE MAPPED AN INVISIBLE GRID ONTO THE GARDEN, BASED ON THE FENCE POSTS.

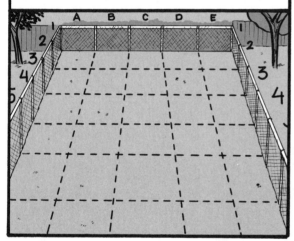

WE CALLED IT BATTLESHIT.

DESTROYER IN D-2!

GOT IT!

AND AN OLD SUBMARINE IN E-5!

GOOD XXX NIGHT XXX COOKIE XXX

XX SLEEP...

XX

TIGHT...

XX

WHAT ABOUT US?

OH, YEAH... 'NIGHT DAD. 'NIGHT MOM.

'NIGHT SWEETS...

50

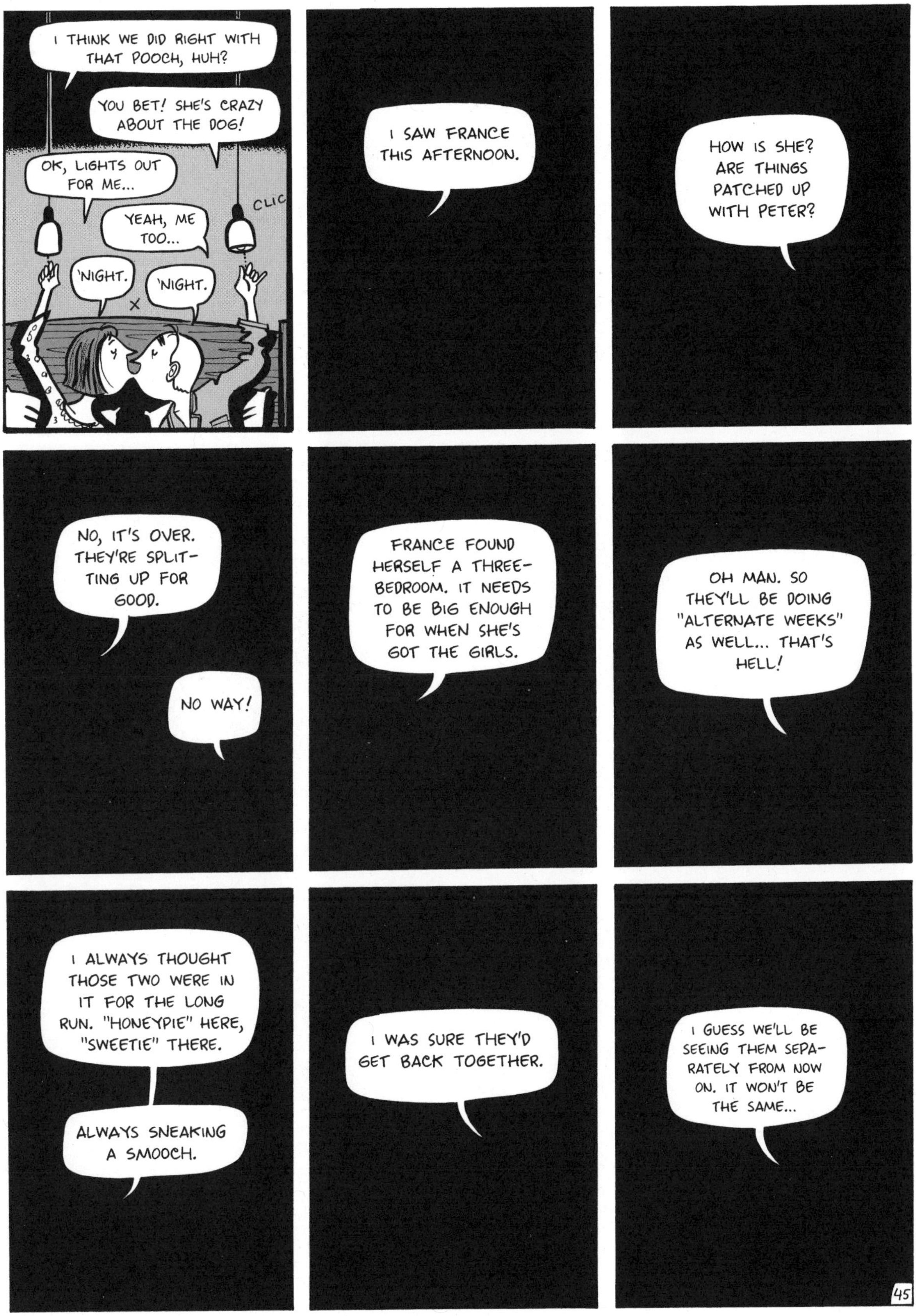
I THINK WE DID RIGHT WITH THAT POOCH, HUH?
YOU BET! SHE'S CRAZY ABOUT THE DOG!
OK, LIGHTS OUT FOR ME...
CLIC
YEAH, ME TOO...
'NIGHT.
'NIGHT.
I SAW FRANCE THIS AFTERNOON.
HOW IS SHE? ARE THINGS PATCHED UP WITH PETER?
NO, IT'S OVER. THEY'RE SPLIT-TING UP FOR GOOD.
NO WAY!
FRANCE FOUND HERSELF A THREE-BEDROOM. IT NEEDS TO BE BIG ENOUGH FOR WHEN SHE'S GOT THE GIRLS.
OH MAN. SO THEY'LL BE DOING "ALTERNATE WEEKS" AS WELL... THAT'S HELL!
I ALWAYS THOUGHT THOSE TWO WERE IN IT FOR THE LONG RUN. "HONEYPIE" HERE, "SWEETIE" THERE.
ALWAYS SNEAKING A SMOOCH.
I WAS SURE THEY'D GET BACK TOGETHER.
I GUESS WE'LL BE SEEING THEM SEPA-RATELY FROM NOW ON. IT WON'T BE THE SAME...
45

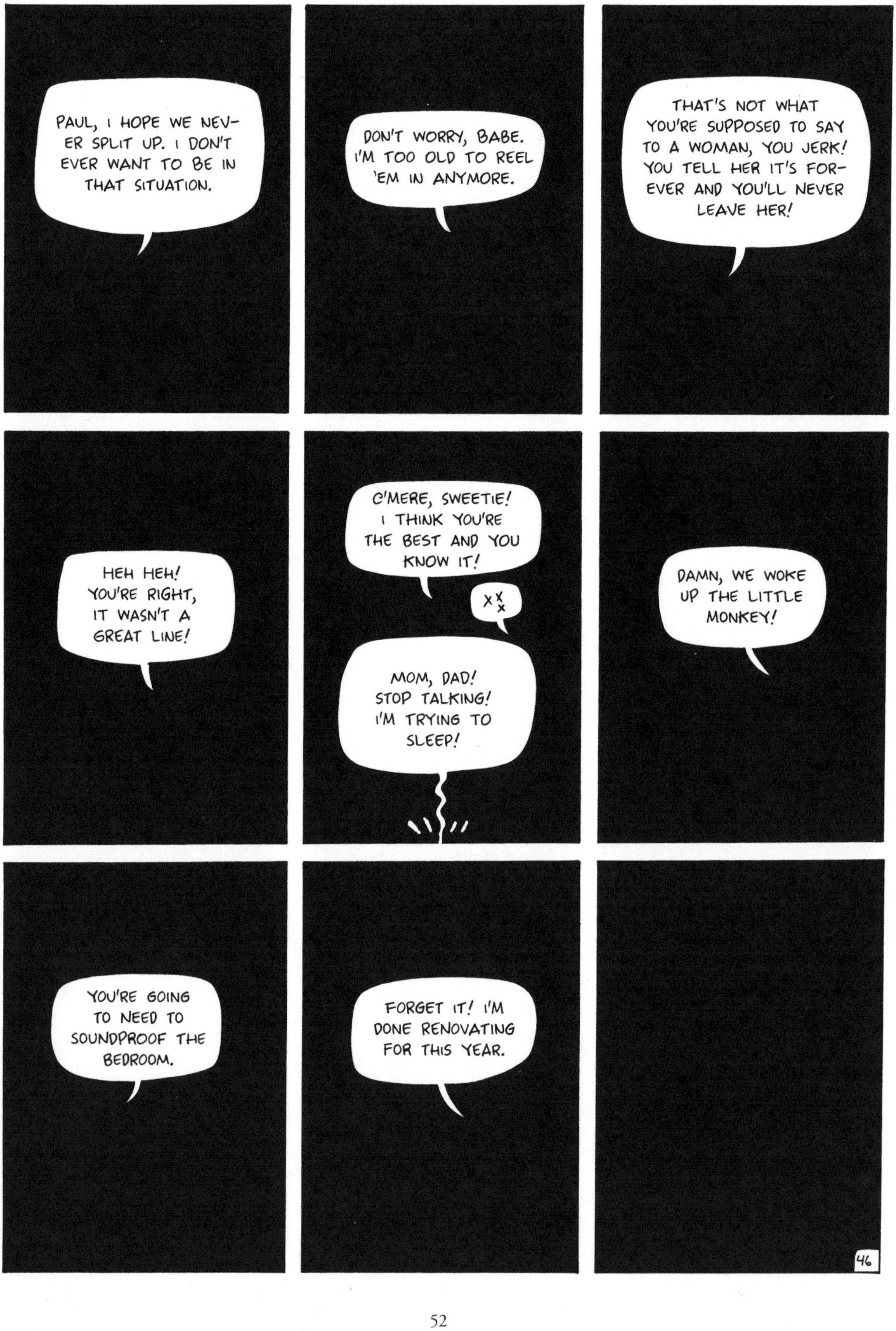
PAUL, I HOPE WE NEVER SPLIT UP. I DON'T EVER WANT TO BE IN THAT SITUATION.
DON'T WORRY, BABE. I'M TOO OLD TO REEL 'EM IN ANYMORE.
THAT'S NOT WHAT YOU'RE SUPPOSED TO SAY TO A WOMAN, YOU JERK! YOU TELL HER IT'S FOREVER AND YOU'LL NEVER LEAVE HER!
HEH HEH! YOU'RE RIGHT, IT WASN'T A GREAT LINE!
C'MERE, SWEETIE! I THINK YOU'RE THE BEST AND YOU KNOW IT!
X X X
MOM, DAD! STOP TALKING! I'M TRYING TO SLEEP!
DAMN, WE WOKE UP THE LITTLE MONKEY!
YOU'RE GOING TO NEED TO SOUNDPROOF THE BEDROOM.
FORGET IT! I'M DONE RENOVATING FOR THIS YEAR.
46

One year later

RRRRRAK

CLICK RRJJRJJJJ

LET'S SEE, WHAT'S HAPPENED OVER THE PAST YEAR?

JJJJR

CLICK

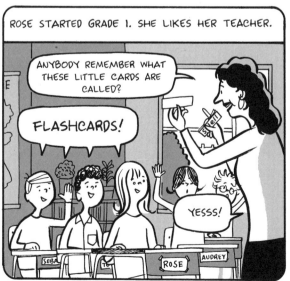

ROSE STARTED GRADE 1. SHE LIKES HER TEACHER.

ANYBODY REMEMBER WHAT THESE LITTLE CARDS ARE CALLED?

FLASHCARDS!

YESSS!

ON NEW YEAR'S EVE, THE WHOLE FAMILY GOT TOGETHER BY THE RIVER TO WATCH THE FIRE-WORKS AND CELEBRATE THE NEW MILLENNIUM.

OOOOH!

MIDNIGHT! POP THAT DAMNED CHAMPAGNE ALREADY!

47

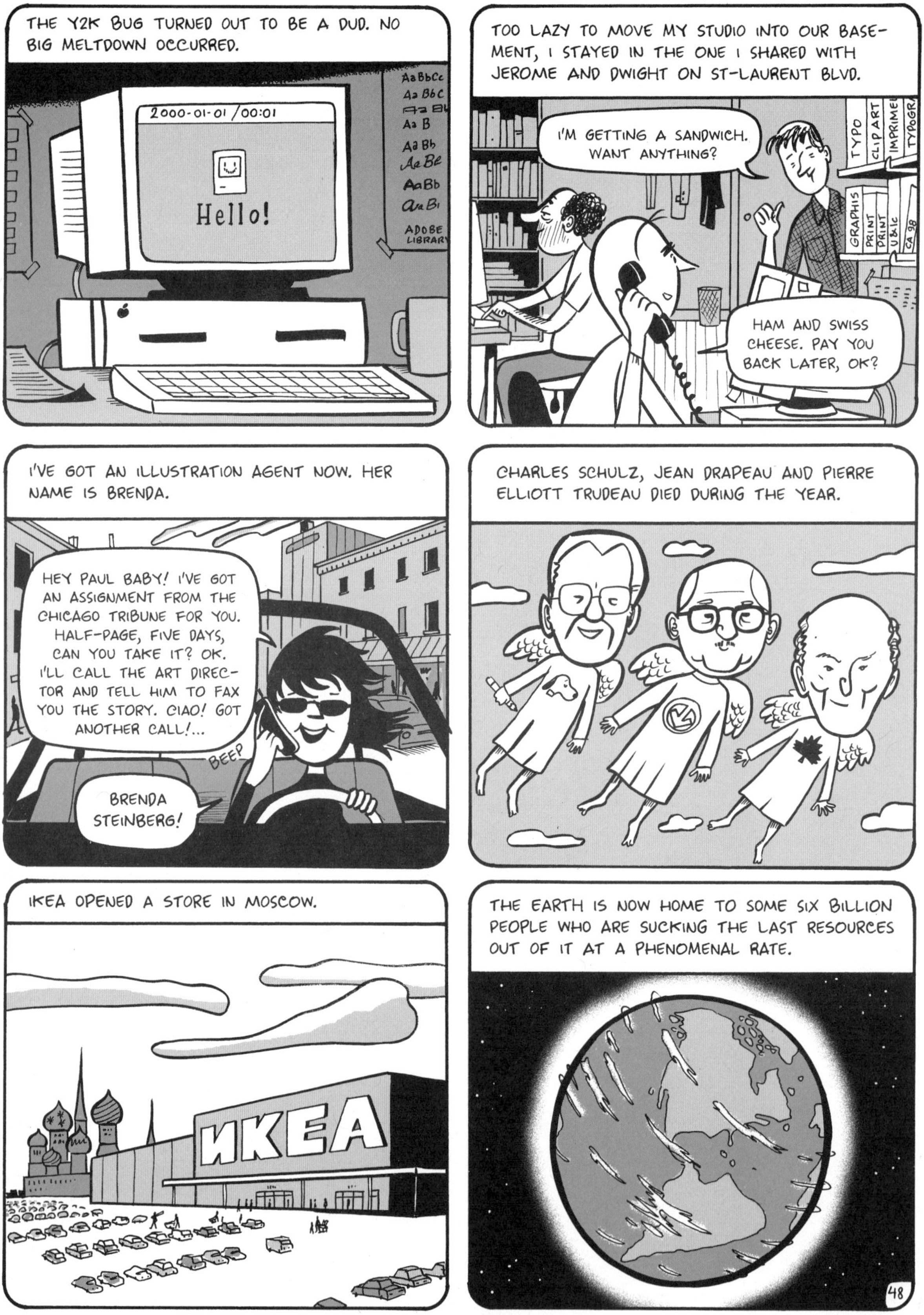
THE Y2K BUG TURNED OUT TO BE A DUD. NO BIG MELTDOWN OCCURRED.
2000-01-01 /00:01
Hello!
ADOBE LIBRARY
TOO LAZY TO MOVE MY STUDIO INTO OUR BASEMENT, I STAYED IN THE ONE I SHARED WITH JEROME AND DWIGHT ON ST-LAURENT BLVD.
I'M GETTING A SANDWICH. WANT ANYTHING?
HAM AND SWISS CHEESE. PAY YOU BACK LATER, OK?
TYPO
CLIP ART
GRAPHIS
PRINT
PRINT
CA 98
I'VE GOT AN ILLUSTRATION AGENT NOW. HER NAME IS BRENDA.
HEY PAUL BABY! I'VE GOT AN ASSIGNMENT FROM THE CHICAGO TRIBUNE FOR YOU. HALF-PAGE, FIVE DAYS, CAN YOU TAKE IT? OK. I'LL CALL THE ART DIRECTOR AND TELL HIM TO FAX YOU THE STORY. CIAO! GOT ANOTHER CALL!...
BEEP
BRENDA STEINBERG!
CHARLES SCHULZ, JEAN DRAPEAU AND PIERRE ELLIOTT TRUDEAU DIED DURING THE YEAR.
IKEA OPENED A STORE IN MOSCOW.
ИKEA
THE EARTH IS NOW HOME TO SOME SIX BILLION PEOPLE WHO ARE SUCKING THE LAST RESOURCES OUT OF IT AT A PHENOMENAL RATE.
48

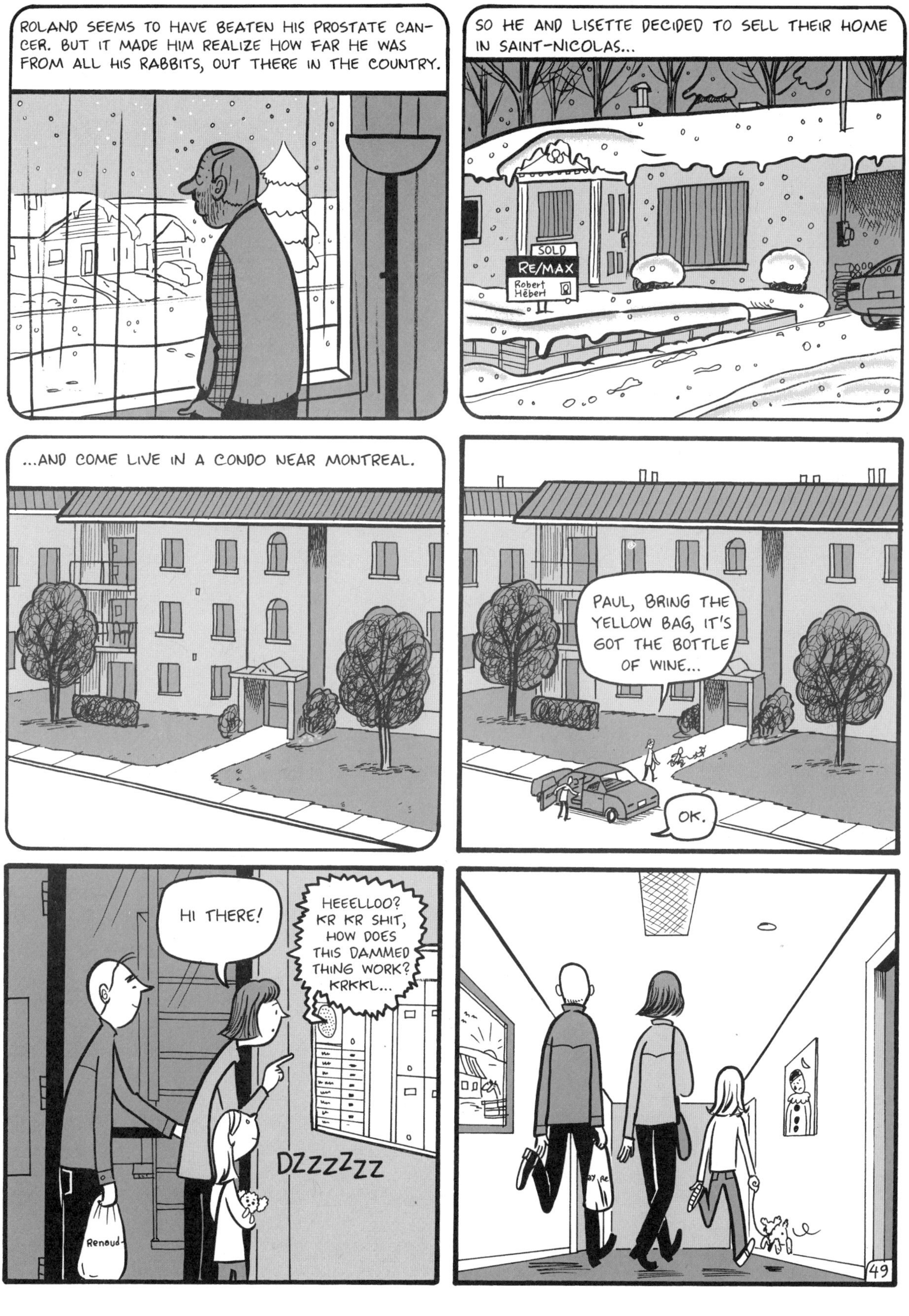
ROLAND SEEMS TO HAVE BEATEN HIS PROSTATE CANCER. BUT IT MADE HIM REALIZE HOW FAR HE WAS FROM ALL HIS RABBITS, OUT THERE IN THE COUNTRY.
SO HE AND LISETTE DECIDED TO SELL THEIR HOME IN SAINT-NICOLAS...
SOLD
RE/MAX
Robert Hébert
...AND COME LIVE IN A CONDO NEAR MONTREAL.
PAUL, BRING THE YELLOW BAG, IT'S GOT THE BOTTLE OF WINE...
OK.
HI THERE!
HEEELLOO? KR KR SHIT, HOW DOES THIS DAMMED THING WORK? KRKKL...
DZZZZZZ
Renaud
49

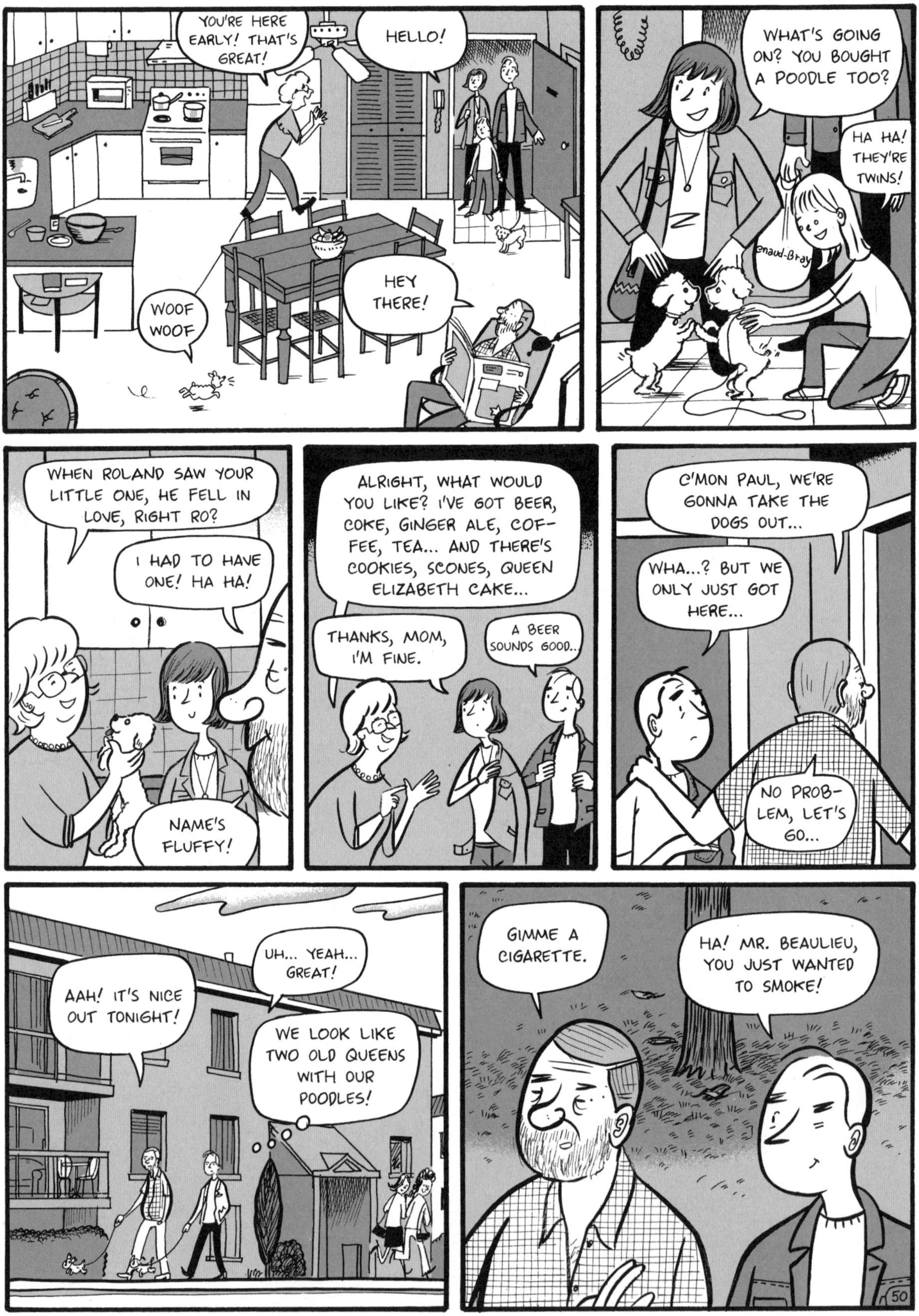
YOU'RE HERE EARLY! THAT'S GREAT!
HELLO!
WOOF WOOF
HEY THERE!
WHAT'S GOING ON? YOU BOUGHT A POODLE TOO?
HA HA! THEY'RE TWINS!
enaud-Bray
WHEN ROLAND SAW YOUR LITTLE ONE, HE FELL IN LOVE, RIGHT RO?
I HAD TO HAVE ONE! HA HA!
NAME'S FLUFFY!
ALRIGHT, WHAT WOULD YOU LIKE? I'VE GOT BEER, COKE, GINGER ALE, COF-FEE, TEA... AND THERE'S COOKIES, SCONES, QUEEN ELIZABETH CAKE...
THANKS, MOM, I'M FINE.
A BEER SOUNDS GOOD...
C'MON PAUL, WE'RE GONNA TAKE THE DOGS OUT...
WHA...? BUT WE ONLY JUST GOT HERE...
NO PROB-LEM, LET'S GO...
AAH! IT'S NICE OUT TONIGHT!
UH... YEAH... GREAT!
WE LOOK LIKE TWO OLD QUEENS WITH OUR POODLES!
GIMME A CIGARETTE.
HA! MR. BEAULIEU, YOU JUST WANTED TO SMOKE!
50

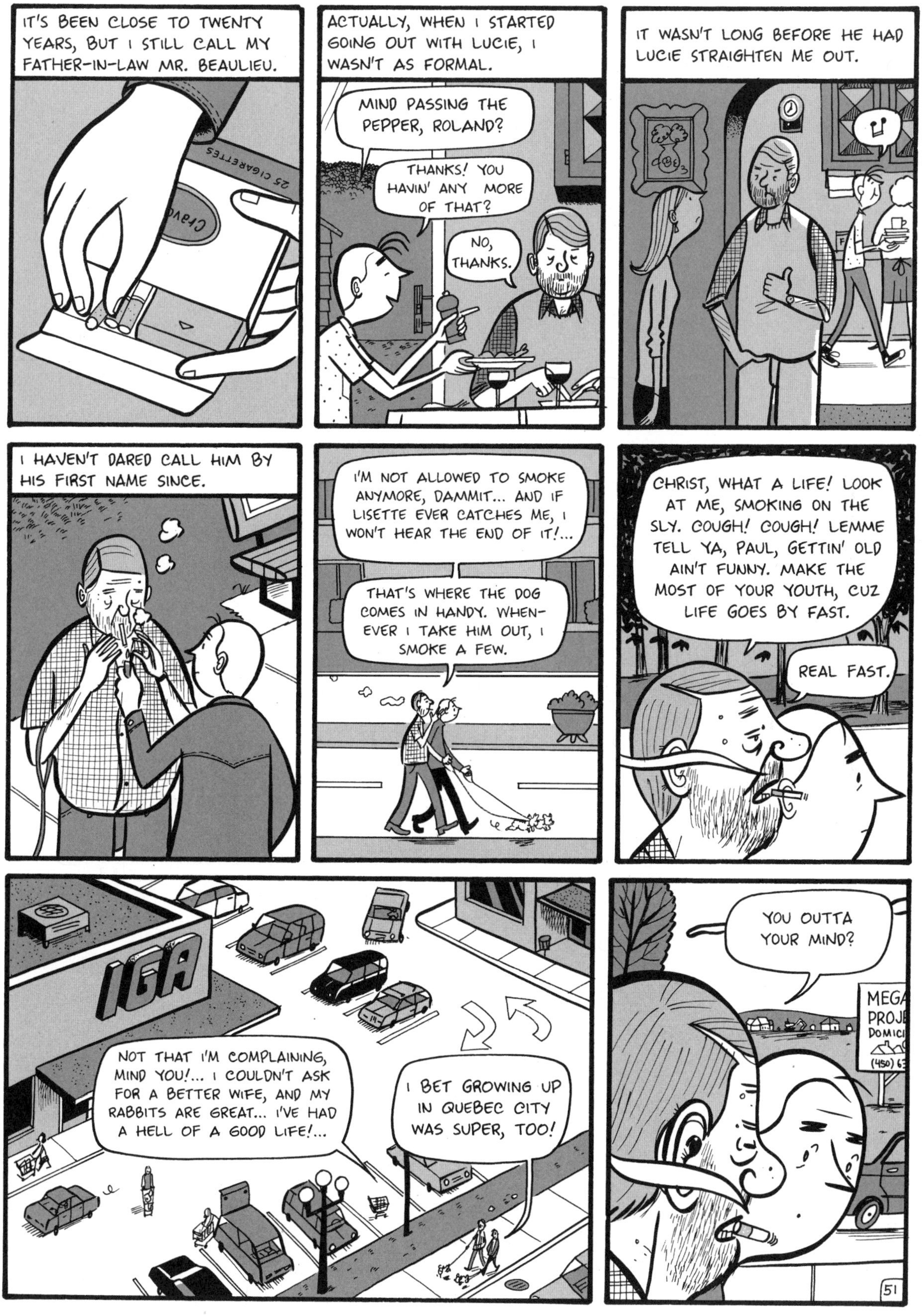
IT'S BEEN CLOSE TO TWENTY YEARS, BUT I STILL CALL MY FATHER-IN-LAW MR. BEAULIEU.
25 CIGARETTES
ACTUALLY, WHEN I STARTED GOING OUT WITH LUCIE, I WASN'T AS FORMAL.
MIND PASSING THE PEPPER, ROLAND?
THANKS! YOU HAVIN' ANY MORE OF THAT?
NO, THANKS.
IT WASN'T LONG BEFORE HE HAD LUCIE STRAIGHTEN ME OUT.
I HAVEN'T DARED CALL HIM BY HIS FIRST NAME SINCE.
I'M NOT ALLOWED TO SMOKE ANYMORE, DAMMIT... AND IF LISETTE EVER CATCHES ME, I WON'T HEAR THE END OF IT!...
THAT'S WHERE THE DOG COMES IN HANDY. WHENEVER I TAKE HIM OUT, I SMOKE A FEW.
CHRIST, WHAT A LIFE! LOOK AT ME, SMOKING ON THE SLY. COUGH! COUGH! LEMME TELL YA, PAUL, GETTIN' OLD AIN'T FUNNY. MAKE THE MOST OF YOUR YOUTH, CUZ LIFE GOES BY FAST.
REAL FAST.
IGA
NOT THAT I'M COMPLAINING, MIND YOU!... I COULDN'T ASK FOR A BETTER WIFE, AND MY RABBITS ARE GREAT... I'VE HAD A HELL OF A GOOD LIFE!...
I BET GROWING UP IN QUEBEC CITY WAS SUPER, TOO!
YOU OUTTA YOUR MIND?
51

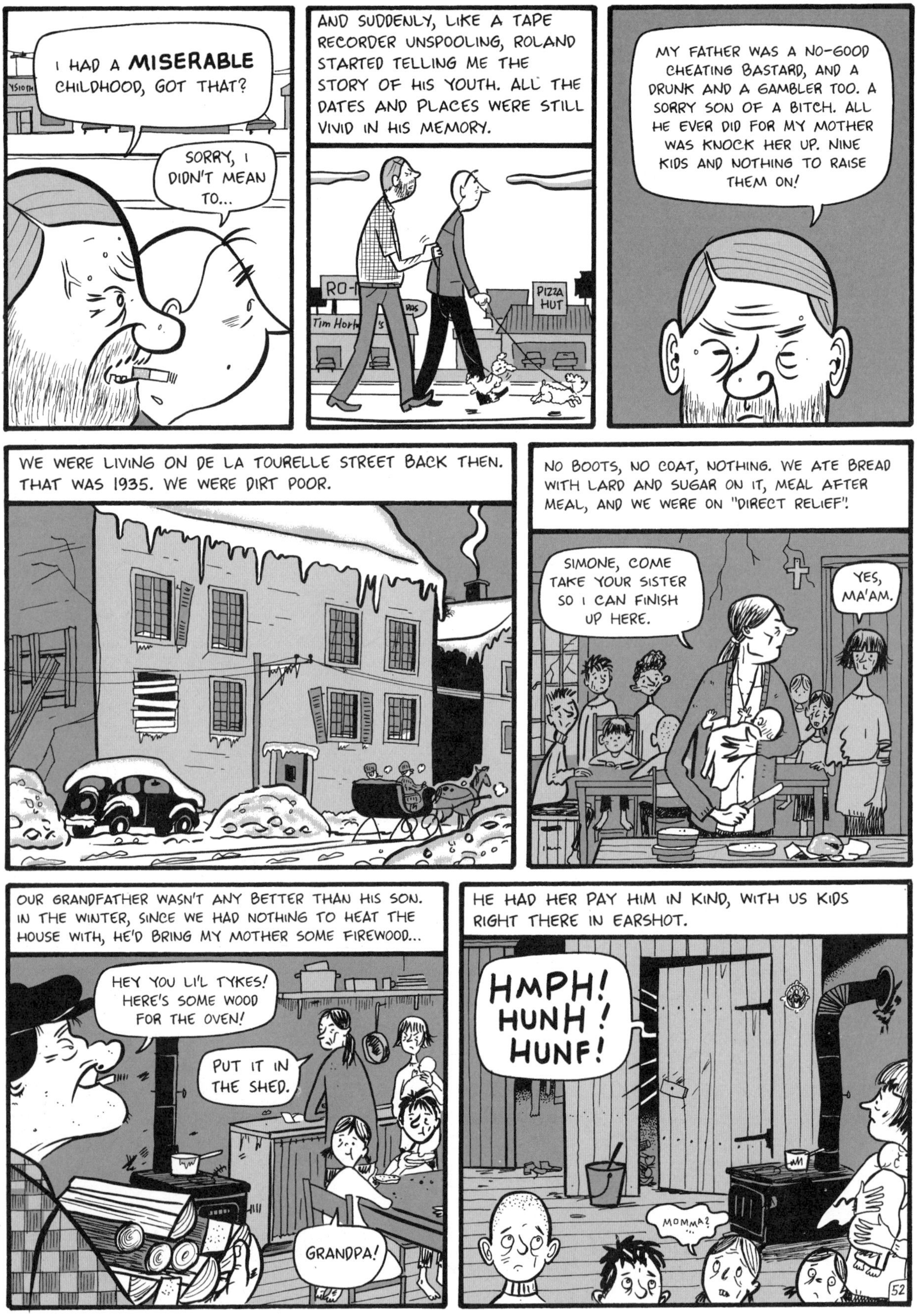
I HAD A **MISERABLE** CHILDHOOD, GOT THAT?
SORRY, I DIDN'T MEAN TO...
AND SUDDENLY, LIKE A TAPE RECORDER UNSPOOLING, ROLAND STARTED TELLING ME THE STORY OF HIS YOUTH. ALL THE DATES AND PLACES WERE STILL VIVID IN HIS MEMORY.
PIZZA HUT
MY FATHER WAS A NO-GOOD CHEATING BASTARD, AND A DRUNK AND A GAMBLER TOO. A SORRY SON OF A BITCH. ALL HE EVER DID FOR MY MOTHER WAS KNOCK HER UP. NINE KIDS AND NOTHING TO RAISE THEM ON!
WE WERE LIVING ON DE LA TOURELLE STREET BACK THEN. THAT WAS 1935. WE WERE DIRT POOR.
NO BOOTS, NO COAT, NOTHING. WE ATE BREAD WITH LARD AND SUGAR ON IT, MEAL AFTER MEAL, AND WE WERE ON "DIRECT RELIEF".
SIMONE, COME TAKE YOUR SISTER SO I CAN FINISH UP HERE.
YES, MA'AM.
OUR GRANDFATHER WASN'T ANY BETTER THAN HIS SON. IN THE WINTER, SINCE WE HAD NOTHING TO HEAT THE HOUSE WITH, HE'D BRING MY MOTHER SOME FIREWOOD...
HEY YOU LI'L TYKES! HERE'S SOME WOOD FOR THE OVEN!
PUT IT IN THE SHED.
GRANDPA!
HE HAD HER PAY HIM IN KIND, WITH US KIDS RIGHT THERE IN EARSHOT.
HMPH! HUNH! HUNF!
MOMMA?
52

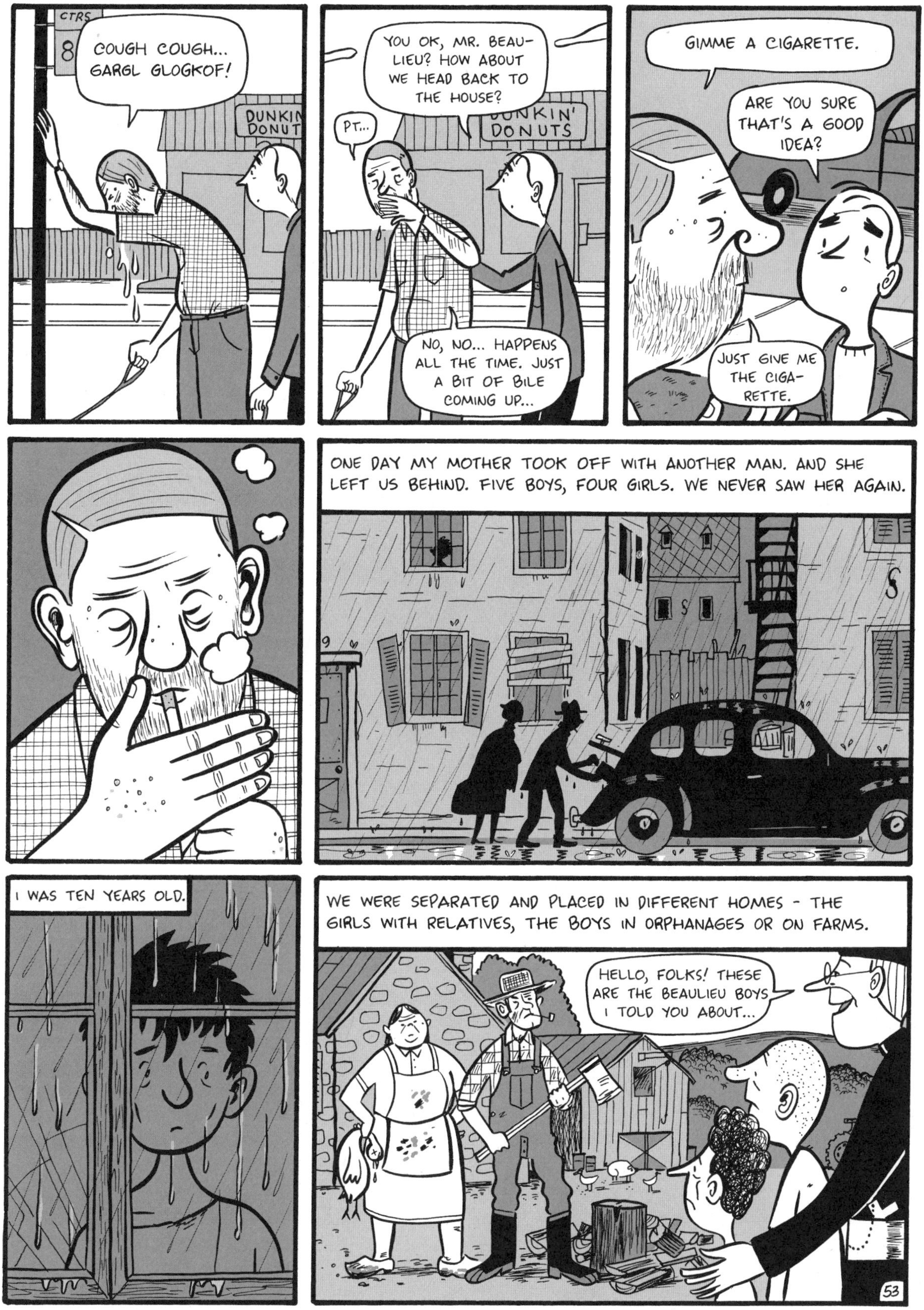
CTRS
8
COUGH COUGH... GARGL GLOGKOF!
DUNKIN DONUT
YOU OK, MR. BEAULIEU? HOW ABOUT WE HEAD BACK TO THE HOUSE?
PT...
DUNKIN' DONUTS
NO, NO... HAPPENS ALL THE TIME. JUST A BIT OF BILE COMING UP...
GIMME A CIGARETTE.
ARE YOU SURE THAT'S A GOOD IDEA?
JUST GIVE ME THE CIGARETTE.
ONE DAY MY MOTHER TOOK OFF WITH ANOTHER MAN. AND SHE LEFT US BEHIND. FIVE BOYS, FOUR GIRLS. WE NEVER SAW HER AGAIN.
I WAS TEN YEARS OLD.
WE WERE SEPARATED AND PLACED IN DIFFERENT HOMES - THE GIRLS WITH RELATIVES, THE BOYS IN ORPHANAGES OR ON FARMS.
HELLO, FOLKS! THESE ARE THE BEAULIEU BOYS I TOLD YOU ABOUT...
53

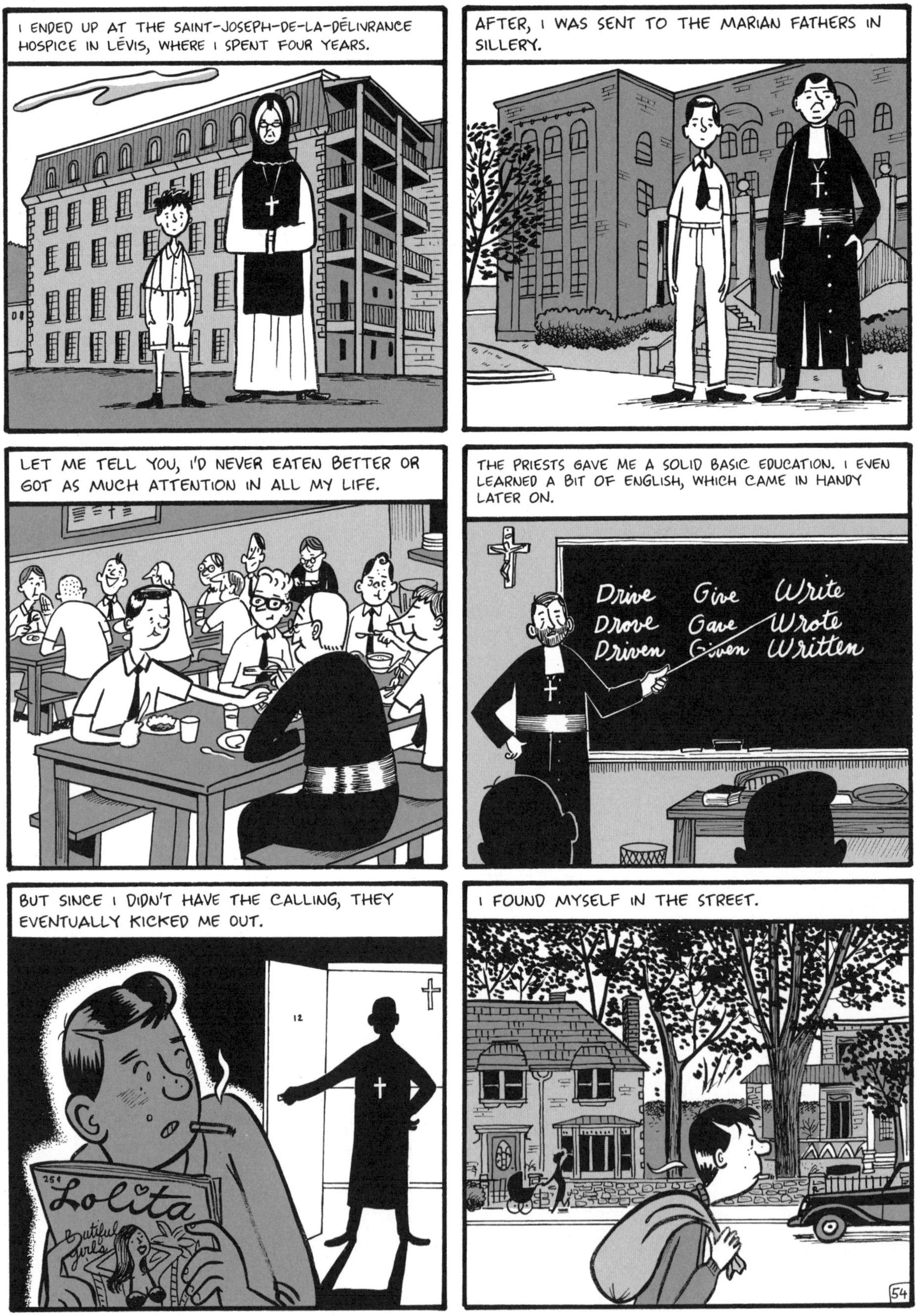
I ENDED UP AT THE SAINT-JOSEPH-DE-LA-DÉLIVRANCE HOSPICE IN LÉVIS, WHERE I SPENT FOUR YEARS.
AFTER, I WAS SENT TO THE MARIAN FATHERS IN SILLERY.
LET ME TELL YOU, I'D NEVER EATEN BETTER OR GOT AS MUCH ATTENTION IN ALL MY LIFE.
THE PRIESTS GAVE ME A SOLID BASIC EDUCATION. I EVEN LEARNED A BIT OF ENGLISH, WHICH CAME IN HANDY LATER ON.
Drive Give Write
Drove Gave Wrote
Driven Given Written
BUT SINCE I DIDN'T HAVE THE CALLING, THEY EVENTUALLY KICKED ME OUT.
25¢
Lolita
12
I FOUND MYSELF IN THE STREET.
54

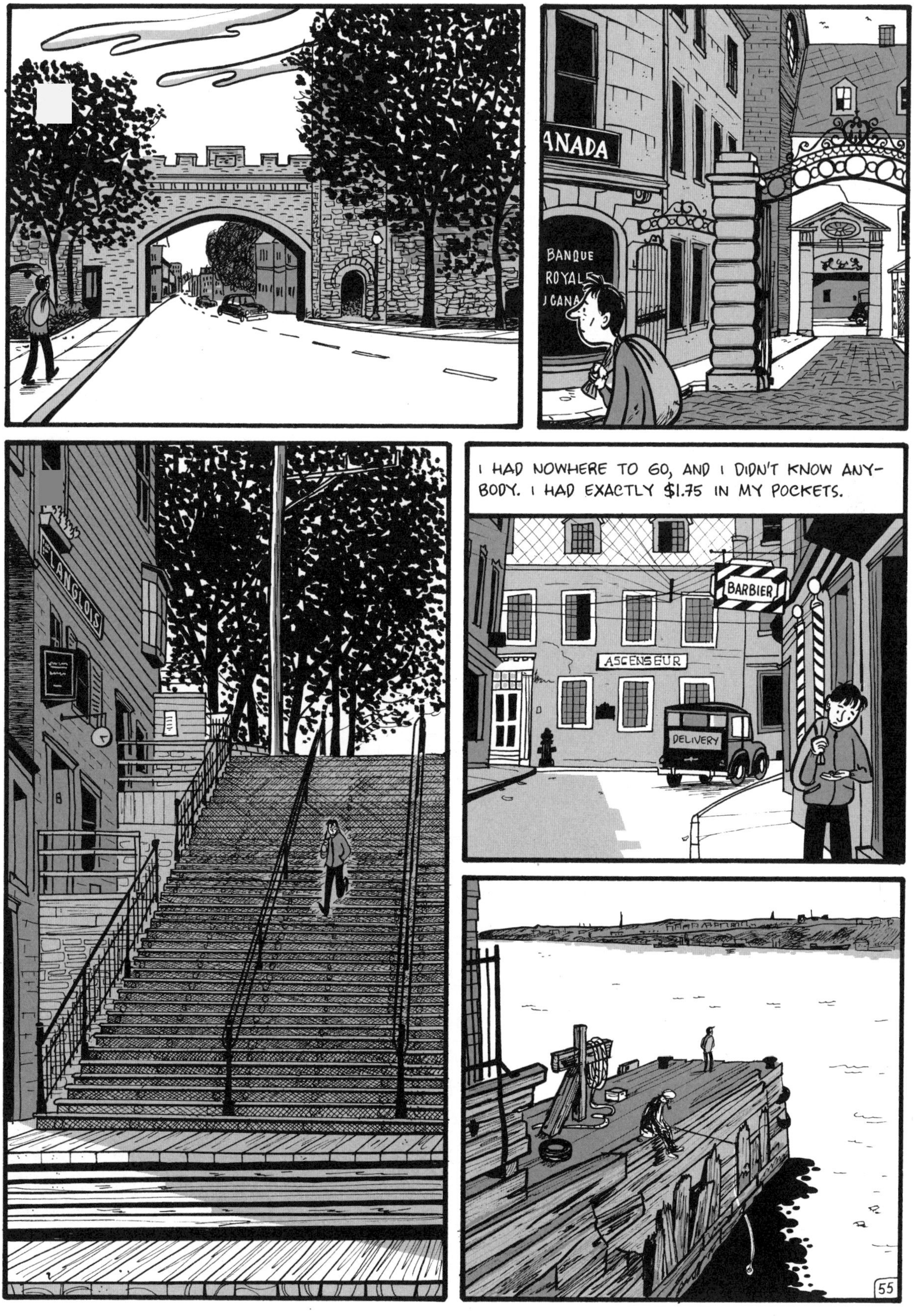
ANADA
BANQUE
LANGLOIS
I HAD NOWHERE TO GO, AND I DIDN'T KNOW ANY-BODY. I HAD EXACTLY $1.75 IN MY POCKETS.
BARBIER
ASCENSEUR
DELIVERY
55

I WENT BACK TO MY FATHER.

HE WAS ALREADY IN BAD SHAPE WHEN I WAS A KID. BUT NOW HE WAS A TOTAL WRECK.

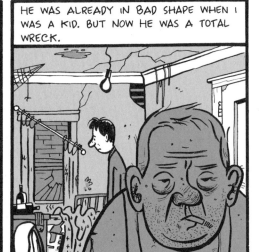

FROM THE LOOKS OF IT, HE'D CONTINUED TO DO THE ONLY TWO THINGS HE KNEW HOW: GAMBLE...

...AND DRINK.

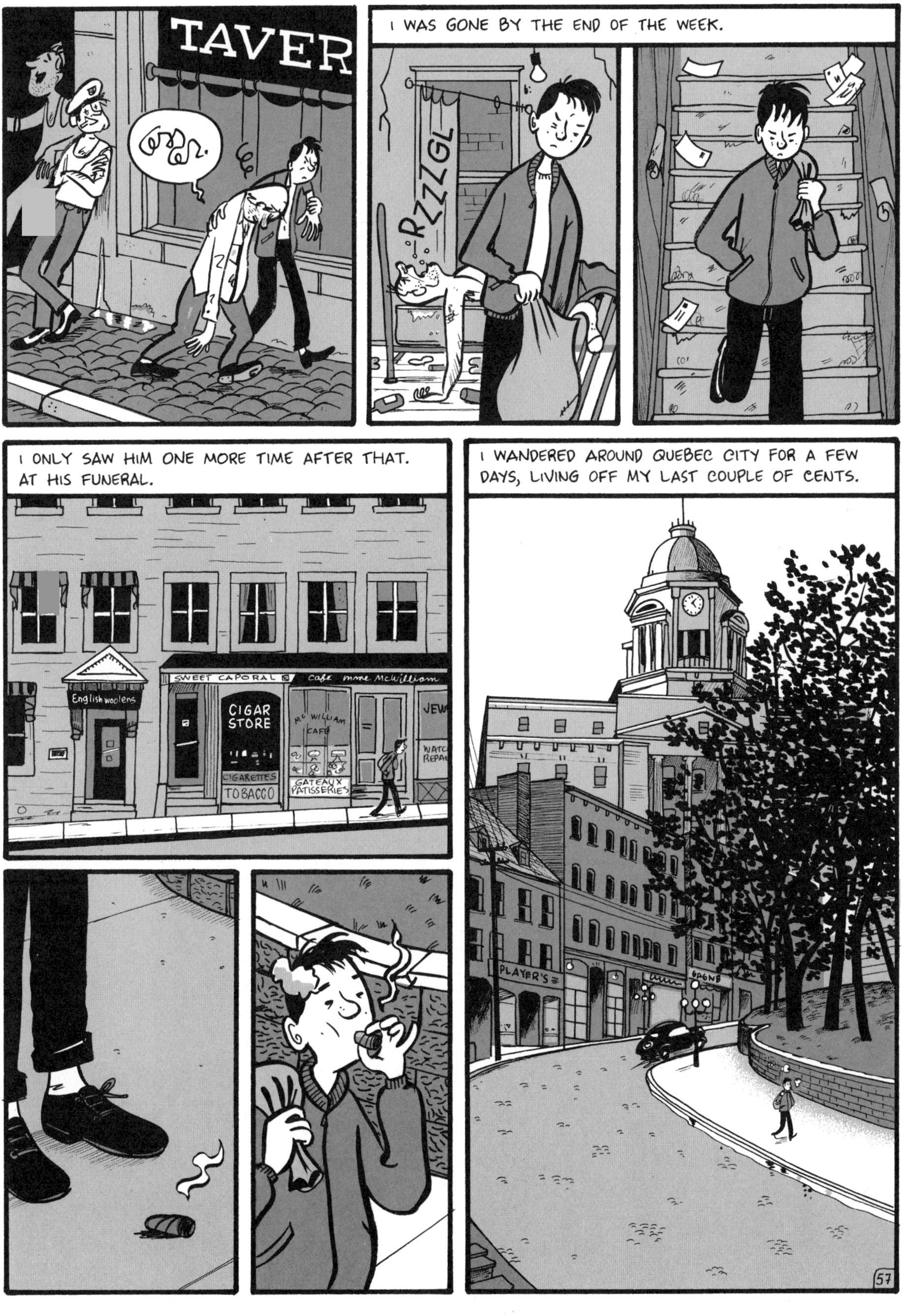

TAVER
I WAS GONE BY THE END OF THE WEEK.
RZZZGL
I ONLY SAW HIM ONE MORE TIME AFTER THAT. AT HIS FUNERAL.
SWEET CAPORAL
Café mme McWilliam
English woolens
CIGAR STORE
CIGARETTES
TOBACCO
McWILLIAM CAFÉ
GATEAUX PATISSERIES
WATC REPAI
I WANDERED AROUND QUEBEC CITY FOR A FEW DAYS, LIVING OFF MY LAST COUPLE OF CENTS.
PLAYER'S
57

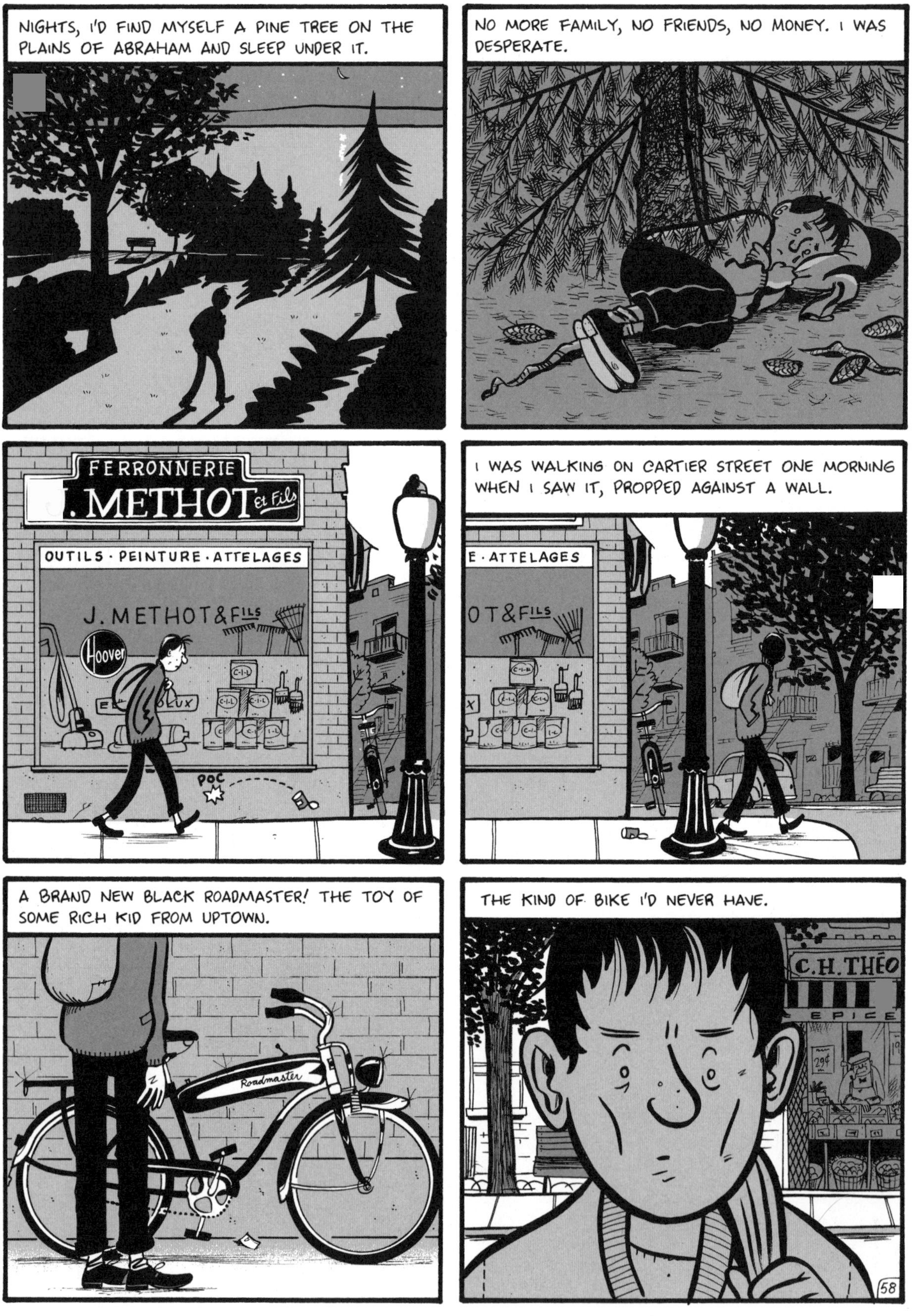
NIGHTS, I'D FIND MYSELF A PINE TREE ON THE PLAINS OF ABRAHAM AND SLEEP UNDER IT.
NO MORE FAMILY, NO FRIENDS, NO MONEY. I WAS DESPERATE.
FERRONNERIE
METHOT Et Fils
OUTILS · PEINTURE · ATTELAGES
J. METHOT & FILS
Hoover
POC
I WAS WALKING ON CARTIER STREET ONE MORNING WHEN I SAW IT, PROPPED AGAINST A WALL.
E · ATTELAGES
OT & FILS
A BRAND NEW BLACK ROADMASTER! THE TOY OF SOME RICH KID FROM UPTOWN.
Roadmaster
THE KIND OF BIKE I'D NEVER HAVE.
C.H.THÉO
EPICE
29¢
58

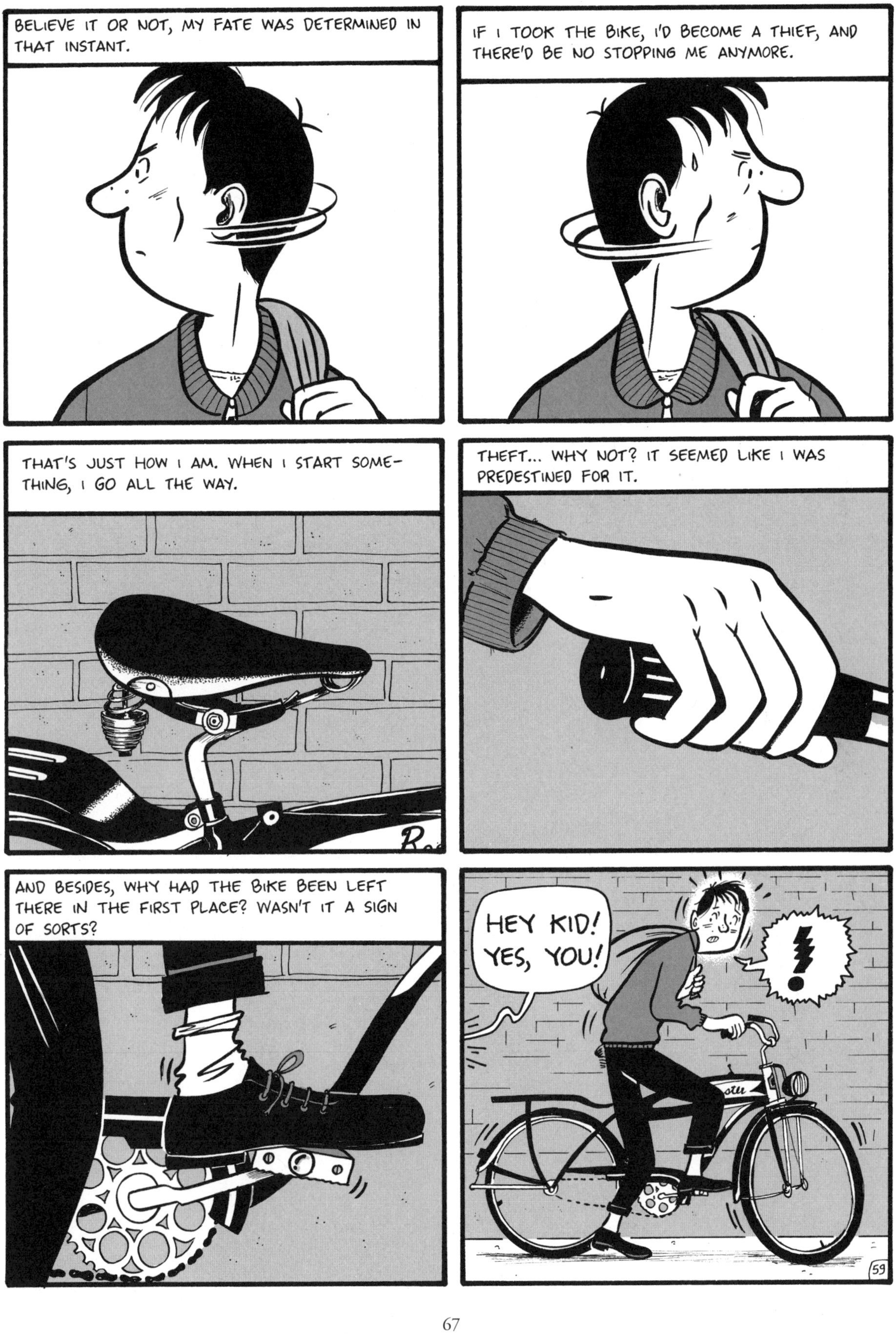
BELIEVE IT OR NOT, MY FATE WAS DETERMINED IN THAT INSTANT.
IF I TOOK THE BIKE, I'D BECOME A THIEF, AND THERE'D BE NO STOPPING ME ANYMORE.
THAT'S JUST HOW I AM. WHEN I START SOME-THING, I GO ALL THE WAY.
THEFT... WHY NOT? IT SEEMED LIKE I WAS PREDESTINED FOR IT.
AND BESIDES, WHY HAD THE BIKE BEEN LEFT THERE IN THE FIRST PLACE? WASN'T IT A SIGN OF SORTS?
HEY KID! YES, YOU!
!
59

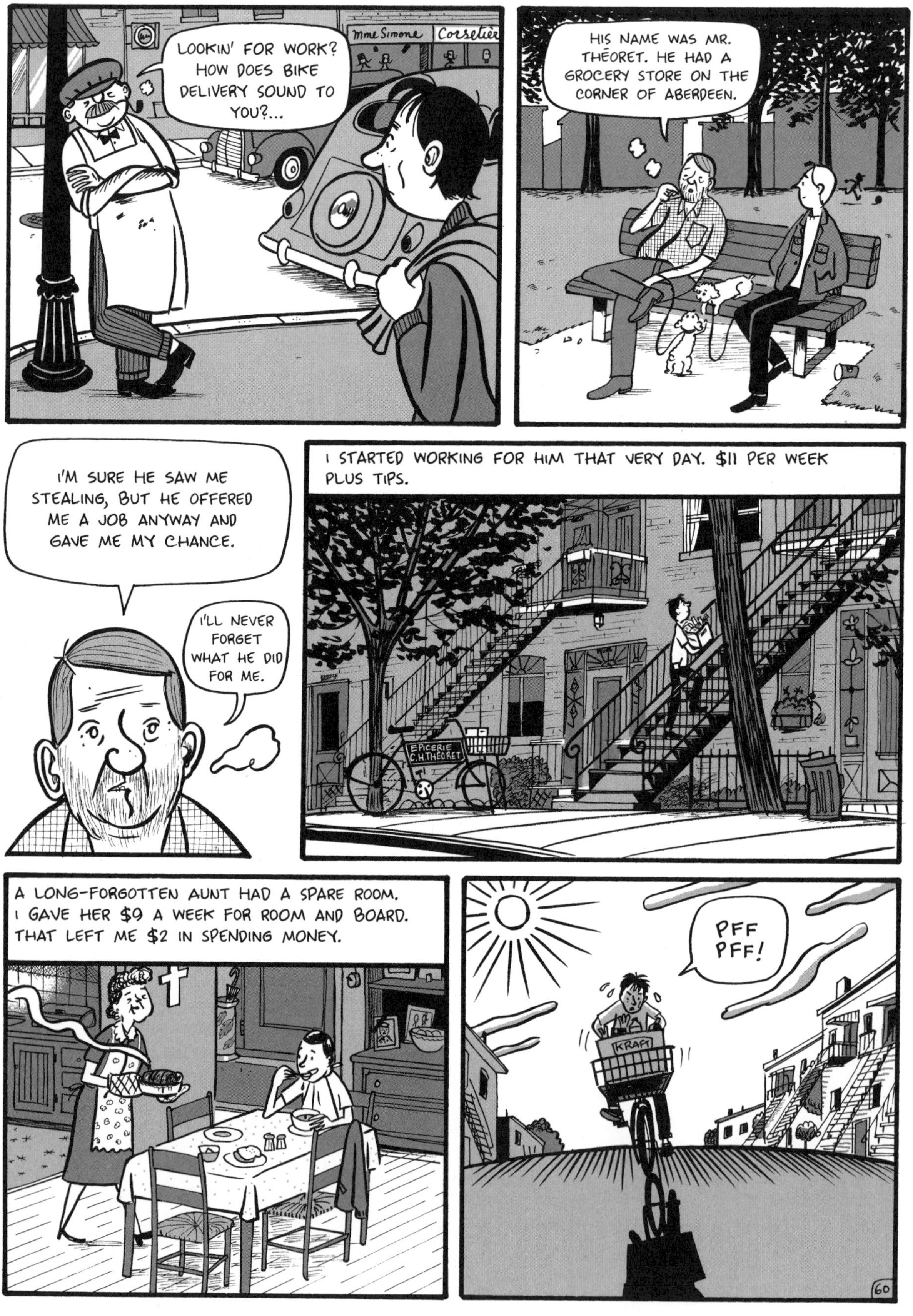
Mme Simone
Corsetier
LOOKIN' FOR WORK? HOW DOES BIKE DELIVERY SOUND TO YOU?...
HIS NAME WAS MR. THÉORET. HE HAD A GROCERY STORE ON THE CORNER OF ABERDEEN.
I'M SURE HE SAW ME STEALING, BUT HE OFFERED ME A JOB ANYWAY AND GAVE ME MY CHANCE.
I'LL NEVER FORGET WHAT HE DID FOR ME.
I STARTED WORKING FOR HIM THAT VERY DAY. $11 PER WEEK PLUS TIPS.
EPICERIE C.H.THEORET
A LONG-FORGOTTEN AUNT HAD A SPARE ROOM. I GAVE HER $9 A WEEK FOR ROOM AND BOARD. THAT LEFT ME $2 IN SPENDING MONEY.
PFF PFF!
KRAFT
60

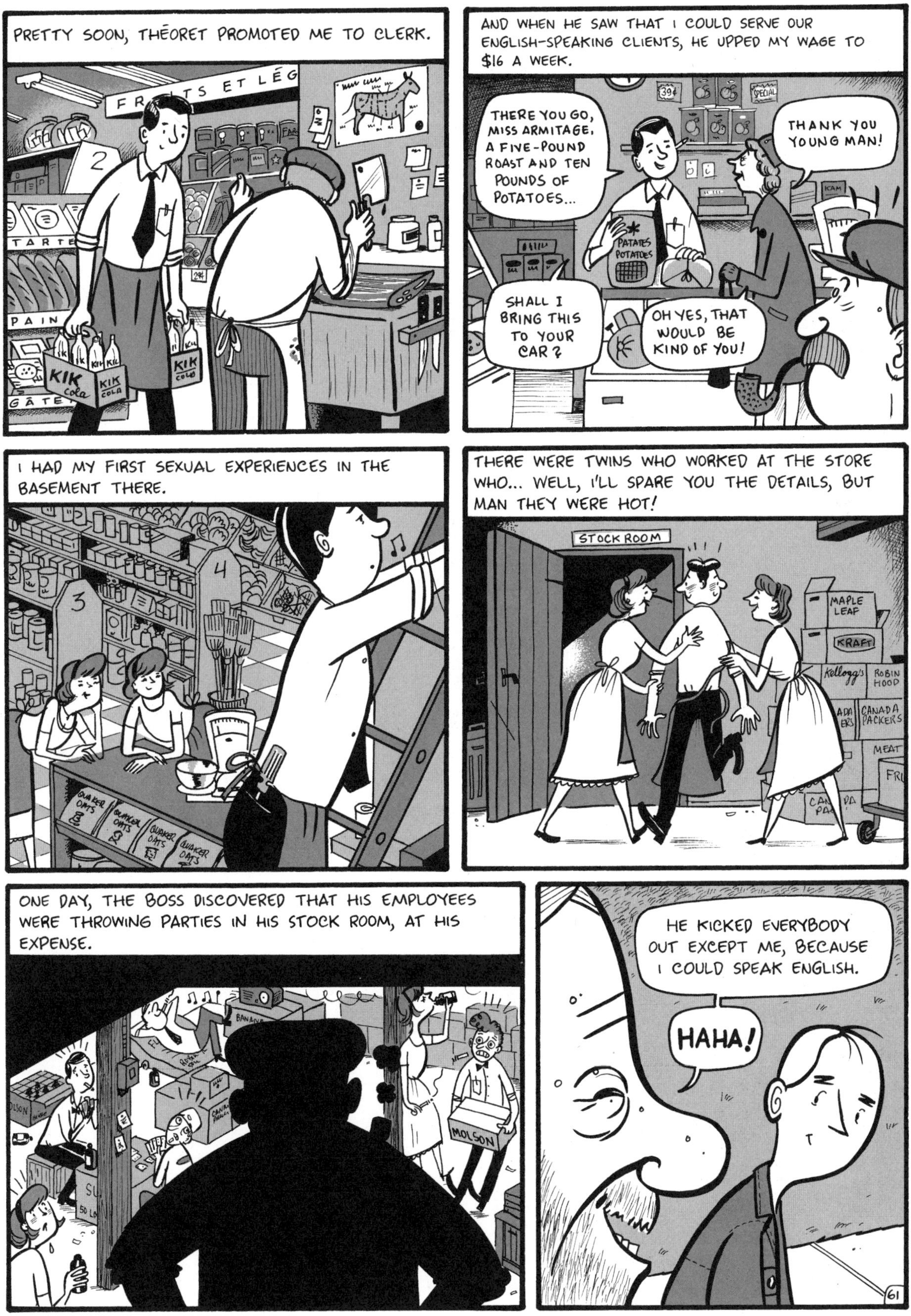
PRETTY SOON, THÉORET PROMOTED ME TO CLERK.
TARTE
PAIN
KIK cola
AND WHEN HE SAW THAT I COULD SERVE OUR ENGLISH-SPEAKING CLIENTS, HE UPPED MY WAGE TO $16 A WEEK.
THERE YOU GO, MISS ARMITAGE, A FIVE-POUND ROAST AND TEN POUNDS OF POTATOES...
THANK YOU YOUNG MAN!
SHALL I BRING THIS TO YOUR CAR?
OH YES, THAT WOULD BE KIND OF YOU!
PATATES POTATOES
SPECIAL
39¢
I HAD MY FIRST SEXUAL EXPERIENCES IN THE BASEMENT THERE.
QUAKER OATS
THERE WERE TWINS WHO WORKED AT THE STORE WHO... WELL, I'LL SPARE YOU THE DETAILS, BUT MAN THEY WERE HOT!
STOCK ROOM
MAPLE LEAF
KRAFT
Kellogg's
ROBIN HOOD
CANADA PACKERS
MEAT
ONE DAY, THE BOSS DISCOVERED THAT HIS EMPLOYEES WERE THROWING PARTIES IN HIS STOCK ROOM, AT HIS EXPENSE.
MOLSON
HE KICKED EVERYBODY OUT EXCEPT ME, BECAUSE I COULD SPEAK ENGLISH.
HAHA!
61

WHEN I WAS 19, I DECIDED TO TRY MY HAND AT TREE-CUTTING IN THE CAMPS UP AT LAC-SAINT-JEAN. $26 A WEEK. IT WAS GREAT MONEY, BUT THE WORK WAS EXHAUSTING. I LASTED SEVEN MONTHS.

I WENT BACK TO THÉORET'S, AND THAT'S WHERE I MET LISETTE. SHE WAS THE DAUGHTER OF A CLIENT, MRS. GAGNON.

YOUR MOTHER-IN-LAW WAS A BEAUTY IN THOSE DAYS! WE GOT MARRIED IN '57.

WHEN SUPERMARKETS APPEARED, LOCAL GROCERY STORES TOOK A HIT. THÉORET CLOSED SHOP AND I FOUND MYSELF WORK AS A TRAVELLING SALESMAN FOR AN OFFICE SUPPLY DISTRIBUTOR. $35 A WEEK PLUS COMMISSIONS.

I HAD A CRAZY RUN. I COVERED VICTORIAVILLE TO GASPÉ, PLUS NEW BRUNSWICK! I WAS NEVER HOME.

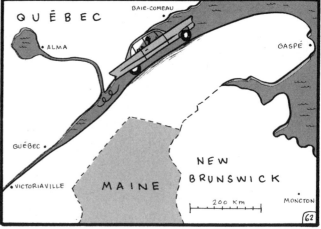

QUÉBEC

BAIE-COMEAU

ALMA

GASPÉ

QUÉBEC

VICTORIAVILLE

MAINE

NEW BRUNSWICK

MONCTON

200 KM

62

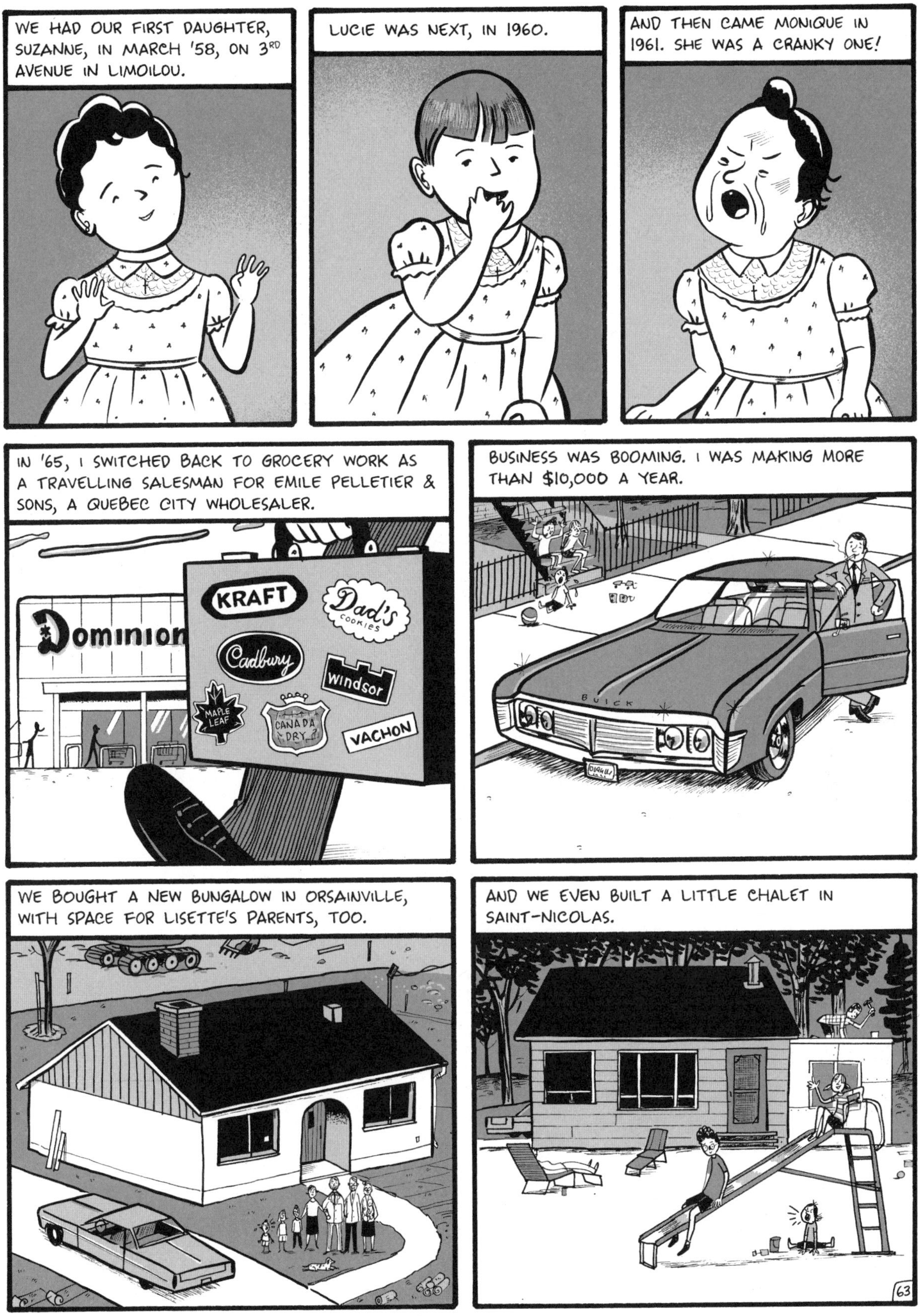
WE HAD OUR FIRST DAUGHTER, SUZANNE, IN MARCH '58, ON 3RD AVENUE IN LIMOILOU.
LUCIE WAS NEXT, IN 1960.
AND THEN CAME MONIQUE IN 1961. SHE WAS A CRANKY ONE!
IN '65, I SWITCHED BACK TO GROCERY WORK AS A TRAVELLING SALESMAN FOR EMILE PELLETIER & SONS, A QUEBEC CITY WHOLESALER.
Dominion
KRAFT
Dad's COOKIES
Cadbury
windsor
MAPLE LEAF
CANADA DRY
VACHON
BUSINESS WAS BOOMING. I WAS MAKING MORE THAN $10,000 A YEAR.
BUICK
WE BOUGHT A NEW BUNGALOW IN ORSAINVILLE, WITH SPACE FOR LISETTE'S PARENTS, TOO.
AND WE EVEN BUILT A LITTLE CHALET IN SAINT-NICOLAS.
63

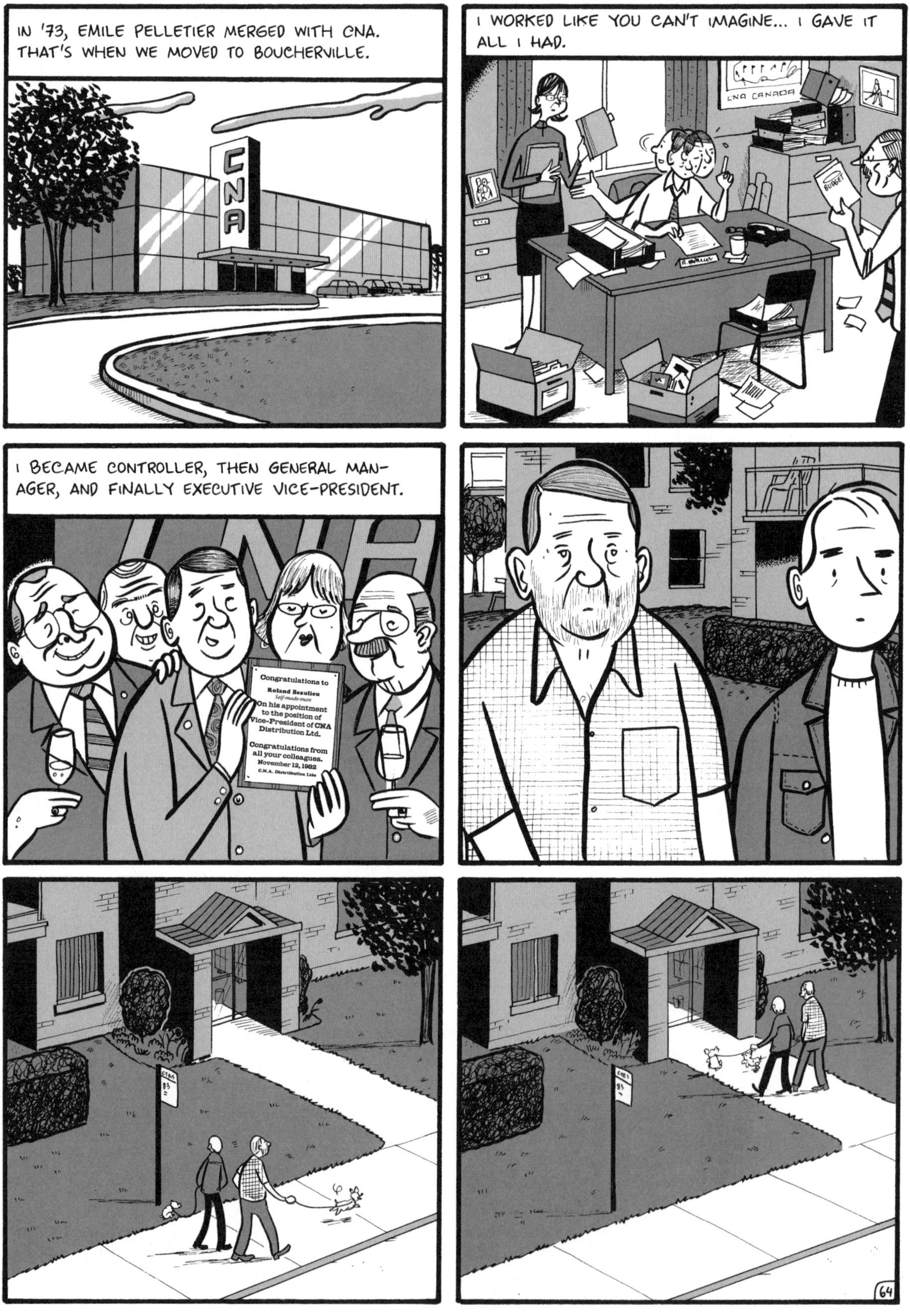
IN '73, EMILE PELLETIER MERGED WITH CNA. THAT'S WHEN WE MOVED TO BOUCHERVILLE.
CNA
I WORKED LIKE YOU CAN'T IMAGINE... I GAVE IT ALL I HAD.
CNA CANADA
BUDGET
I BECAME CONTROLLER, THEN GENERAL MANAGER, AND FINALLY EXECUTIVE VICE-PRESIDENT.
Congratulations to
Roland Beaulieu
Self-made-man
On his appointment to the position of Vice-President of CNA Distribution Ltd.
Congratulations from all your colleagues.
November 12, 1982
C.N.A. Distribution Ltée
64

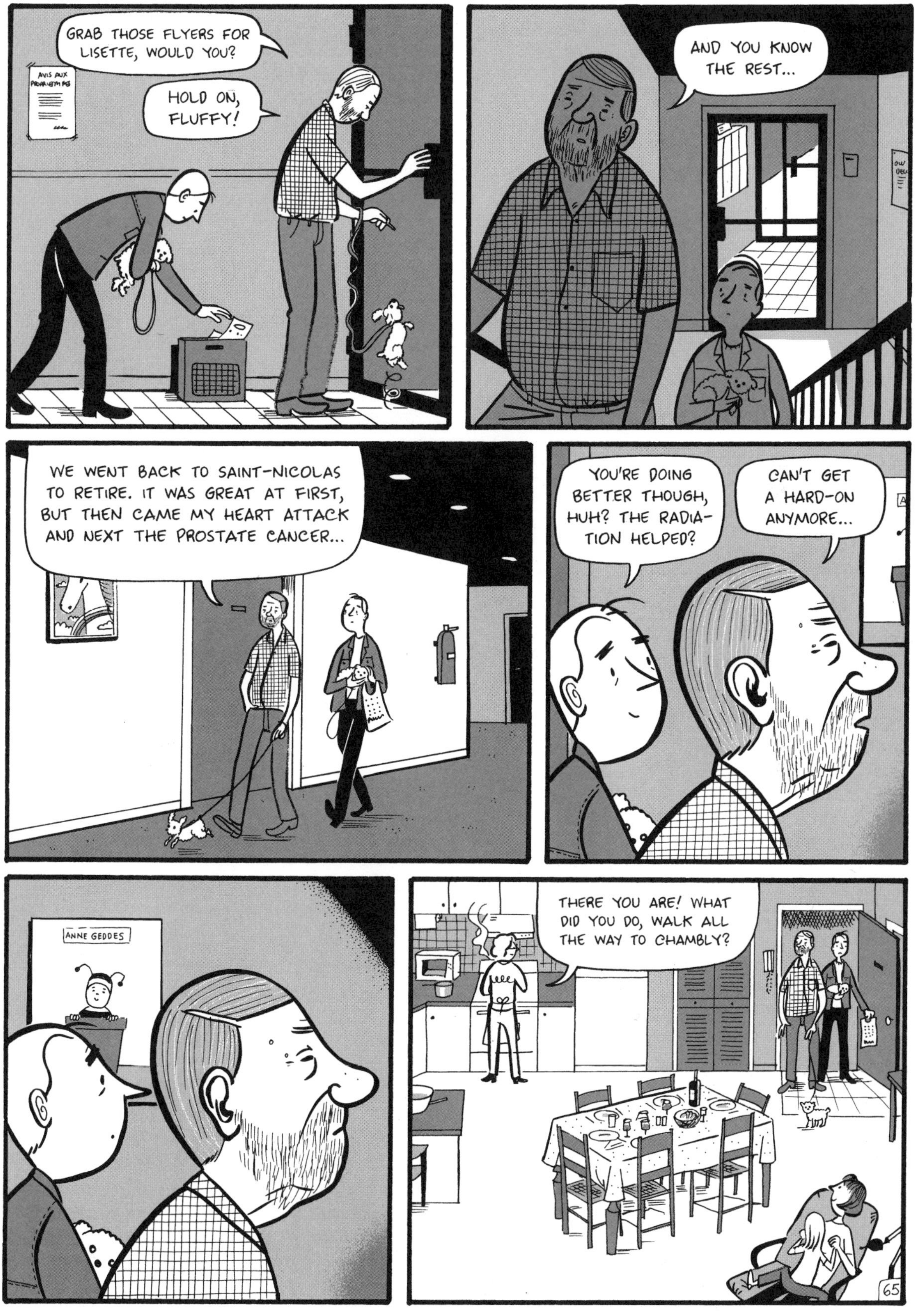
AVIS AUX PROPRIÉTAIRES
GRAB THOSE FLYERS FOR LISETTE, WOULD YOU?
HOLD ON, FLUFFY!
AND YOU KNOW THE REST...
WE WENT BACK TO SAINT-NICOLAS TO RETIRE. IT WAS GREAT AT FIRST, BUT THEN CAME MY HEART ATTACK AND NEXT THE PROSTATE CANCER...
YOU'RE DOING BETTER THOUGH, HUH? THE RADIATION HELPED?
CAN'T GET A HARD-ON ANYMORE...
ANNE GEDDES
THERE YOU ARE! WHAT DID YOU DO, WALK ALL THE WAY TO CHAMBLY?
65

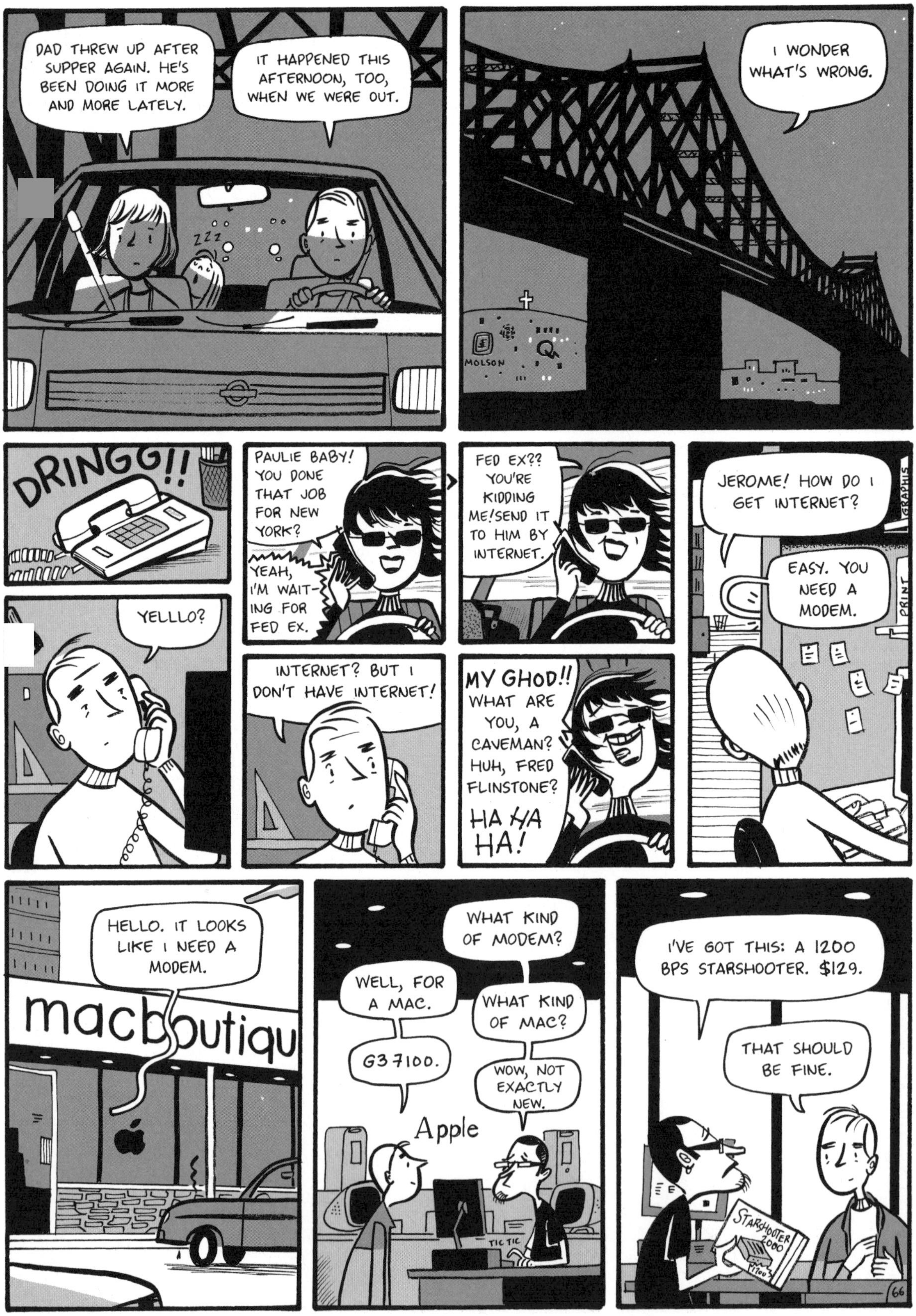
DAD THREW UP AFTER SUPPER AGAIN. HE'S BEEN DOING IT MORE AND MORE LATELY.
IT HAPPENED THIS AFTERNOON, TOO, WHEN WE WERE OUT.
ZZZ
I WONDER WHAT'S WRONG.
MOLSON
DRINGG!!
YELLLO?
PAULIE BABY! YOU DONE THAT JOB FOR NEW YORK?
YEAH, I'M WAITING FOR FED EX.
FED EX?? YOU'RE KIDDING ME! SEND IT TO HIM BY INTERNET.
INTERNET? BUT I DON'T HAVE INTERNET!
MY GHOD!! WHAT ARE YOU, A CAVEMAN? HUH, FRED FLINSTONE?
HA HA HA!
JEROME! HOW DO I GET INTERNET?
EASY. YOU NEED A MODEM.
GRAPHIS
PRINT
HELLO. IT LOOKS LIKE I NEED A MODEM.
macboutiqu
WHAT KIND OF MODEM?
WELL, FOR A MAC.
WHAT KIND OF MAC?
G3 7100.
WOW, NOT EXACTLY NEW.
Apple
TIC TIC
I'VE GOT THIS: A 1200 BPS STARSHOOTER. $129.
THAT SHOULD BE FINE.
STARSHOOTER 2000

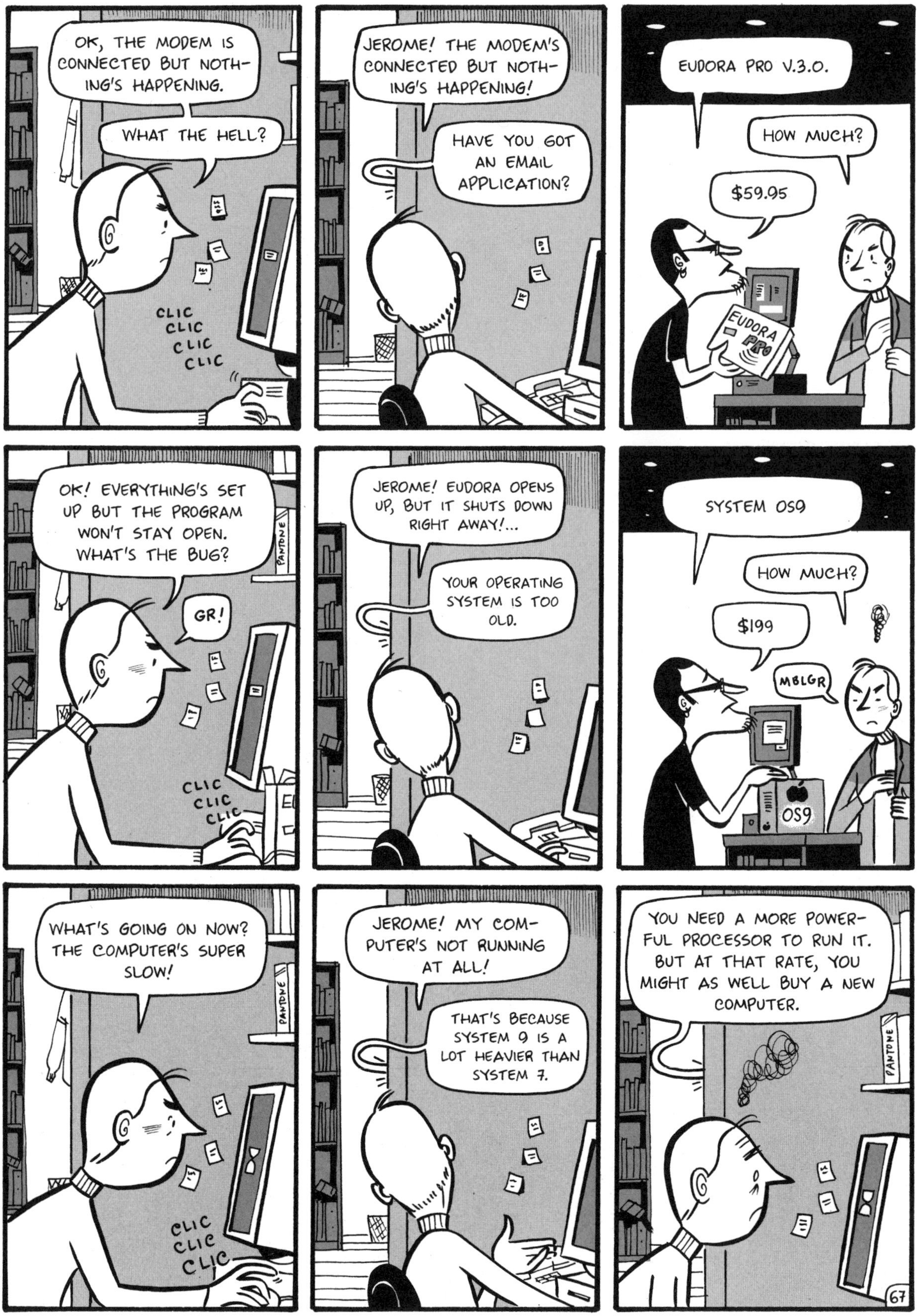
OK, THE MODEM IS CONNECTED BUT NOTHING'S HAPPENING.
WHAT THE HELL?
CLIC CLIC CLIC CLIC
JEROME! THE MODEM'S CONNECTED BUT NOTHING'S HAPPENING!
HAVE YOU GOT AN EMAIL APPLICATION?
EUDORA PRO V.3.0.
HOW MUCH?
$59.95
EUDORA PRO
OK! EVERYTHING'S SET UP BUT THE PROGRAM WON'T STAY OPEN. WHAT'S THE BUG?
GR!
PANTONE
CLIC CLIC CLIC
JEROME! EUDORA OPENS UP, BUT IT SHUTS DOWN RIGHT AWAY!...
YOUR OPERATING SYSTEM IS TOO OLD.
SYSTEM OS9
HOW MUCH?
$199
MBLGR
OS9
WHAT'S GOING ON NOW? THE COMPUTER'S SUPER SLOW!
PANTONE
CLIC CLIC CLIC
JEROME! MY COMPUTER'S NOT RUNNING AT ALL!
THAT'S BECAUSE SYSTEM 9 IS A LOT HEAVIER THAN SYSTEM 7.
YOU NEED A MORE POWERFUL PROCESSOR TO RUN IT. BUT AT THAT RATE, YOU MIGHT AS WELL BUY A NEW COMPUTER.
PANTONE
67

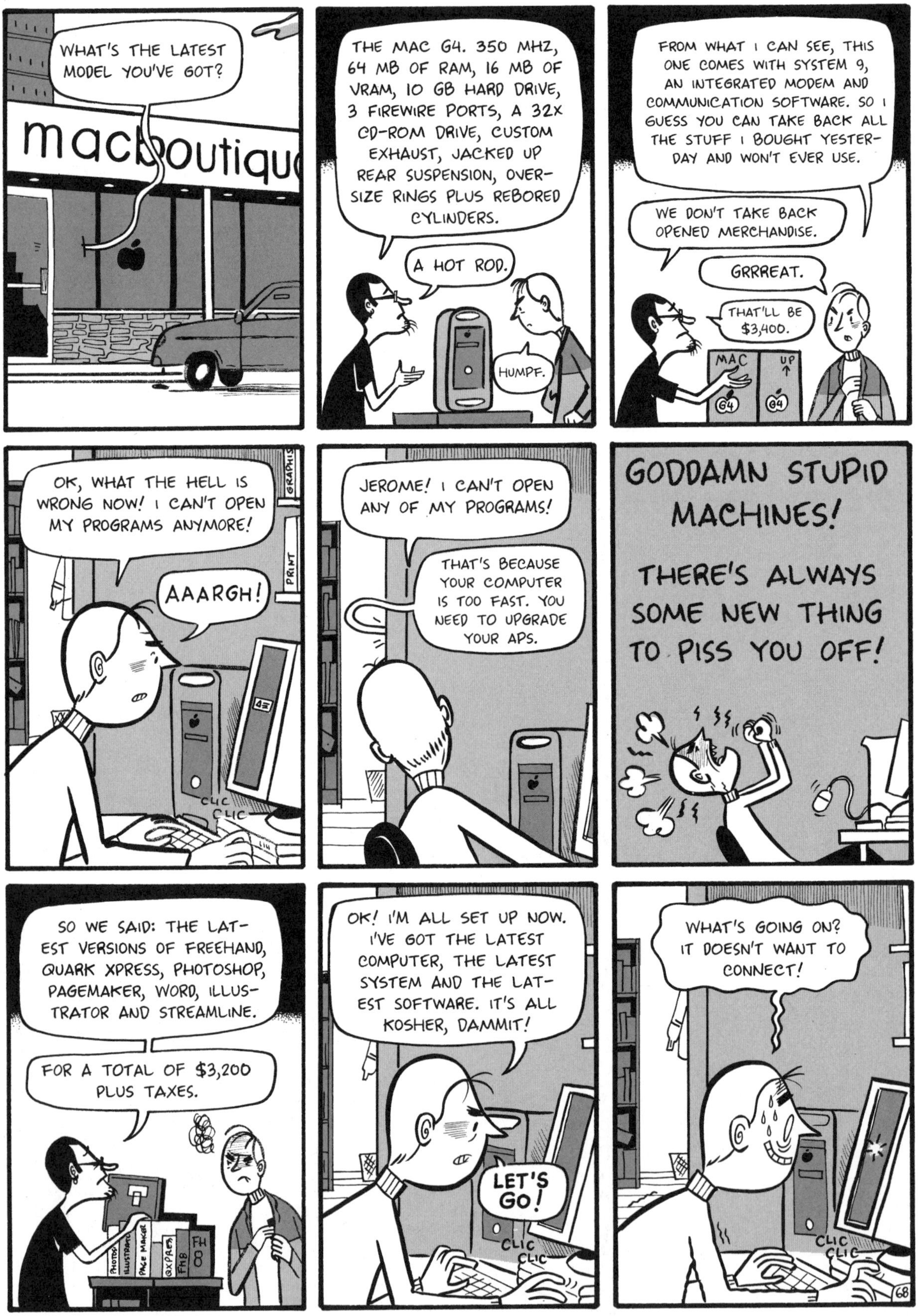
WHAT'S THE LATEST MODEL YOU'VE GOT?
macboutique
THE MAC G4. 350 MHZ, 64 MB OF RAM, 16 MB OF VRAM, 10 GB HARD DRIVE, 3 FIREWIRE PORTS, A 32X CD-ROM DRIVE, CUSTOM EXHAUST, JACKED UP REAR SUSPENSION, OVERSIZE RINGS PLUS REBORED CYLINDERS.
A HOT ROD.
HUMPF.
FROM WHAT I CAN SEE, THIS ONE COMES WITH SYSTEM 9, AN INTEGRATED MODEM AND COMMUNICATION SOFTWARE. SO I GUESS YOU CAN TAKE BACK ALL THE STUFF I BOUGHT YESTERDAY AND WON'T EVER USE.
WE DON'T TAKE BACK OPENED MERCHANDISE.
GRRREAT.
THAT'LL BE $3,400.
MAC
UP
G4
OK, WHAT THE HELL IS WRONG NOW! I CAN'T OPEN MY PROGRAMS ANYMORE!
AAARGH!
GRAPHIS
PRINT
CLIC CLIC
JEROME! I CAN'T OPEN ANY OF MY PROGRAMS!
THAT'S BECAUSE YOUR COMPUTER IS TOO FAST. YOU NEED TO UPGRADE YOUR APS.
GODDAMN STUPID MACHINES!
THERE'S ALWAYS SOME NEW THING TO PISS YOU OFF!
SO WE SAID: THE LATEST VERSIONS OF FREEHAND, QUARK XPRESS, PHOTOSHOP, PAGEMAKER, WORD, ILLUSTRATOR AND STREAMLINE.
FOR A TOTAL OF $3,200 PLUS TAXES.
FH 8
OK! I'M ALL SET UP NOW. I'VE GOT THE LATEST COMPUTER, THE LATEST SYSTEM AND THE LATEST SOFTWARE. IT'S ALL KOSHER, DAMMIT!
LET'S GO!
CLIC CLIC
WHAT'S GOING ON? IT DOESN'T WANT TO CONNECT!
CLIC CLIC
68

DEEP BREATH...
RELAX.
JEROME! I CAN'T CONNECT TO THE INTERNET!
COURSE NOT. YOU NEED AN ISP, LIKE DLINK OR CYBERCOM.
RIGHT. WHY DIDN'T I THINK OF THAT?
SILLY ME...
TAC TAC TAC
WELCOME TO CYBERCOM CANADA. TO SPEAK WITH A REPRESENTATIVE, PRESS 1.
1
IF YOU'RE CALLING FROM A TOUCHTONE PHONE, PRESS 4.
4
IF YOUR PLACE OF BUSINESS IS NOT INUKJUAK, PRESS 3.
3
IF YOU'RE A VEGETARIAN, PRESS 8. IF NOT, PRESS 6.
6
IF YOU'RE WEARING PANTS, PRESS 2.
2
BEEP
ONE MOMENT, PLEASE.
VOOOLARE, OH OH, CANTARE, OH OH OH OH, NEL BLU DIPINTO DI BLU, FELICE DI STARE LASSÙ...
...YOUR CALL IS IMPORTANT TO US. A REPRESENTATIVE WILL ANSWER YOUR CALL AS SOON AS POSSIBLE... ONDO PIAN PIANO SPARIVA LONTANO LAGGIÙ...
CLICK. HELLO, THIS IS SEBASTIAN. THANK YOU FOR CHOOSING CYBERCOM CANADA FOR YOUR TELEPHONE AND NETWORKING NEEDS. WE LOVE WORKING WITH YOU, WE VALUE YOUR BUSINESS AND WE KISS THE GROUND BENEATH YOUR FEET. WE WILL GO OUT OF OUR WAY TO PROVIDE QUALITY CUSTOMER SERVICE AND MAKE THIS PHONE CALL THE BEST MOMENT OF YOUR LIFE. WHAT CAN I DO FOR YOU?
OK, LISTEN, I JUST WANT TO OPEN AN INTERNET ACCOUNT.
OF COURSE. WE'LL CONFIGURE A CONFIGURATIVE CONFIGURATION. WHAT KIND OF COMPUTER DO YOU HAVE?
MAC.
EXCELLENT. GO INTO YOUR NETWORK.
WHERE?
GO TO APPLE → SYSTEM PREFERENCES → NETWORK.
ALRIGHT.
CLIC CLIC CLIC
GO INTO YOUR TCP/IP...
WHERE?
CLICK ON "CONFIGURE."
CLIC
ALRIGHT.
ENTER 1234567 AND YOUR IPV4.
CLIC
ALRIGHT.
ENTER 67.154.690 AS YOUR IP ADDRESS.
CLIC
WHERE?
UNDER PPPOE, FOR PROVIDER TYPE CYBERCOM.
CLIC
DONE.
CLIC
FOR PROXIES, TYPE FTP.
OK.
CLIC CLIC
CLIC
HAVE YOU GOT AN EMAIL NAME?
NO.
CHOOSE ONE.
PAUL.
IT'S ALREADY IN USE. CHOOSE ANOTHER.
OK...PAUL 2?
NO, SOMEBODY'S GOT IT ALREADY. ANOTHER?
PAUL38!
SORRY, TAKEN.
AAARH! PAUL 6934567 ZAT OK??
YES, THANKS.
69

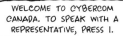

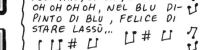

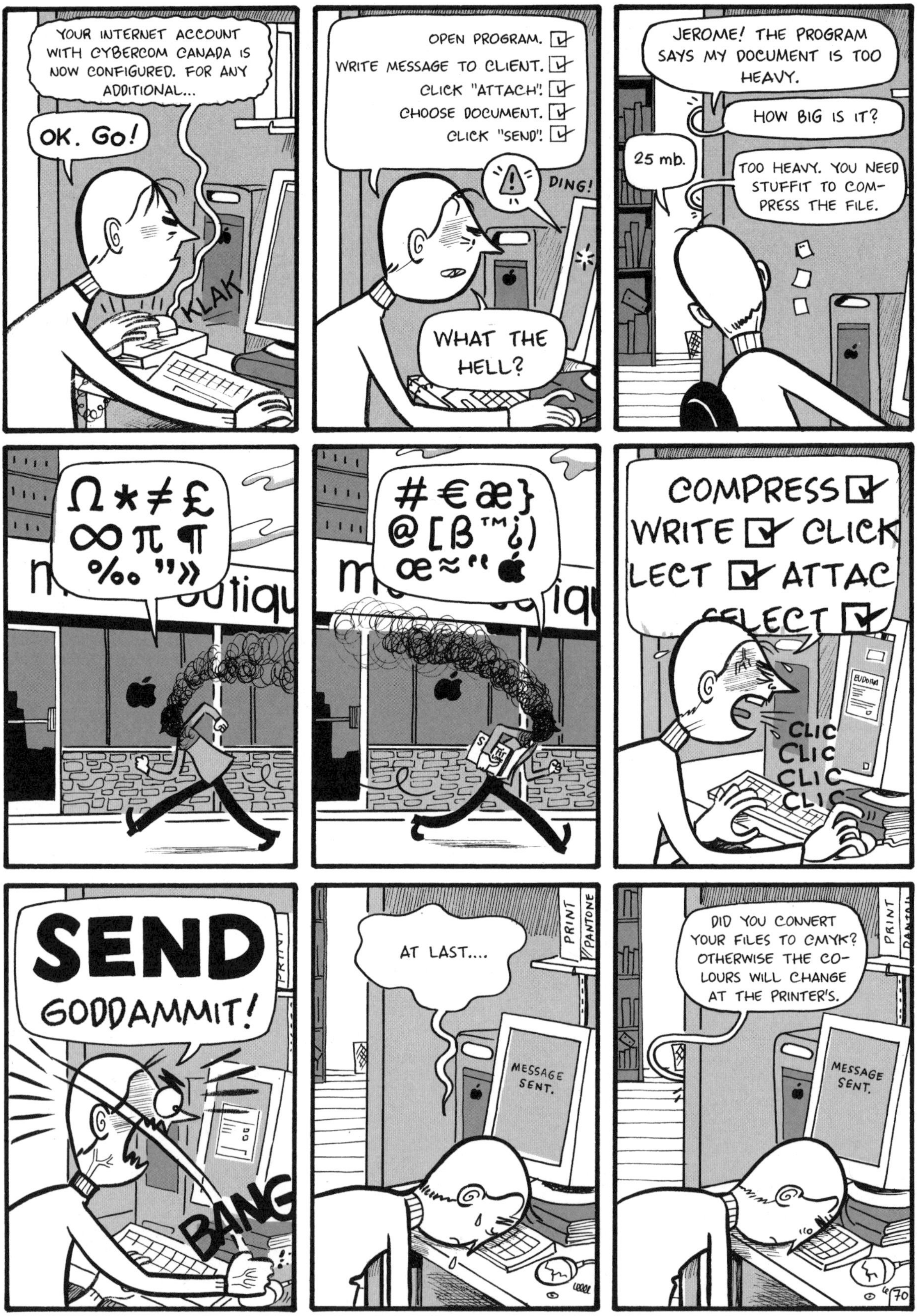
YOUR INTERNET ACCOUNT WITH CYBERCOM CANADA IS NOW CONFIGURED. FOR ANY ADDITIONAL...
OK. GO!
KLAK
OPEN PROGRAM. ☑
WRITE MESSAGE TO CLIENT. ☑
CLICK "ATTACH". ☑
CHOOSE DOCUMENT. ☑
CLICK "SEND". ☑
DING!
WHAT THE HELL?
JEROME! THE PROGRAM SAYS MY DOCUMENT IS TOO HEAVY.
HOW BIG IS IT?
25 mb.
TOO HEAVY. YOU NEED STUFFIT TO COMPRESS THE FILE.
Ω * ≠ £ ∞ π ¶ ‰ " »
€ æ } @ [ß ™ ¿) œ ≈ "
COMPRESS ☑
WRITE ☑ CLICK
LECT ☑ ATTAC
SELECT ☑
EUDORA
CLIC
CLIC
CLIC
CLIC
SEND GODDAMMIT!
BANG
PRINT
AT LAST....
PRINT
PANTONE
MESSAGE SENT.
DID YOU CONVERT YOUR FILES TO CMYK? OTHERWISE THE COLOURS WILL CHANGE AT THE PRINTER'S.
PRINT
MESSAGE SENT.

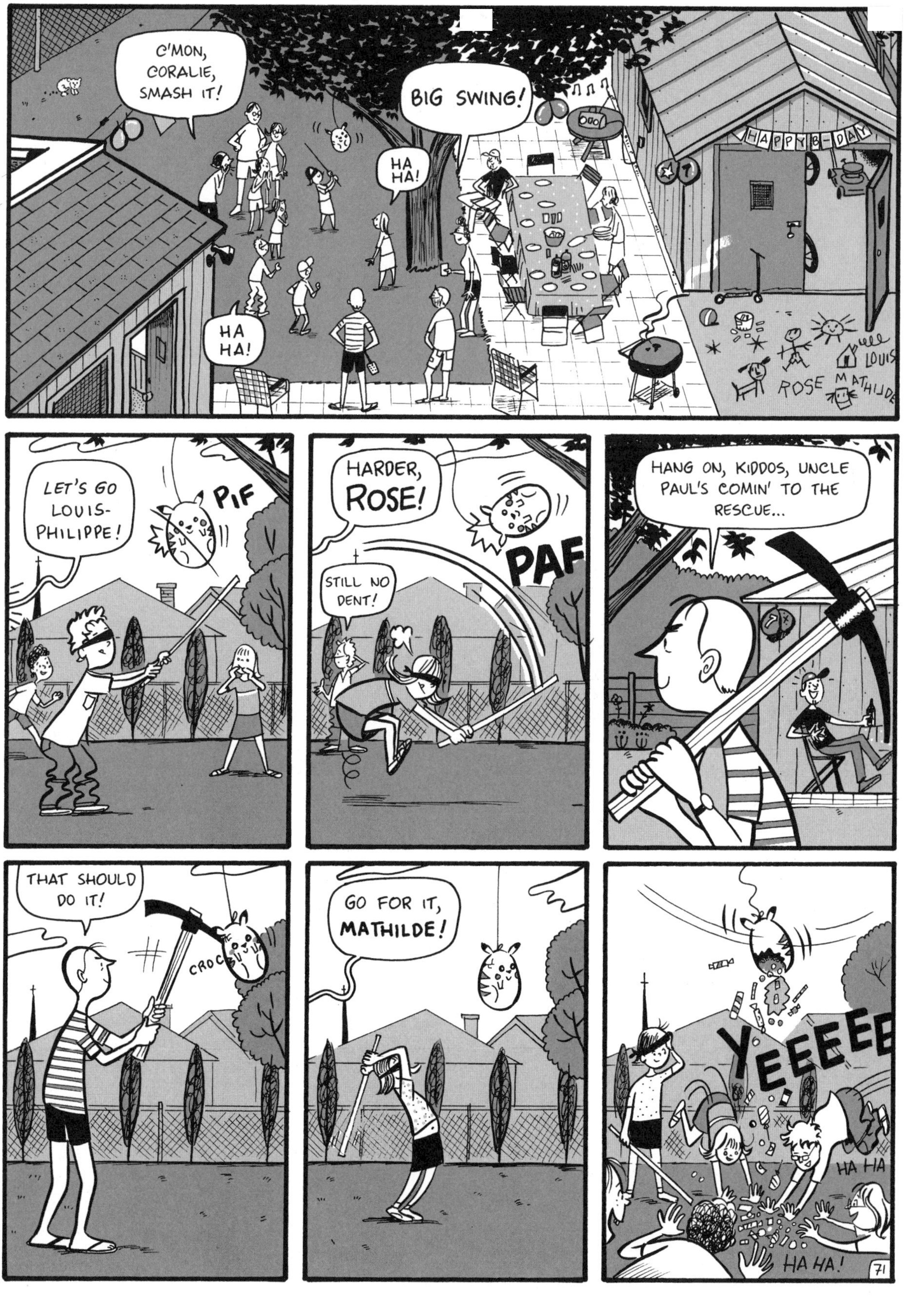
C'MON, CORALIE, SMASH IT!
HA HA!
HA HA!
BIG SWING!
HAPPY B-DAY
ROSE
LOUIS
MATHILDE
LET'S GO LOUIS-PHILIPPE!
PIF
HARDER, ROSE!
STILL NO DENT!
PAF
HANG ON, KIDDOS, UNCLE PAUL'S COMIN' TO THE RESCUE...
THAT SHOULD DO IT!
CROC
GO FOR IT, MATHILDE!
YEEEEE
HA HA
HA HA!
71

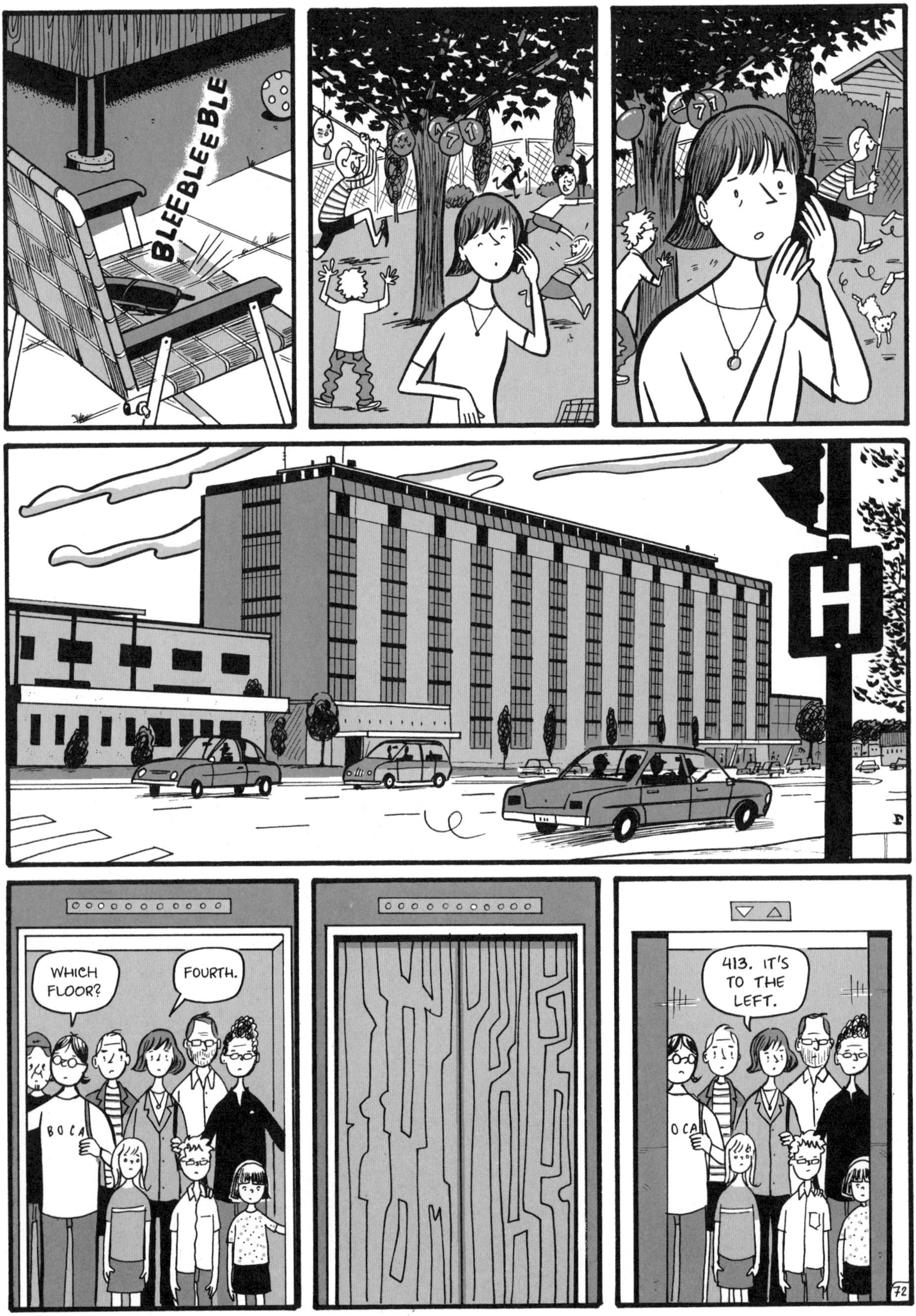
BLEEBLEEBLE
WHICH FLOOR?
FOURTH.
413. IT'S TO THE LEFT.
72

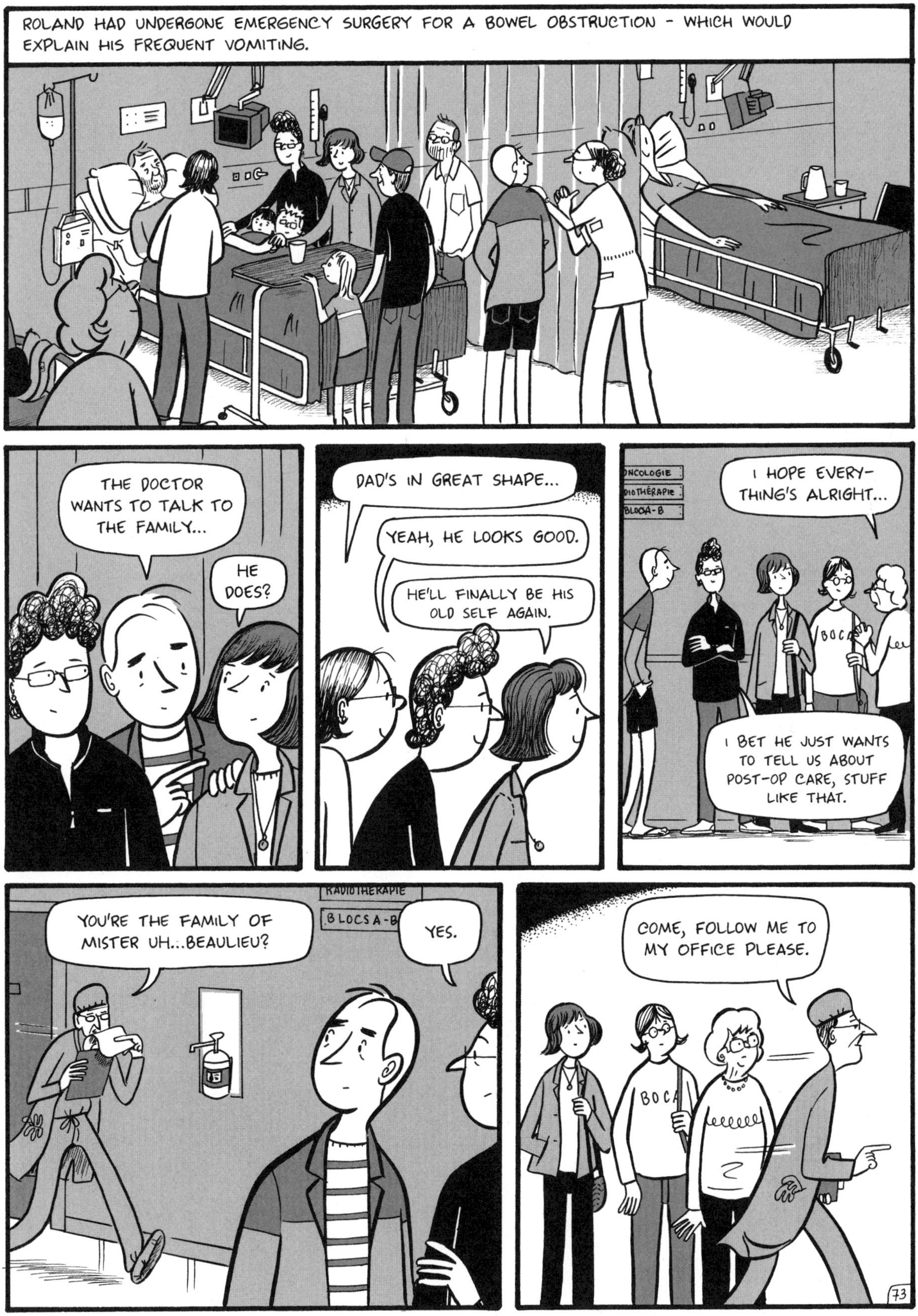

ROLAND HAD UNDERGONE EMERGENCY SURGERY FOR A BOWEL OBSTRUCTION - WHICH WOULD EXPLAIN HIS FREQUENT VOMITING.
THE DOCTOR WANTS TO TALK TO THE FAMILY...
HE DOES?
DAD'S IN GREAT SHAPE...
YEAH, HE LOOKS GOOD.
HE'LL FINALLY BE HIS OLD SELF AGAIN.
ONCOLOGIE
DIOTHÉRAPIE
BLOCSA-B
I HOPE EVERYTHING'S ALRIGHT...
I BET HE JUST WANTS TO TELL US ABOUT POST-OP CARE, STUFF LIKE THAT.
RADIOTHERAPIE
BLOCS A-B
YOU'RE THE FAMILY OF MISTER UH...BEAULIEU?
YES.
COME, FOLLOW ME TO MY OFFICE PLEASE.
73

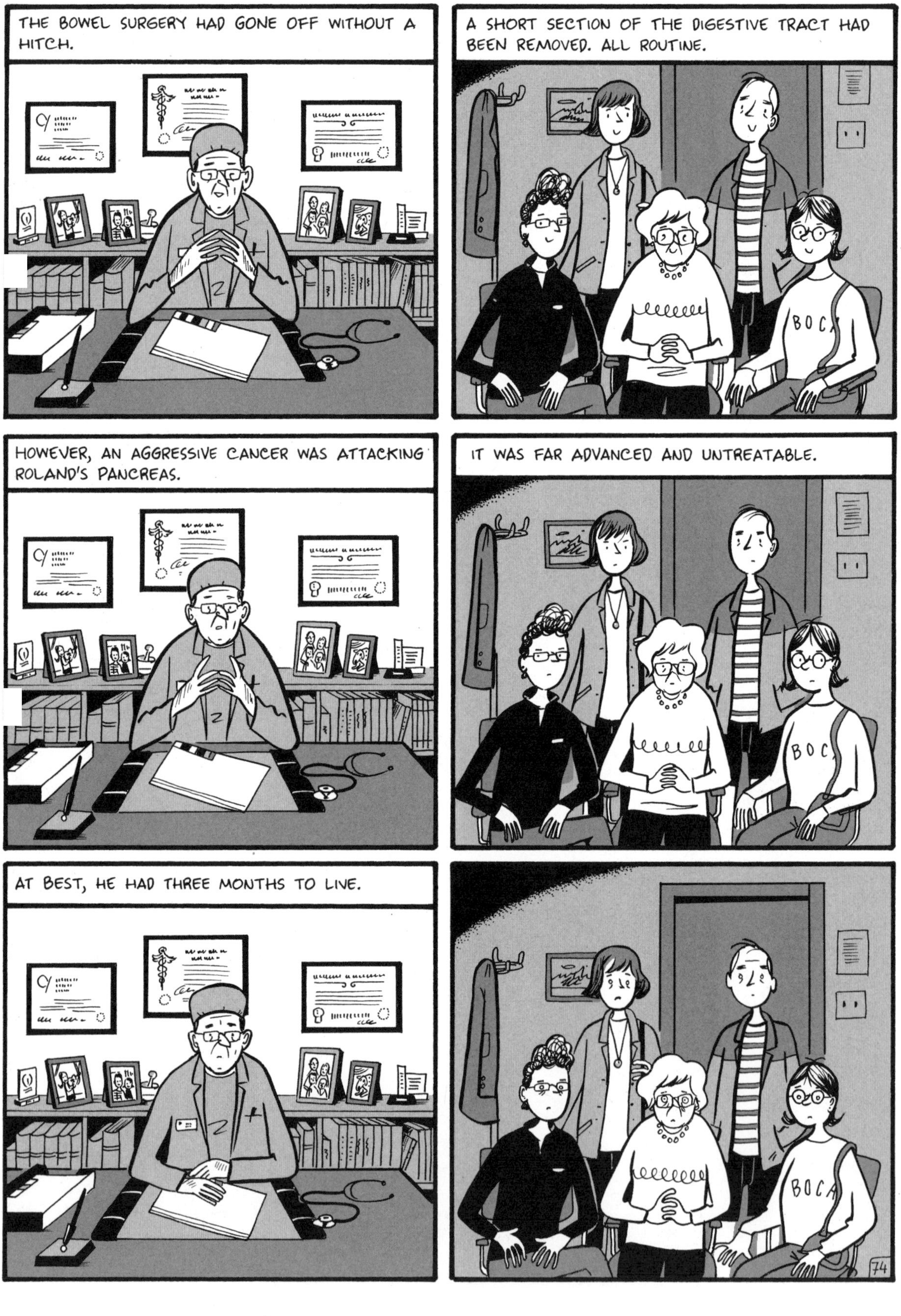
THE BOWEL SURGERY HAD GONE OFF WITHOUT A HITCH.
A SHORT SECTION OF THE DIGESTIVE TRACT HAD BEEN REMOVED. ALL ROUTINE.
BOCA
HOWEVER, AN AGGRESSIVE CANCER WAS ATTACKING ROLAND'S PANCREAS.
IT WAS FAR ADVANCED AND UNTREATABLE.
BOCA
AT BEST, HE HAD THREE MONTHS TO LIVE.
BOCA
74

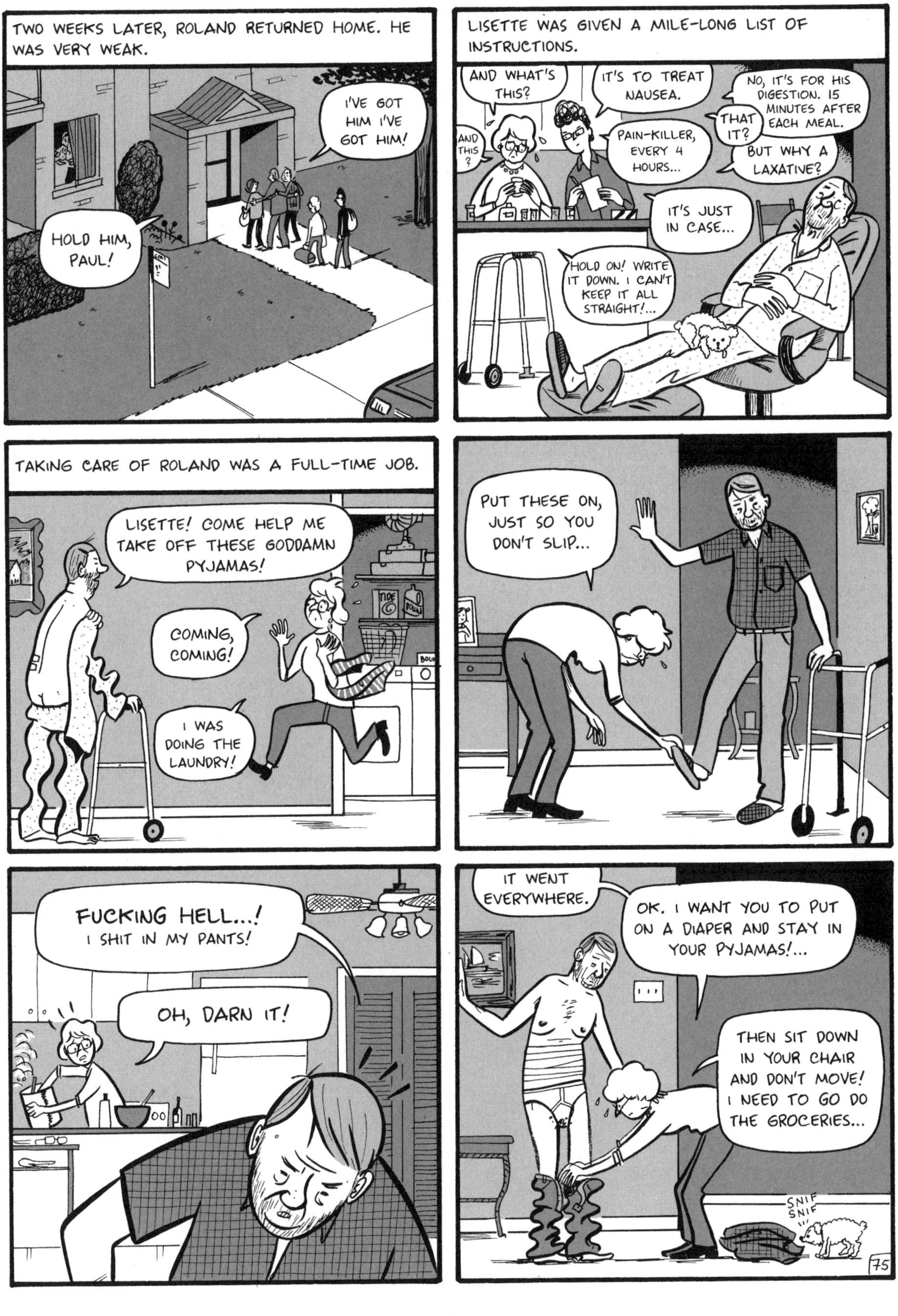
TWO WEEKS LATER, ROLAND RETURNED HOME. HE WAS VERY WEAK.
I'VE GOT HIM I'VE GOT HIM!
HOLD HIM, PAUL!
LISETTE WAS GIVEN A MILE-LONG LIST OF INSTRUCTIONS.
AND WHAT'S THIS?
IT'S TO TREAT NAUSEA.
AND THIS?
PAIN-KILLER, EVERY 4 HOURS...
THAT IT?
NO, IT'S FOR HIS DIGESTION. 15 MINUTES AFTER EACH MEAL.
BUT WHY A LAXATIVE?
IT'S JUST IN CASE...
HOLD ON! WRITE IT DOWN. I CAN'T KEEP IT ALL STRAIGHT!...
TAKING CARE OF ROLAND WAS A FULL-TIME JOB.
LISETTE! COME HELP ME TAKE OFF THESE GODDAMN PYJAMAS!
COMING, COMING!
I WAS DOING THE LAUNDRY!
PUT THESE ON, JUST SO YOU DON'T SLIP...
FUCKING HELL...! I SHIT IN MY PANTS!
OH, DARN IT!
IT WENT EVERYWHERE.
OK. I WANT YOU TO PUT ON A DIAPER AND STAY IN YOUR PYJAMAS!...
THEN SIT DOWN IN YOUR CHAIR AND DON'T MOVE! I NEED TO GO DO THE GROCERIES...
SNIF SNIF
75

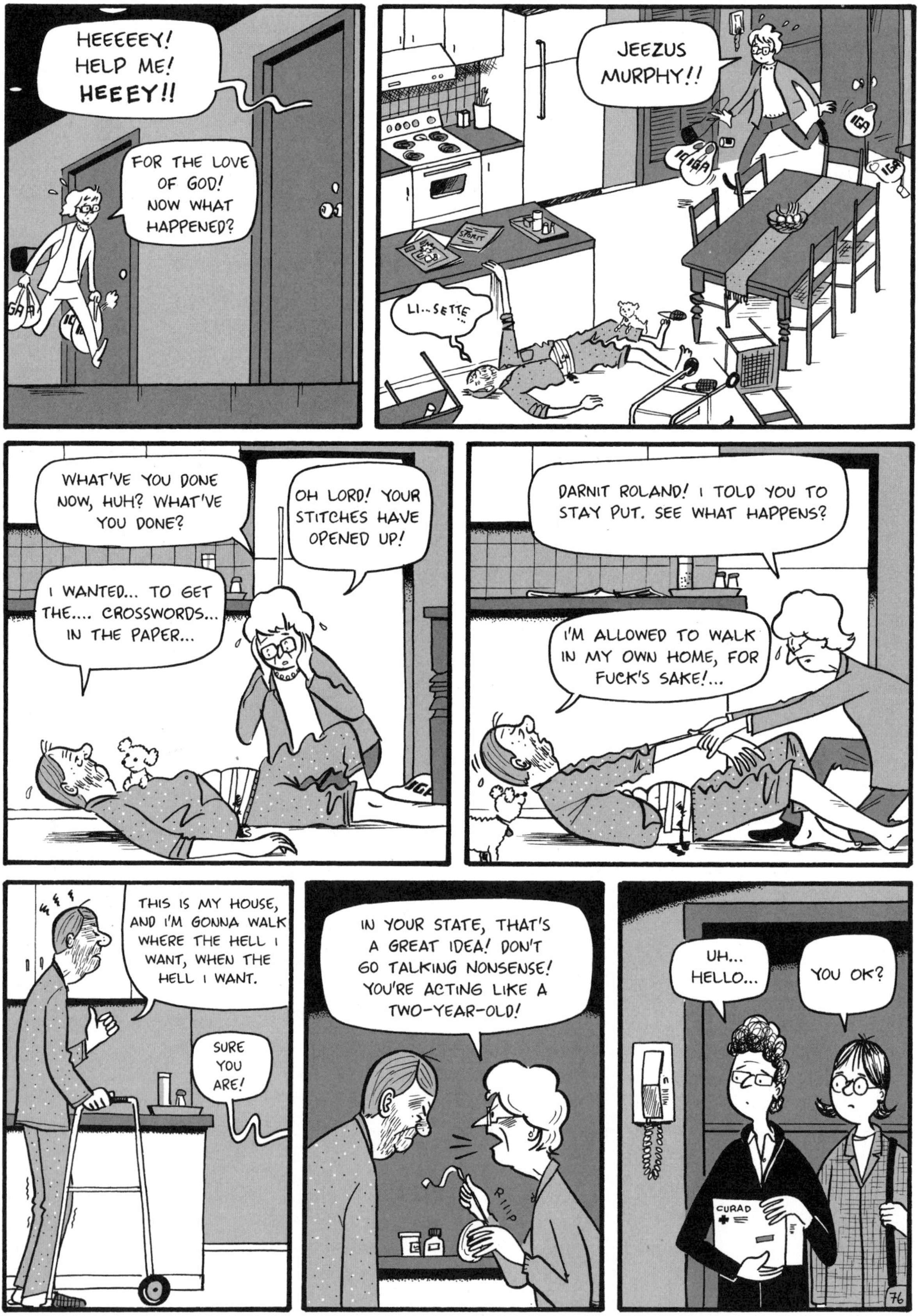
HEEEEEY! HELP ME! HEEEY!!
FOR THE LOVE OF GOD! NOW WHAT HAPPENED?
JEEZUS MURPHY!!
LI...SETTE
WHAT'VE YOU DONE NOW, HUH? WHAT'VE YOU DONE?
I WANTED... TO GET THE.... CROSSWORDS... IN THE PAPER...
OH LORD! YOUR STITCHES HAVE OPENED UP!
DARNIT ROLAND! I TOLD YOU TO STAY PUT. SEE WHAT HAPPENS?
I'M ALLOWED TO WALK IN MY OWN HOME, FOR FUCK'S SAKE!...
THIS IS MY HOUSE, AND I'M GONNA WALK WHERE THE HELL I WANT, WHEN THE HELL I WANT.
SURE YOU ARE!
IN YOUR STATE, THAT'S A GREAT IDEA! DON'T GO TALKING NONSENSE! YOU'RE ACTING LIKE A TWO-YEAR-OLD!
RIIIP
UH... HELLO...
YOU OK?
CURAD
76

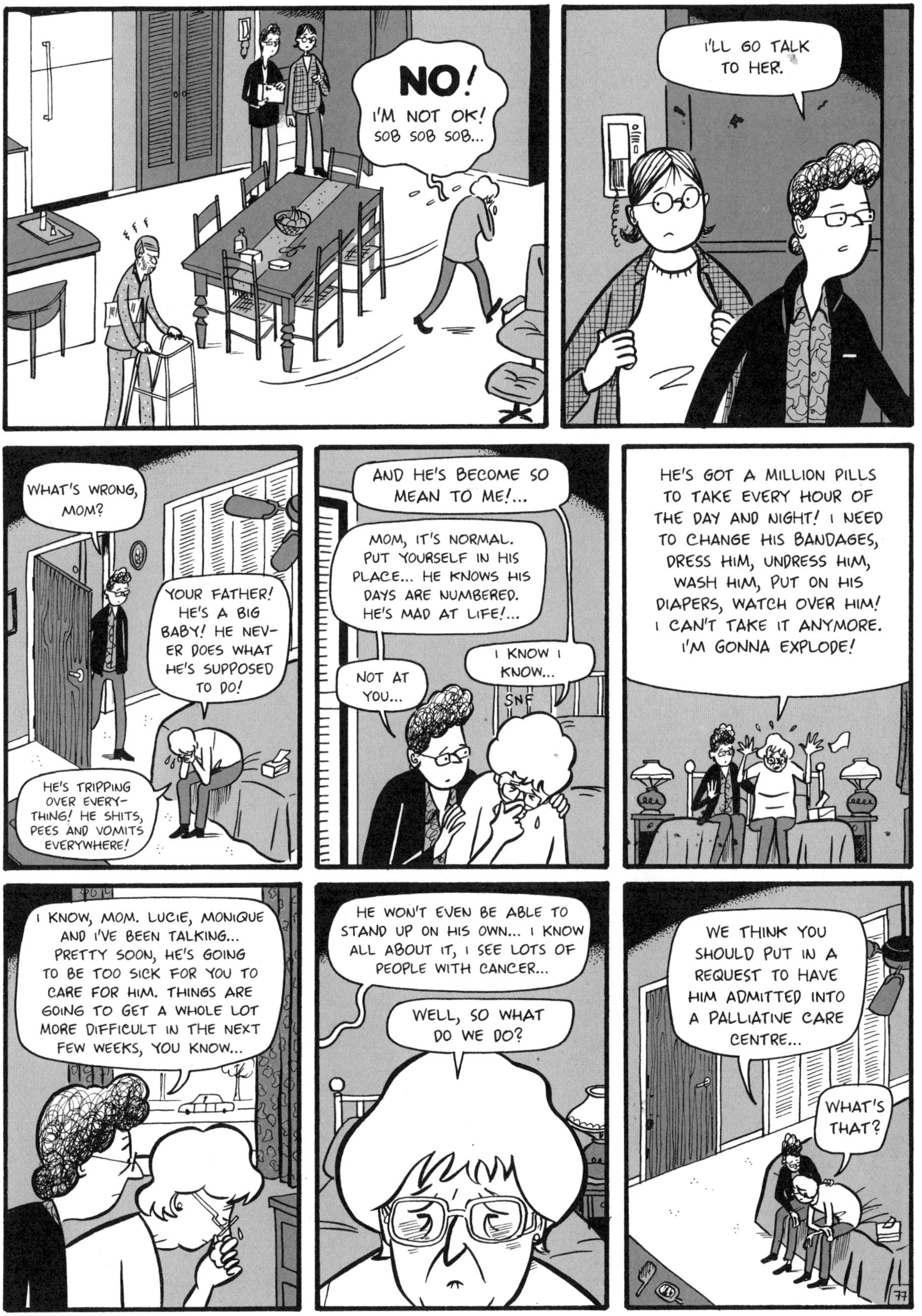
NO! I'M NOT OK! SOB SOB SOB...
I'LL GO TALK TO HER.
WHAT'S WRONG, MOM?
YOUR FATHER! HE'S A BIG BABY! HE NEVER DOES WHAT HE'S SUPPOSED TO DO!
HE'S TRIPPING OVER EVERYTHING! HE SHITS, PEES AND VOMITS EVERYWHERE!
AND HE'S BECOME SO MEAN TO ME!...
MOM, IT'S NORMAL. PUT YOURSELF IN HIS PLACE... HE KNOWS HIS DAYS ARE NUMBERED. HE'S MAD AT LIFE!...
NOT AT YOU...
I KNOW I KNOW...
SNF
HE'S GOT A MILLION PILLS TO TAKE EVERY HOUR OF THE DAY AND NIGHT! I NEED TO CHANGE HIS BANDAGES, DRESS HIM, UNDRESS HIM, WASH HIM, PUT ON HIS DIAPERS, WATCH OVER HIM! I CAN'T TAKE IT ANYMORE. I'M GONNA EXPLODE!
I KNOW, MOM. LUCIE, MONIQUE AND I'VE BEEN TALKING... PRETTY SOON, HE'S GOING TO BE TOO SICK FOR YOU TO CARE FOR HIM. THINGS ARE GOING TO GET A WHOLE LOT MORE DIFFICULT IN THE NEXT FEW WEEKS, YOU KNOW...
HE WON'T EVEN BE ABLE TO STAND UP ON HIS OWN... I KNOW ALL ABOUT IT, I SEE LOTS OF PEOPLE WITH CANCER...
WELL, SO WHAT DO WE DO?
WE THINK YOU SHOULD PUT IN A REQUEST TO HAVE HIM ADMITTED INTO A PALLIATIVE CARE CENTRE...
WHAT'S THAT?
77

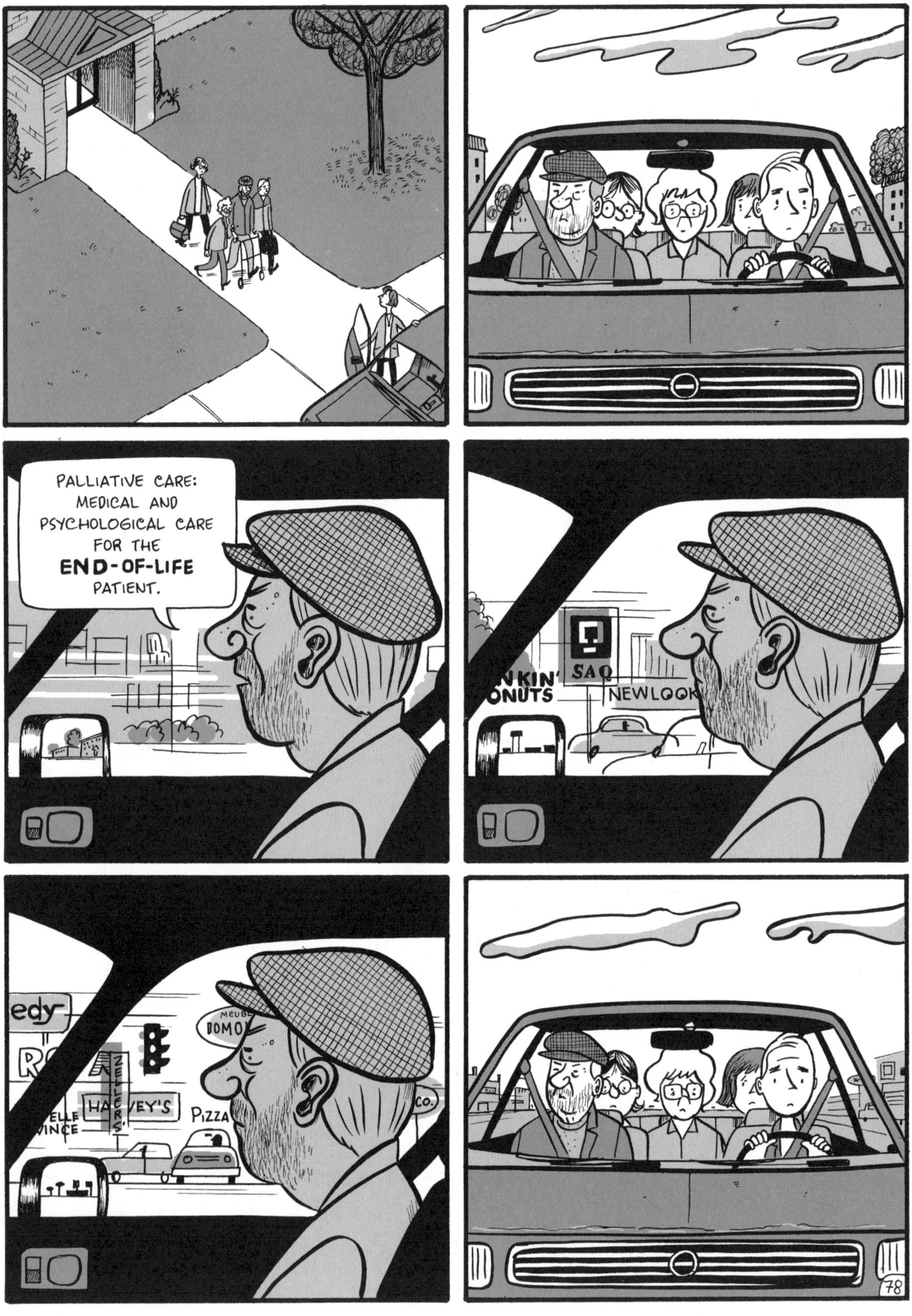
PALLIATIVE CARE: MEDICAL AND PSYCHOLOGICAL CARE FOR THE **END-OF-LIFE** PATIENT.
SAQ
NEWLOOK
ZELLERS'
PIZZA
78

September

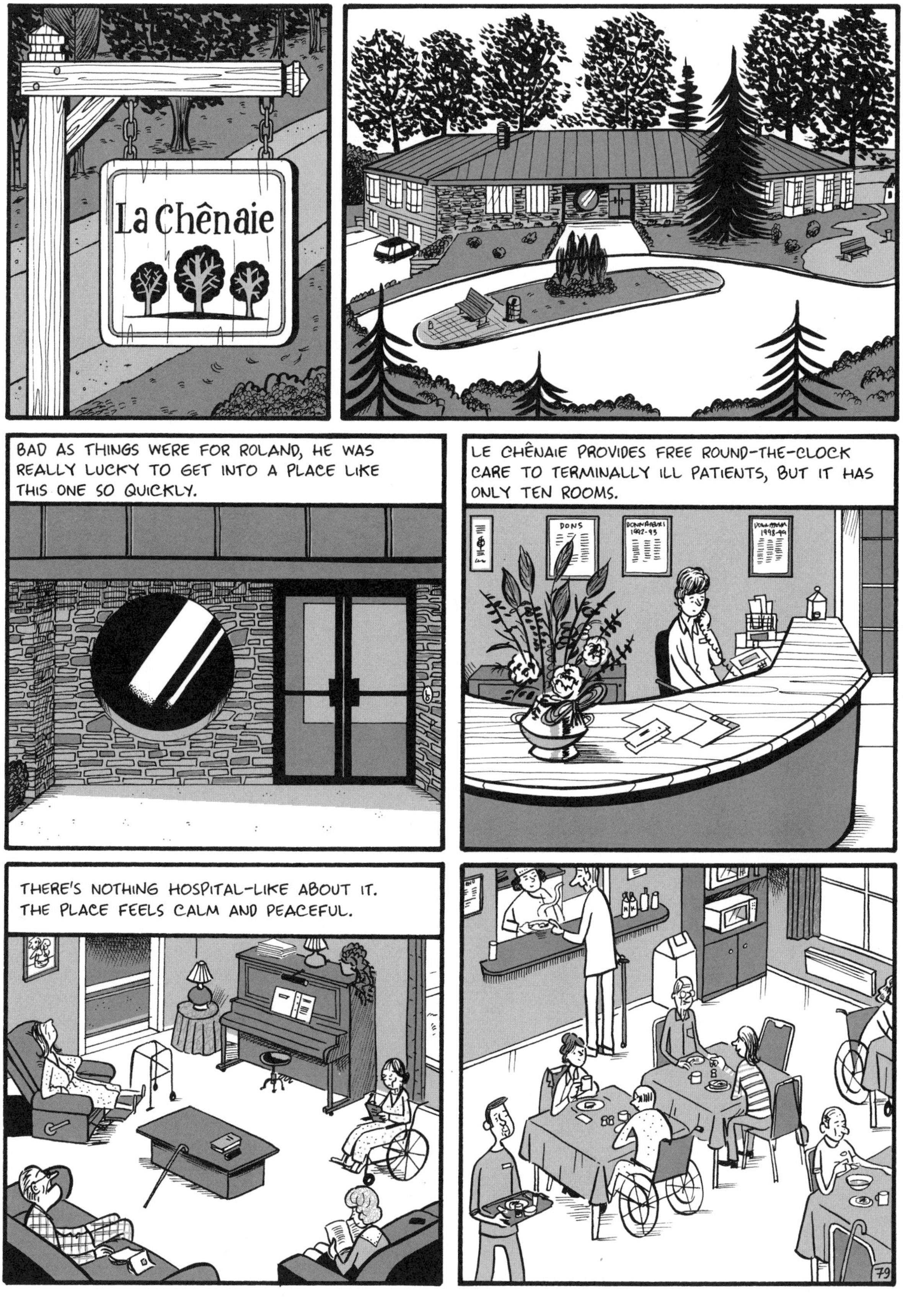
La Chênaie
BAD AS THINGS WERE FOR ROLAND, HE WAS REALLY LUCKY TO GET INTO A PLACE LIKE THIS ONE SO QUICKLY.
LE CHÊNAIE PROVIDES FREE ROUND-THE-CLOCK CARE TO TERMINALLY ILL PATIENTS, BUT IT HAS ONLY TEN ROOMS.
DONS
THERE'S NOTHING HOSPITAL-LIKE ABOUT IT. THE PLACE FEELS CALM AND PEACEFUL.
79

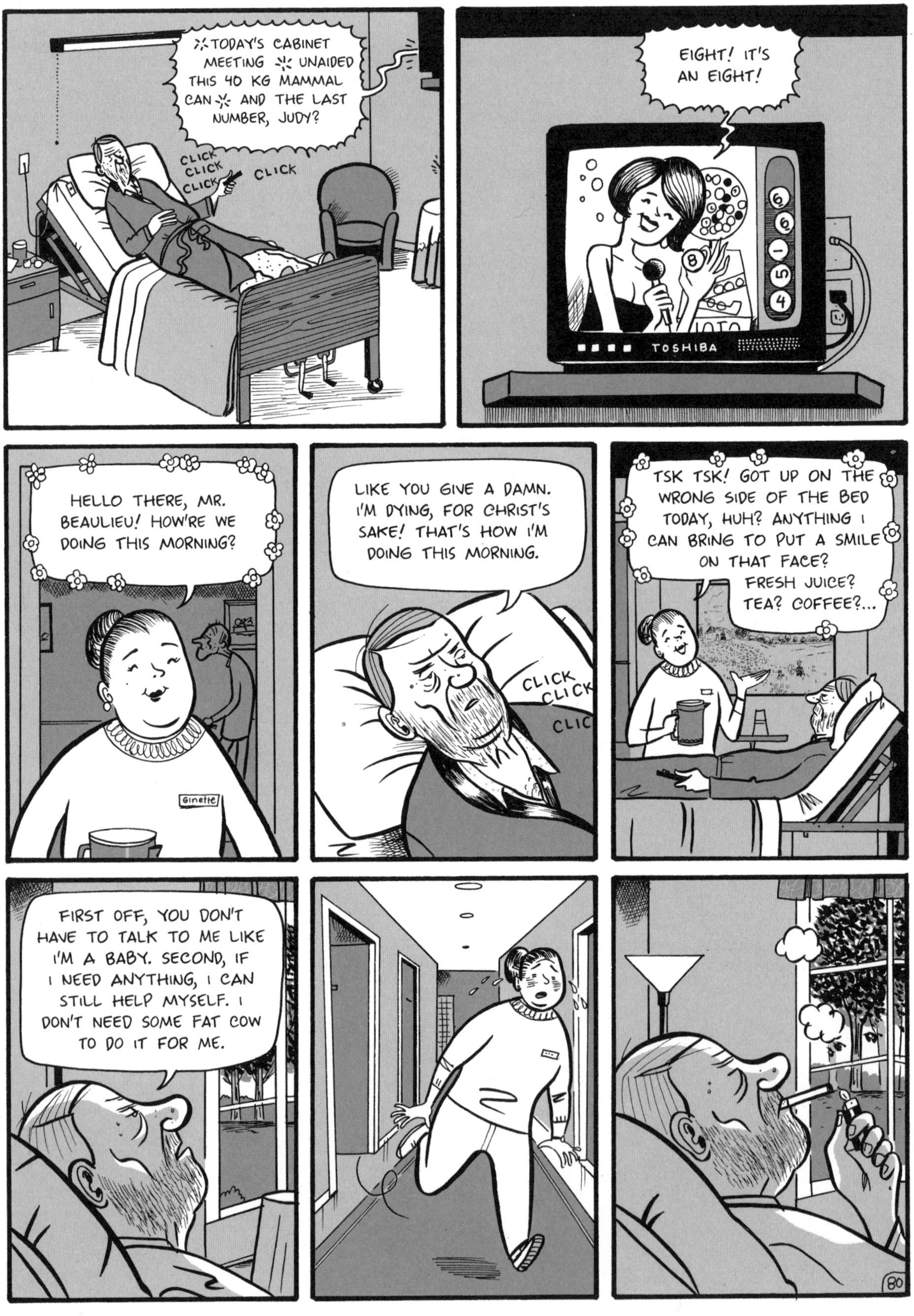
TODAY'S CABINET MEETING UNAIDED THIS 40 KG MAMMAL CAN AND THE LAST NUMBER, JUDY?
CLICK CLICK CLICK
CLICK
EIGHT! IT'S AN EIGHT!
TOSHIBA
HELLO THERE, MR. BEAULIEU! HOW'RE WE DOING THIS MORNING?
Ginette
LIKE YOU GIVE A DAMN. I'M DYING, FOR CHRIST'S SAKE! THAT'S HOW I'M DOING THIS MORNING.
CLICK CLICK
CLIC
TSK TSK! GOT UP ON THE WRONG SIDE OF THE BED TODAY, HUH? ANYTHING I CAN BRING TO PUT A SMILE ON THAT FACE?
FRESH JUICE? TEA? COFFEE?...
FIRST OFF, YOU DON'T HAVE TO TALK TO ME LIKE I'M A BABY. SECOND, IF I NEED ANYTHING, I CAN STILL HELP MYSELF. I DON'T NEED SOME FAT COW TO DO IT FOR ME.
80

HELLO MR. BEAULIEU! HOW WOULD YOU LIKE ME TO PLAY SOMETHING FOR YOU?

YOU CAN CHOOSE CLASSICAL, POP OR EVEN JAZZ!

HOW ABOUT YOU TAKE THAT TOY PIANO AND GET LOST!

HELLO, MISTER BEAULIEU.

MY NAME IS NORMAN. I'M A DOCTOR HERE AT THE CENTRE, AND I'M RESPONSIBLE FOR THE STAFF AS WELL.

D'YOU MIND? SMOKING'S NOT ALLOWED INDOORS.

YOU CAN SMOKE OUTSIDE ON THE PORCHES.

PST.

DIXIE

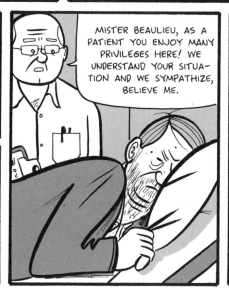

MISTER BEAULIEU, AS A PATIENT YOU ENJOY MANY PRIVILEGES HERE! WE UNDERSTAND YOUR SITUATION AND WE SYMPATHIZE, BELIEVE ME.

BUT THERE'S ONE THING THAT WE WILL NOT TOLERATE, AND THAT IS ANY VERBAL ABUSE OR OTHER MISTREATMENT OF OUR VOLUNTEERS.

81

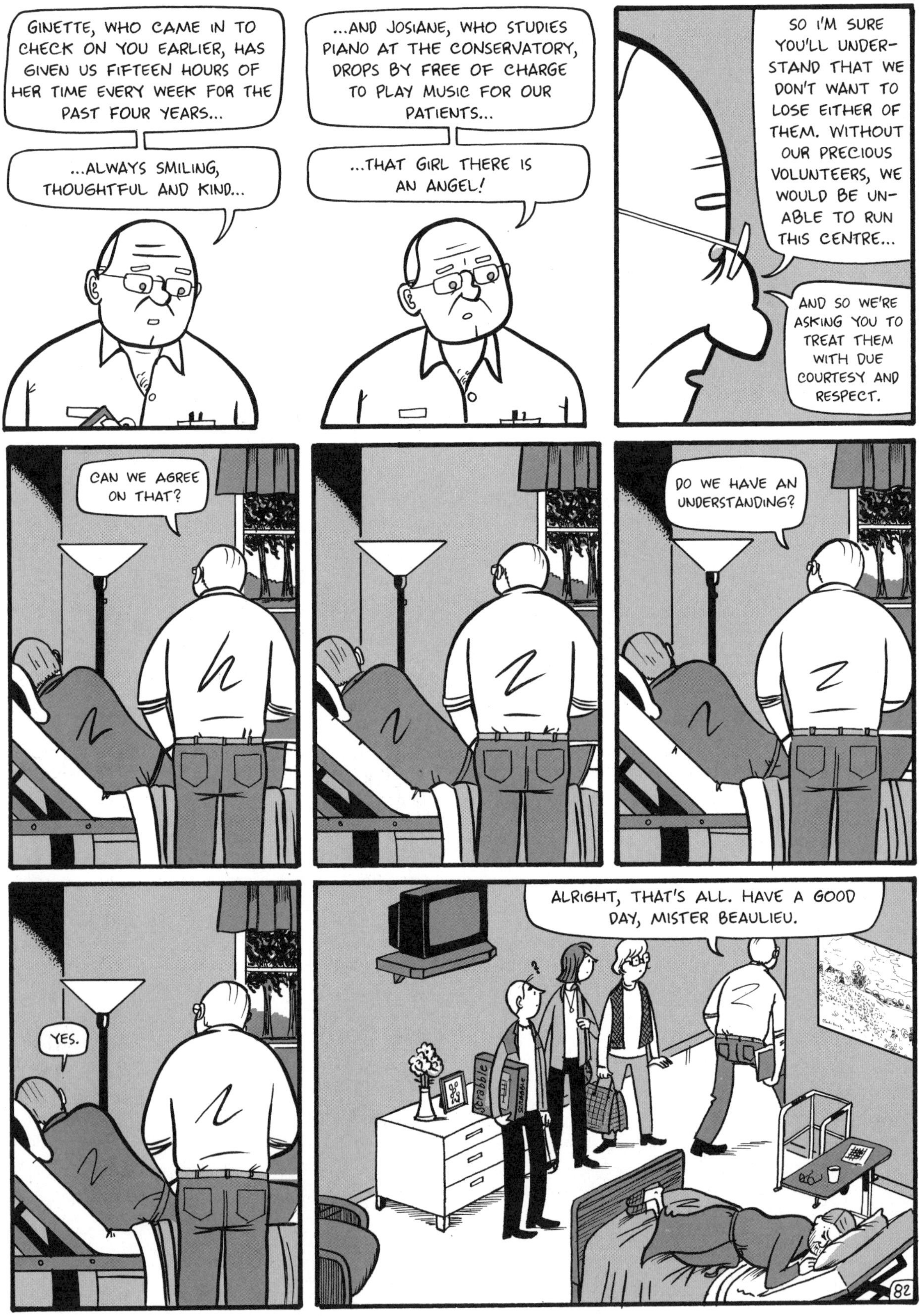
GINETTE, WHO CAME IN TO CHECK ON YOU EARLIER, HAS GIVEN US FIFTEEN HOURS OF HER TIME EVERY WEEK FOR THE PAST FOUR YEARS...
...ALWAYS SMILING, THOUGHTFUL AND KIND...
...AND JOSIANE, WHO STUDIES PIANO AT THE CONSERVATORY, DROPS BY FREE OF CHARGE TO PLAY MUSIC FOR OUR PATIENTS...
...THAT GIRL THERE IS AN ANGEL!
SO I'M SURE YOU'LL UNDERSTAND THAT WE DON'T WANT TO LOSE EITHER OF THEM. WITHOUT OUR PRECIOUS VOLUNTEERS, WE WOULD BE UNABLE TO RUN THIS CENTRE...
AND SO WE'RE ASKING YOU TO TREAT THEM WITH DUE COURTESY AND RESPECT.
CAN WE AGREE ON THAT?
DO WE HAVE AN UNDERSTANDING?
YES.
ALRIGHT, THAT'S ALL. HAVE A GOOD DAY, MISTER BEAULIEU.
Scrabble
82

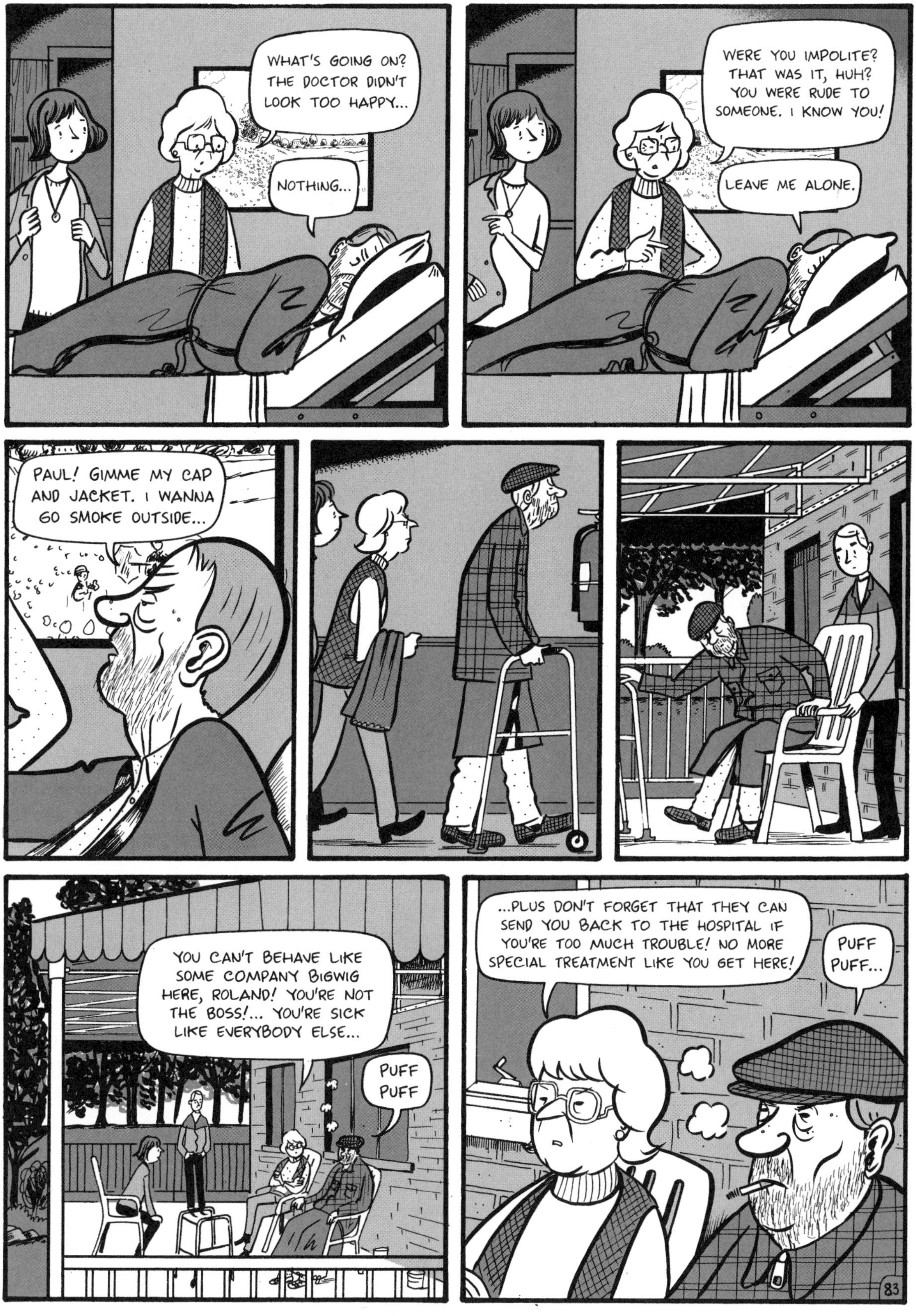
WHAT'S GOING ON? THE DOCTOR DIDN'T LOOK TOO HAPPY...
NOTHING...
WERE YOU IMPOLITE? THAT WAS IT, HUH? YOU WERE RUDE TO SOMEONE. I KNOW YOU!
LEAVE ME ALONE.
PAUL! GIMME MY CAP AND JACKET. I WANNA GO SMOKE OUTSIDE...
YOU CAN'T BEHAVE LIKE SOME COMPANY BIGWIG HERE, ROLAND! YOU'RE NOT THE BOSS!... YOU'RE SICK LIKE EVERYBODY ELSE...
PUFF PUFF
...PLUS DON'T FORGET THAT THEY CAN SEND YOU BACK TO THE HOSPITAL IF YOU'RE TOO MUCH TROUBLE! NO MORE SPECIAL TREATMENT LIKE YOU GET HERE!
PUFF PUFF...
83

October

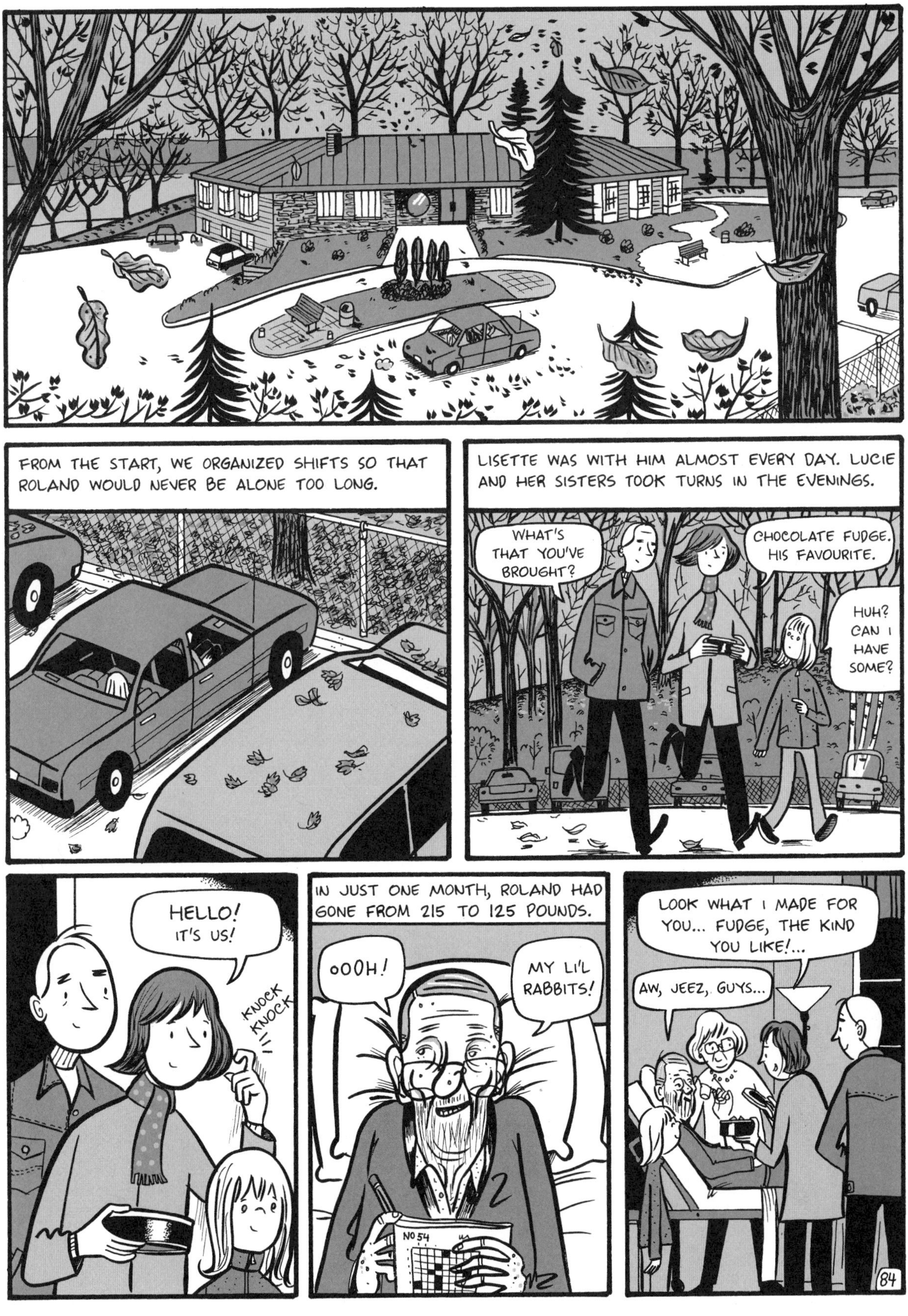
FROM THE START, WE ORGANIZED SHIFTS SO THAT ROLAND WOULD NEVER BE ALONE TOO LONG.
LISETTE WAS WITH HIM ALMOST EVERY DAY. LUCIE AND HER SISTERS TOOK TURNS IN THE EVENINGS.
WHAT'S THAT YOU'VE BROUGHT?
CHOCOLATE FUDGE. HIS FAVOURITE.
HUH? CAN I HAVE SOME?
HELLO! IT'S US!
KNOCK KNOCK
IN JUST ONE MONTH, ROLAND HAD GONE FROM 215 TO 125 POUNDS.
OOOH!
MY LI'L RABBITS!
NO 54
LOOK WHAT I MADE FOR YOU... FUDGE, THE KIND YOU LIKE!...
AW, JEEZ, GUYS...
84

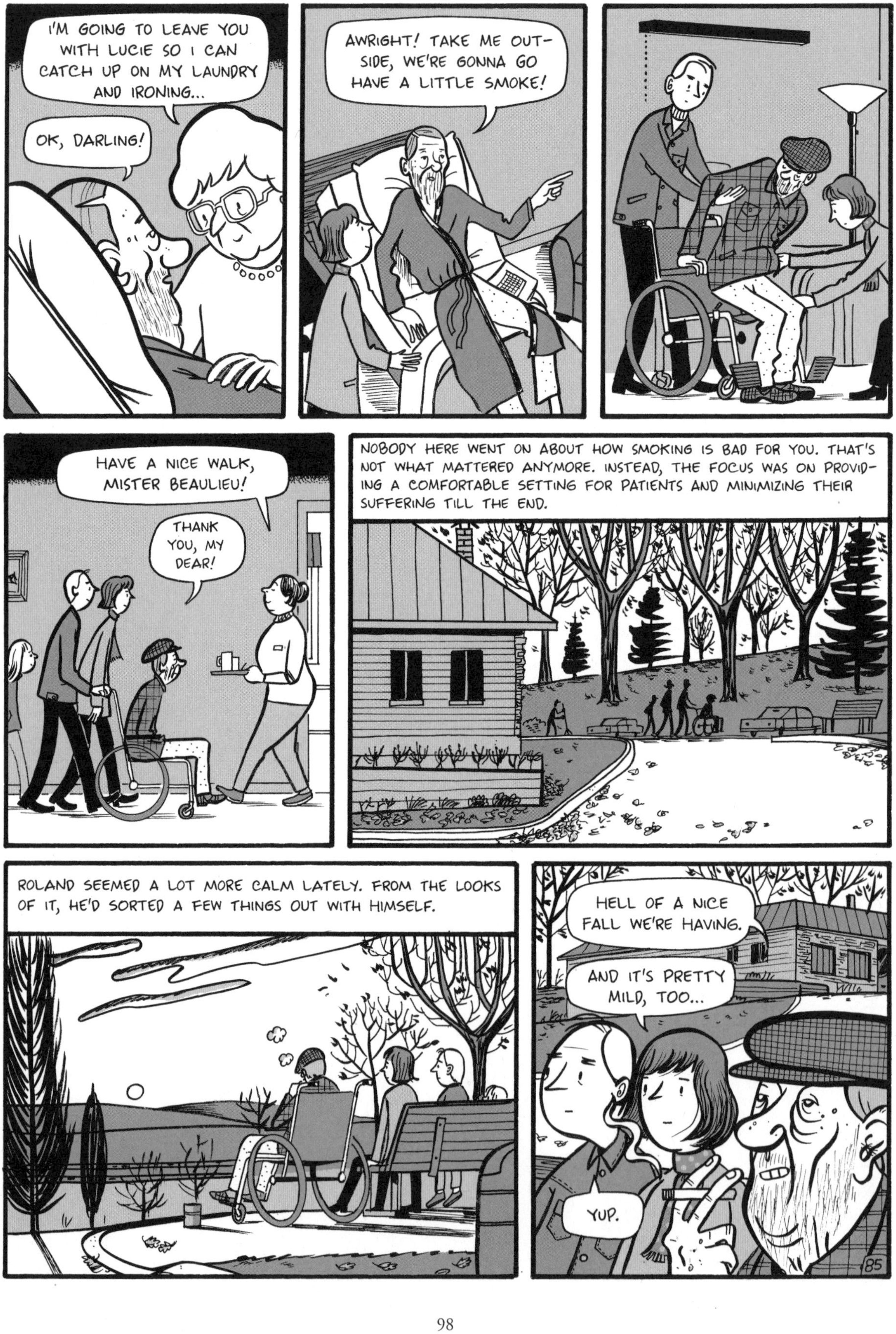
I'M GOING TO LEAVE YOU WITH LUCIE SO I CAN CATCH UP ON MY LAUNDRY AND IRONING...
OK, DARLING!
AWRIGHT! TAKE ME OUT-SIDE, WE'RE GONNA GO HAVE A LITTLE SMOKE!
HAVE A NICE WALK, MISTER BEAULIEU!
THANK YOU, MY DEAR!
NOBODY HERE WENT ON ABOUT HOW SMOKING IS BAD FOR YOU. THAT'S NOT WHAT MATTERED ANYMORE. INSTEAD, THE FOCUS WAS ON PROVID-ING A COMFORTABLE SETTING FOR PATIENTS AND MINIMIZING THEIR SUFFERING TILL THE END.
ROLAND SEEMED A LOT MORE CALM LATELY. FROM THE LOOKS OF IT, HE'D SORTED A FEW THINGS OUT WITH HIMSELF.
HELL OF A NICE FALL WE'RE HAVING.
AND IT'S PRETTY MILD, TOO...
YUP.
85

AT LEAST I DON'T NEED TO RAKE ANY LEAVES ANYMORE.

HA HA NO!

NO MORE LEAF RAKING EVER AGAIN...

PLOC

I CAN HARDLY BELIEVE HOW BIG YOU'RE GETTING, ROSIE-PIE!

I'M 115 CENTIMETRES!

HOW MUCH IS THAT IN FEET?

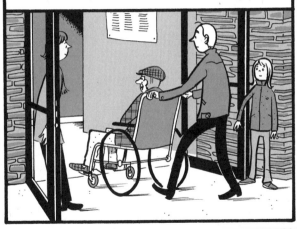

OUR EVENINGS WITH ROLAND ALWAYS FOLLOWED THE SAME PATTERN: 1) A CIGARETTE, 2) TEA AND SCRABBLE, 3) CIGARETTE NR. 2, 4) BED.

BEING AN INCREDIBLY ORGANIZED PERSON, ROLAND LIKED THE ROUTINE OF IT.

SPICE GIRLS

I'LL HAVE A TEA!

LET ME GET THAT, MR. BEAULIEU.

86

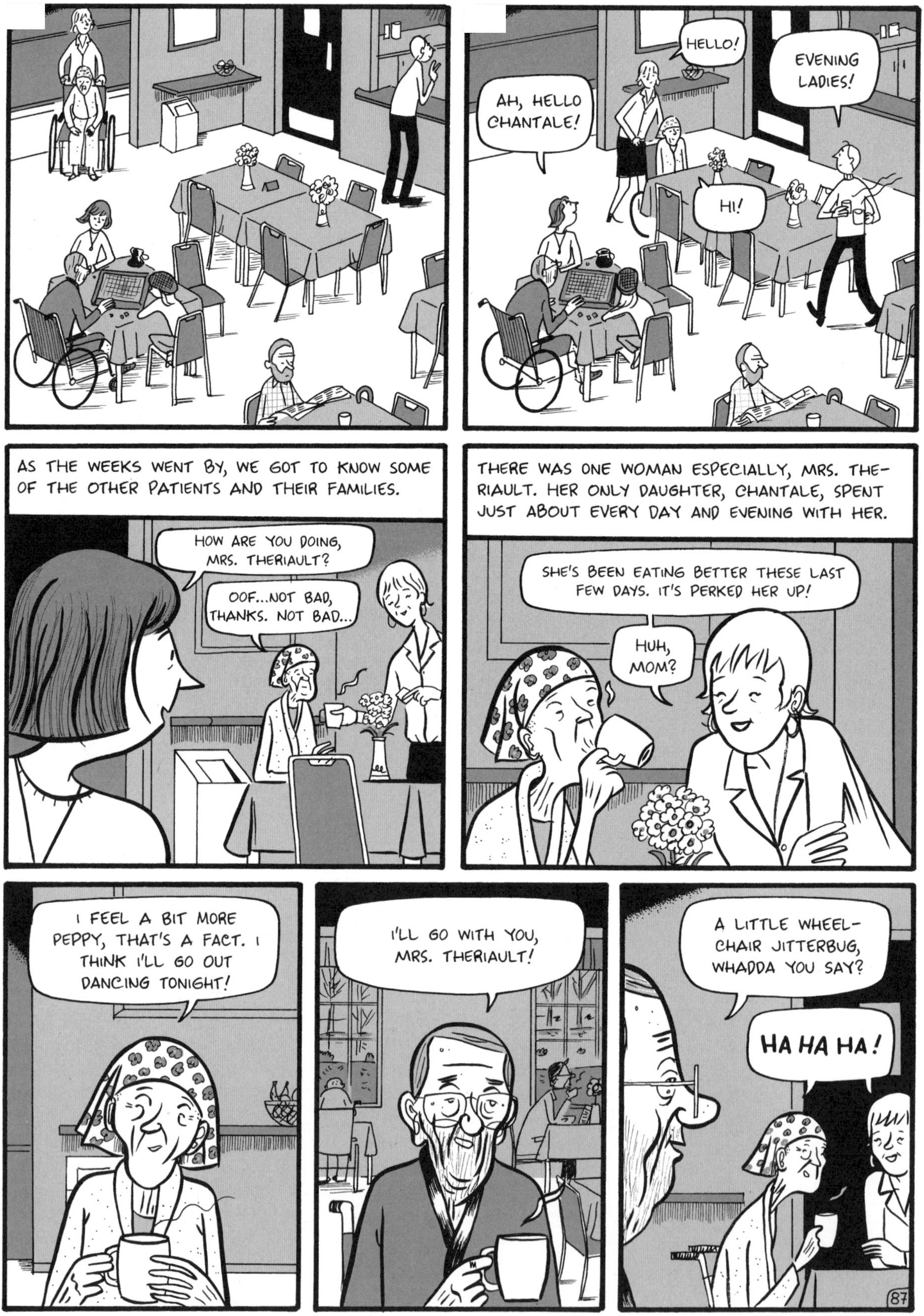
HELLO!
AH, HELLO CHANTALE!
EVENING LADIES!
HI!
AS THE WEEKS WENT BY, WE GOT TO KNOW SOME OF THE OTHER PATIENTS AND THEIR FAMILIES.
HOW ARE YOU DOING, MRS. THERIAULT?
OOF...NOT BAD, THANKS. NOT BAD...
THERE WAS ONE WOMAN ESPECIALLY, MRS. THERIAULT. HER ONLY DAUGHTER, CHANTALE, SPENT JUST ABOUT EVERY DAY AND EVENING WITH HER.
SHE'S BEEN EATING BETTER THESE LAST FEW DAYS. IT'S PERKED HER UP!
HUH, MOM?
I FEEL A BIT MORE PEPPY, THAT'S A FACT. I THINK I'LL GO OUT DANCING TONIGHT!
I'LL GO WITH YOU, MRS. THERIAULT!
A LITTLE WHEELCHAIR JITTERBUG, WHADDA YOU SAY?
HA HA HA!
87

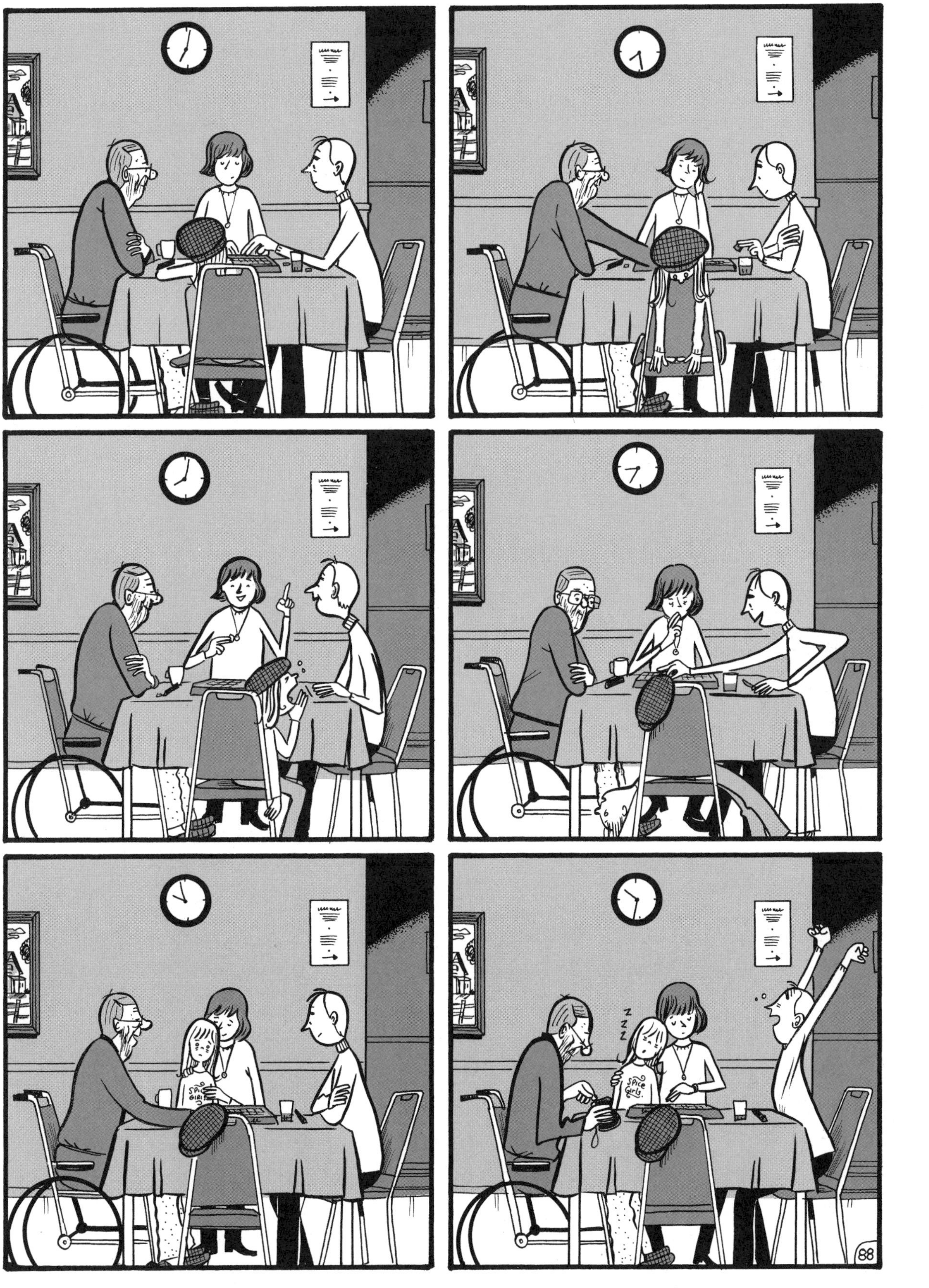
SPICE GIRLS
Z Z Z
SPICE GIRLS
88

MAXWELL HOUSE
89

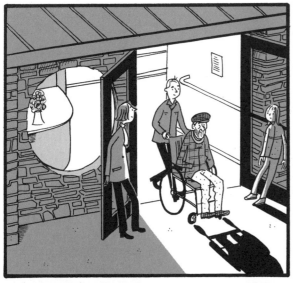

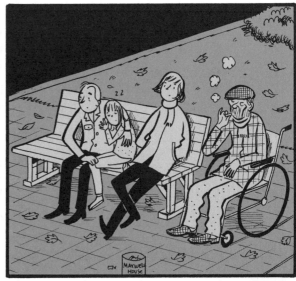

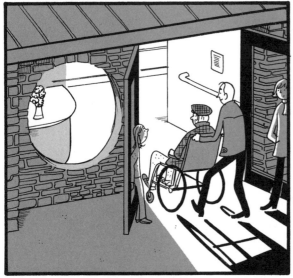

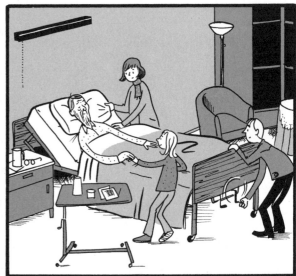

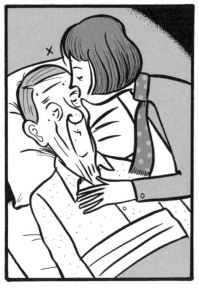

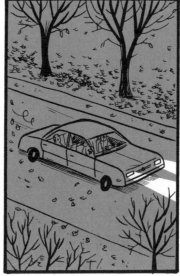

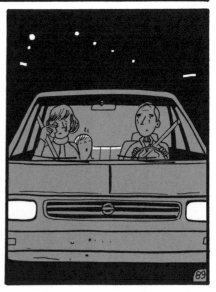

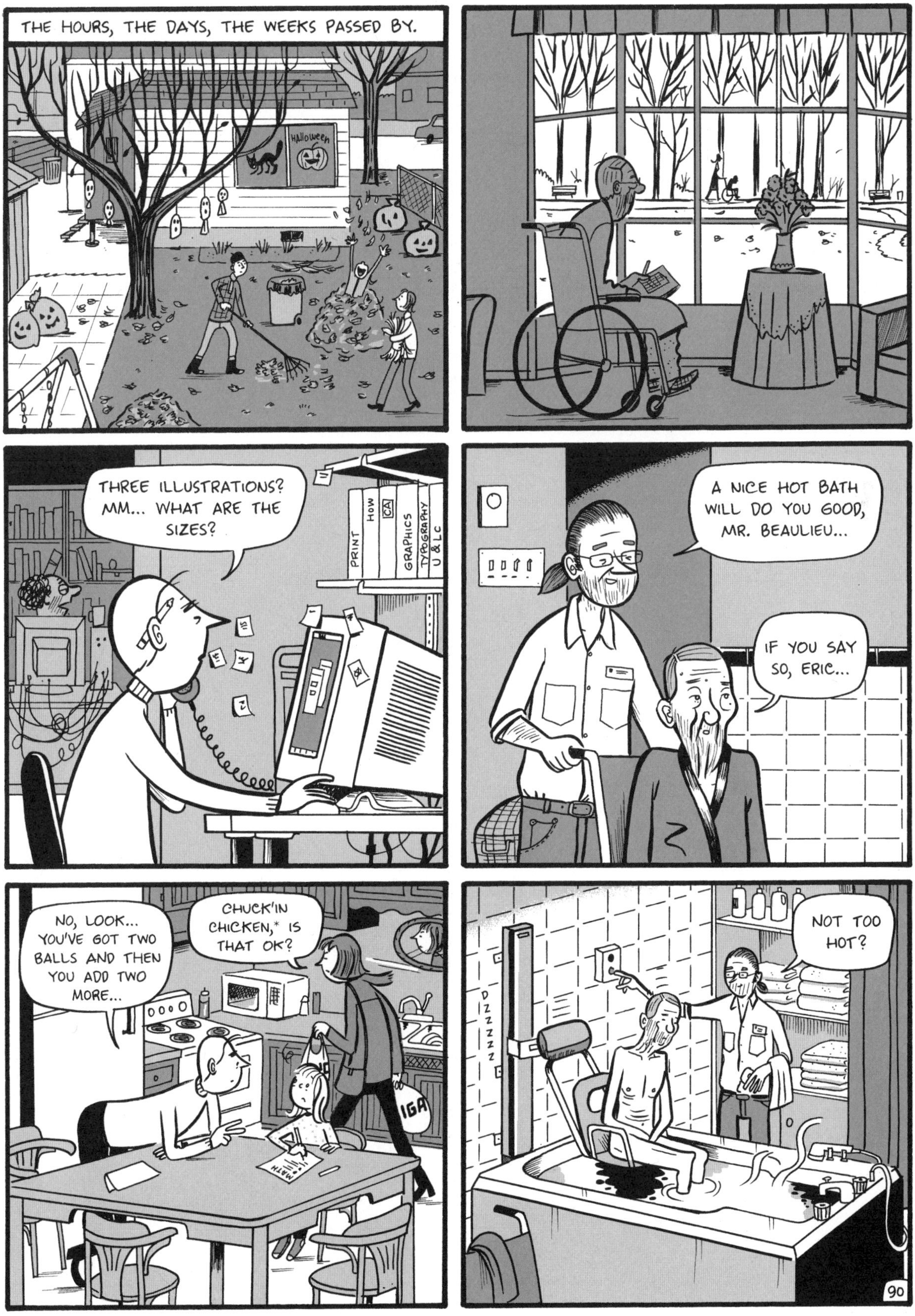
THE HOURS, THE DAYS, THE WEEKS PASSED BY.
Halloween
THREE ILLUSTRATIONS? MM... WHAT ARE THE SIZES?
PRINT
HOW
CA
GRAPHICS
TYPOGRAPHY
U&LC
A NICE HOT BATH WILL DO YOU GOOD, MR. BEAULIEU...
IF YOU SAY SO, ERIC...
NO, LOOK... YOU'VE GOT TWO BALLS AND THEN YOU ADD TWO MORE...
CHUCK'IN CHICKEN,* IS THAT OK?
IGA
MATH
NOT TOO HOT?
90

* TAKE A CHICKEN, CHUCK IT IN THE OVEN.

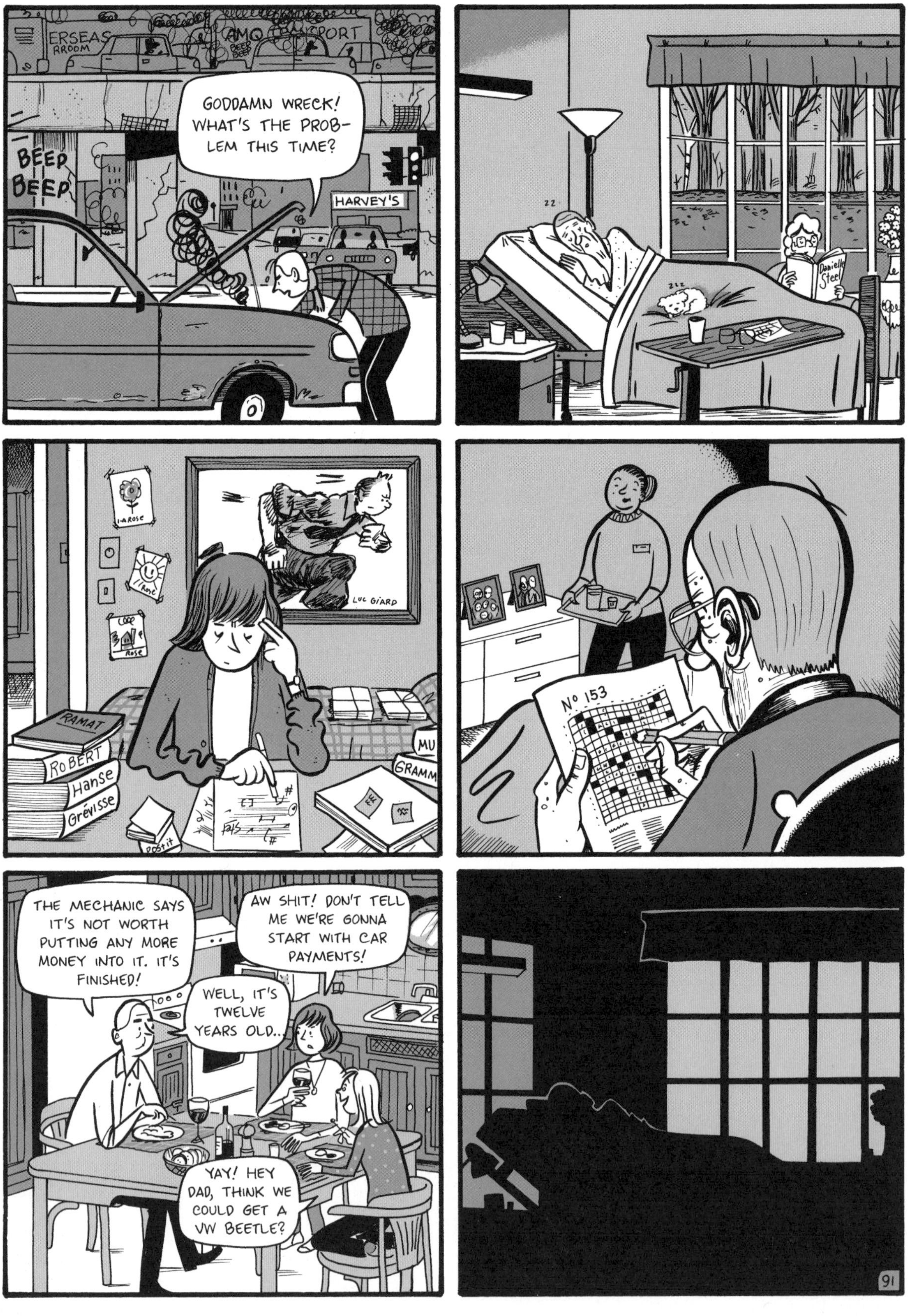

BEEP BEEP
GODDAMN WRECK! WHAT'S THE PROBLEM THIS TIME?
HARVEY'S
Danielle Steel
LUC GIARD
RAMAT
ROBERT
Hanse
Grévisse
GRAMM
Nº 153
THE MECHANIC SAYS IT'S NOT WORTH PUTTING ANY MORE MONEY INTO IT. IT'S FINISHED!
AW SHIT! DON'T TELL ME WE'RE GONNA START WITH CAR PAYMENTS!
WELL, IT'S TWELVE YEARS OLD...
YAY! HEY DAD, THINK WE COULD GET A VW BEETLE?
91

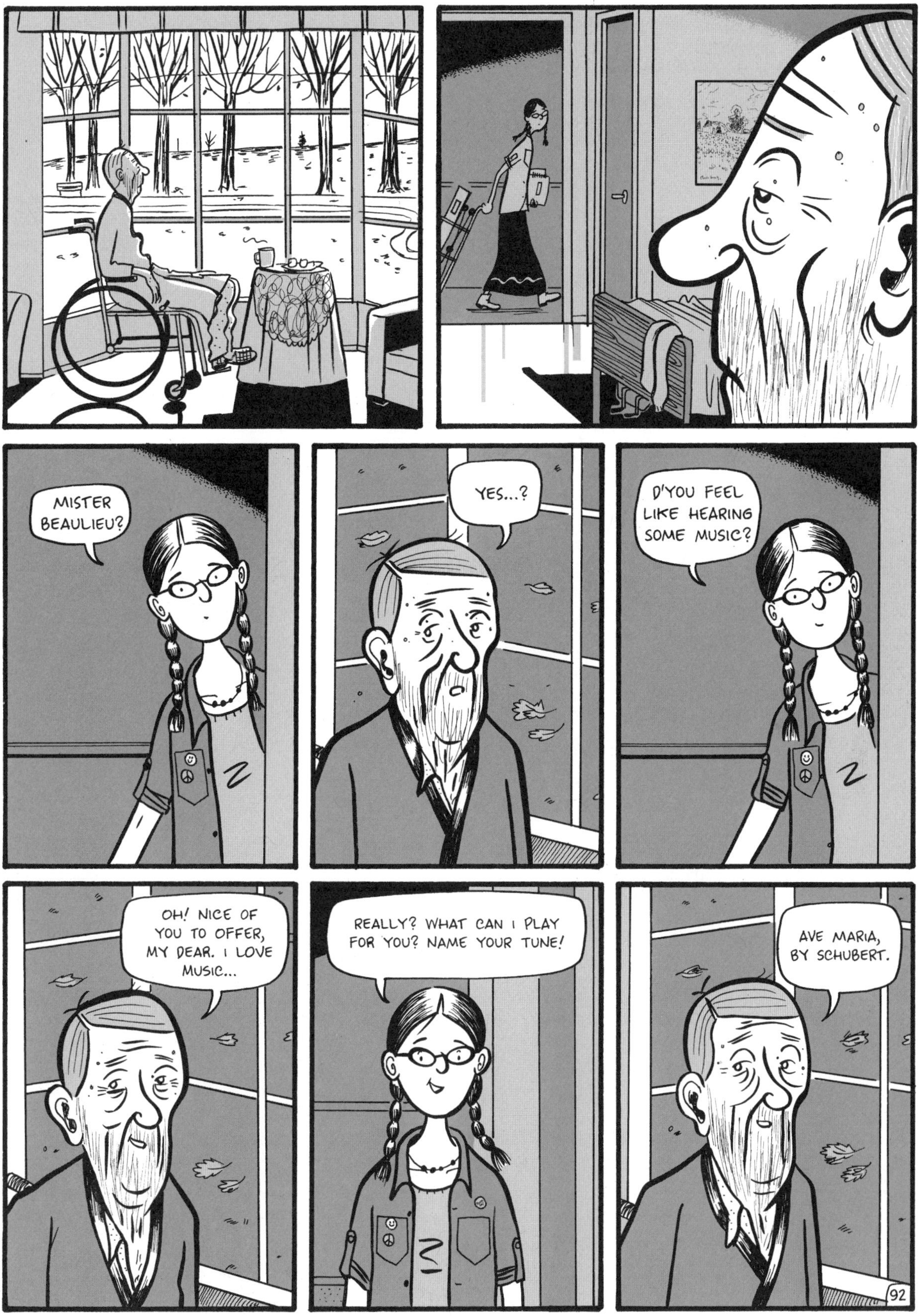

MISTER BEAULIEU?
YES...?
D'YOU FEEL LIKE HEARING SOME MUSIC?
OH! NICE OF YOU TO OFFER, MY DEAR. I LOVE MUSIC...
REALLY? WHAT CAN I PLAY FOR YOU? NAME YOUR TUNE!
AVE MARIA, BY SCHUBERT.
92

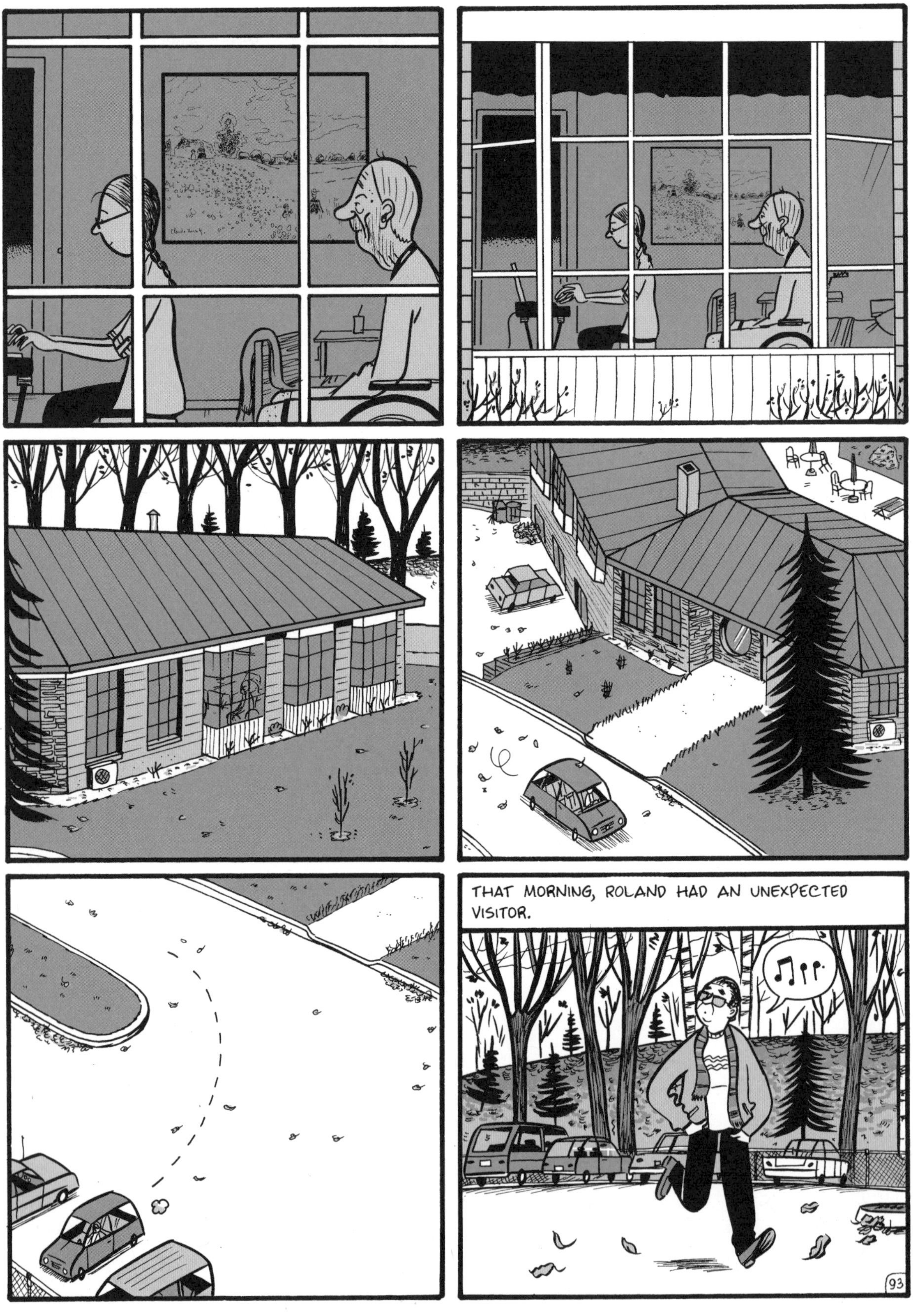
THAT MORNING, ROLAND HAD AN UNEXPECTED VISITOR.
93

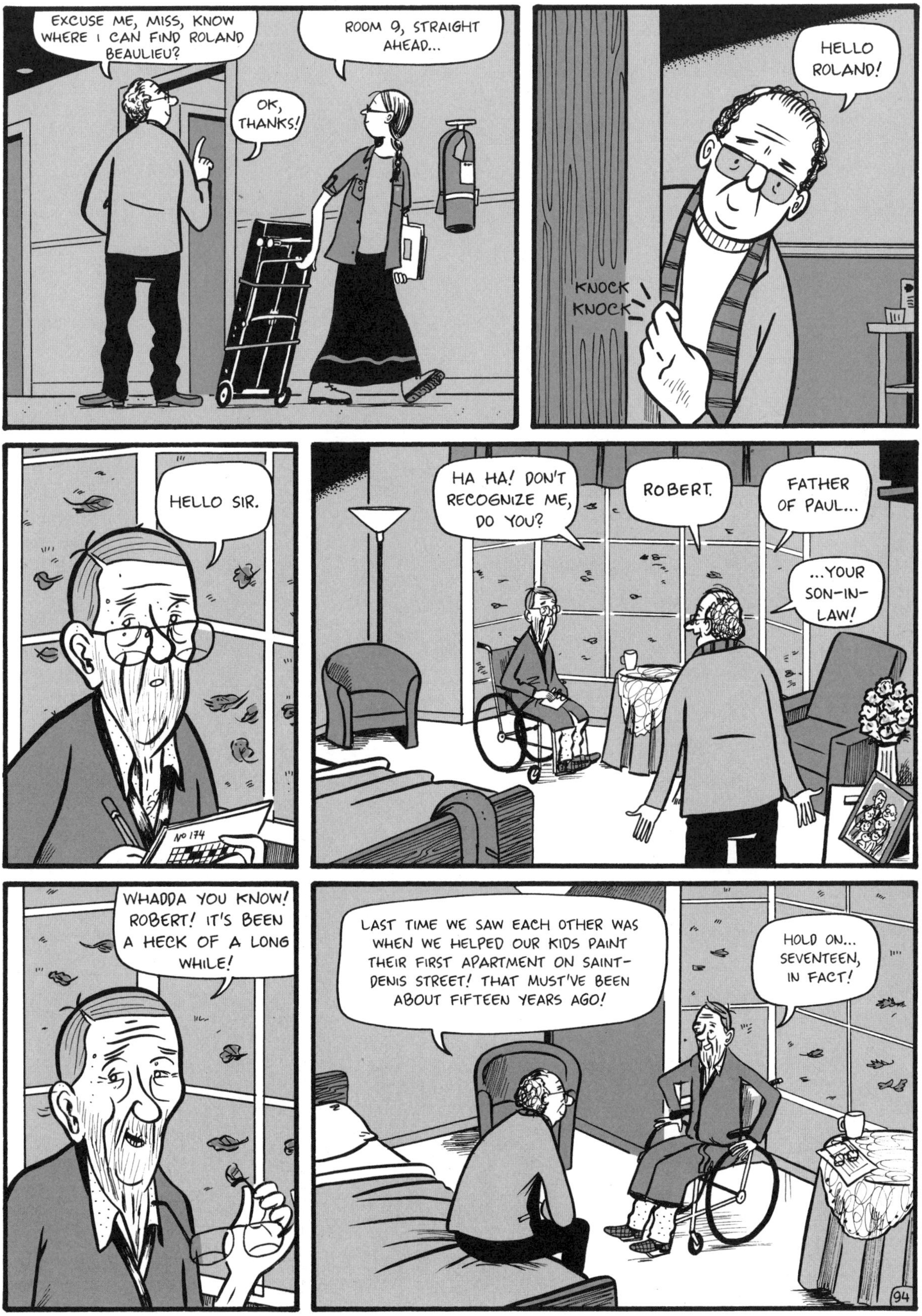
EXCUSE ME, MISS, KNOW WHERE I CAN FIND ROLAND BEAULIEU?
ROOM 9, STRAIGHT AHEAD...
OK, THANKS!
HELLO ROLAND!
KNOCK KNOCK
HELLO SIR.
Nº 174
HA HA! DON'T RECOGNIZE ME, DO YOU?
ROBERT.
FATHER OF PAUL...
...YOUR SON-IN-LAW!
WHADDA YOU KNOW! ROBERT! IT'S BEEN A HECK OF A LONG WHILE!
LAST TIME WE SAW EACH OTHER WAS WHEN WE HELPED OUR KIDS PAINT THEIR FIRST APARTMENT ON SAINT-DENIS STREET! THAT MUST'VE BEEN ABOUT FIFTEEN YEARS AGO!
HOLD ON... SEVENTEEN, IN FACT!
94

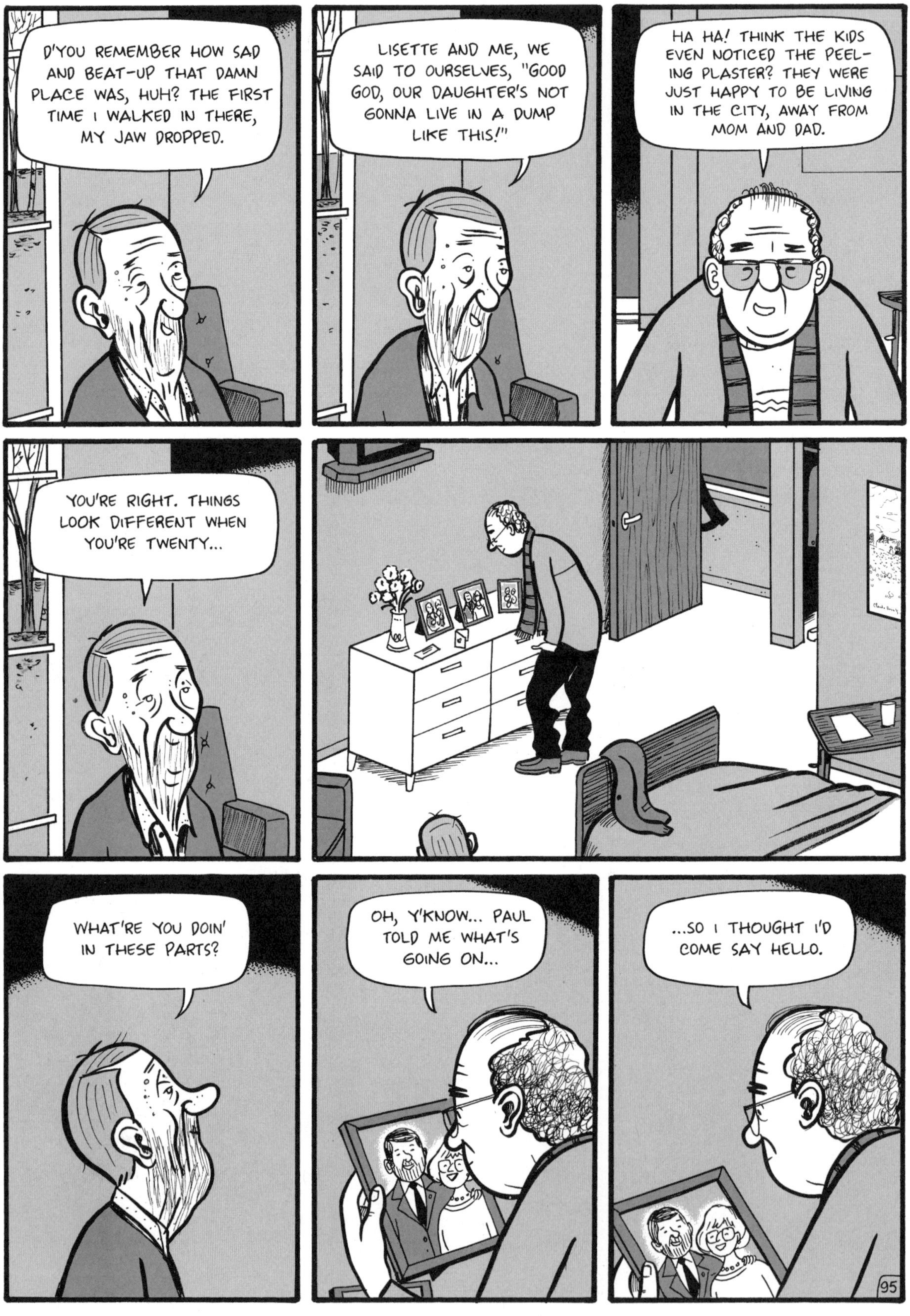
D'YOU REMEMBER HOW SAD AND BEAT-UP THAT DAMN PLACE WAS, HUH? THE FIRST TIME I WALKED IN THERE, MY JAW DROPPED.
LISETTE AND ME, WE SAID TO OURSELVES, "GOOD GOD, OUR DAUGHTER'S NOT GONNA LIVE IN A DUMP LIKE THIS!"
HA HA! THINK THE KIDS EVEN NOTICED THE PEELING PLASTER? THEY WERE JUST HAPPY TO BE LIVING IN THE CITY, AWAY FROM MOM AND DAD.
YOU'RE RIGHT. THINGS LOOK DIFFERENT WHEN YOU'RE TWENTY...
WHAT'RE YOU DOIN' IN THESE PARTS?
OH, Y'KNOW... PAUL TOLD ME WHAT'S GOING ON...
...SO I THOUGHT I'D COME SAY HELLO.
95

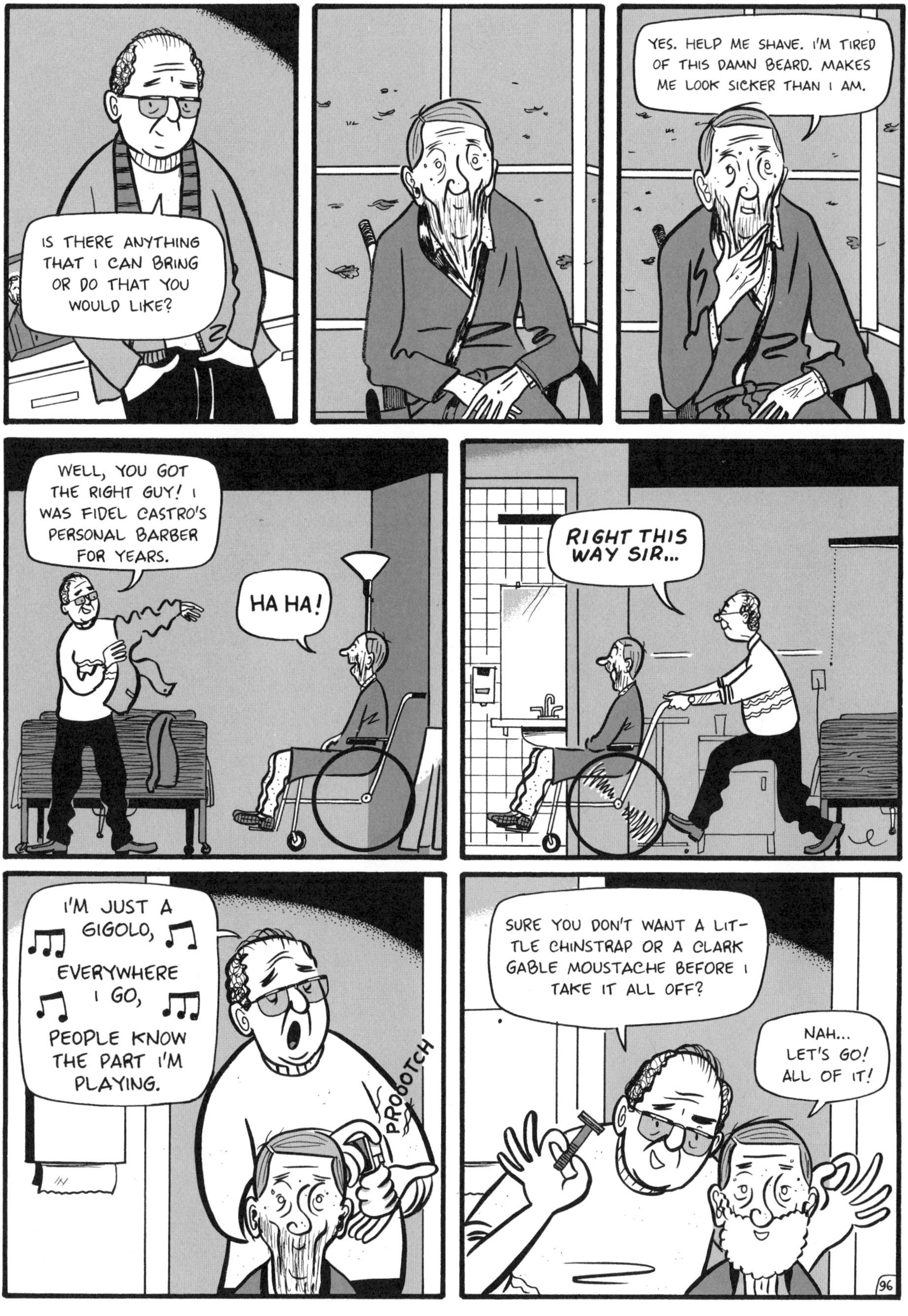
IS THERE ANYTHING THAT I CAN BRING OR DO THAT YOU WOULD LIKE?
YES. HELP ME SHAVE. I'M TIRED OF THIS DAMN BEARD. MAKES ME LOOK SICKER THAN I AM.
WELL, YOU GOT THE RIGHT GUY! I WAS FIDEL CASTRO'S PERSONAL BARBER FOR YEARS.
HA HA!
RIGHT THIS WAY SIR...
I'M JUST A GIGOLO, EVERYWHERE I GO, PEOPLE KNOW THE PART I'M PLAYING.
PROOOTCH
SURE YOU DON'T WANT A LITTLE CHINSTRAP OR A CLARK GABLE MOUSTACHE BEFORE I TAKE IT ALL OFF?
NAH... LET'S GO! ALL OF IT!
96

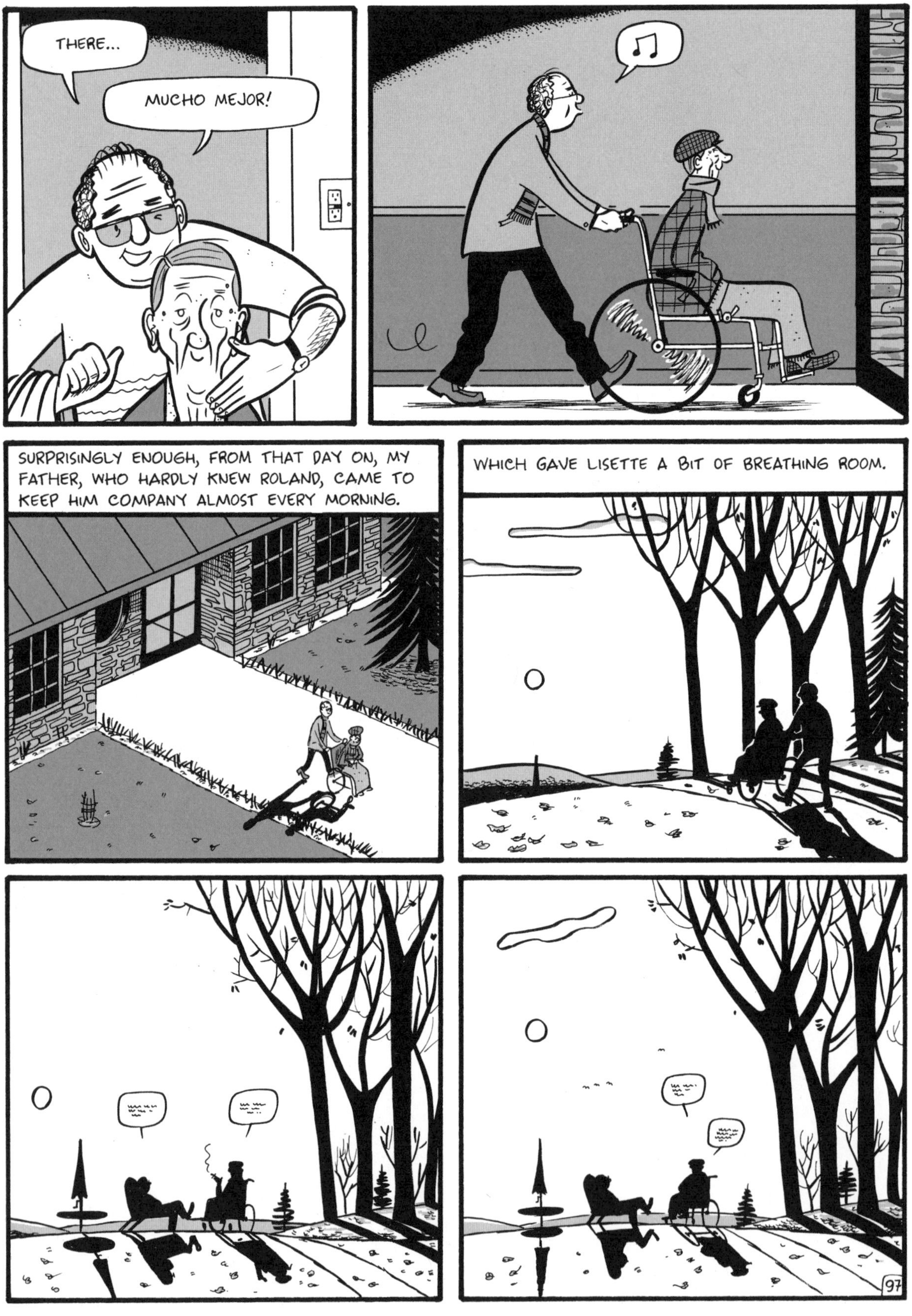

THERE...
MUCHO MEJOR!
♫
SURPRISINGLY ENOUGH, FROM THAT DAY ON, MY FATHER, WHO HARDLY KNEW ROLAND, CAME TO KEEP HIM COMPANY ALMOST EVERY MORNING.
WHICH GAVE LISETTE A BIT OF BREATHING ROOM.
97

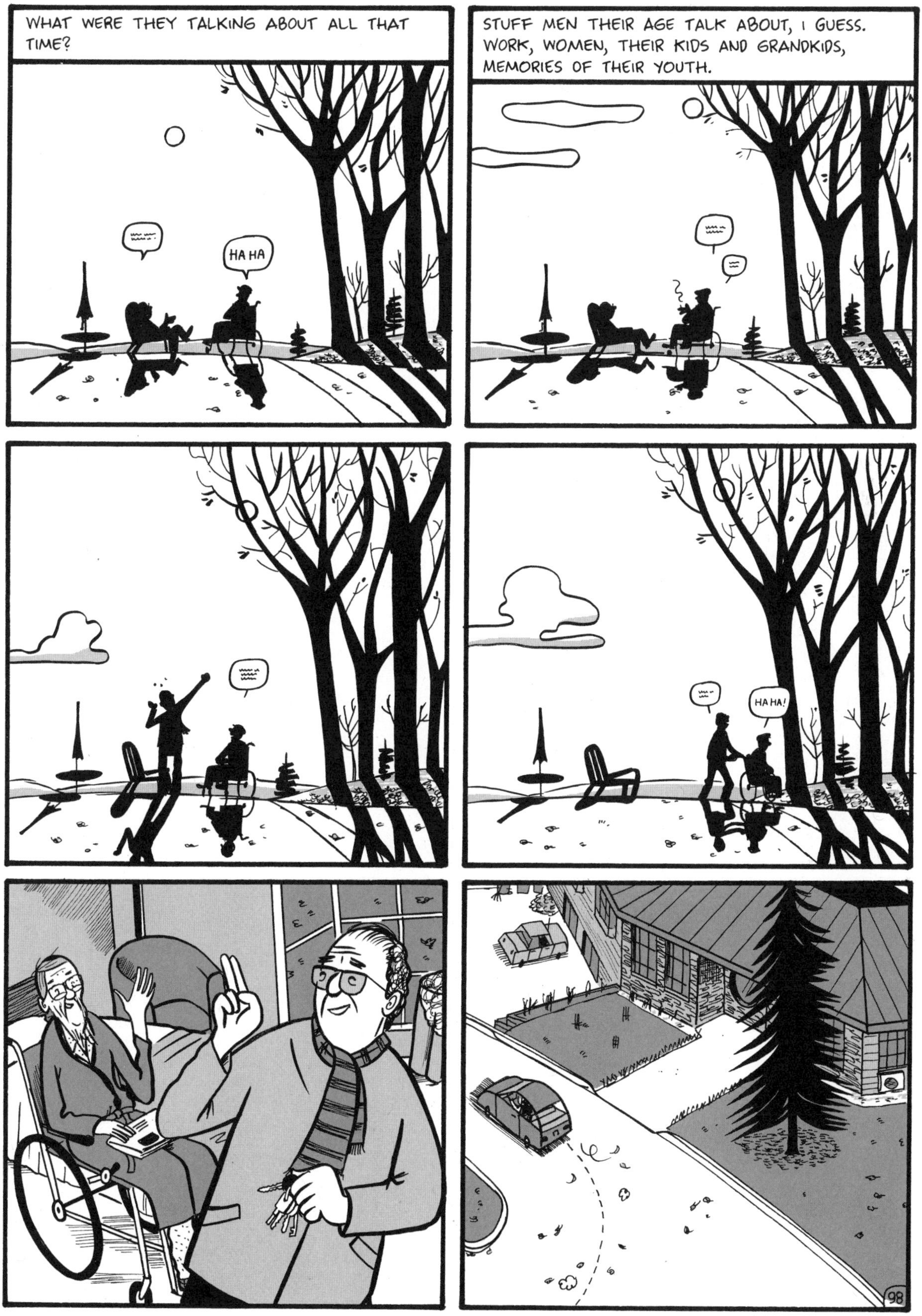

WHAT WERE THEY TALKING ABOUT ALL THAT TIME?
HA HA
STUFF MEN THEIR AGE TALK ABOUT, I GUESS. WORK, WOMEN, THEIR KIDS AND GRANDKIDS, MEMORIES OF THEIR YOUTH.
HA HA!
98

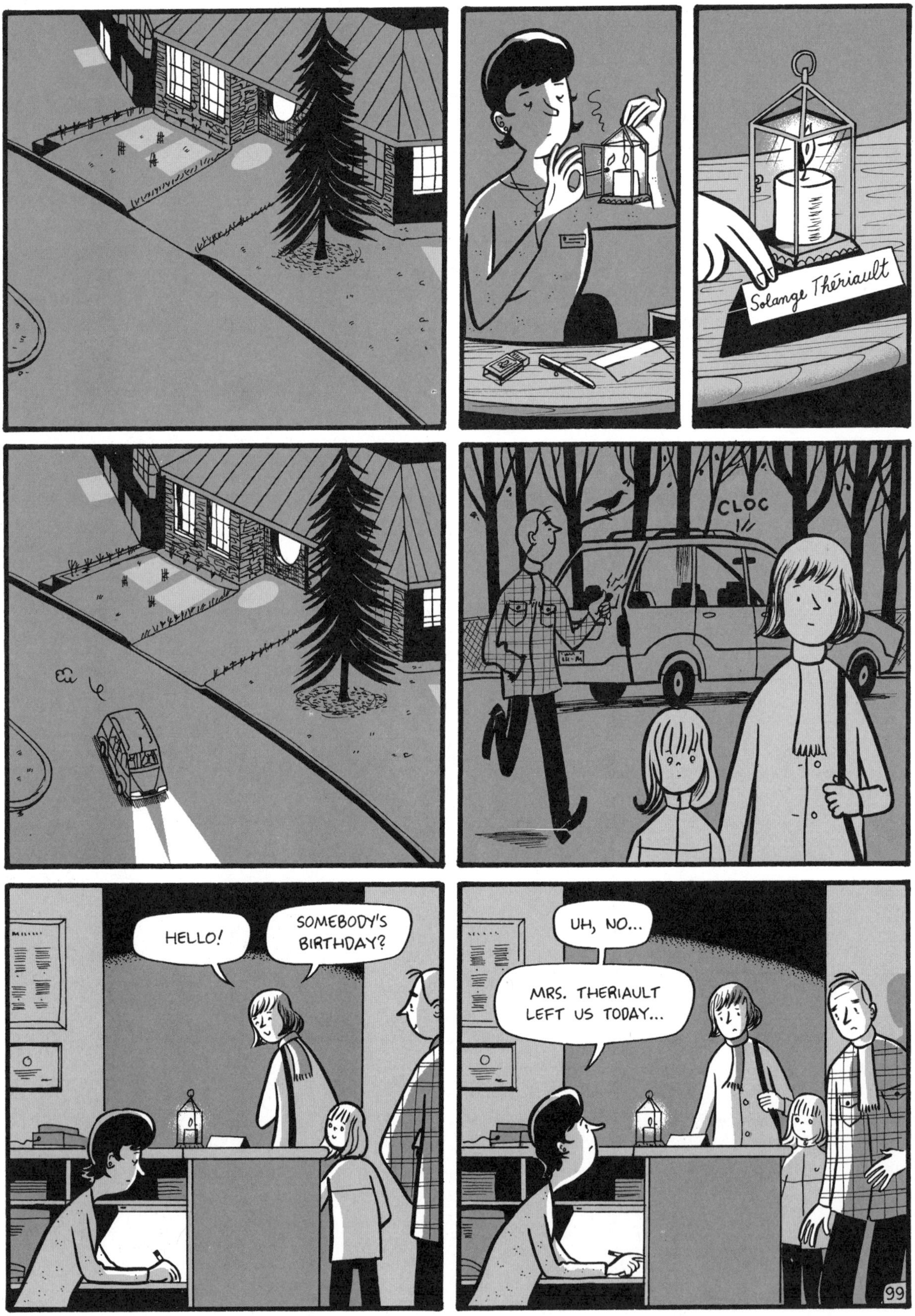
Solange Thériault
CLOC
HELLO!
SOMEBODY'S BIRTHDAY?
UH, NO...
MRS. THERIAULT LEFT US TODAY...
99

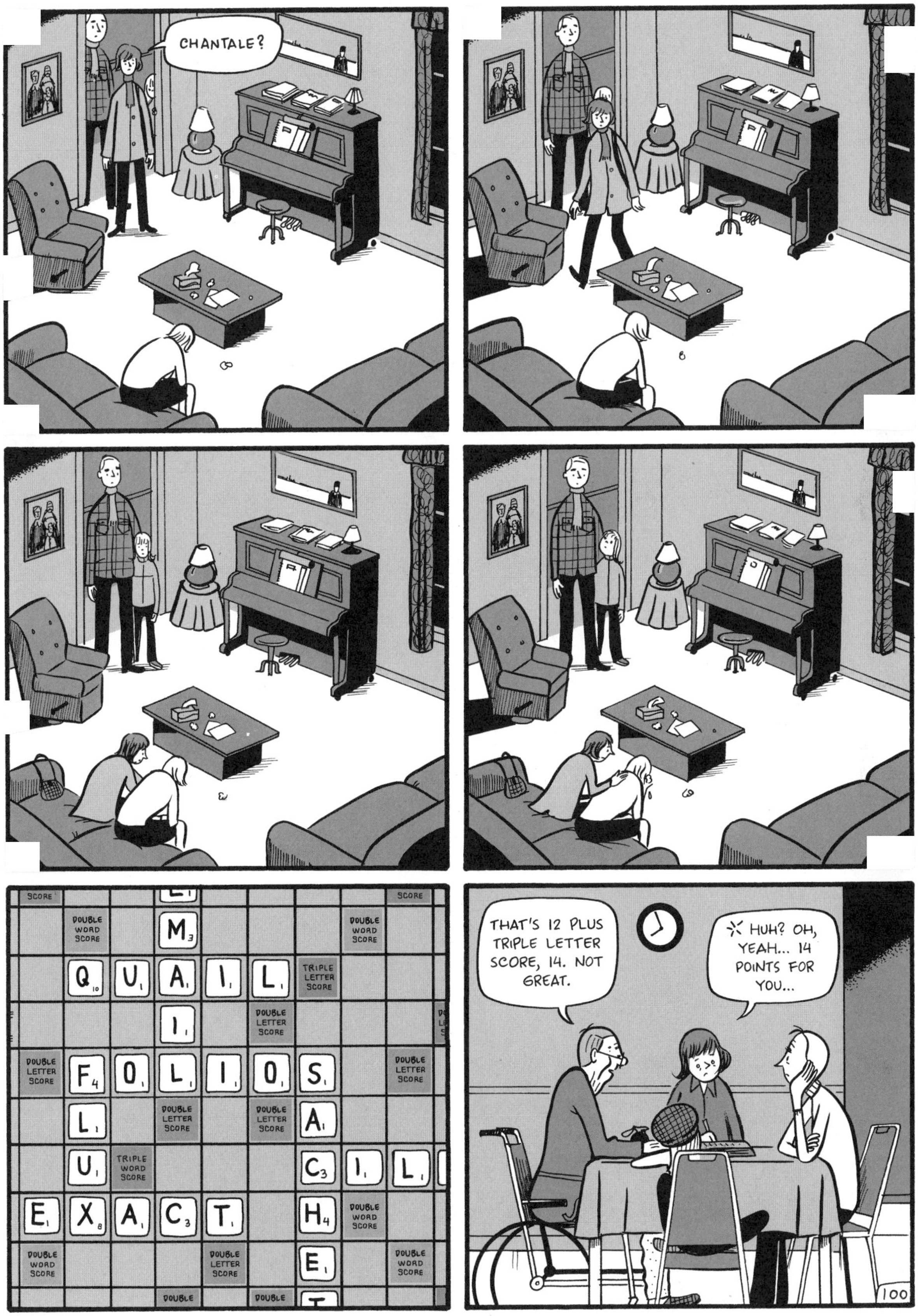
CHANTALE?
QUAIL
FOLIOS
EXACT
THAT'S 12 PLUS TRIPLE LETTER SCORE, 14. NOT GREAT.
HUH? OH, YEAH... 14 POINTS FOR YOU...
100

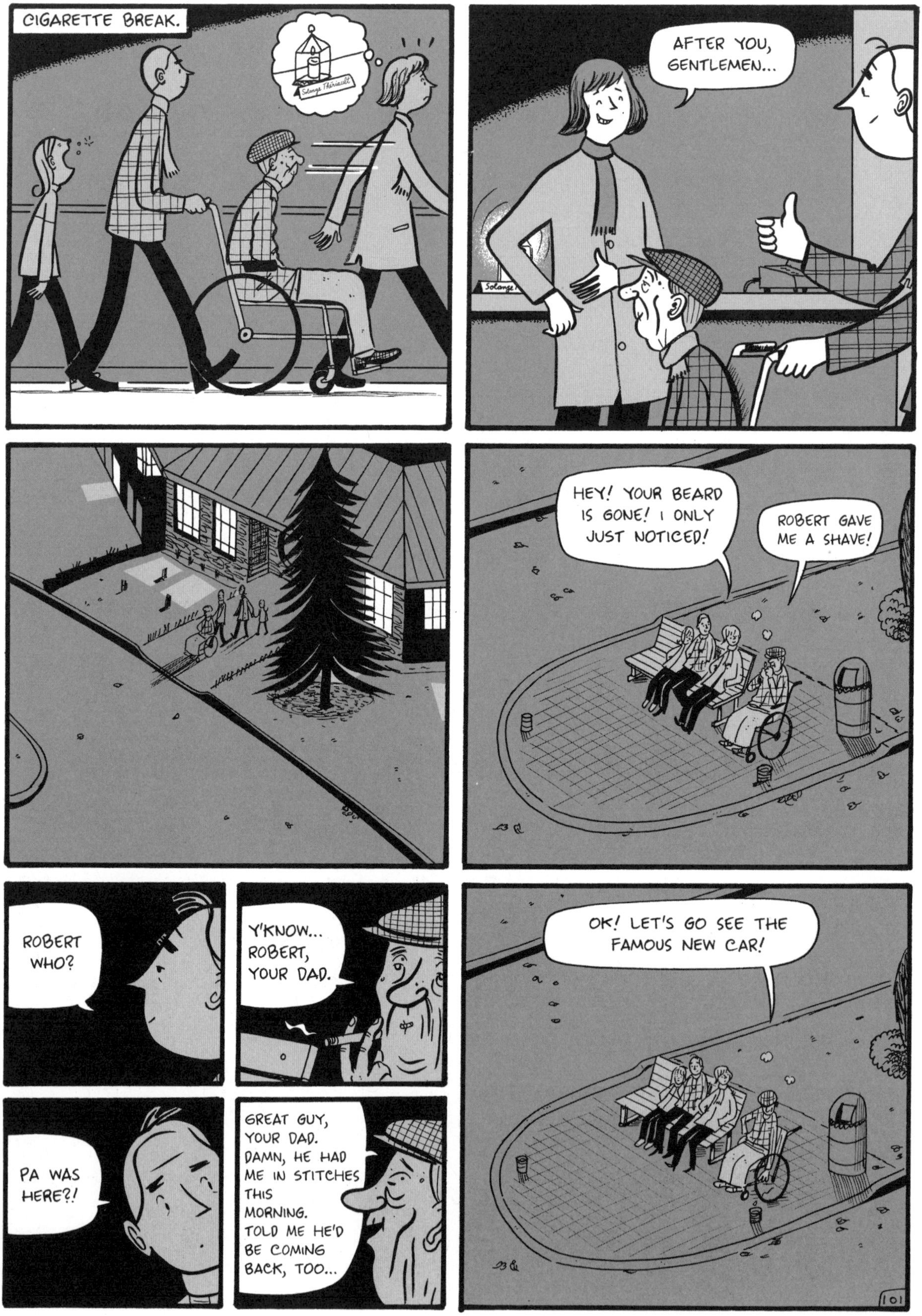
CIGARETTE BREAK.
Solange Thériault
AFTER YOU, GENTLEMEN...
Solange
HEY! YOUR BEARD IS GONE! I ONLY JUST NOTICED!
ROBERT GAVE ME A SHAVE!
ROBERT WHO?
Y'KNOW... ROBERT, YOUR DAD.
PA WAS HERE?!
GREAT GUY, YOUR DAD. DAMN, HE HAD ME IN STITCHES THIS MORNING. TOLD ME HE'D BE COMING BACK, TOO...
OK! LET'S GO SEE THE FAMOUS NEW CAR!
101

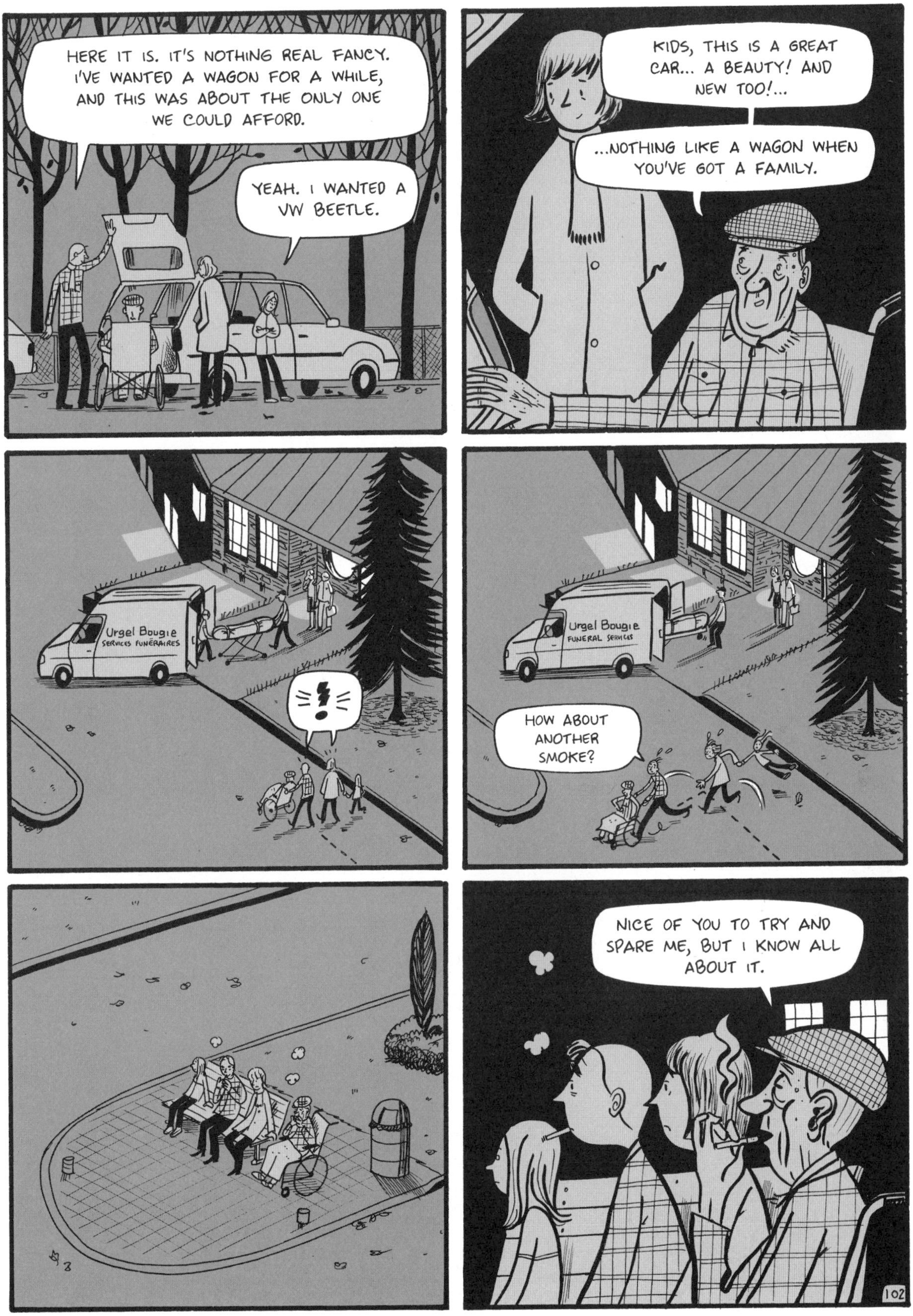
HERE IT IS. IT'S NOTHING REAL FANCY. I'VE WANTED A WAGON FOR A WHILE, AND THIS WAS ABOUT THE ONLY ONE WE COULD AFFORD.
YEAH. I WANTED A VW BEETLE.
KIDS, THIS IS A GREAT CAR... A BEAUTY! AND NEW TOO!...
...NOTHING LIKE A WAGON WHEN YOU'VE GOT A FAMILY.
Urgel Bougie
SERVICES FUNÉRAIRES
Urgel Bougie
FUNERAL SERVICES
HOW ABOUT ANOTHER SMOKE?
NICE OF YOU TO TRY AND SPARE ME, BUT I KNOW ALL ABOUT IT.
102

November

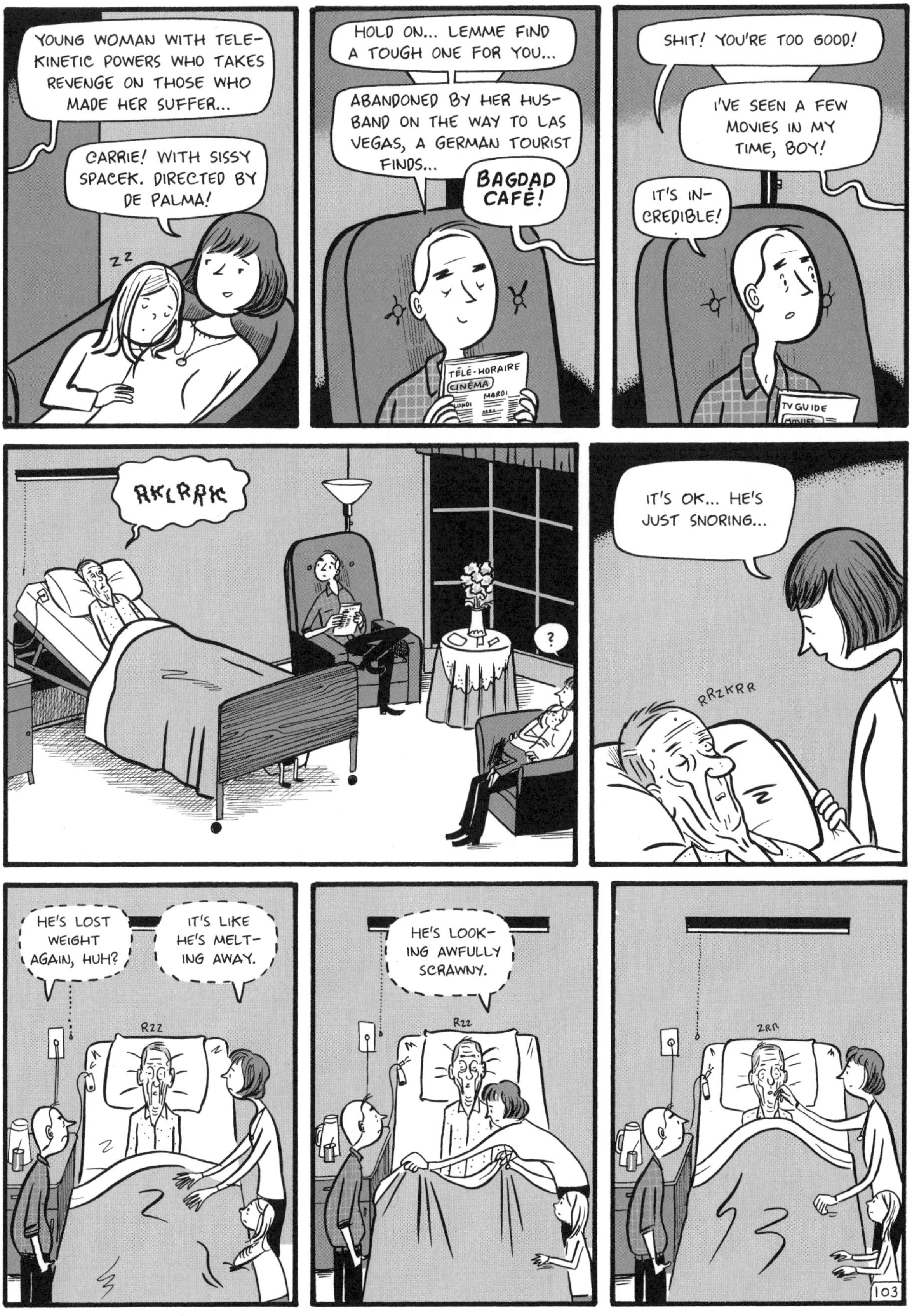
YOUNG WOMAN WITH TELE-KINETIC POWERS WHO TAKES REVENGE ON THOSE WHO MADE HER SUFFER...
CARRIE! WITH SISSY SPACEK. DIRECTED BY DE PALMA!
ZZ
HOLD ON... LEMME FIND A TOUGH ONE FOR YOU...
ABANDONED BY HER HUS-BAND ON THE WAY TO LAS VEGAS, A GERMAN TOURIST FINDS...
BAGDAD CAFÉ!
TÉLÉ-HORAIRE
CINÉMA
SHIT! YOU'RE TOO GOOD!
I'VE SEEN A FEW MOVIES IN MY TIME, BOY!
IT'S IN-CREDIBLE!
TV GUIDE
RKLRRK
?
IT'S OK... HE'S JUST SNORING...
RRZKRR
HE'S LOST WEIGHT AGAIN, HUH?
IT'S LIKE HE'S MELT-ING AWAY.
RZZ
HE'S LOOK-ING AWFULLY SCRAWNY.
RZZ
ZRR
103

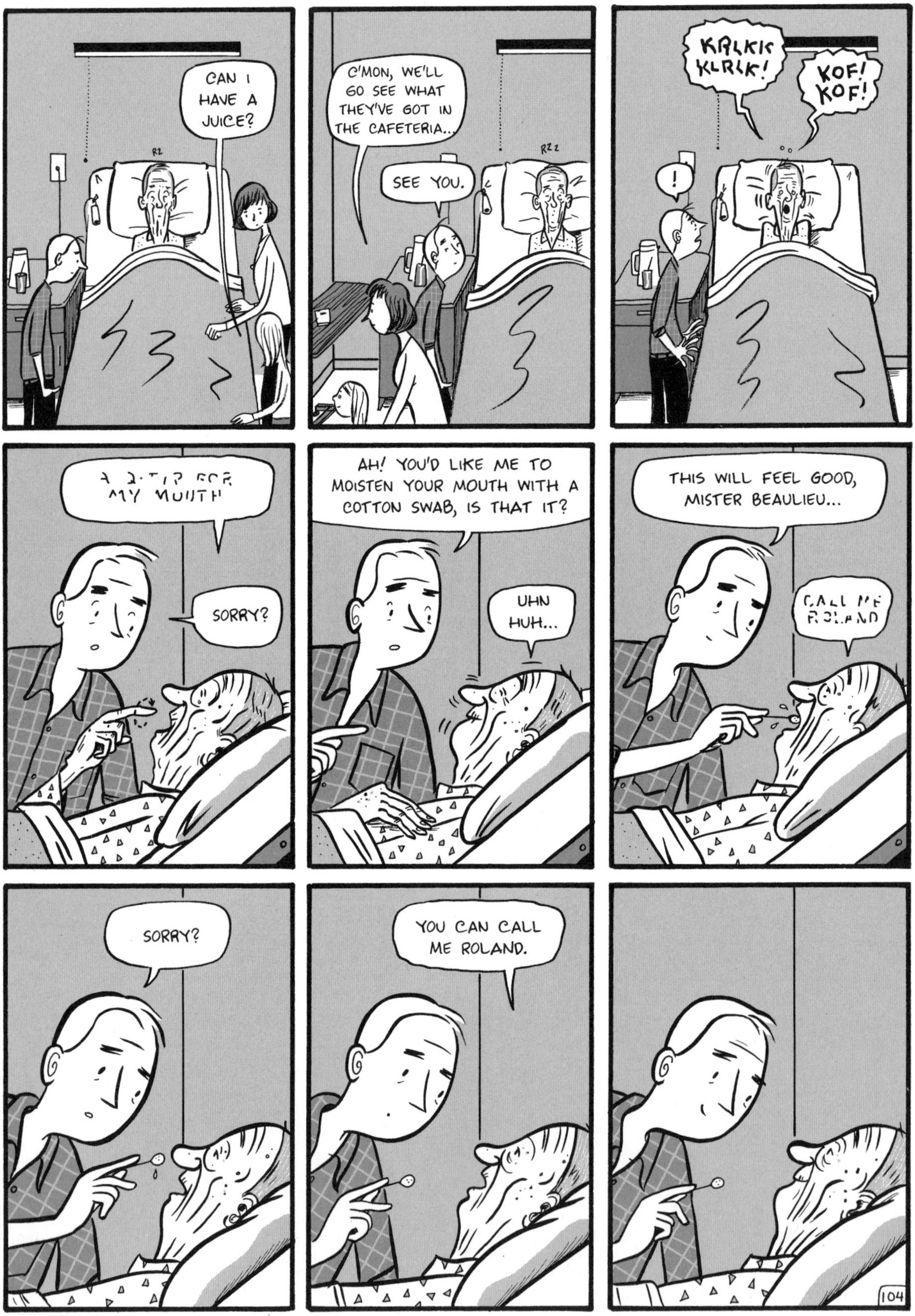
RZ
CAN I HAVE A JUICE?
C'MON, WE'LL GO SEE WHAT THEY'VE GOT IN THE CAFETERIA...
SEE YOU.
RZZ
KRLKIK KLRLK!
KOF! KOF!
!
A Q-TIP FOR MY MOUTH
SORRY?
AH! YOU'D LIKE ME TO MOISTEN YOUR MOUTH WITH A COTTON SWAB, IS THAT IT?
UHN HUH...
THIS WILL FEEL GOOD, MISTER BEAULIEU...
CALL ME ROLAND
SORRY?
YOU CAN CALL ME ROLAND.
104

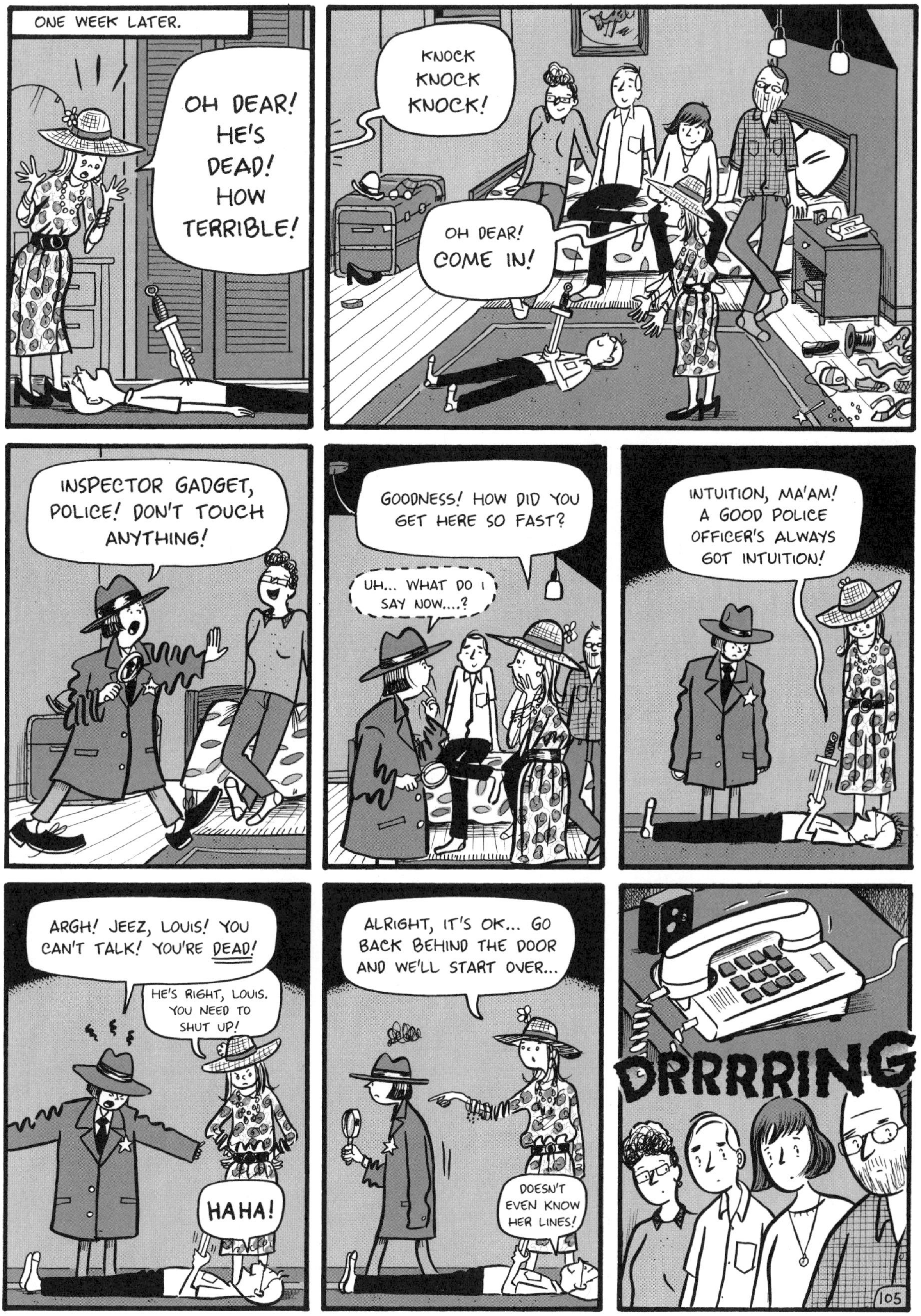
ONE WEEK LATER.
OH DEAR! HE'S DEAD! HOW TERRIBLE!
KNOCK KNOCK KNOCK!
OH DEAR! COME IN!
INSPECTOR GADGET, POLICE! DON'T TOUCH ANYTHING!
GOODNESS! HOW DID YOU GET HERE SO FAST?
UH... WHAT DO I SAY NOW....?
INTUITION, MA'AM! A GOOD POLICE OFFICER'S ALWAYS GOT INTUITION!
ARGH! JEEZ, LOUIS! YOU CAN'T TALK! YOU'RE DEAD!
HE'S RIGHT, LOUIS. YOU NEED TO SHUT UP!
HAHA!
ALRIGHT, IT'S OK... GO BACK BEHIND THE DOOR AND WE'LL START OVER...
DOESN'T EVEN KNOW HER LINES!
DRRRRING
105

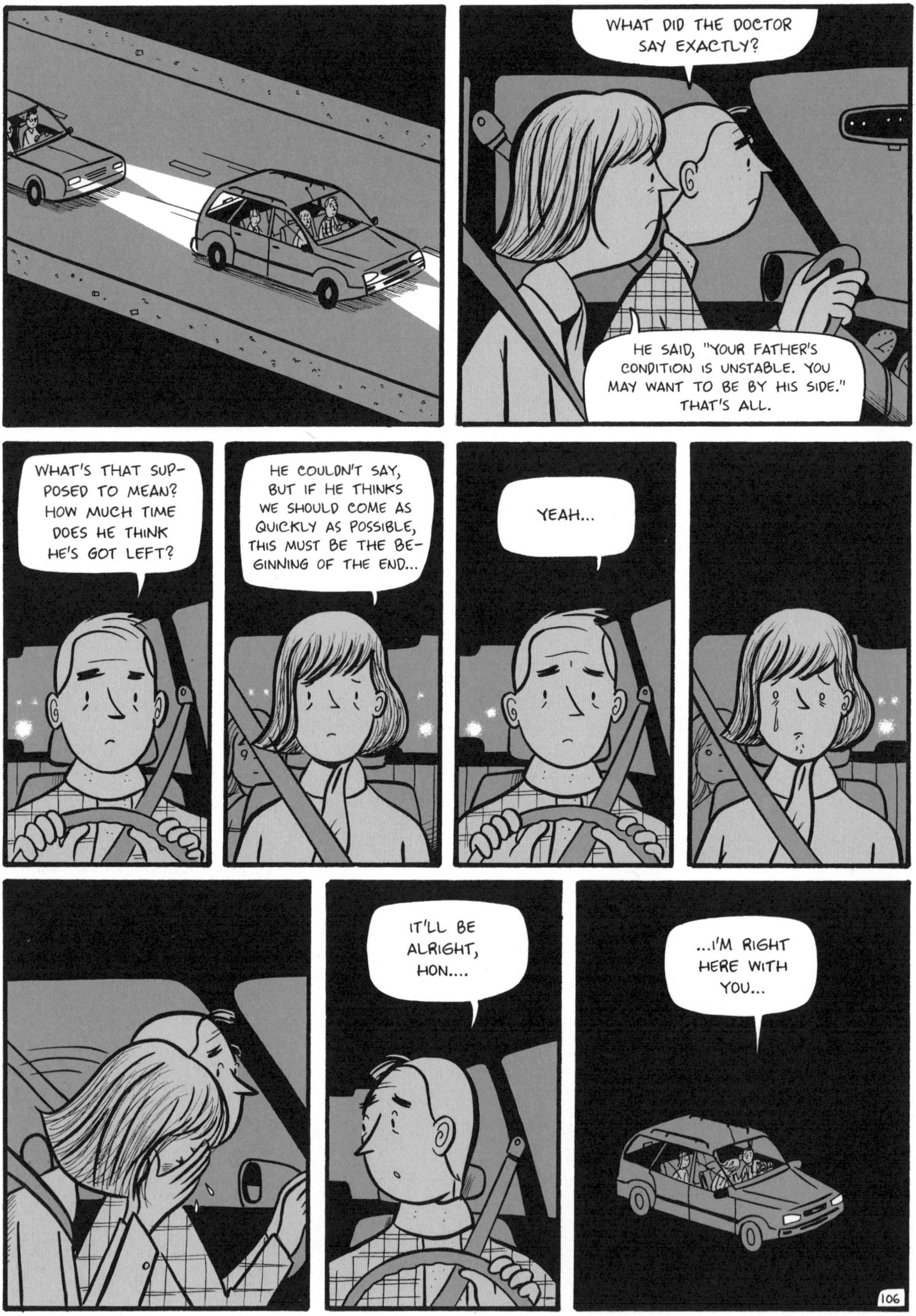
WHAT DID THE DOCTOR SAY EXACTLY?
HE SAID, "YOUR FATHER'S CONDITION IS UNSTABLE. YOU MAY WANT TO BE BY HIS SIDE." THAT'S ALL.
WHAT'S THAT SUP-POSED TO MEAN? HOW MUCH TIME DOES HE THINK HE'S GOT LEFT?
HE COULDN'T SAY, BUT IF HE THINKS WE SHOULD COME AS QUICKLY AS POSSIBLE, THIS MUST BE THE BE-GINNING OF THE END...
YEAH...
IT'LL BE ALRIGHT, HON....
...I'M RIGHT HERE WITH YOU...
106

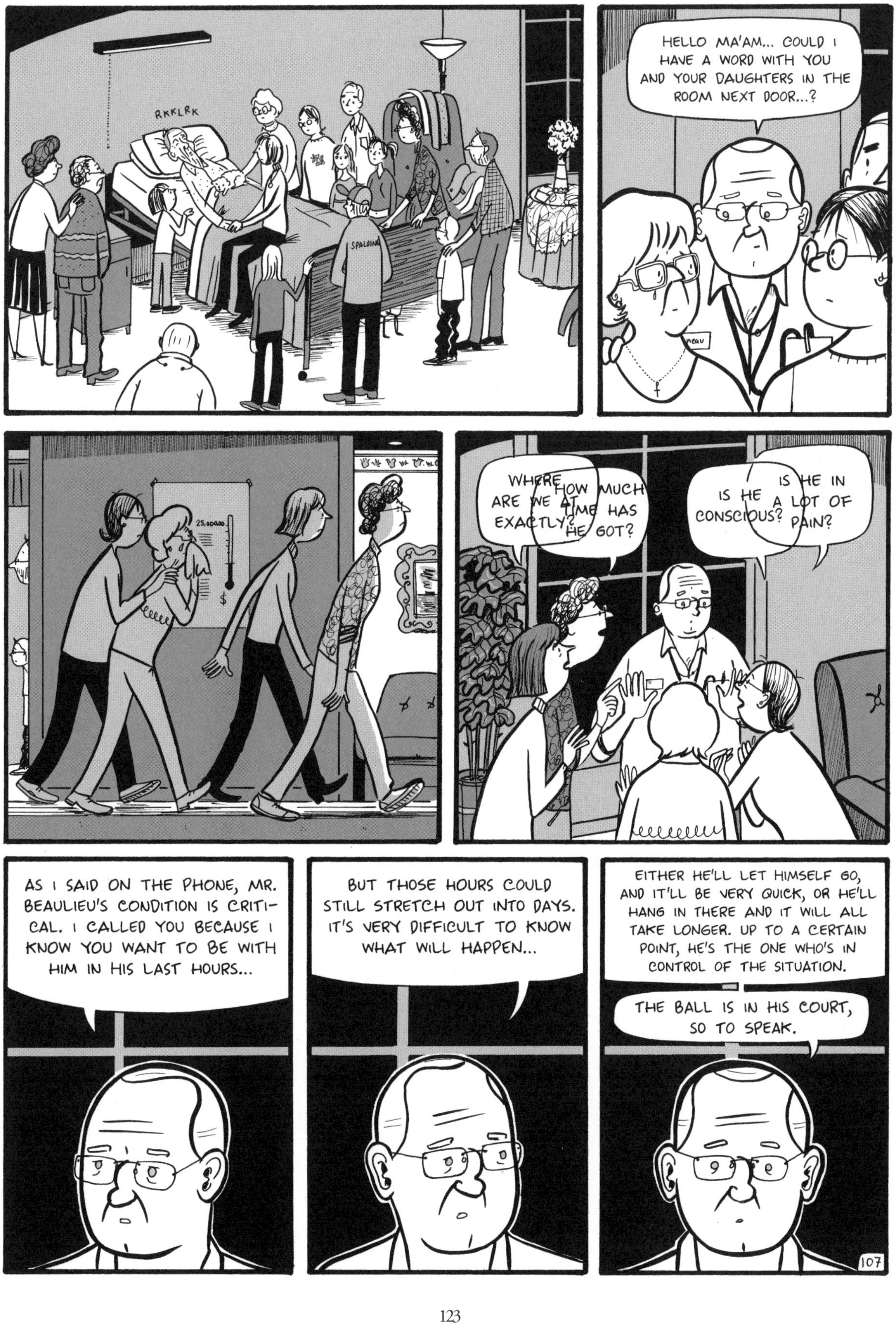
RKKLRK
SPALDING
HELLO MA'AM... COULD I HAVE A WORD WITH YOU AND YOUR DAUGHTERS IN THE ROOM NEXT DOOR...?
WHERE ARE WE AT EXACTLY?
HOW MUCH TIME HAS HE GOT?
IS HE CONSCIOUS?
IS HE IN A LOT OF PAIN?
AS I SAID ON THE PHONE, MR. BEAULIEU'S CONDITION IS CRITICAL. I CALLED YOU BECAUSE I KNOW YOU WANT TO BE WITH HIM IN HIS LAST HOURS...
BUT THOSE HOURS COULD STILL STRETCH OUT INTO DAYS. IT'S VERY DIFFICULT TO KNOW WHAT WILL HAPPEN...
EITHER HE'LL LET HIMSELF GO, AND IT'LL BE VERY QUICK, OR HE'LL HANG IN THERE AND IT WILL ALL TAKE LONGER. UP TO A CERTAIN POINT, HE'S THE ONE WHO'S IN CONTROL OF THE SITUATION.
THE BALL IS IN HIS COURT, SO TO SPEAK.
107

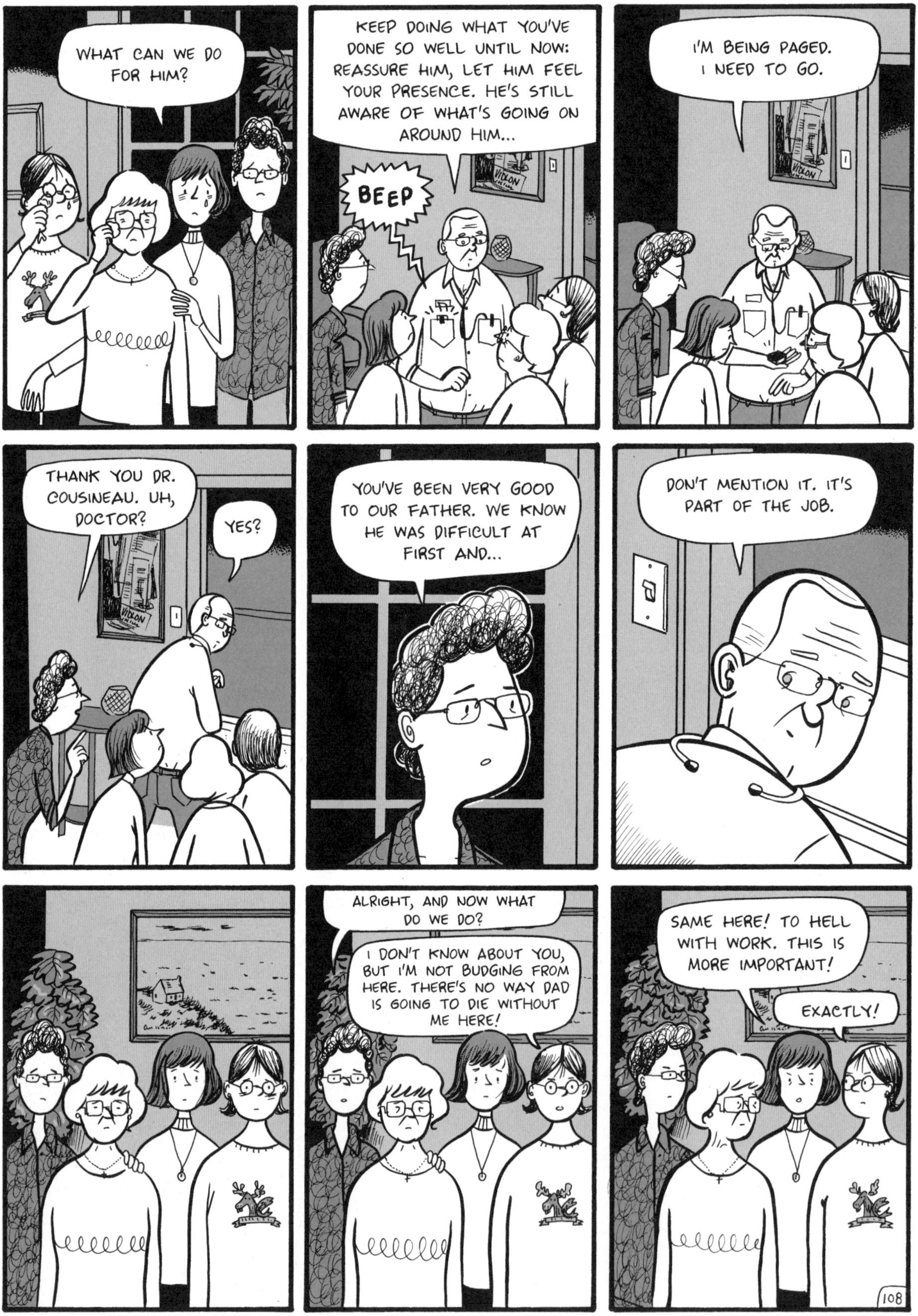
WHAT CAN WE DO FOR HIM?
KEEP DOING WHAT YOU'VE DONE SO WELL UNTIL NOW: REASSURE HIM, LET HIM FEEL YOUR PRESENCE. HE'S STILL AWARE OF WHAT'S GOING ON AROUND HIM...
BEEP
I'M BEING PAGED. I NEED TO GO.
THANK YOU DR. COUSINEAU. UH, DOCTOR?
YES?
YOU'VE BEEN VERY GOOD TO OUR FATHER. WE KNOW HE WAS DIFFICULT AT FIRST AND...
DON'T MENTION IT. IT'S PART OF THE JOB.
ALRIGHT, AND NOW WHAT DO WE DO?
I DON'T KNOW ABOUT YOU, BUT I'M NOT BUDGING FROM HERE. THERE'S NO WAY DAD IS GOING TO DIE WITHOUT ME HERE!
SAME HERE! TO HELL WITH WORK. THIS IS MORE IMPORTANT!
EXACTLY!
108

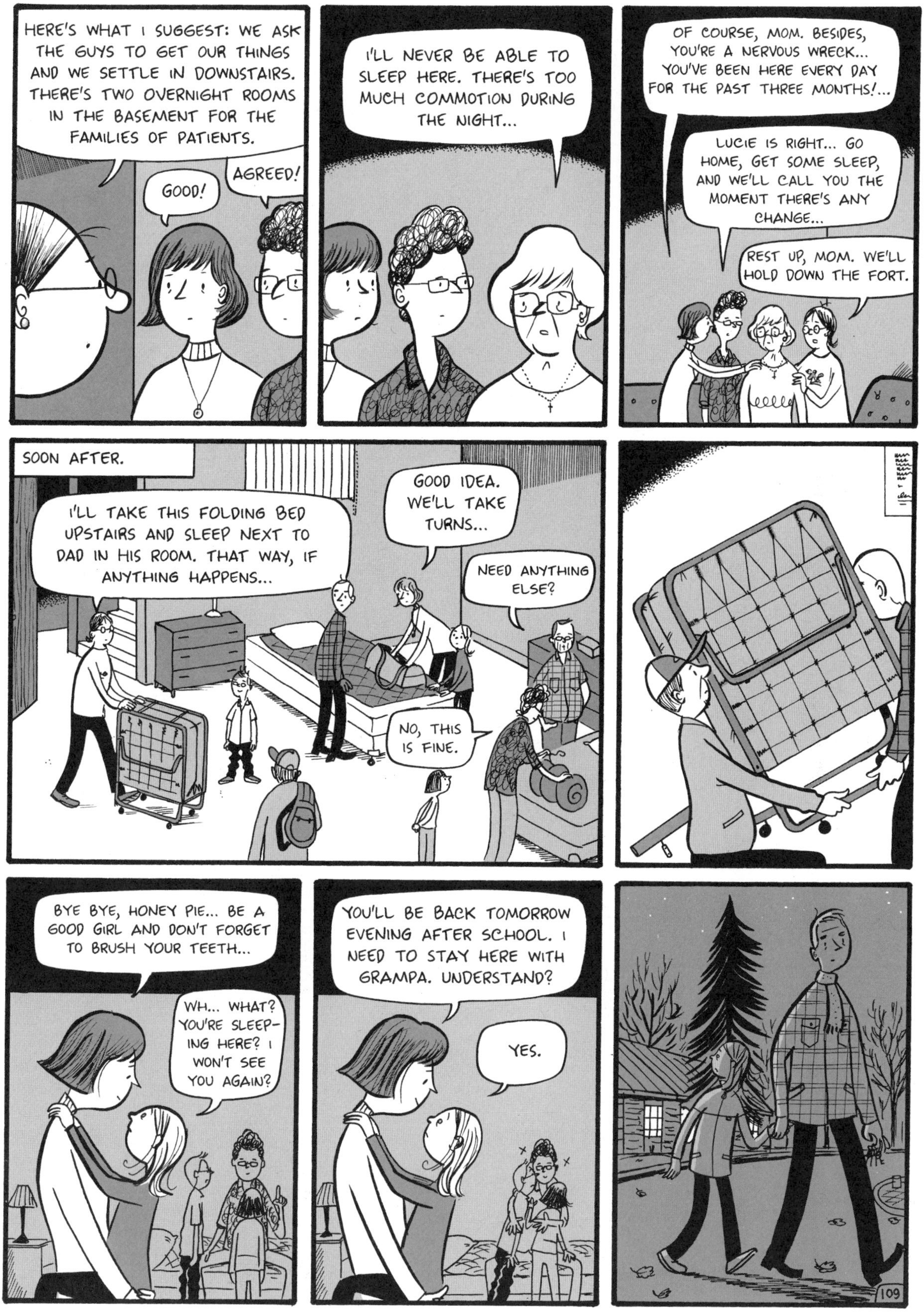
HERE'S WHAT I SUGGEST: WE ASK THE GUYS TO GET OUR THINGS AND WE SETTLE IN DOWNSTAIRS. THERE'S TWO OVERNIGHT ROOMS IN THE BASEMENT FOR THE FAMILIES OF PATIENTS.
GOOD!
AGREED!
I'LL NEVER BE ABLE TO SLEEP HERE. THERE'S TOO MUCH COMMOTION DURING THE NIGHT...
OF COURSE, MOM. BESIDES, YOU'RE A NERVOUS WRECK... YOU'VE BEEN HERE EVERY DAY FOR THE PAST THREE MONTHS!...
LUCIE IS RIGHT... GO HOME, GET SOME SLEEP, AND WE'LL CALL YOU THE MOMENT THERE'S ANY CHANGE...
REST UP, MOM. WE'LL HOLD DOWN THE FORT.
SOON AFTER.
I'LL TAKE THIS FOLDING BED UPSTAIRS AND SLEEP NEXT TO DAD IN HIS ROOM. THAT WAY, IF ANYTHING HAPPENS...
GOOD IDEA. WE'LL TAKE TURNS...
NEED ANYTHING ELSE?
NO, THIS IS FINE.
BYE BYE, HONEY PIE... BE A GOOD GIRL AND DON'T FORGET TO BRUSH YOUR TEETH...
WH... WHAT? YOU'RE SLEEPING HERE? I WON'T SEE YOU AGAIN?
YOU'LL BE BACK TOMORROW EVENING AFTER SCHOOL. I NEED TO STAY HERE WITH GRAMPA. UNDERSTAND?
YES.
109

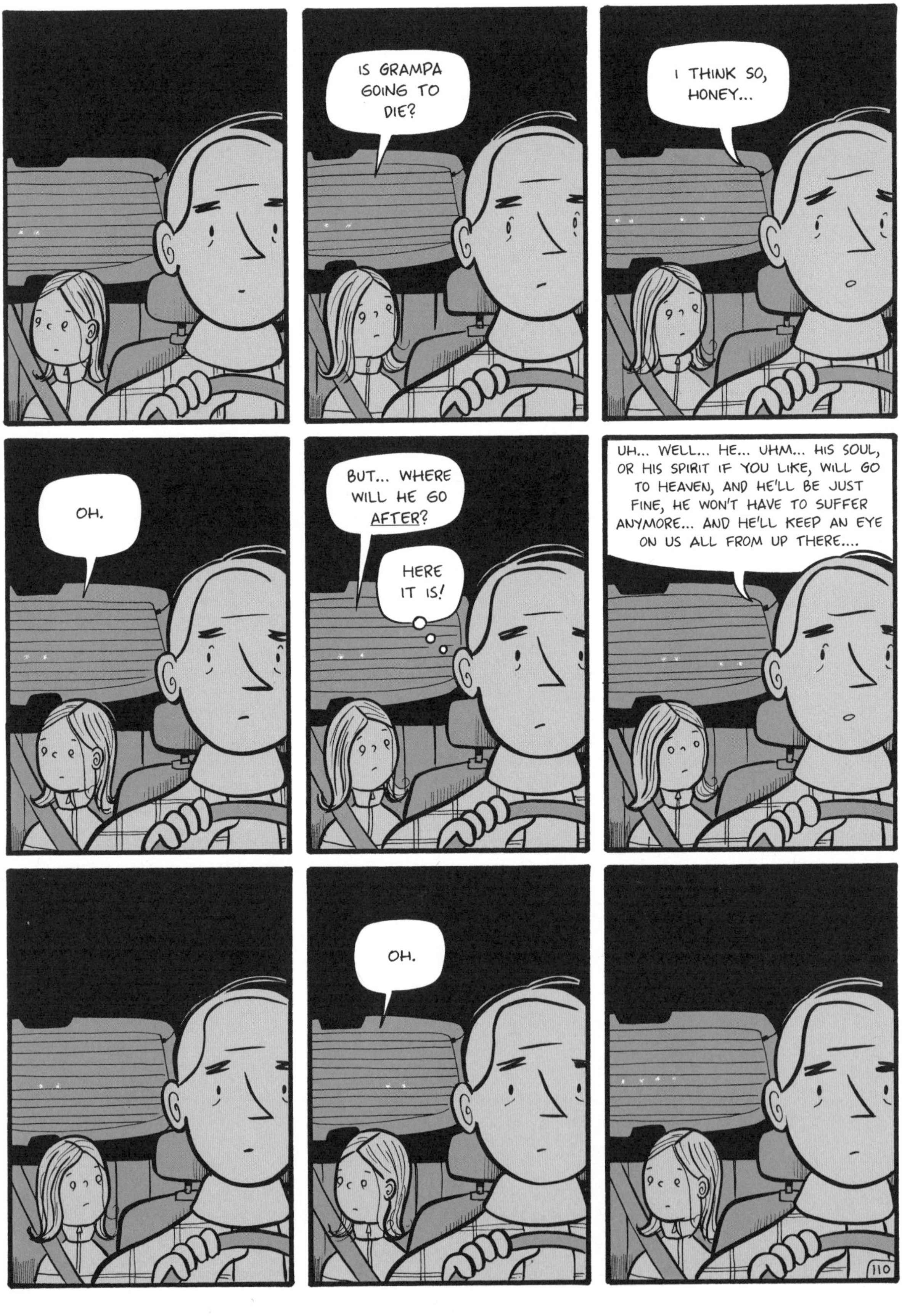
IS GRAMPA GOING TO DIE?
I THINK SO, HONEY...
OH.
BUT... WHERE WILL HE GO AFTER?
HERE IT IS!
UH... WELL... HE... UHM... HIS SOUL, OR HIS SPIRIT IF YOU LIKE, WILL GO TO HEAVEN, AND HE'LL BE JUST FINE, HE WON'T HAVE TO SUFFER ANYMORE... AND HE'LL KEEP AN EYE ON US ALL FROM UP THERE....
OH.
110

Wednesday

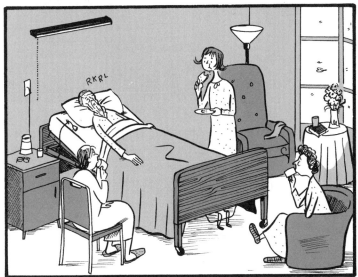

RKRL

MOM WAS RIGHT... THIS IS A HELL OF A PLACE TO SLEEP... THERE'S ALWAYS PEOPLE COMING AND GOING, DOORS SLAMMING...

WELL, THE STAFF HERE NEED TO WORK AT NIGHT TOO. YOU'VE GOTTA ADMIT IT'S A HECK OF A LOT BETTER THAN A HOSPITAL.

I'LL SLIP YOU SOMETHING TOMORROW...

I DON'T WANT YOUR PILLS! I'M SLEEPING HERE TOMORROW NIGHT. I WANT TO BE ALERT IN CASE SOMETHING HAPPENS TO DAD...

HOW WAS LAST NIGHT, MO? DID DAD WAKE UP? DID HE SAY ANYTHING?

NOTHING.

HE DIDN'T EVEN BUDGE. HE'S IN EXACTLY THE SAME POSITION HE WAS IN LAST NIGHT. HIS BREATHING IS SHALLOW AND HE SNORED A BIT. THAT'S ALL.

DO YOU THINK HE CAN HEAR US?
YEAH... MAYBE HE'D LIKE SOME-THING... WATER, I DUNNO...
HOLD ON... I'LL GIVE IT A TRY...
...DAD...
ARE YOU THIRSTY? WOULD YOU LIKE ANYTHING?
¿SÍ.
HE SAID YES!
QUICK! WATER!
TER! ICK!
NOT THAT GLASS, IT ISN'T FRESH!
JEEZUS, WHERE ARE THE BENDY STRAWS!!
WE NEED TO PROP HIM UP.
HERE! THIS ONE'S FRESH!
AH! GOT'EM!
C'MON, DAD... HAVE A SIP...
MAYBE HE CAN'T FEEL THE STRAW ON HIS LIP...
AH?!
YESSSS!
WAY TO GO!
112

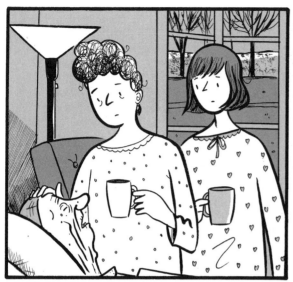

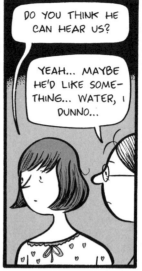

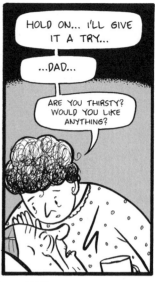

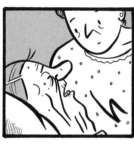

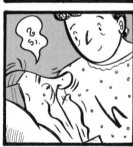

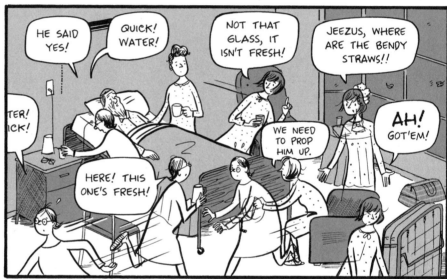

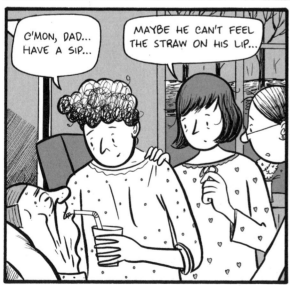

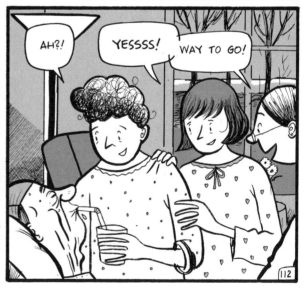

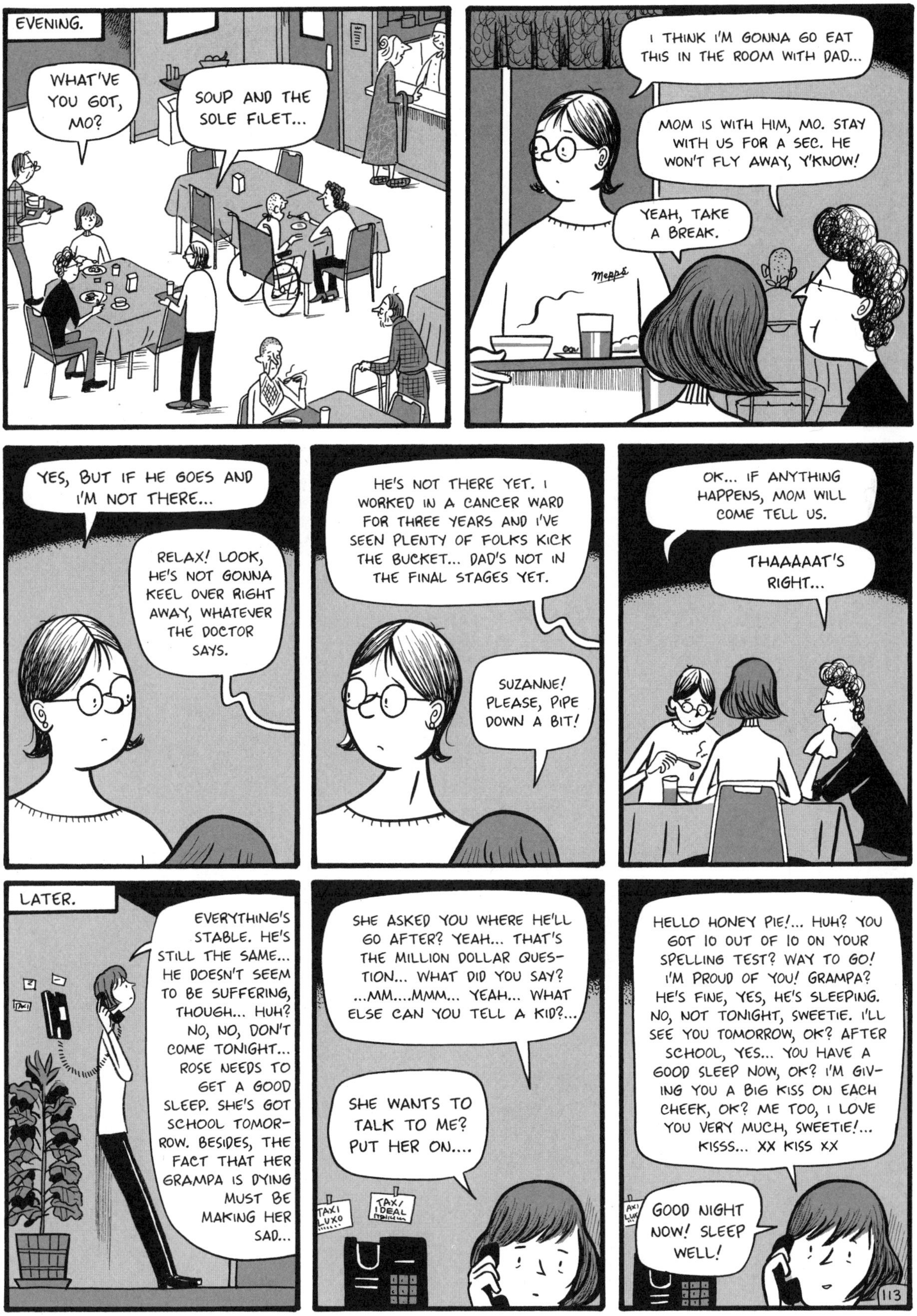
EVENING.
WHAT'VE YOU GOT, MO?
SOUP AND THE SOLE FILET...
I THINK I'M GONNA GO EAT THIS IN THE ROOM WITH DAD...
MOM IS WITH HIM, MO. STAY WITH US FOR A SEC. HE WON'T FLY AWAY, Y'KNOW!
YEAH, TAKE A BREAK.
YES, BUT IF HE GOES AND I'M NOT THERE...
RELAX! LOOK, HE'S NOT GONNA KEEL OVER RIGHT AWAY, WHATEVER THE DOCTOR SAYS.
HE'S NOT THERE YET. I WORKED IN A CANCER WARD FOR THREE YEARS AND I'VE SEEN PLENTY OF FOLKS KICK THE BUCKET... DAD'S NOT IN THE FINAL STAGES YET.
SUZANNE! PLEASE, PIPE DOWN A BIT!
OK... IF ANYTHING HAPPENS, MOM WILL COME TELL US.
THAAAAAT'S RIGHT...
LATER.
EVERYTHING'S STABLE. HE'S STILL THE SAME... HE DOESN'T SEEM TO BE SUFFERING, THOUGH... HUH? NO, NO, DON'T COME TONIGHT... ROSE NEEDS TO GET A GOOD SLEEP. SHE'S GOT SCHOOL TOMORROW. BESIDES, THE FACT THAT HER GRAMPA IS DYING MUST BE MAKING HER SAD...
SHE ASKED YOU WHERE HE'LL GO AFTER? YEAH... THAT'S THE MILLION DOLLAR QUESTION... WHAT DID YOU SAY? ...MM....MMM... YEAH... WHAT ELSE CAN YOU TELL A KID?...
SHE WANTS TO TALK TO ME? PUT HER ON....
TAXI LUXO
TAXI IDEAL
HELLO HONEY PIE!... HUH? YOU GOT 10 OUT OF 10 ON YOUR SPELLING TEST? WAY TO GO! I'M PROUD OF YOU! GRAMPA? HE'S FINE, YES, HE'S SLEEPING. NO, NOT TONIGHT, SWEETIE. I'LL SEE YOU TOMORROW, OK? AFTER SCHOOL, YES... YOU HAVE A GOOD SLEEP NOW, OK? I'M GIVING YOU A BIG KISS ON EACH CHEEK, OK? ME TOO, I LOVE YOU VERY MUCH, SWEETIE!... KISSS... XX KISS XX
GOOD NIGHT NOW! SLEEP WELL!
113

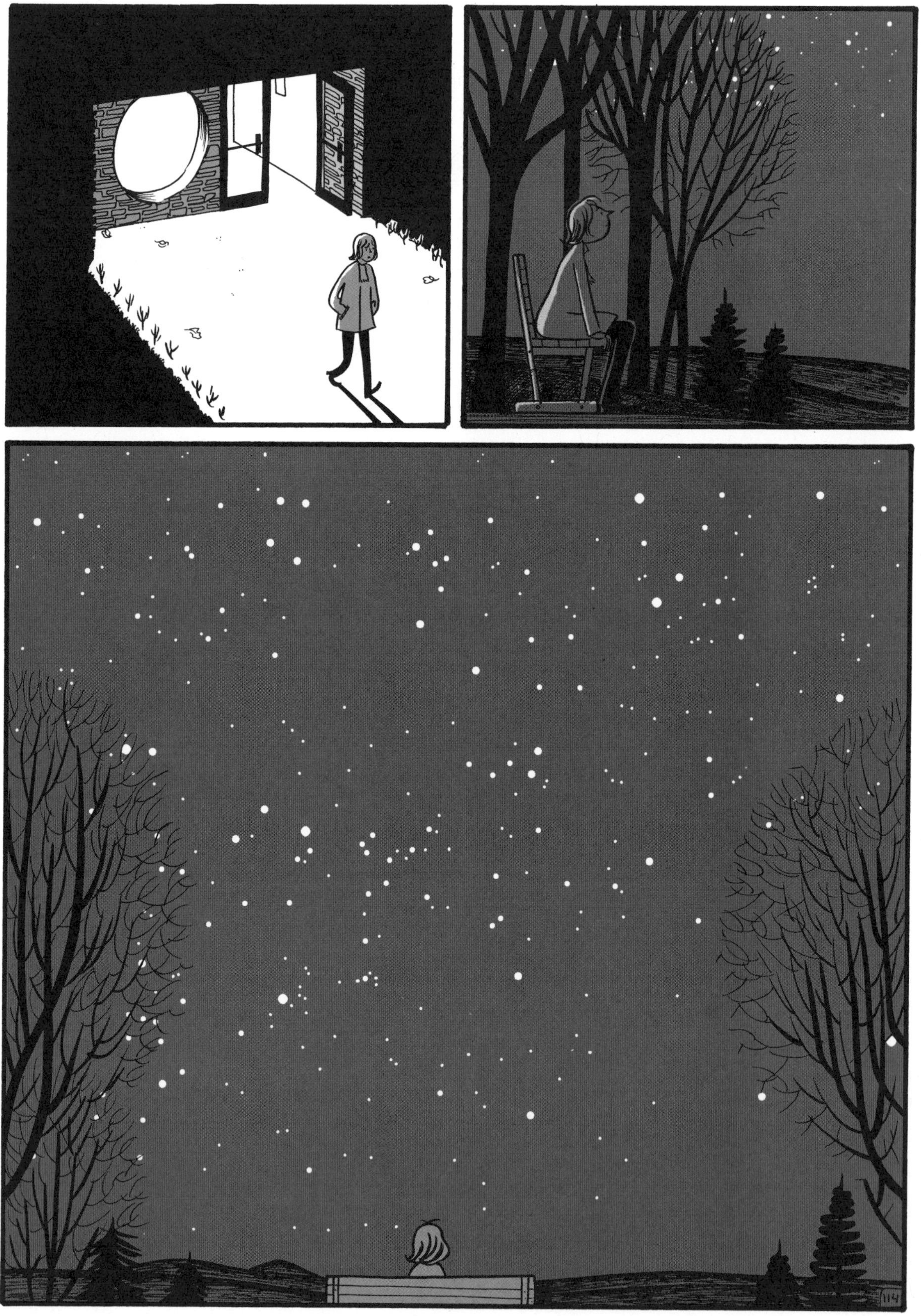

Thursday

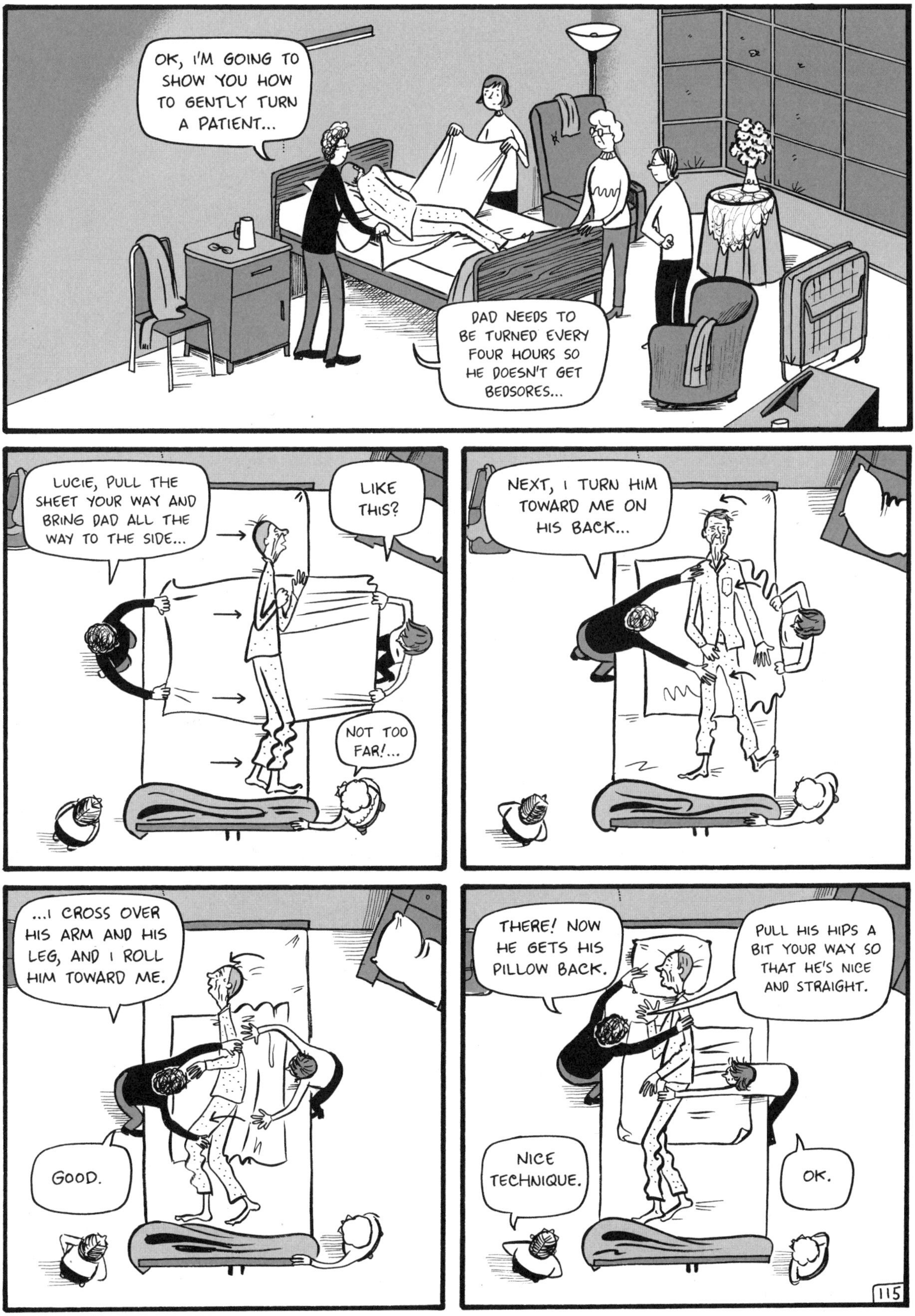
OK, I'M GOING TO SHOW YOU HOW TO GENTLY TURN A PATIENT...
DAD NEEDS TO BE TURNED EVERY FOUR HOURS SO HE DOESN'T GET BEDSORES...
LUCIE, PULL THE SHEET YOUR WAY AND BRING DAD ALL THE WAY TO THE SIDE...
LIKE THIS?
NOT TOO FAR!...
NEXT, I TURN HIM TOWARD ME ON HIS BACK...
...I CROSS OVER HIS ARM AND HIS LEG, AND I ROLL HIM TOWARD ME.
GOOD.
THERE! NOW HE GETS HIS PILLOW BACK.
PULL HIS HIPS A BIT YOUR WAY SO THAT HE'S NICE AND STRAIGHT.
NICE TECHNIQUE.
OK.
115

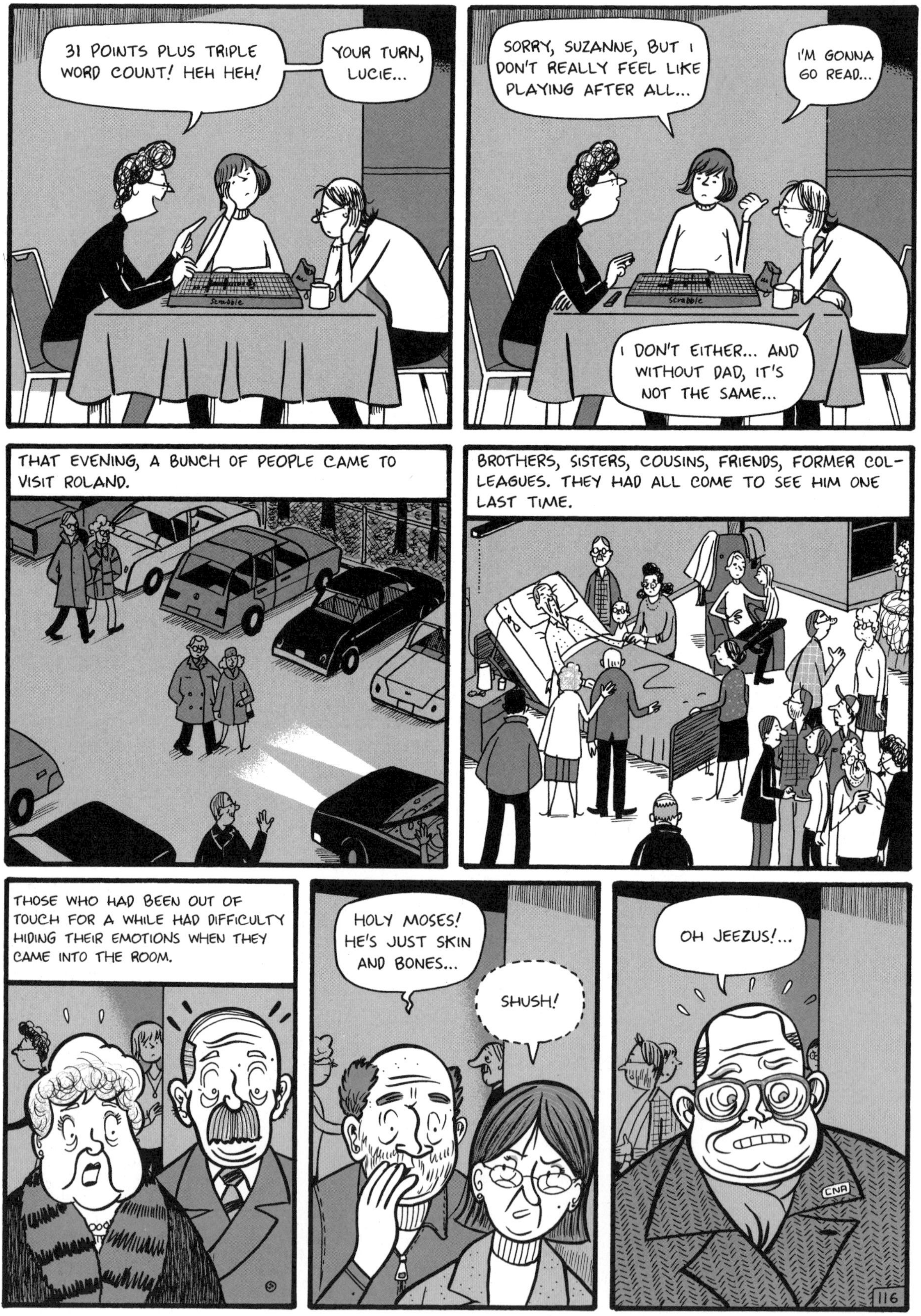
31 POINTS PLUS TRIPLE WORD COUNT! HEH HEH!
YOUR TURN, LUCIE...
SORRY, SUZANNE, BUT I DON'T REALLY FEEL LIKE PLAYING AFTER ALL...
I'M GONNA GO READ...
I DON'T EITHER... AND WITHOUT DAD, IT'S NOT THE SAME...
THAT EVENING, A BUNCH OF PEOPLE CAME TO VISIT ROLAND.
BROTHERS, SISTERS, COUSINS, FRIENDS, FORMER COLLEAGUES. THEY HAD ALL COME TO SEE HIM ONE LAST TIME.
THOSE WHO HAD BEEN OUT OF TOUCH FOR A WHILE HAD DIFFICULTY HIDING THEIR EMOTIONS WHEN THEY CAME INTO THE ROOM.
HOLY MOSES! HE'S JUST SKIN AND BONES...
SHUSH!
OH JEEZUS!...
116

VISITING SOMEONE WHO'S DYING IS COMPLETELY DIFFERENT FROM VISITING SOMEONE WHO'S RECOVERING. WHEN A PERSON IS CONVALESCING, YOU CAN CHEER THEM ON, JOKE AROUND AND TALK ABOUT THE FUTURE.

DON'T WORRY SEBASTIAN! WE'LL WIN THE COLLEGE CUP NEXT YEAR!

WE'RE GONNA MAKE'EM PAY! HA HA!

YEAH!!!

BUT WHAT DO YOU SAY TO SOMEONE WHO'S DYING?

NICE BIG ROOM YOU'VE GOT HERE, ROLAND...

...CLEAN AS A WHISTLE...

...YEAH...

...SPOT- LESS.

KRKLRK

BY 10 P.M., ALL THE VISITORS WERE GONE.

WHEW! PEACE AND QUIET!

I COULDN'T HAVE TALKED FOR AN- OTHER MINUTE!

WHY DON'T YOU GIRLS GO GET SOME AIR...

GOOD IDEA, MOM.

I'M COMING!

ME TOO!

THERE WERE FOLKS TONIGHT THAT I HAVEN'T SEEN IN DECADES!

DAD'S OLD OFFICE COLLEAGUES, FOR INSTANCE...

DID YOU NOTICE MR. VIAU'S FACE WHEN HE SAW DAD?

YEAH! OLD VIAU ISN'T TOO SUBTLE.

117

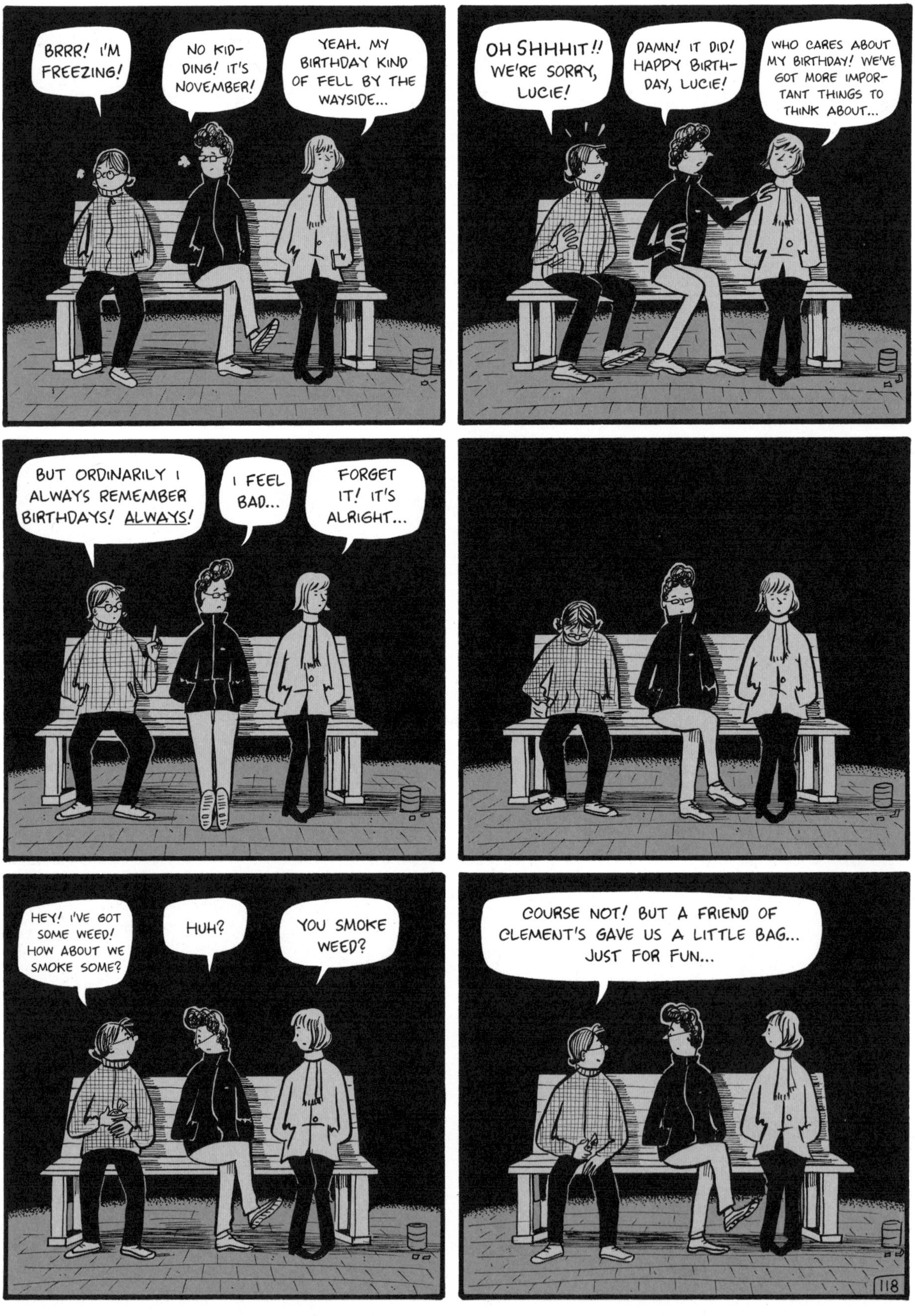
BRRR! I'M FREEZING!
NO KID-DING! IT'S NOVEMBER!
YEAH. MY BIRTHDAY KIND OF FELL BY THE WAYSIDE...
OH SHHHIT!! WE'RE SORRY, LUCIE!
DAMN! IT DID! HAPPY BIRTH-DAY, LUCIE!
WHO CARES ABOUT MY BIRTHDAY! WE'VE GOT MORE IMPOR-TANT THINGS TO THINK ABOUT...
BUT ORDINARILY I ALWAYS REMEMBER BIRTHDAYS! ALWAYS!
I FEEL BAD...
FORGET IT! IT'S ALRIGHT...
HEY! I'VE GOT SOME WEED! HOW ABOUT WE SMOKE SOME?
HUH?
YOU SMOKE WEED?
COURSE NOT! BUT A FRIEND OF CLEMENT'S GAVE US A LITTLE BAG... JUST FOR FUN...
118

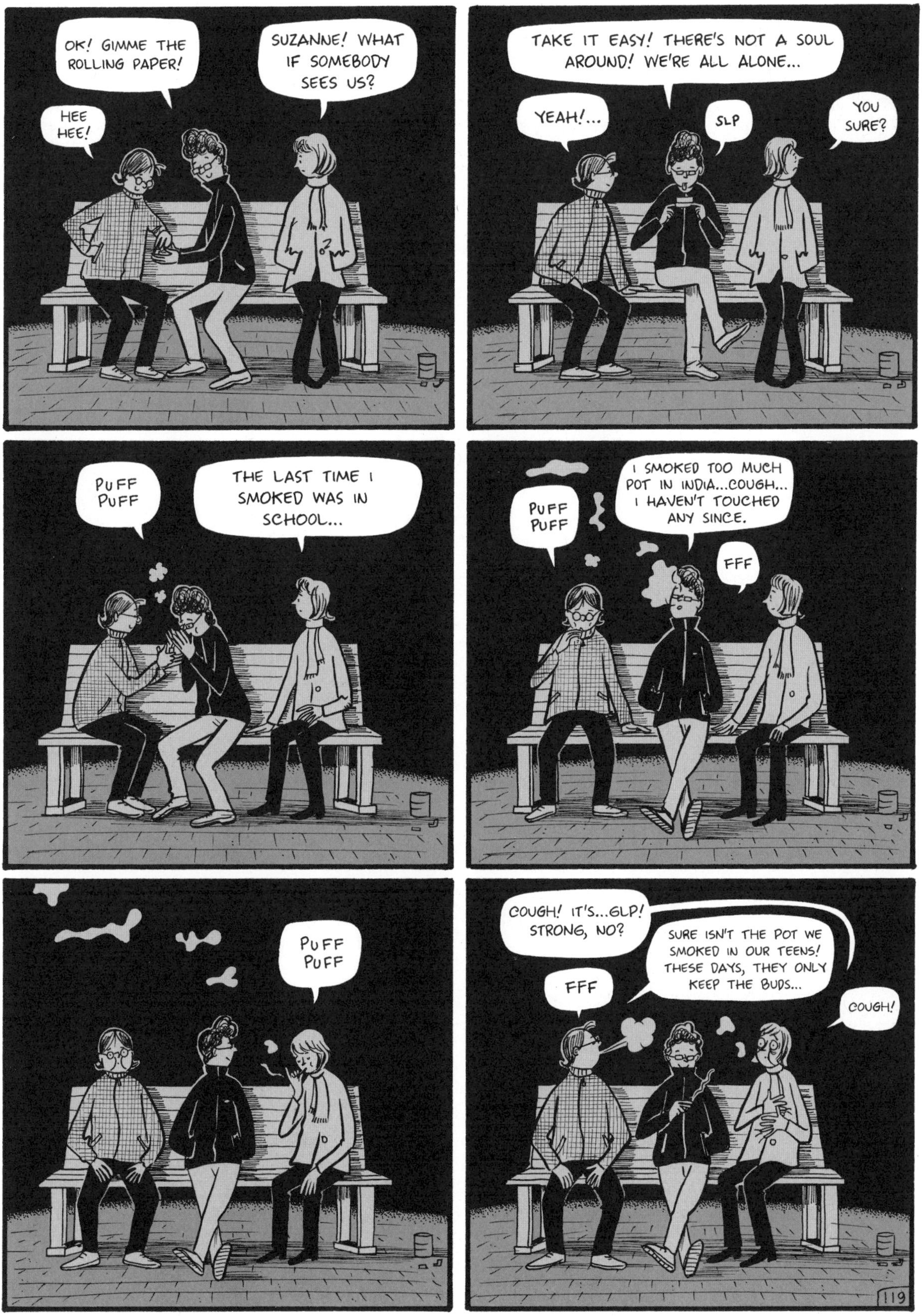
OK! GIMME THE ROLLING PAPER!
HEE HEE!
SUZANNE! WHAT IF SOMEBODY SEES US?
TAKE IT EASY! THERE'S NOT A SOUL AROUND! WE'RE ALL ALONE...
YEAH!...
SLP
YOU SURE?
PUFF PUFF
THE LAST TIME I SMOKED WAS IN SCHOOL...
I SMOKED TOO MUCH POT IN INDIA...COUGH... I HAVEN'T TOUCHED ANY SINCE.
PUFF PUFF
FFF
PUFF PUFF
COUGH! IT'S...GLP! STRONG, NO?
SURE ISN'T THE POT WE SMOKED IN OUR TEENS! THESE DAYS, THEY ONLY KEEP THE BUDS...
FFF
COUGH!
119

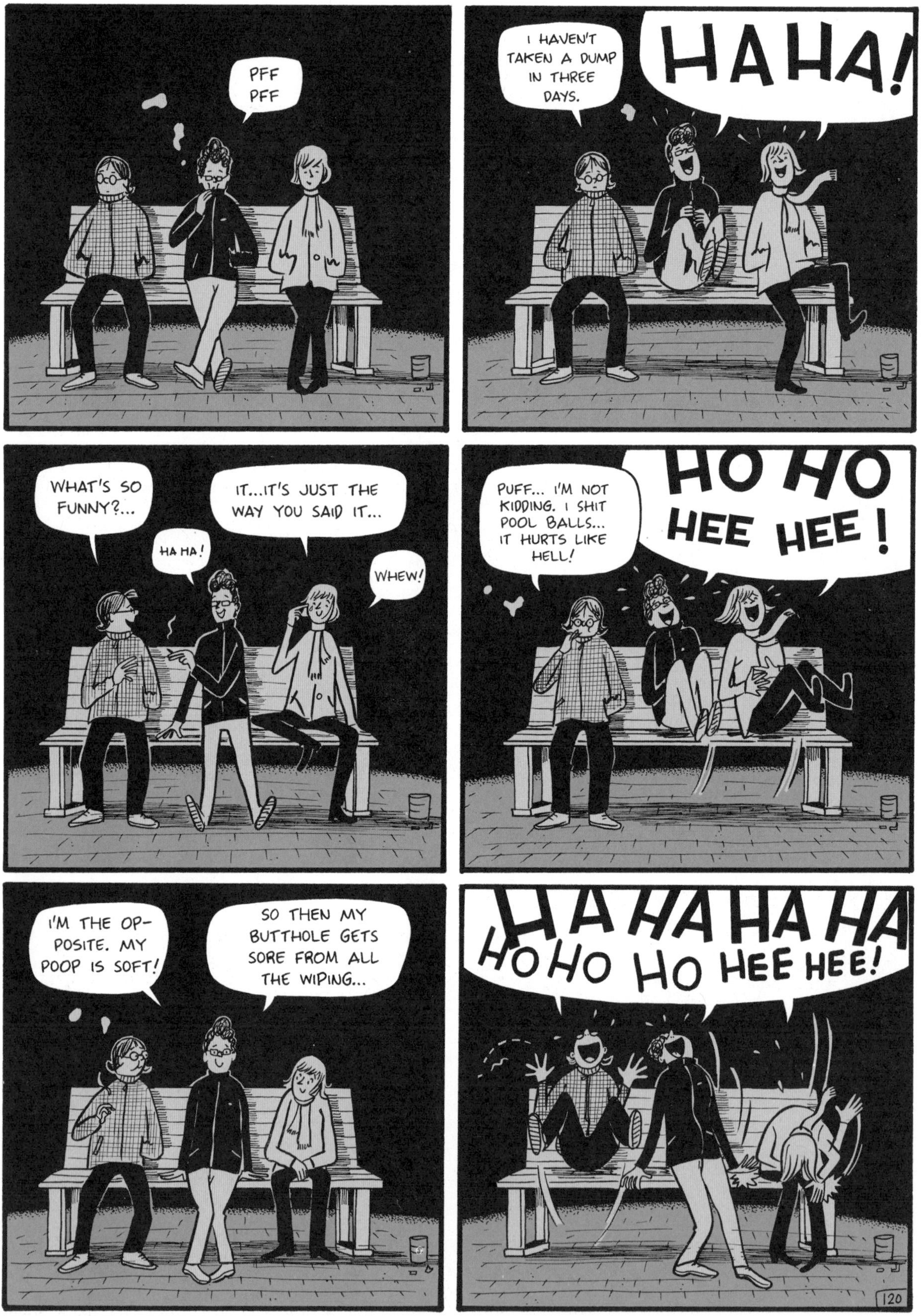
PFF
PFF
I HAVEN'T TAKEN A DUMP IN THREE DAYS.
HAHA!
WHAT'S SO FUNNY?...
HA HA!
IT...IT'S JUST THE WAY YOU SAID IT...
WHEW!
PUFF... I'M NOT KIDDING. I SHIT POOL BALLS... IT HURTS LIKE HELL!
HO HO HEE HEE!
I'M THE OP-POSITE. MY POOP IS SOFT!
SO THEN MY BUTTHOLE GETS SORE FROM ALL THE WIPING...
HA HA HA HA HA
HO HO HO HEE HEE!
120

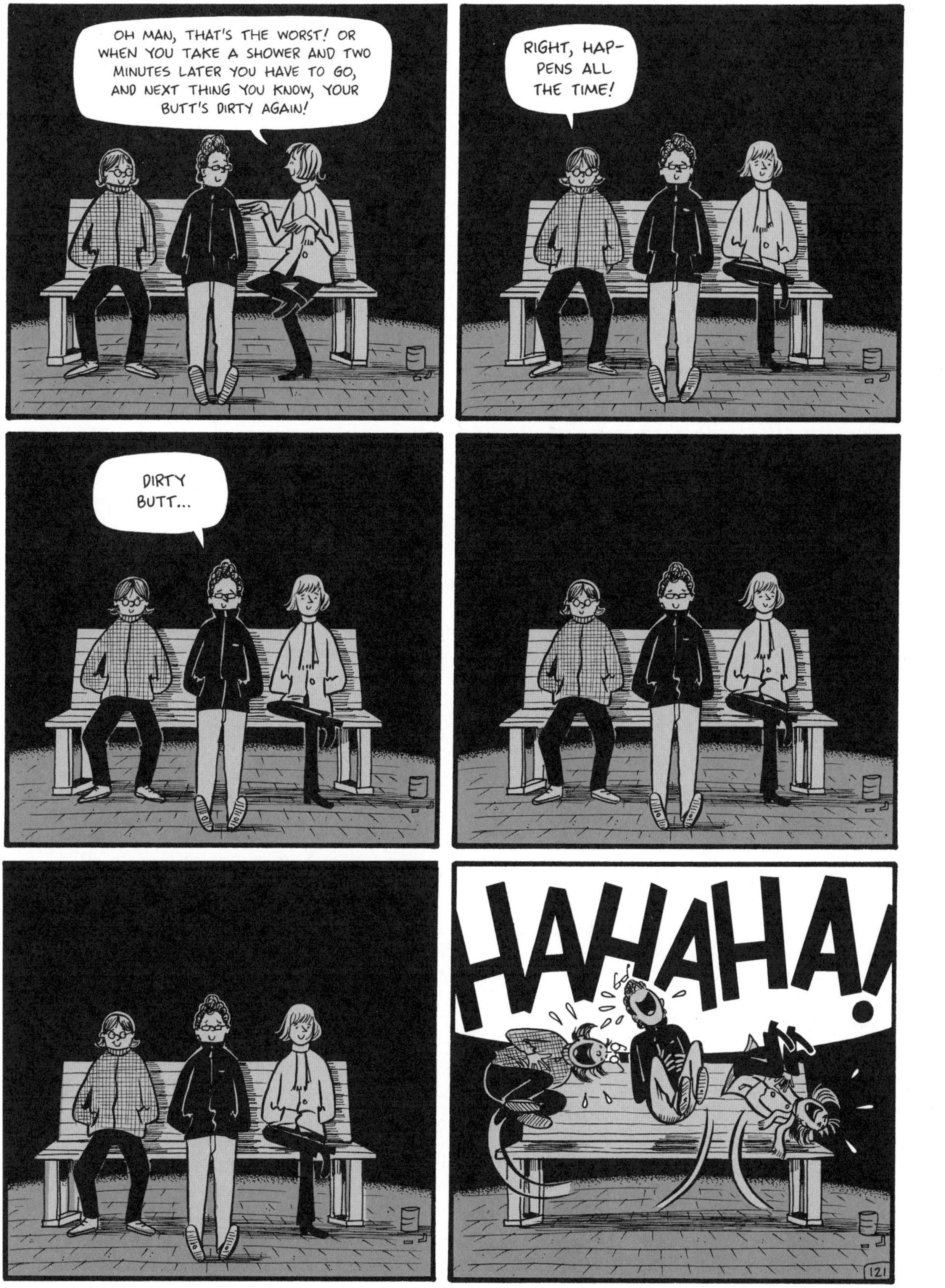
OH MAN, THAT'S THE WORST! OR WHEN YOU TAKE A SHOWER AND TWO MINUTES LATER YOU HAVE TO GO, AND NEXT THING YOU KNOW, YOUR BUTT'S DIRTY AGAIN!
RIGHT, HAPPENS ALL THE TIME!
DIRTY BUTT...
HAHAHA!
121

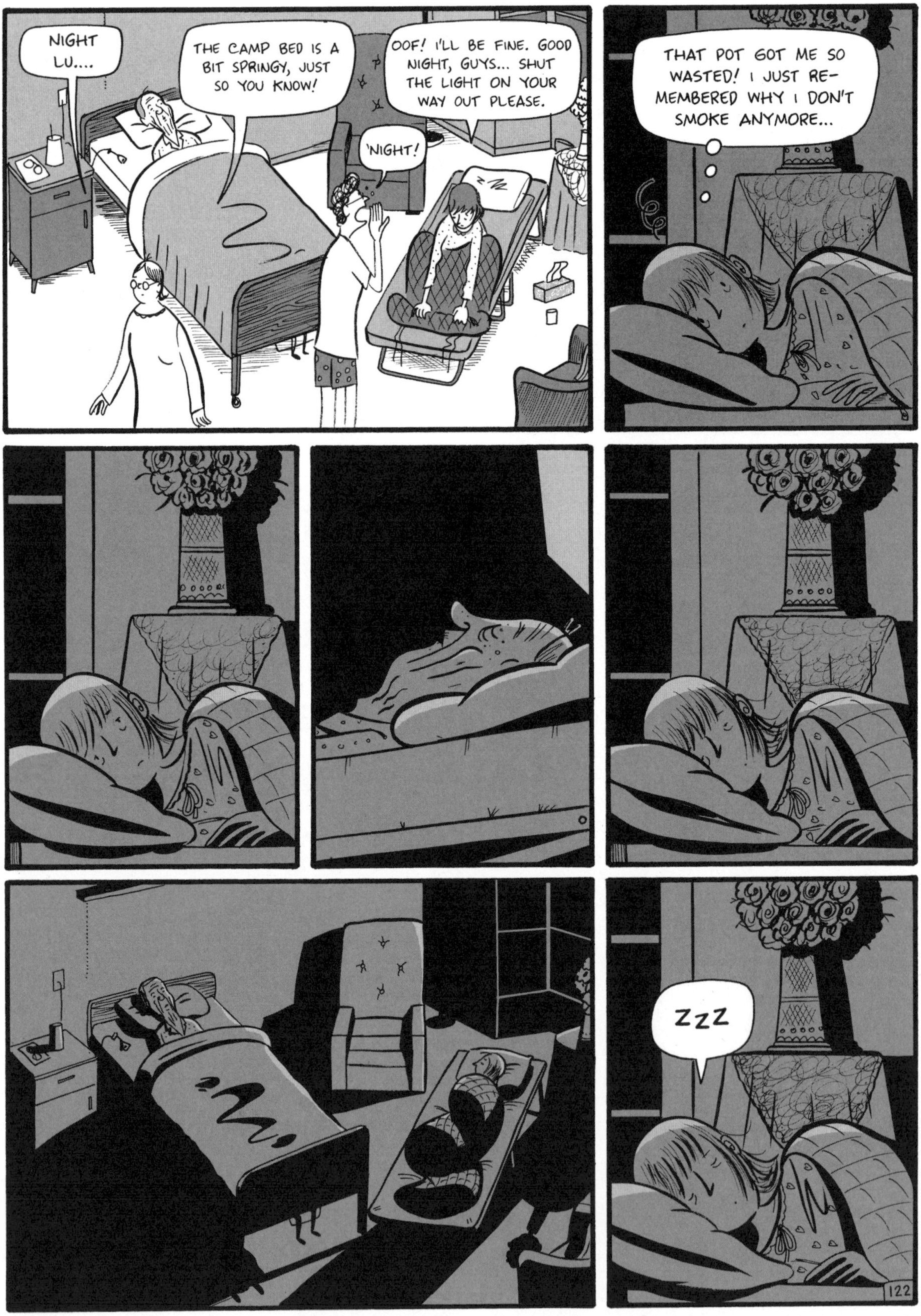
NIGHT LU....
THE CAMP BED IS A BIT SPRINGY, JUST SO YOU KNOW!
OOF! I'LL BE FINE. GOOD NIGHT, GUYS... SHUT THE LIGHT ON YOUR WAY OUT PLEASE.
'NIGHT!
THAT POT GOT ME SO WASTED! I JUST REMEMBERED WHY I DON'T SMOKE ANYMORE...
ZZZ
122

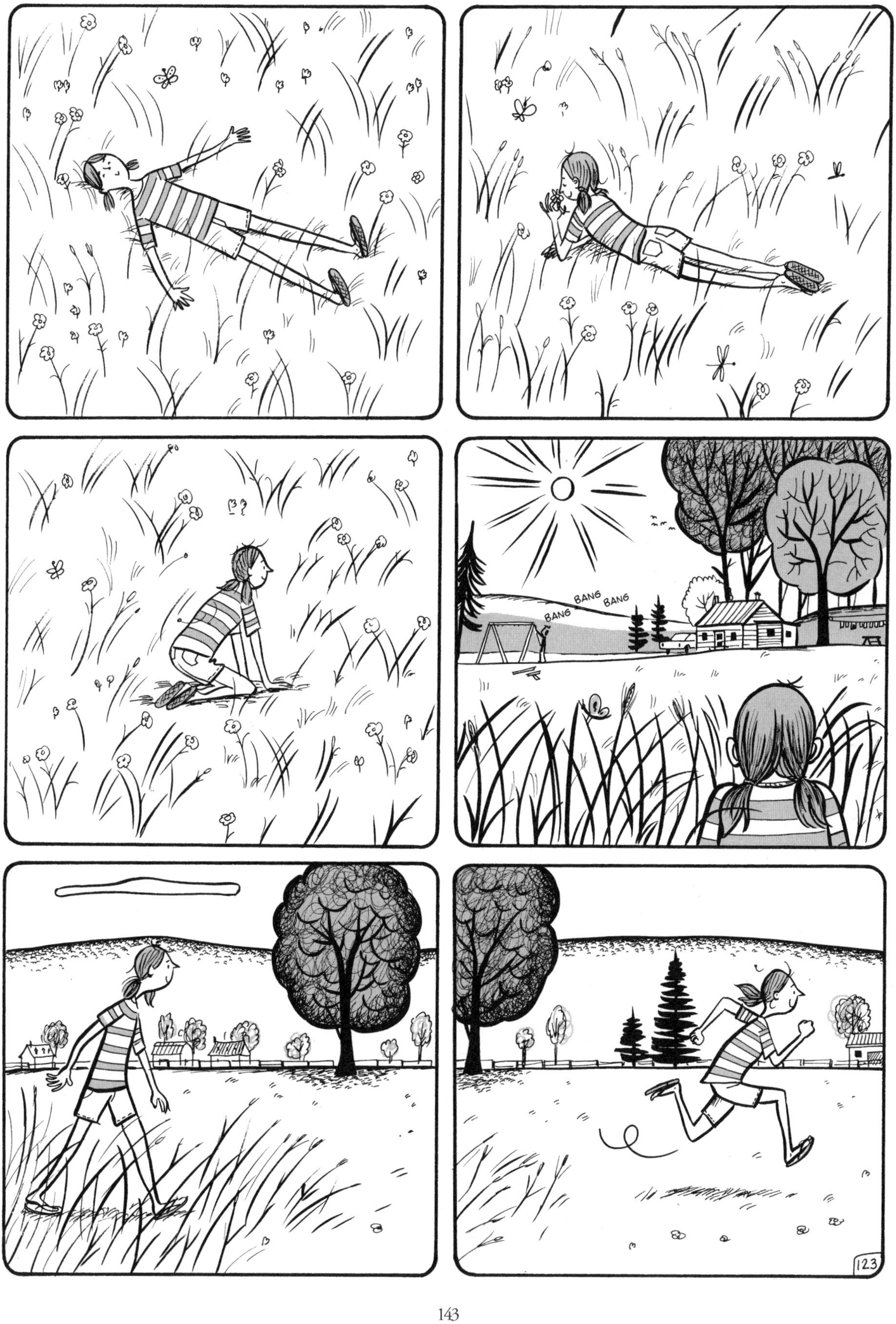
BANG
BANG
BANG
123

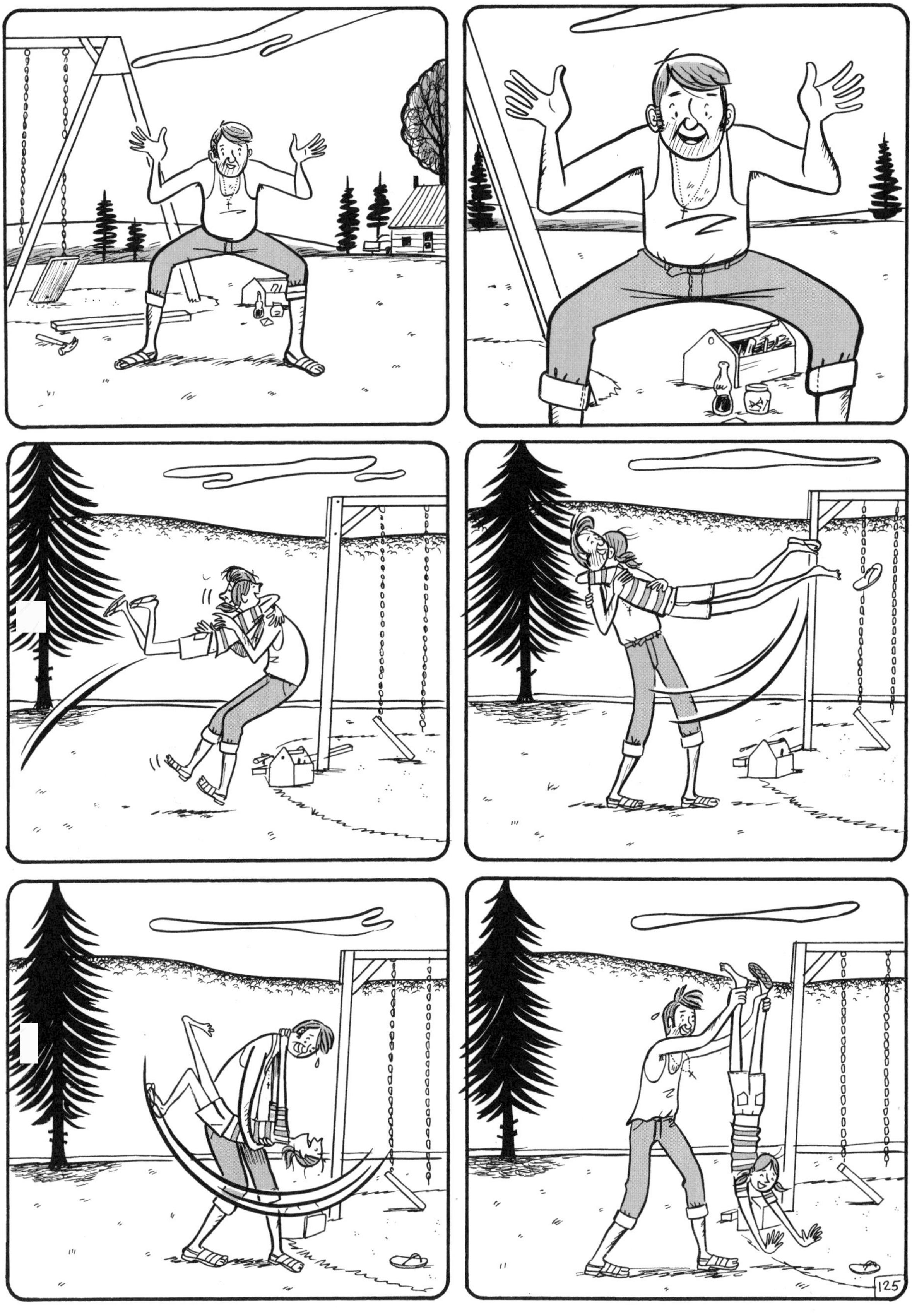
125

AVE MARIA
AVE MARIA
KRAK
KRAK
KRAK
AVE MA
KRAK
127

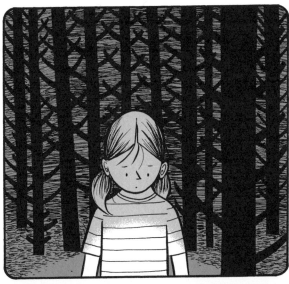

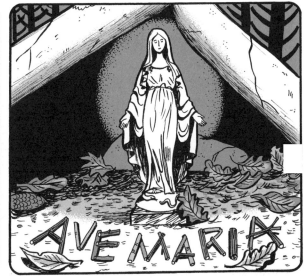

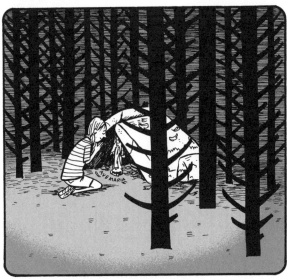

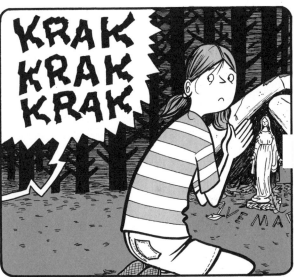

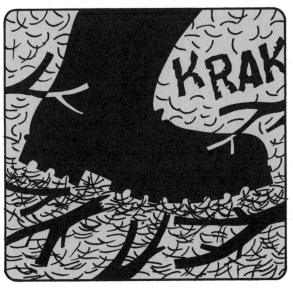

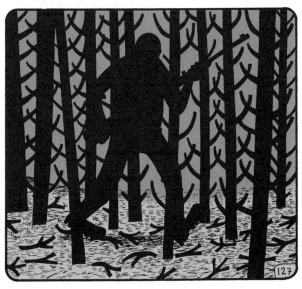

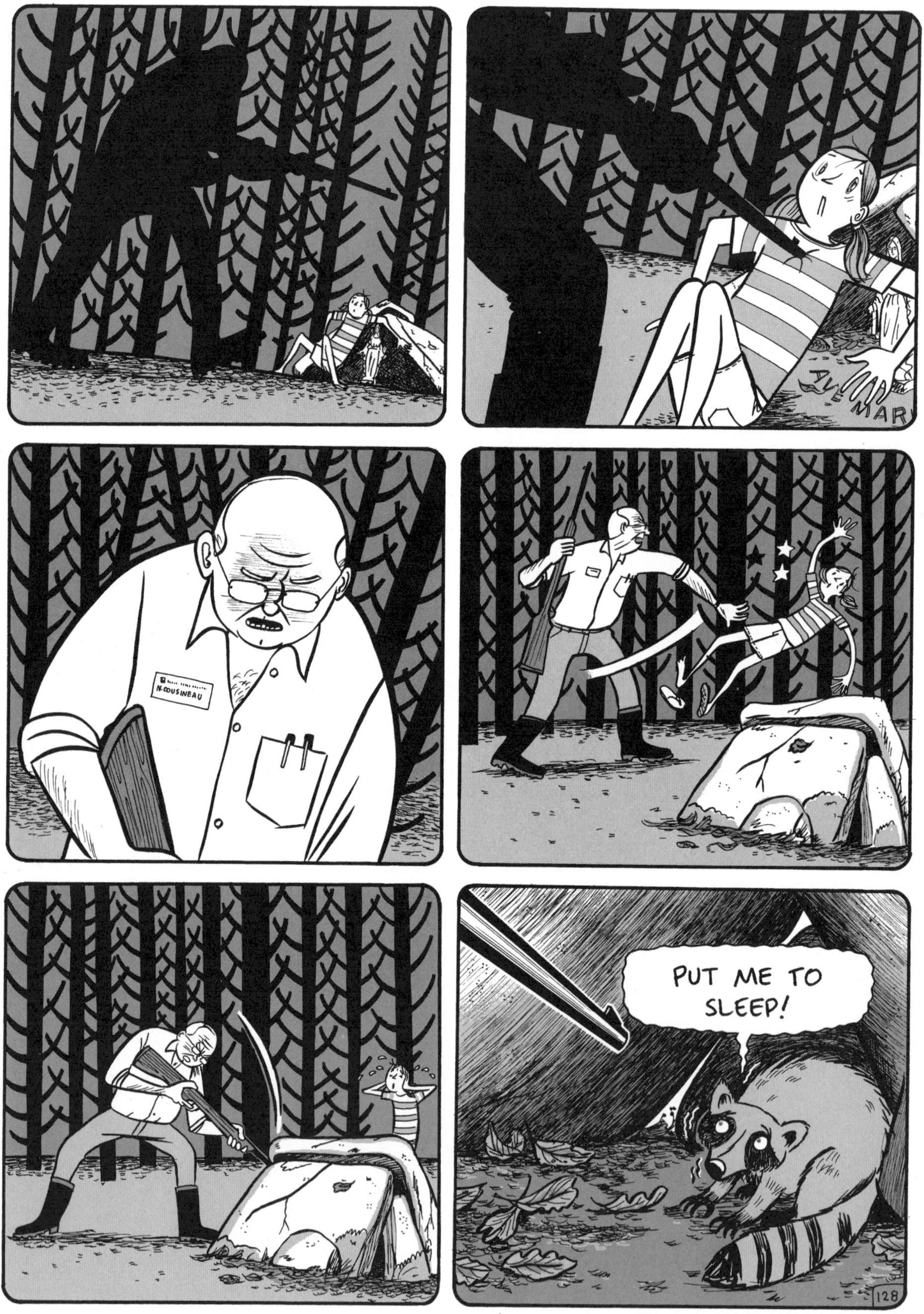
N.COUSINEAU
PUT ME TO SLEEP!
128

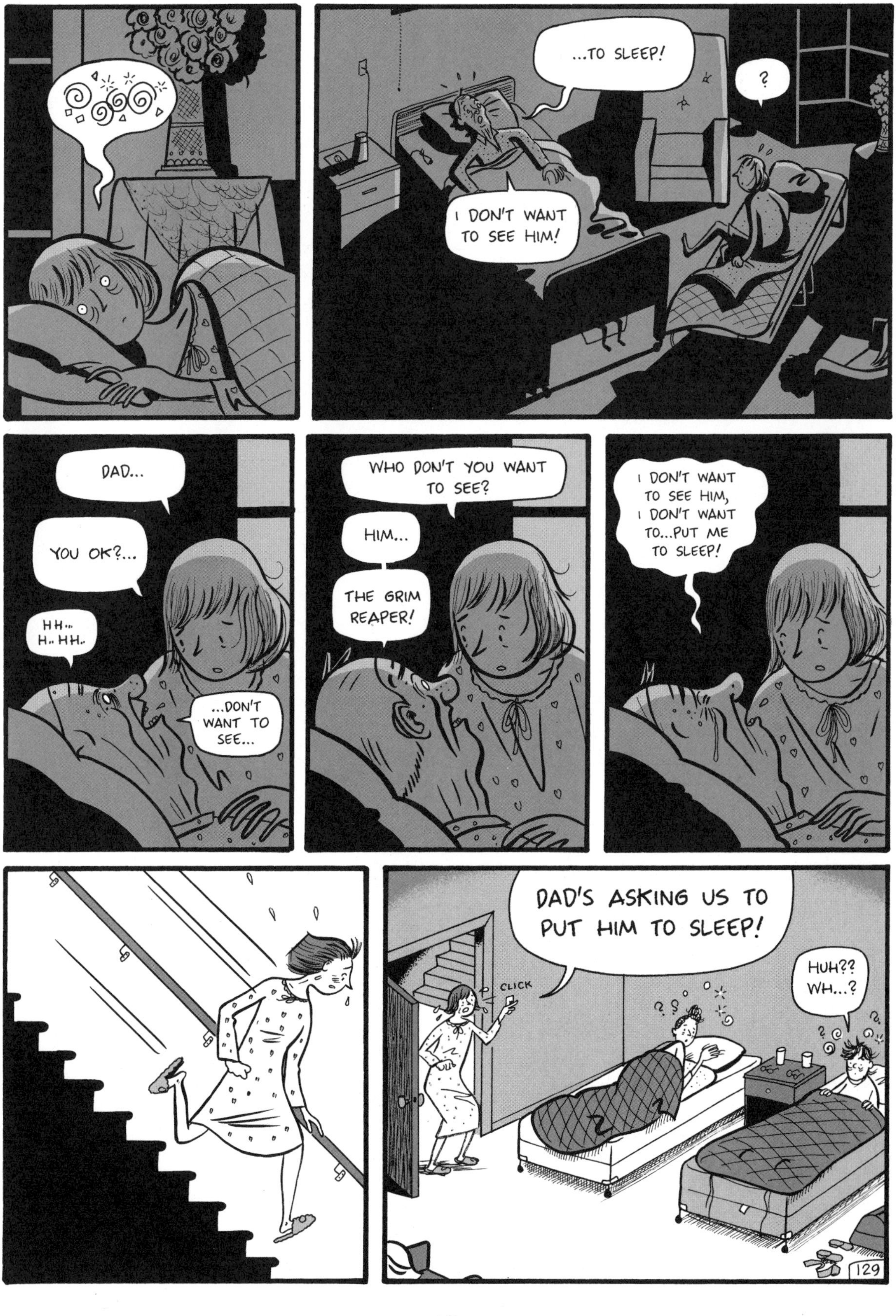
...TO SLEEP!
?
I DON'T WANT TO SEE HIM!
DAD...
YOU OK?...
HH... H.. HH..
...DON'T WANT TO SEE...
WHO DON'T YOU WANT TO SEE?
HIM...
THE GRIM REAPER!
I DON'T WANT TO SEE HIM, I DON'T WANT TO...PUT ME TO SLEEP!
DAD'S ASKING US TO PUT HIM TO SLEEP!
CLICK
HUH?? WH...?
129

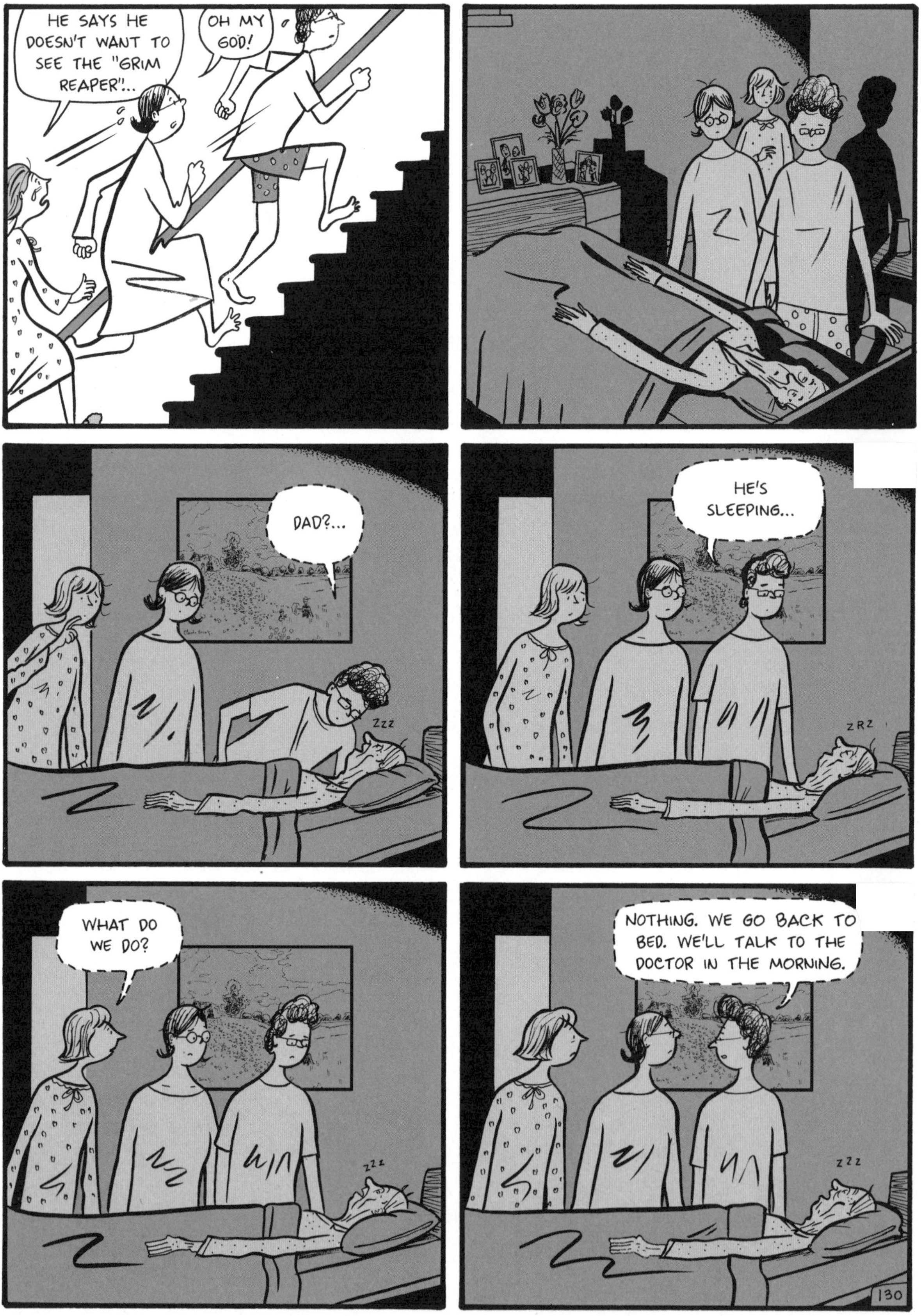
HE SAYS HE DOESN'T WANT TO SEE THE "GRIM REAPER"...
OH MY GOD!
DAD?...
ZZZ
HE'S SLEEPING...
ZRZ
WHAT DO WE DO?
ZZZ
NOTHING. WE GO BACK TO BED. WE'LL TALK TO THE DOCTOR IN THE MORNING.
ZZZ
130

Friday

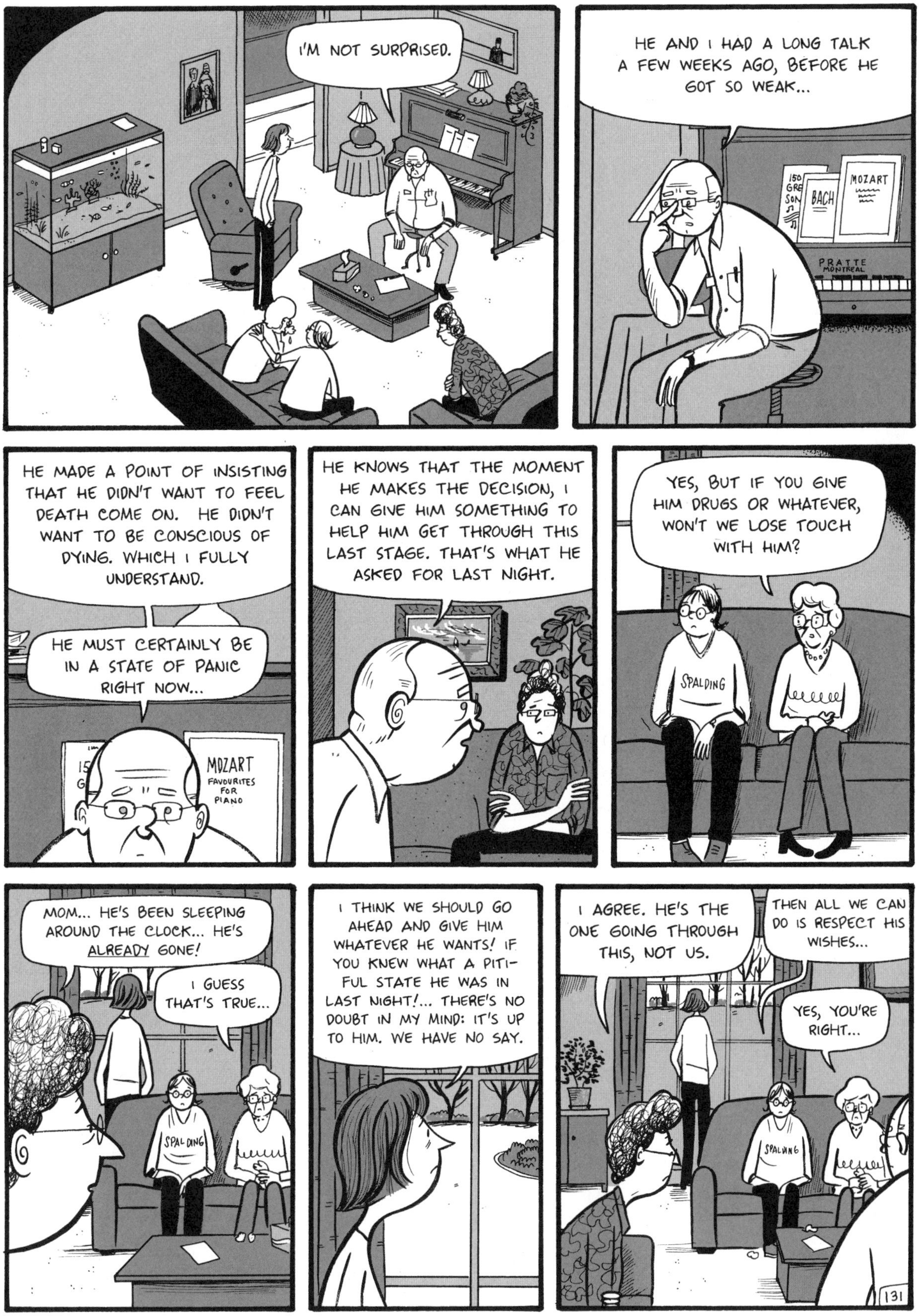
I'M NOT SURPRISED.
HE AND I HAD A LONG TALK A FEW WEEKS AGO, BEFORE HE GOT SO WEAK...
MOZART
BACH
PRATTE MONTREAL
HE MADE A POINT OF INSISTING THAT HE DIDN'T WANT TO FEEL DEATH COME ON. HE DIDN'T WANT TO BE CONSCIOUS OF DYING. WHICH I FULLY UNDERSTAND.
HE MUST CERTAINLY BE IN A STATE OF PANIC RIGHT NOW...
MOZART FAVOURITES FOR PIANO
HE KNOWS THAT THE MOMENT HE MAKES THE DECISION, I CAN GIVE HIM SOMETHING TO HELP HIM GET THROUGH THIS LAST STAGE. THAT'S WHAT HE ASKED FOR LAST NIGHT.
YES, BUT IF YOU GIVE HIM DRUGS OR WHATEVER, WON'T WE LOSE TOUCH WITH HIM?
SPALDING
MOM... HE'S BEEN SLEEPING AROUND THE CLOCK... HE'S ALREADY GONE!
I GUESS THAT'S TRUE...
SPALDING
I THINK WE SHOULD GO AHEAD AND GIVE HIM WHATEVER HE WANTS! IF YOU KNEW WHAT A PITIFUL STATE HE WAS IN LAST NIGHT!... THERE'S NO DOUBT IN MY MIND: IT'S UP TO HIM. WE HAVE NO SAY.
I AGREE. HE'S THE ONE GOING THROUGH THIS, NOT US.
THEN ALL WE CAN DO IS RESPECT HIS WISHES...
YES, YOU'RE RIGHT...
SPALDING
131

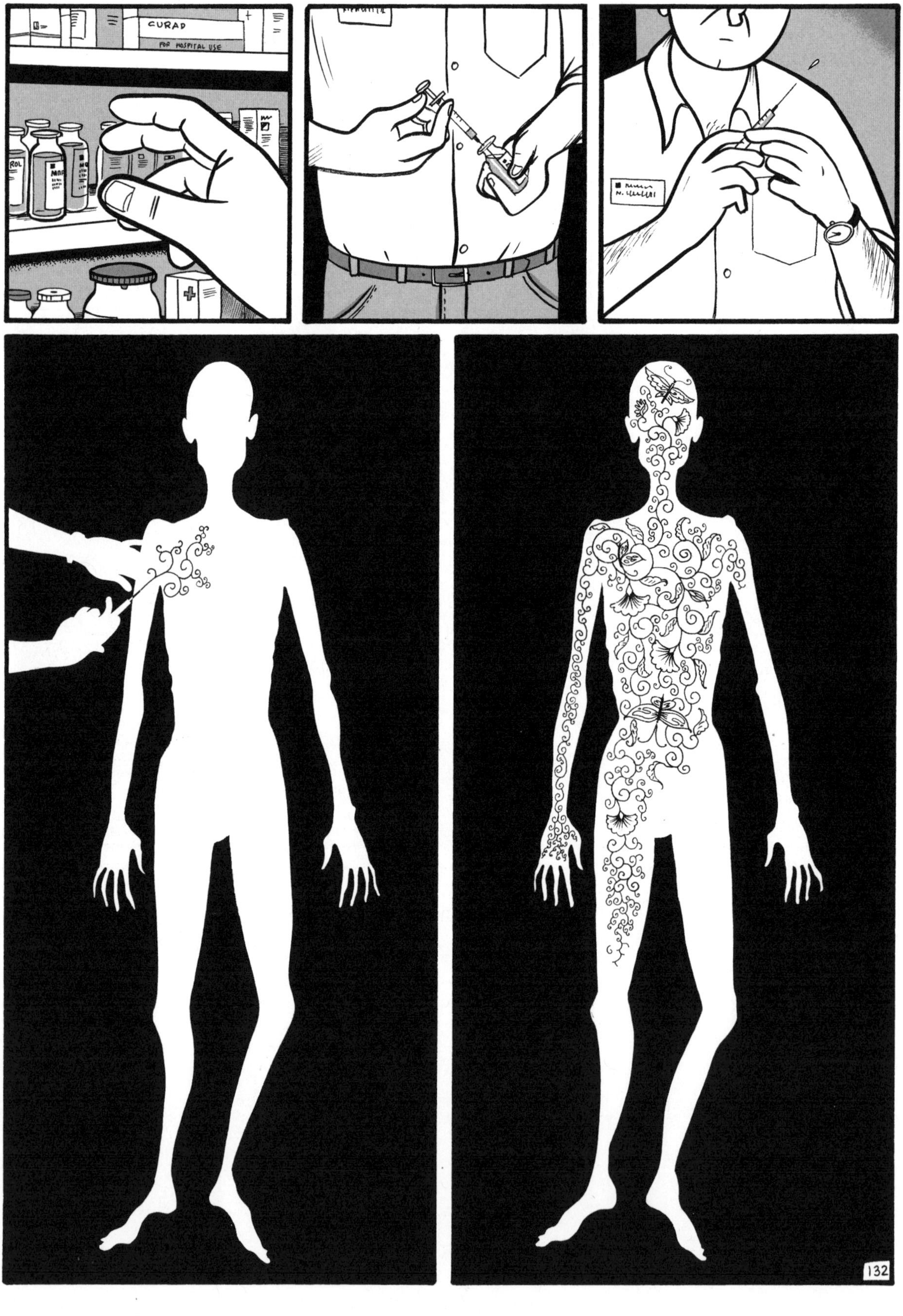
CURAD
FOR HOSPITAL USE
132

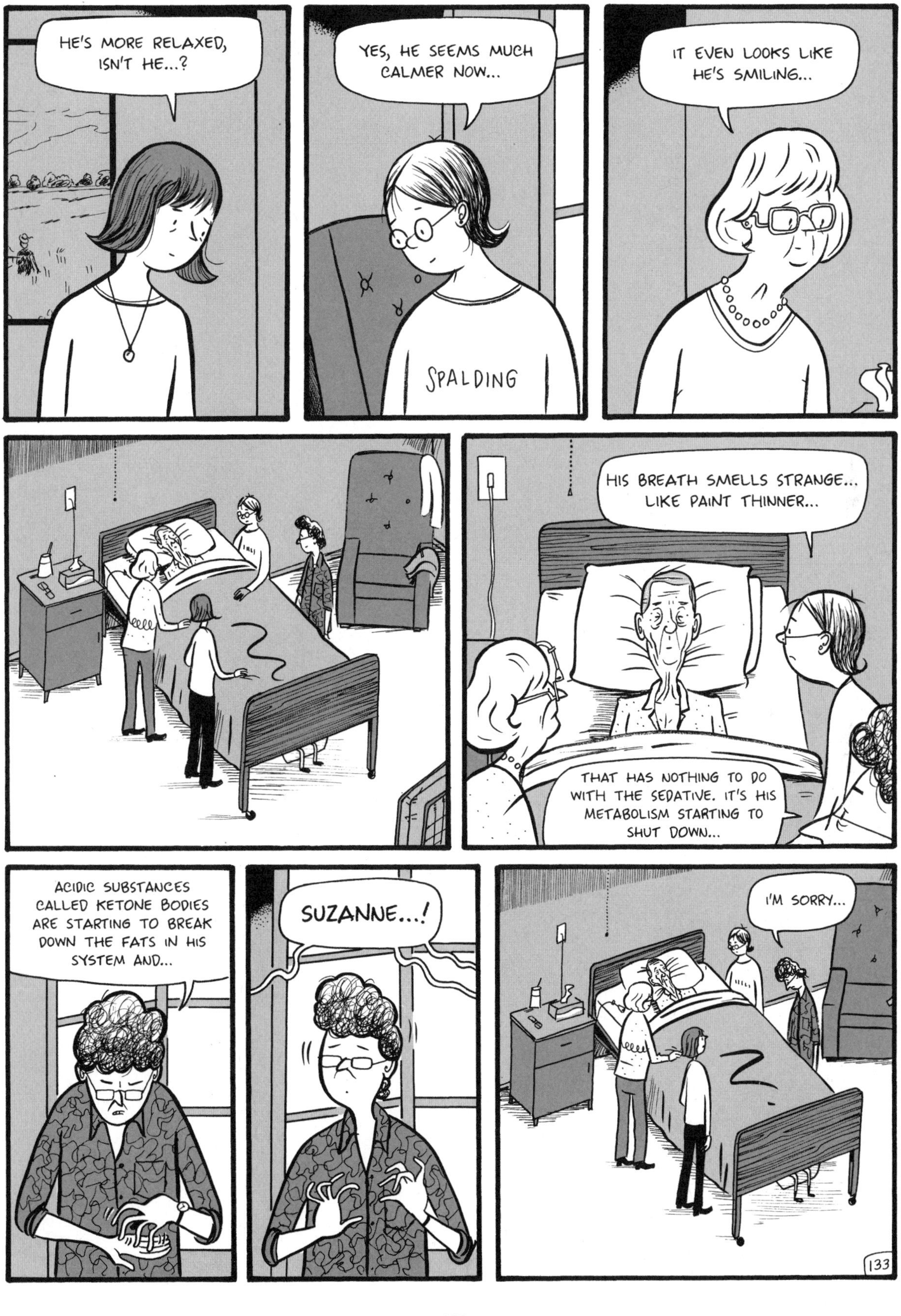
HE'S MORE RELAXED, ISN'T HE...?
YES, HE SEEMS MUCH CALMER NOW...
SPALDING
IT EVEN LOOKS LIKE HE'S SMILING...
HIS BREATH SMELLS STRANGE... LIKE PAINT THINNER...
THAT HAS NOTHING TO DO WITH THE SEDATIVE. IT'S HIS METABOLISM STARTING TO SHUT DOWN...
ACIDIC SUBSTANCES CALLED KETONE BODIES ARE STARTING TO BREAK DOWN THE FATS IN HIS SYSTEM AND...
SUZANNE...!
I'M SORRY...
133

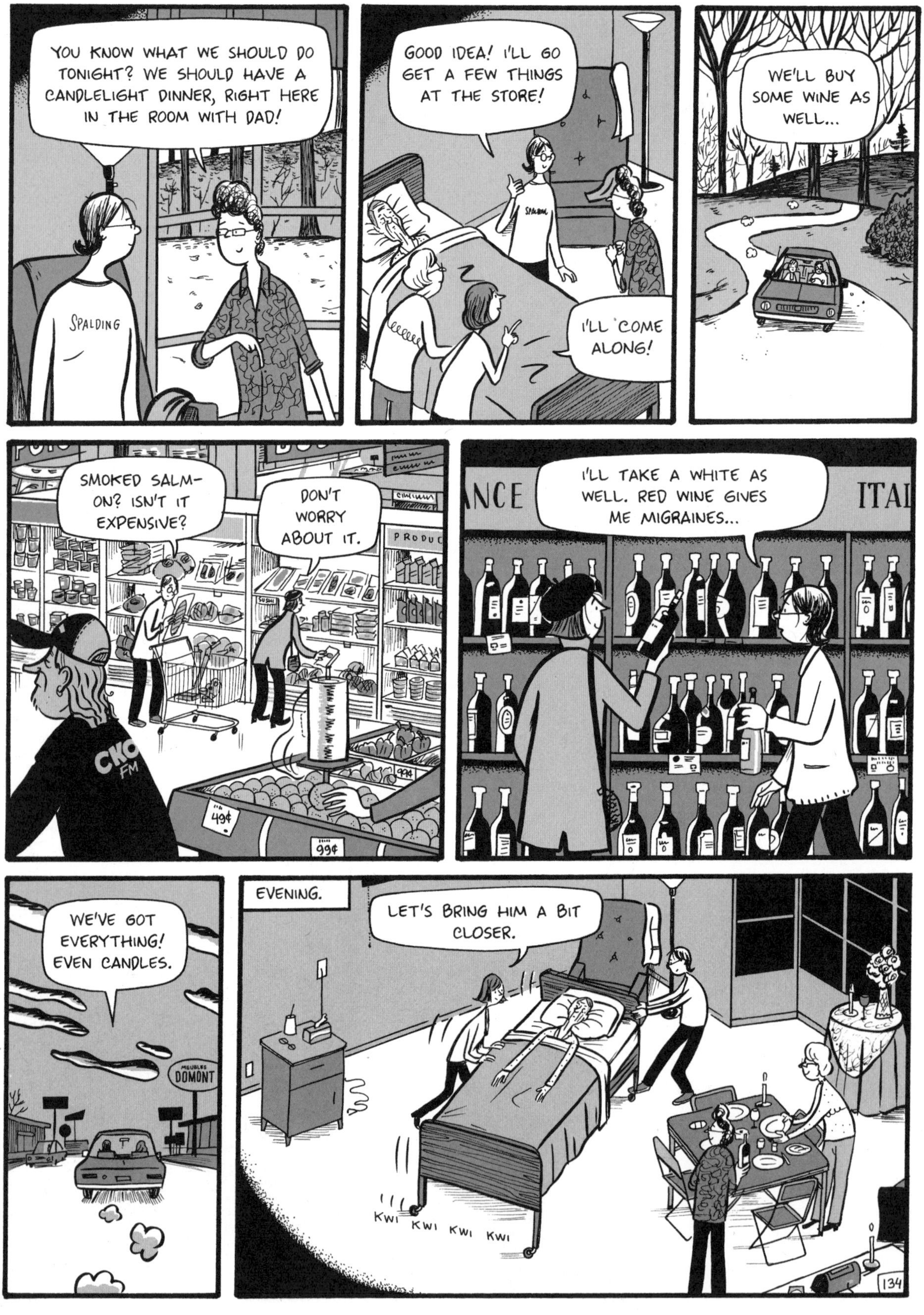
YOU KNOW WHAT WE SHOULD DO TONIGHT? WE SHOULD HAVE A CANDLELIGHT DINNER, RIGHT HERE IN THE ROOM WITH DAD!
SPALDING
GOOD IDEA! I'LL GO GET A FEW THINGS AT THE STORE!
I'LL COME ALONG!
WE'LL BUY SOME WINE AS WELL...
SMOKED SALMON? ISN'T IT EXPENSIVE?
DON'T WORRY ABOUT IT.
CKO FM
49¢
99¢
I'LL TAKE A WHITE AS WELL. RED WINE GIVES ME MIGRAINES...
ITAL
WE'VE GOT EVERYTHING! EVEN CANDLES.
DOMONT
EVENING.
LET'S BRING HIM A BIT CLOSER.
KWI KWI KWI KWI
134

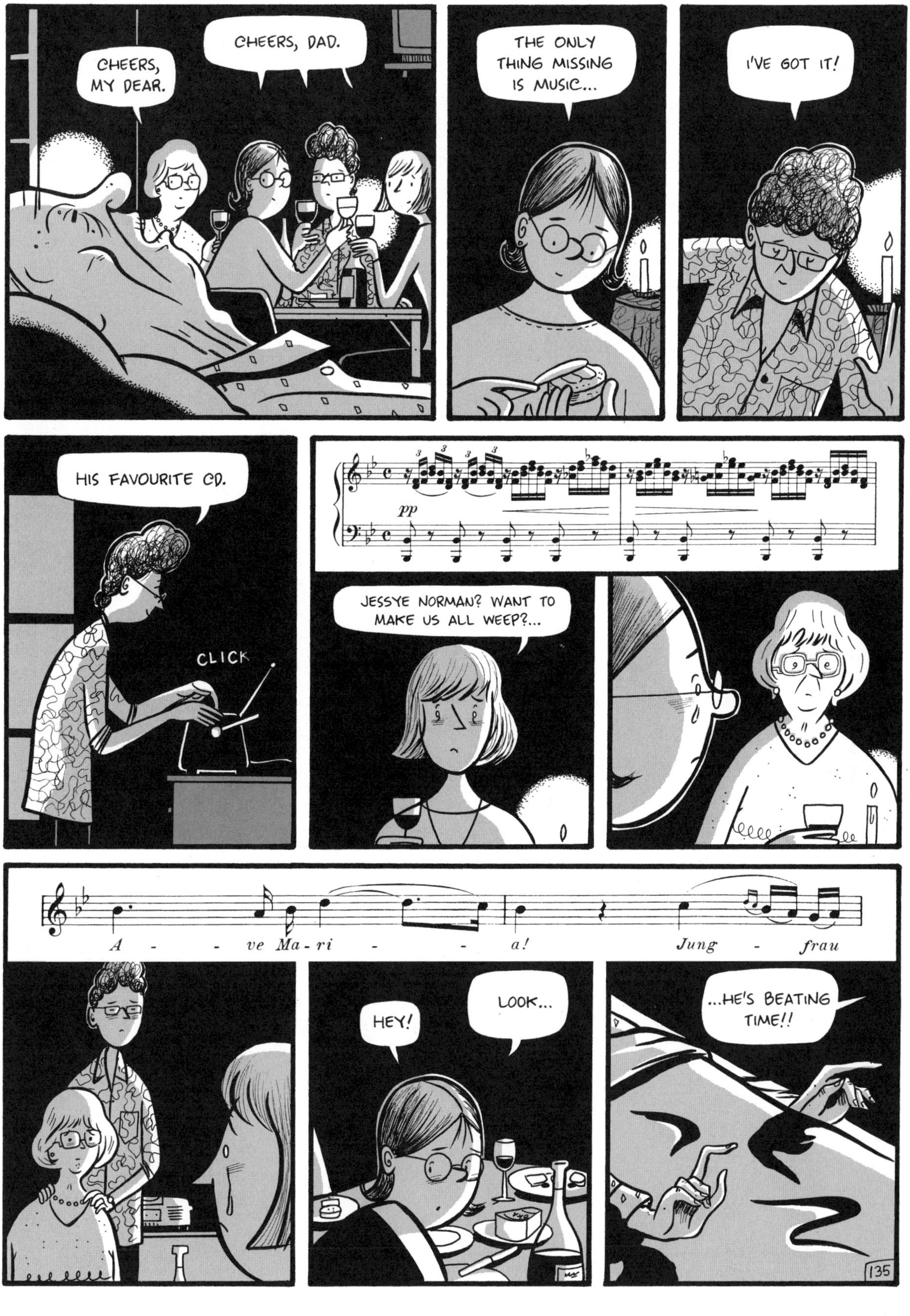
CHEERS, MY DEAR.
CHEERS, DAD.
THE ONLY THING MISSING IS MUSIC...
I'VE GOT IT!
HIS FAVOURITE CD.
CLICK
pp
JESSYE NORMAN? WANT TO MAKE US ALL WEEP?...
A - - ve Ma - ri - - a! Jung - frau
HEY!
LOOK...
...HE'S BEATING TIME!!
135

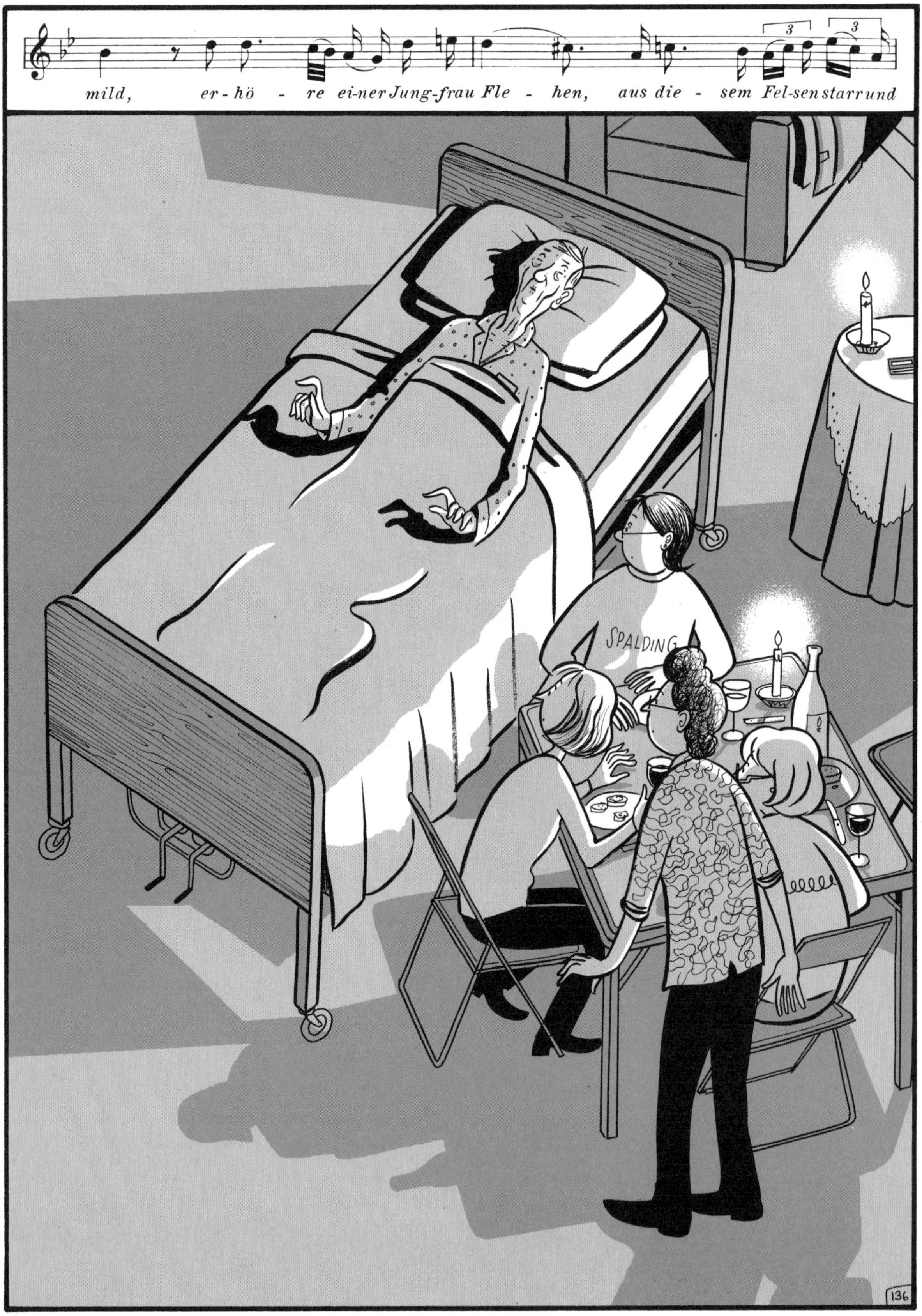
mild, er - hö - re ei-ner Jung-frau Fle - hen, aus die - sem Fel-sen starr und
SPALDING
136

Saturday

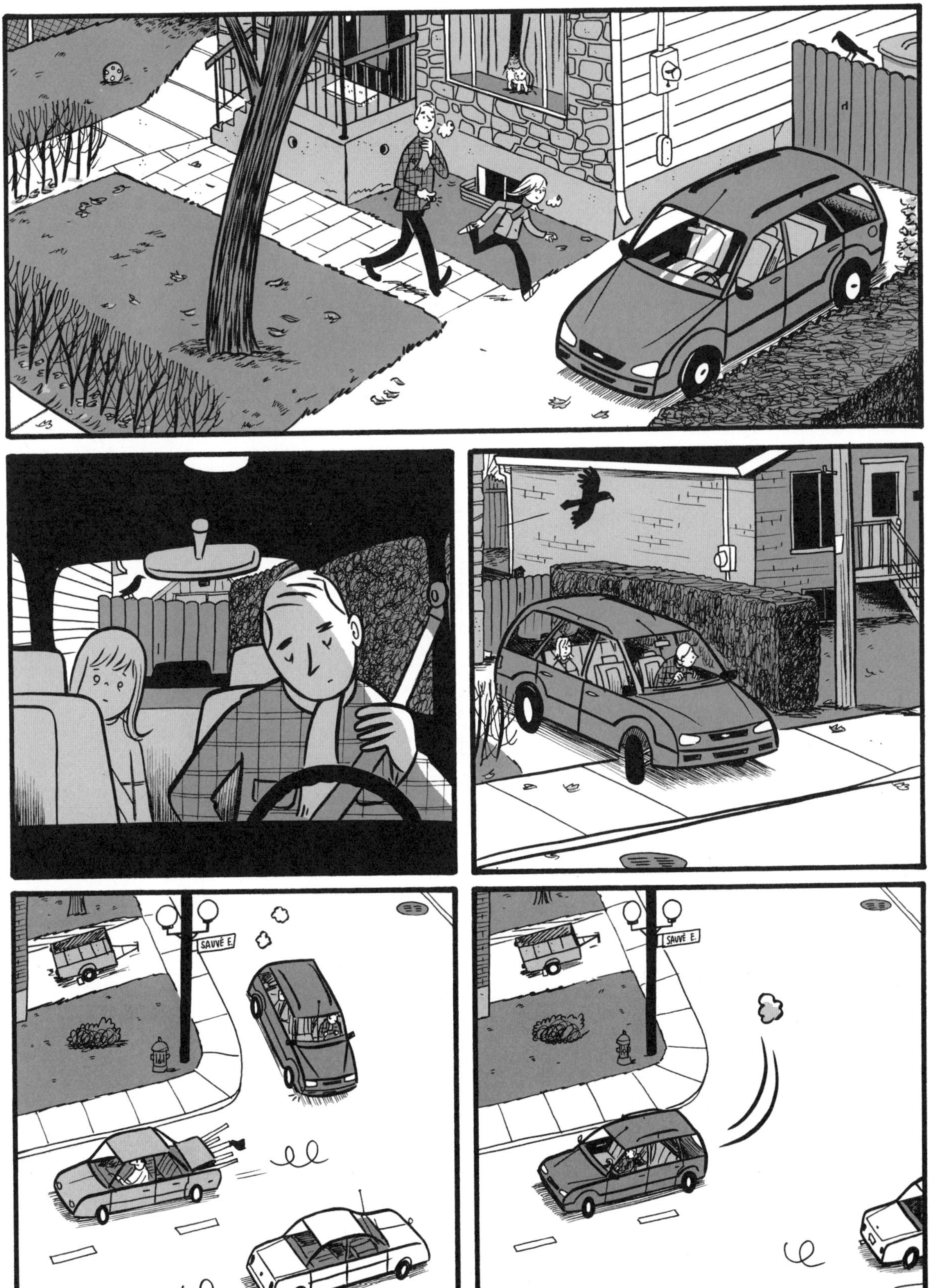
SAUVÉ E.
SAUVÉ E.
137

COLLEGE AHUNTSIC
Ultramar
88.7
EPANNEUR
DU COIN
Saint-Hubert
Legendre
Ultrama
SPECIAL
1.99
ROBERT
ROBERT
40
OUEST
EST
RANSPORT SPECIA
S ET LÉGUME
AL · QUÉBEC · MOUS
50) 992-600
Tunnel Louis-H.-
LaFontaine
SOYEZ VISIBLES
138

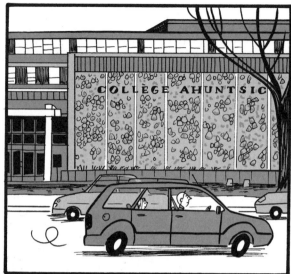

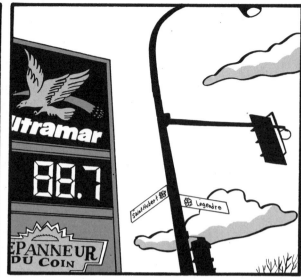

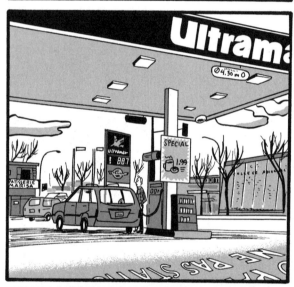

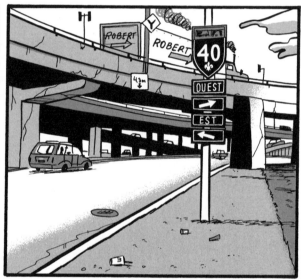

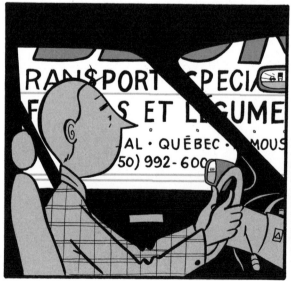

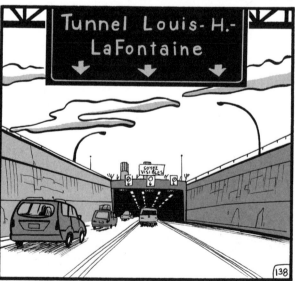

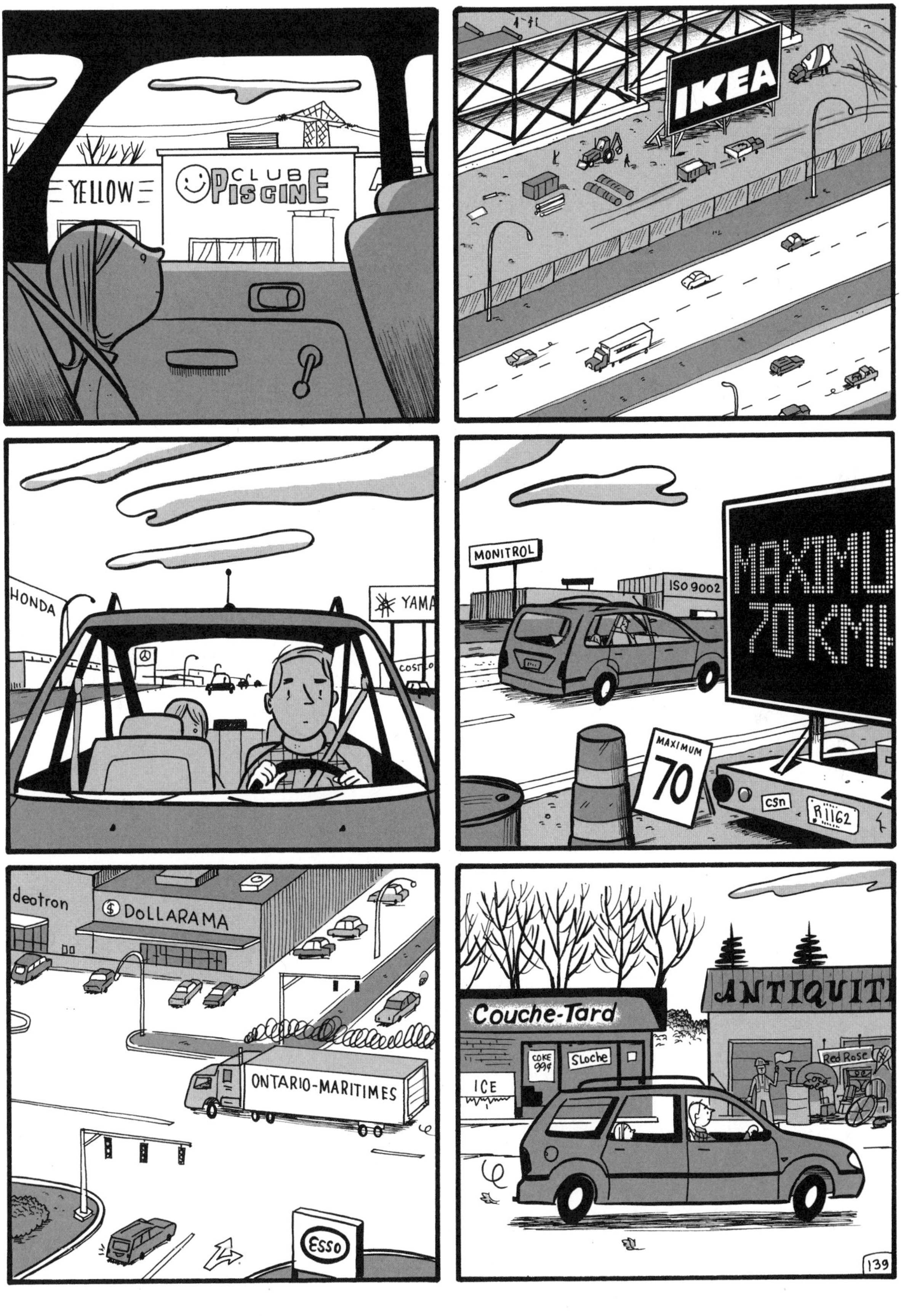
YELLOW
CLUB PISCINE
IKEA
HONDA
YAMA
MONITROL
ISO 9002
MAXIMU
70 KM
MAXIMUM
70
CSN
R1162
deotron
DOLLARAMA
ONTARIO-MARITIMES
ESSO
Couche-Tard
COKE 99¢
Sloche
ICE
ANTIQUIT
Red Rose
139

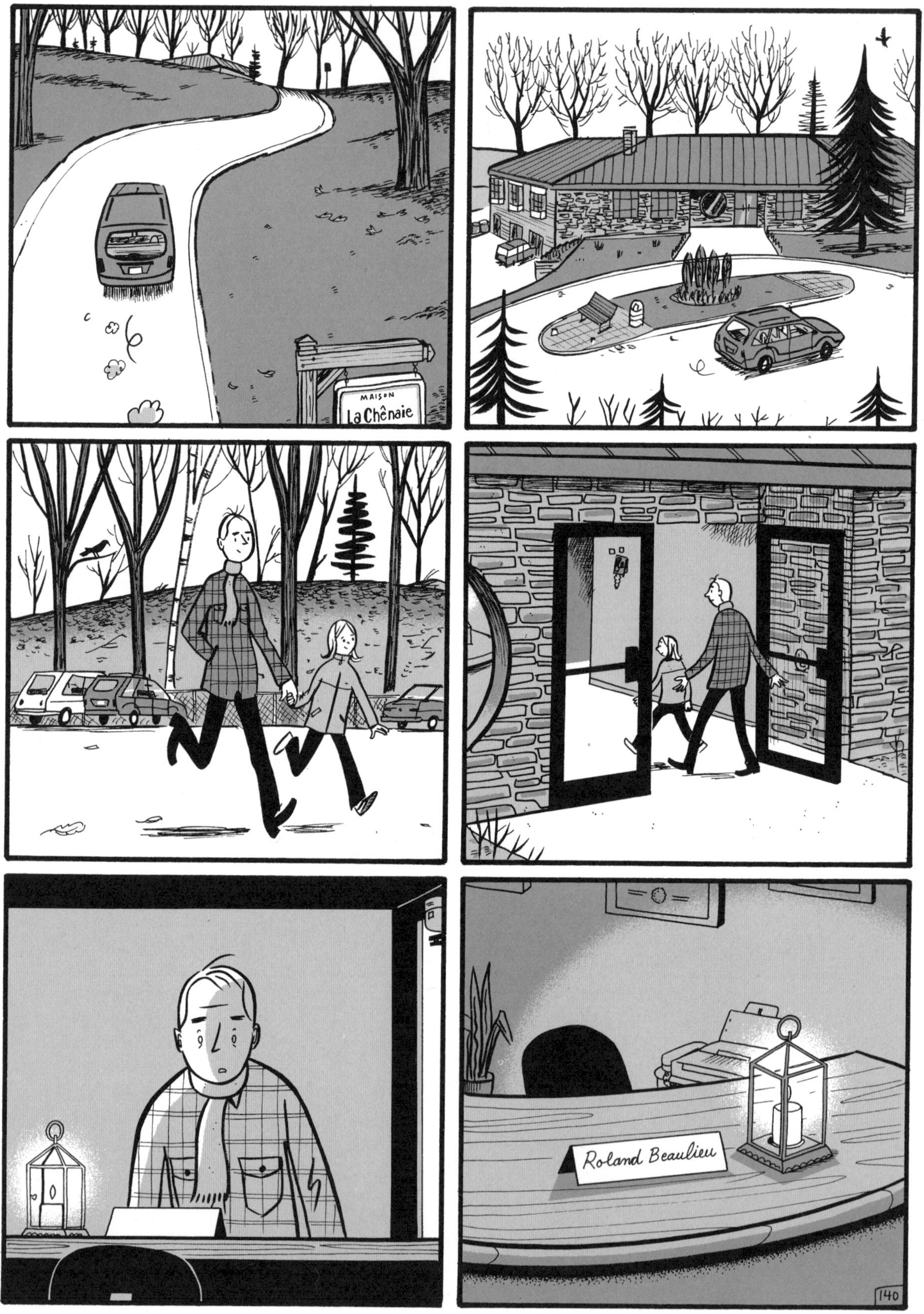
MAISON
La Chênaie
Roland Beaulieu
140

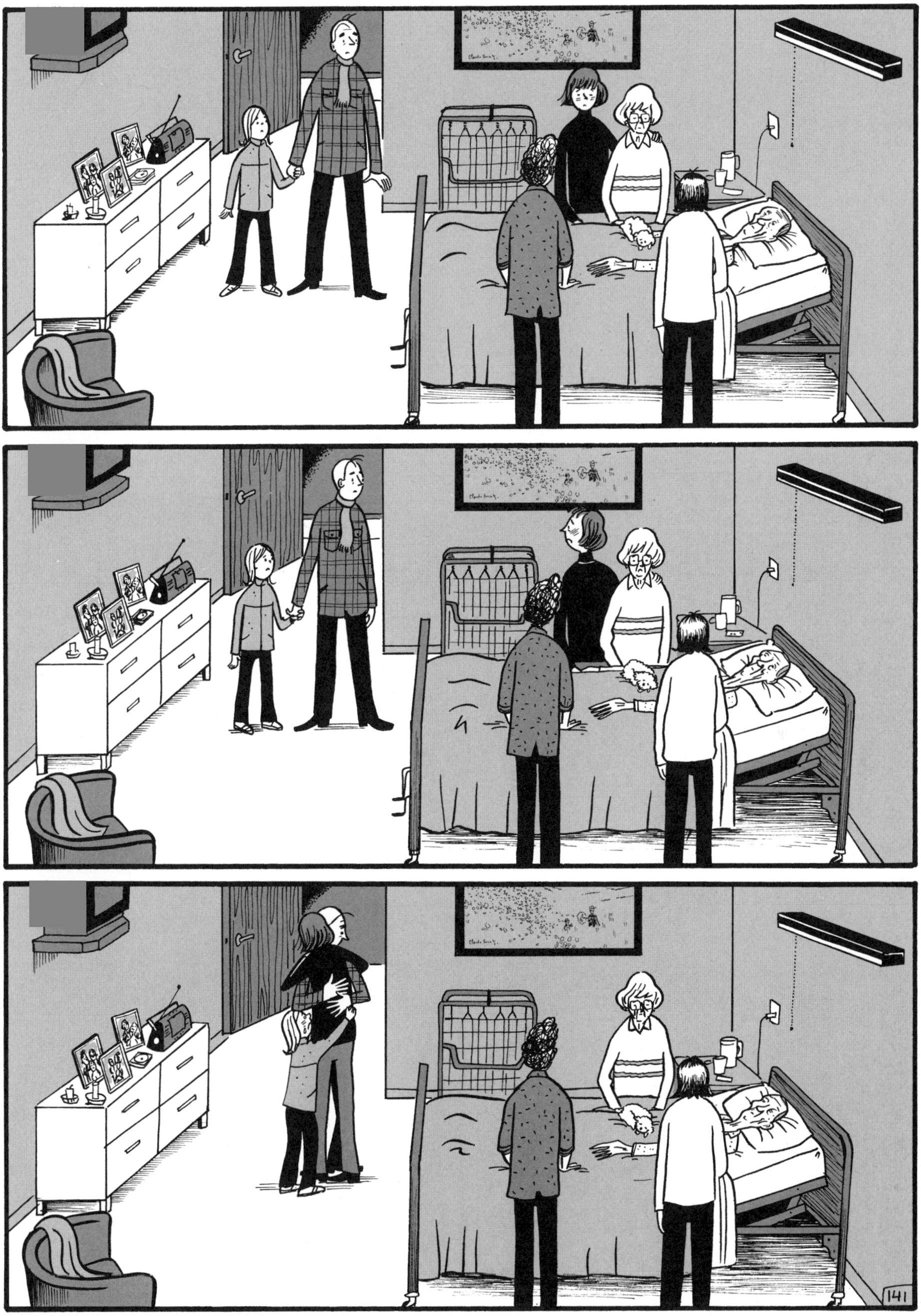
141

WE STAYED THERE FOR A WHILE, STANDING IN SILENCE, CONTEMPLATING ROLAND.

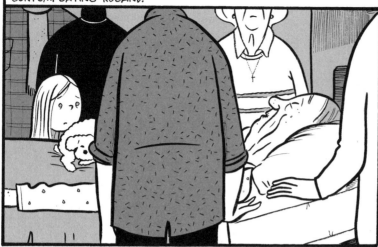

HE LOOKED WELL. IN FACT, HE LOOKED BETTER DEAD THAN HE HAD ALIVE. HIS FACE CONVEYED A REAL SENSE OF RELEASE AND RELIEF.

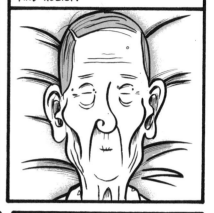

ROLAND, THE MAN WHO NEVER LEFT ANYTHING TO CHANCE, HAD PLANNED HIS "AFTER DEATH" WITH CARE.

DETAILED INSTRUCTIONS WERE NOTED ON A BLUE SHEET OF PAPER LEFT FOR US IN PLAIN VIEW IN HIS NIGHT TABLE DRAWER.

THE HEADING READ: "TO DO AFTER MY DEATH."

1) CALL REQUIEM FUNERAL HOME AT (450) 555-1212.

ALL WE NEEDED TO DO WAS FOLLOW HIS INSTRUCTIONS, AND THE WHOLE PROCESS, FROM THE TRANSFER OF THE BODY THROUGH TO THE FUNERAL SERVICE AND BURIAL, WOULD BE SET IN MOTION AUTOMATICALLY.

AND INDEED, A HALF-HOUR AFTER WE CALLED, TWO EMPLOYEES FROM THE REQUIEM FUNERAL HOME ARRIVED IN A DARK VAN.

142

ONE OF THEM PLACED A ROSE ON ROLAND'S CHEST AND SPOKE A FEW WORDS TO MARK THE OCCASION.

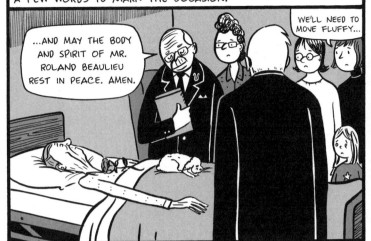

...AND MAY THE BODY AND SPIRIT OF MR. ROLAND BEAULIEU REST IN PEACE. AMEN.

WE'LL NEED TO MOVE FLUFFY...

WE LEFT THE ROOM SO WE WOULDN'T HAVE TO SEE THEM PLACE THE BODY IN THE BAG.

C'MON, ROSE, WE'LL LET THEM TAKE CARE OF GRAMPA...

WHAT'RE THEY DOING TO HIM?

AND THEN WE WATCHED THE VAN LEAVE.

CLANG.

RRRRR

143

WE RETURNED TO THE ROOM.

SUDDENLY, IT NO LONGER HAD THE SAME MEANING. WITH ITS CENTRE OF INTEREST GONE, IT WAS A SIMPLE HOSPITAL ROOM AGAIN.

THERE WAS NOTHING LEFT FOR US TO DO THERE.

DO YOU HAVE ANY SPACE LEFT IN THERE?

YES, PLENTY.

WE EMPTIED THE WHOLE ROOM IN LESS THAN FIVE MINUTES.

SCRABBLE

I WANT HIS HAT!

EXIT ▶

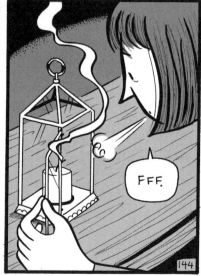

FFF.

144

Epilogue

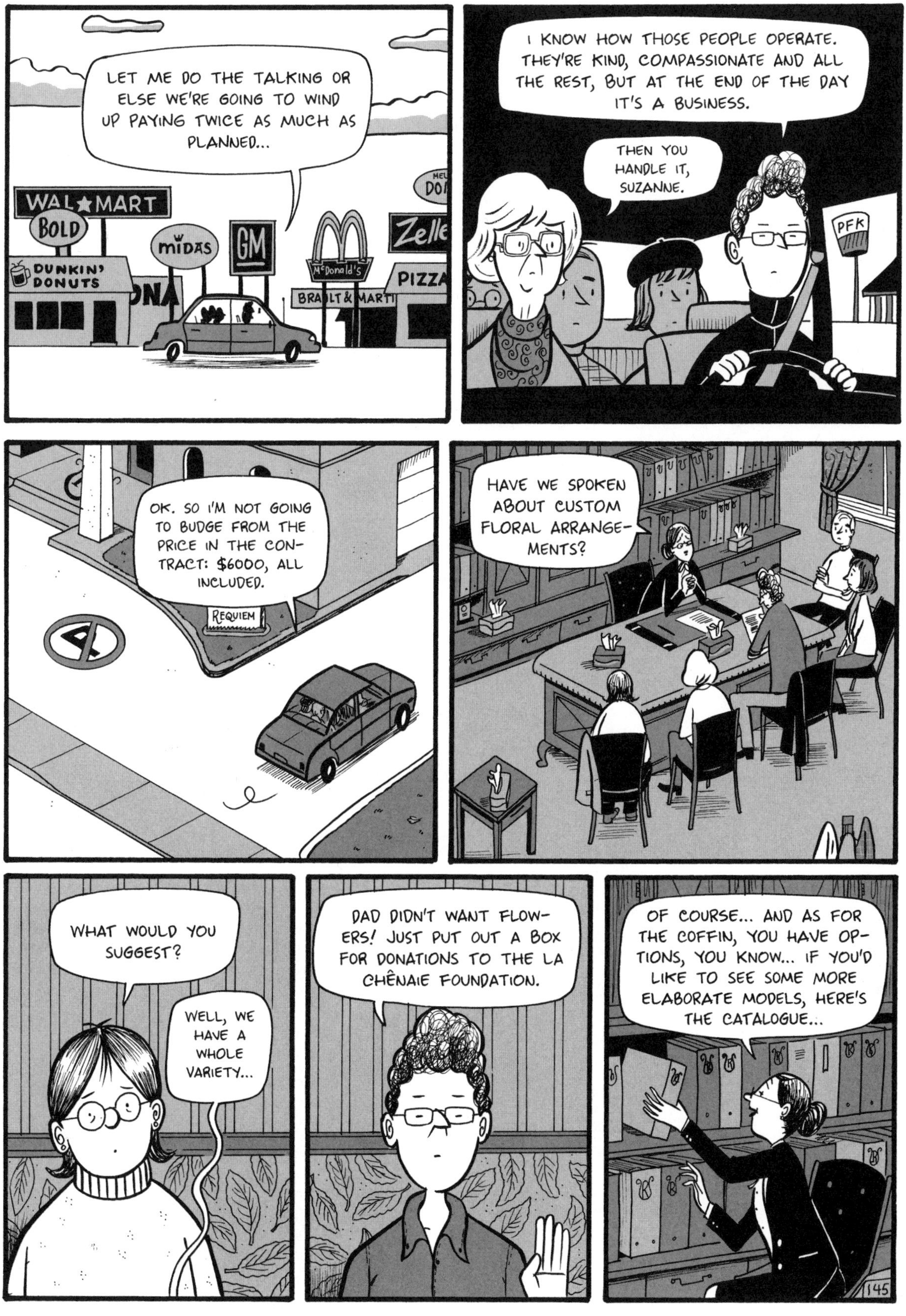
LET ME DO THE TALKING OR ELSE WE'RE GOING TO WIND UP PAYING TWICE AS MUCH AS PLANNED...
WAL★MART
BOLD
DUNKIN' DONUTS
midas
GM
McDonald's
Zellers
PIZZA
BRAULT & MARTINEAU
I KNOW HOW THOSE PEOPLE OPERATE. THEY'RE KIND, COMPASSIONATE AND ALL THE REST, BUT AT THE END OF THE DAY IT'S A BUSINESS.
THEN YOU HANDLE IT, SUZANNE.
PFK
OK. SO I'M NOT GOING TO BUDGE FROM THE PRICE IN THE CONTRACT: $6000, ALL INCLUDED.
REQUIEM
HAVE WE SPOKEN ABOUT CUSTOM FLORAL ARRANGEMENTS?
WHAT WOULD YOU SUGGEST?
WELL, WE HAVE A WHOLE VARIETY...
DAD DIDN'T WANT FLOWERS! JUST PUT OUT A BOX FOR DONATIONS TO THE LA CHÊNAIE FOUNDATION.
OF COURSE... AND AS FOR THE COFFIN, YOU HAVE OPTIONS, YOU KNOW... IF YOU'D LIKE TO SEE SOME MORE ELABORATE MODELS, HERE'S THE CATALOGUE...
145

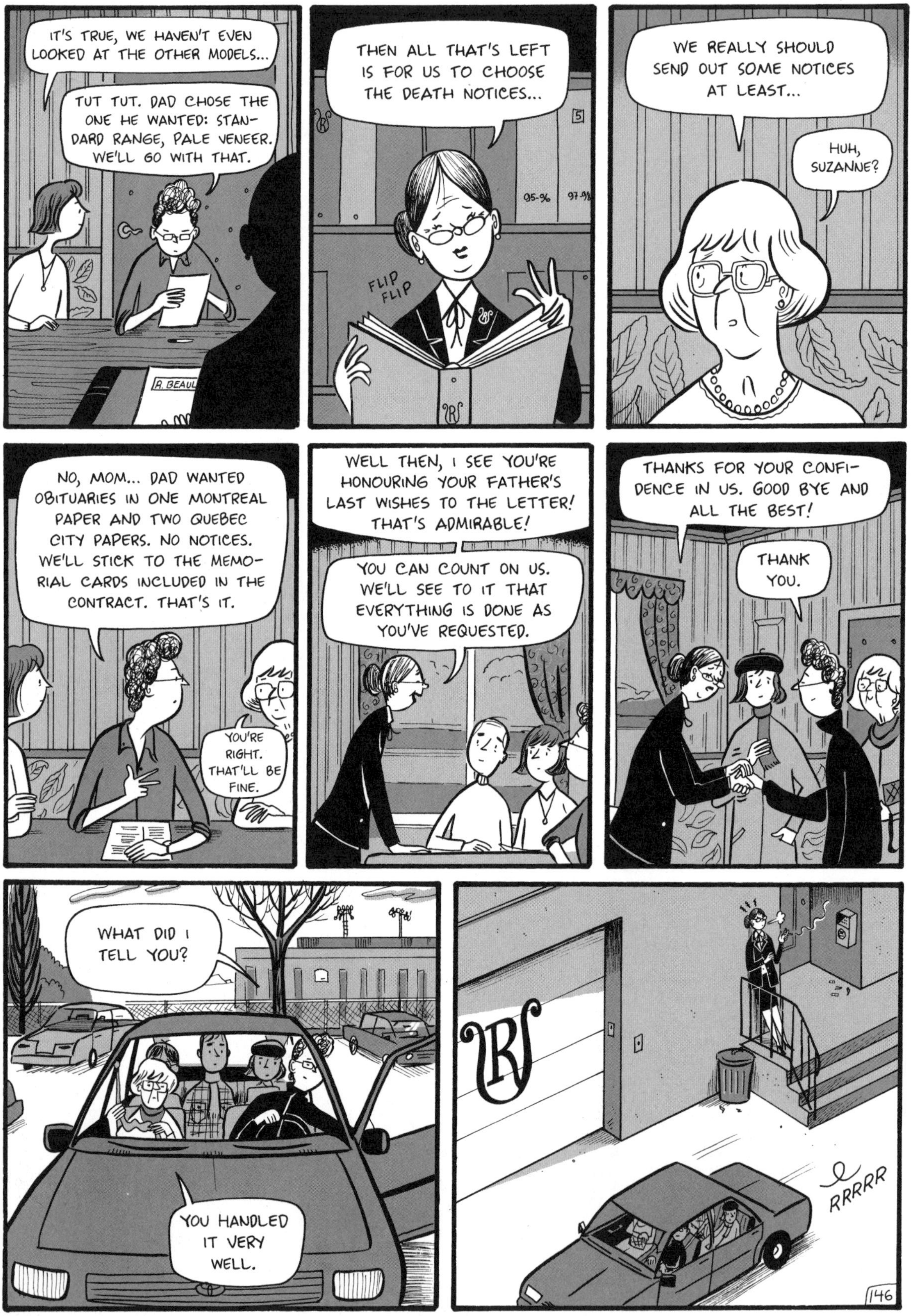

IT'S TRUE, WE HAVEN'T EVEN LOOKED AT THE OTHER MODELS...
TUT TUT. DAD CHOSE THE ONE HE WANTED: STANDARD RANGE, PALE VENEER. WE'LL GO WITH THAT.
A. BEAUL
THEN ALL THAT'S LEFT IS FOR US TO CHOOSE THE DEATH NOTICES...
FLIP FLIP
WE REALLY SHOULD SEND OUT SOME NOTICES AT LEAST...
HUH, SUZANNE?
NO, MOM... DAD WANTED OBITUARIES IN ONE MONTREAL PAPER AND TWO QUEBEC CITY PAPERS. NO NOTICES. WE'LL STICK TO THE MEMORIAL CARDS INCLUDED IN THE CONTRACT. THAT'S IT.
YOU'RE RIGHT. THAT'LL BE FINE.
WELL THEN, I SEE YOU'RE HONOURING YOUR FATHER'S LAST WISHES TO THE LETTER! THAT'S ADMIRABLE!
YOU CAN COUNT ON US. WE'LL SEE TO IT THAT EVERYTHING IS DONE AS YOU'VE REQUESTED.
THANKS FOR YOUR CONFIDENCE IN US. GOOD BYE AND ALL THE BEST!
THANK YOU.
WHAT DID I TELL YOU?
YOU HANDLED IT VERY WELL.
RRRRR
146

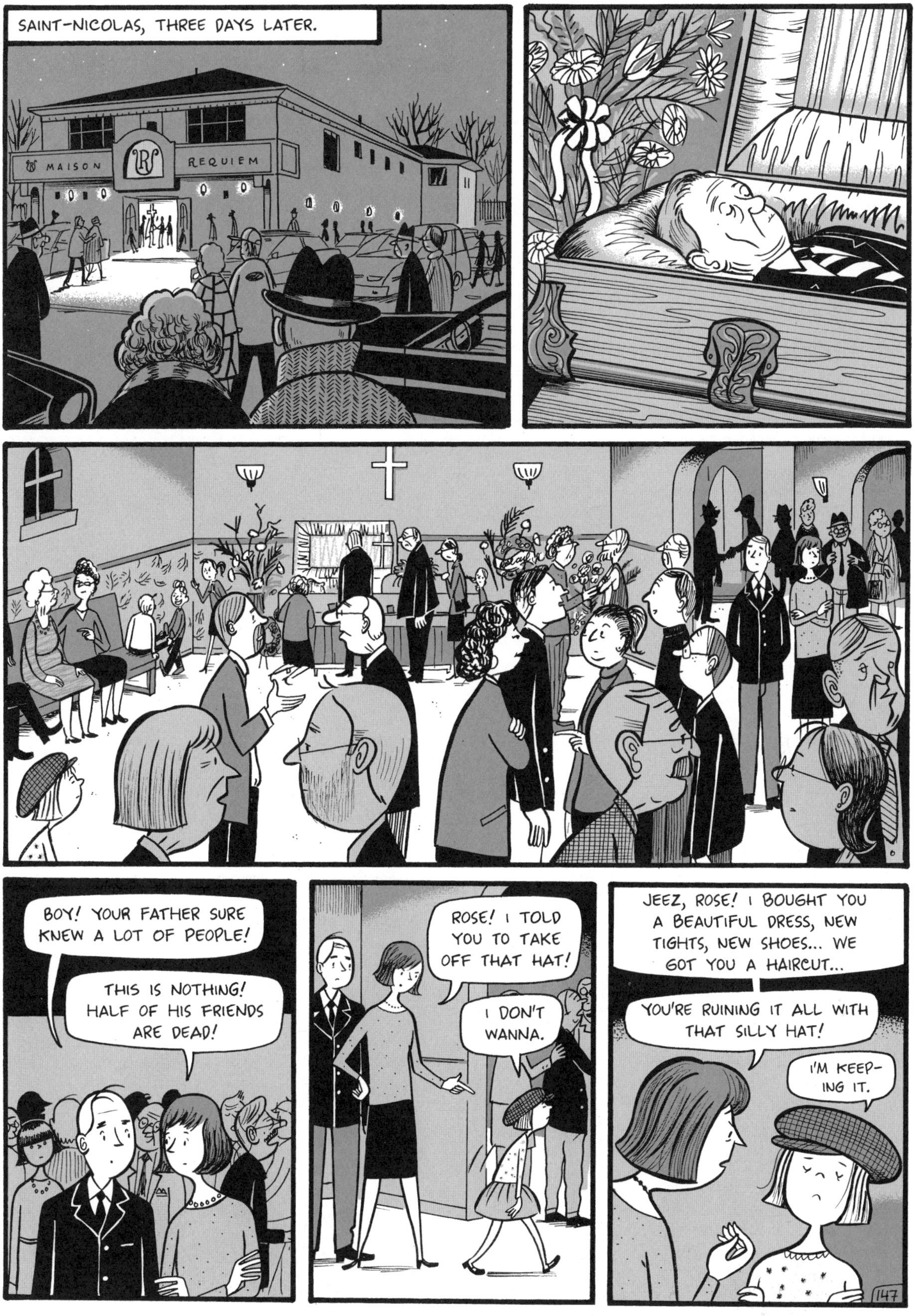
SAINT-NICOLAS, THREE DAYS LATER.
MAISON REQUIEM
BOY! YOUR FATHER SURE KNEW A LOT OF PEOPLE!
THIS IS NOTHING! HALF OF HIS FRIENDS ARE DEAD!
ROSE! I TOLD YOU TO TAKE OFF THAT HAT!
I DON'T WANNA.
JEEZ, ROSE! I BOUGHT YOU A BEAUTIFUL DRESS, NEW TIGHTS, NEW SHOES... WE GOT YOU A HAIRCUT...
YOU'RE RUINING IT ALL WITH THAT SILLY HAT!
I'M KEEP-ING IT.
147

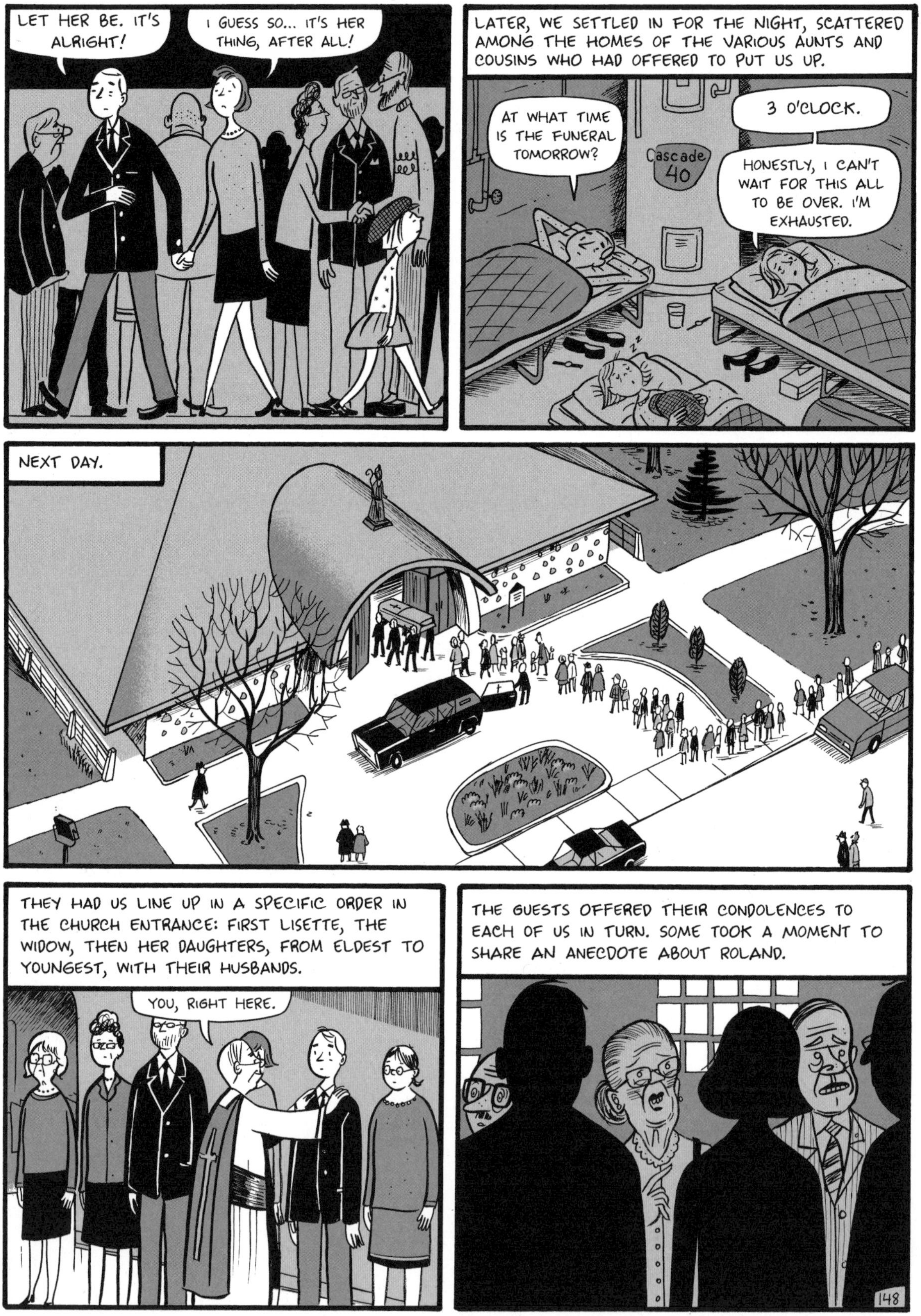
LET HER BE. IT'S ALRIGHT!
I GUESS SO... IT'S HER THING, AFTER ALL!
LATER, WE SETTLED IN FOR THE NIGHT, SCATTERED AMONG THE HOMES OF THE VARIOUS AUNTS AND COUSINS WHO HAD OFFERED TO PUT US UP.
AT WHAT TIME IS THE FUNERAL TOMORROW?
Cascade 40
3 O'CLOCK.
HONESTLY, I CAN'T WAIT FOR THIS ALL TO BE OVER. I'M EXHAUSTED.
NEXT DAY.
THEY HAD US LINE UP IN A SPECIFIC ORDER IN THE CHURCH ENTRANCE: FIRST LISETTE, THE WIDOW, THEN HER DAUGHTERS, FROM ELDEST TO YOUNGEST, WITH THEIR HUSBANDS.
YOU, RIGHT HERE.
THE GUESTS OFFERED THEIR CONDOLENCES TO EACH OF US IN TURN. SOME TOOK A MOMENT TO SHARE AN ANECDOTE ABOUT ROLAND.
148

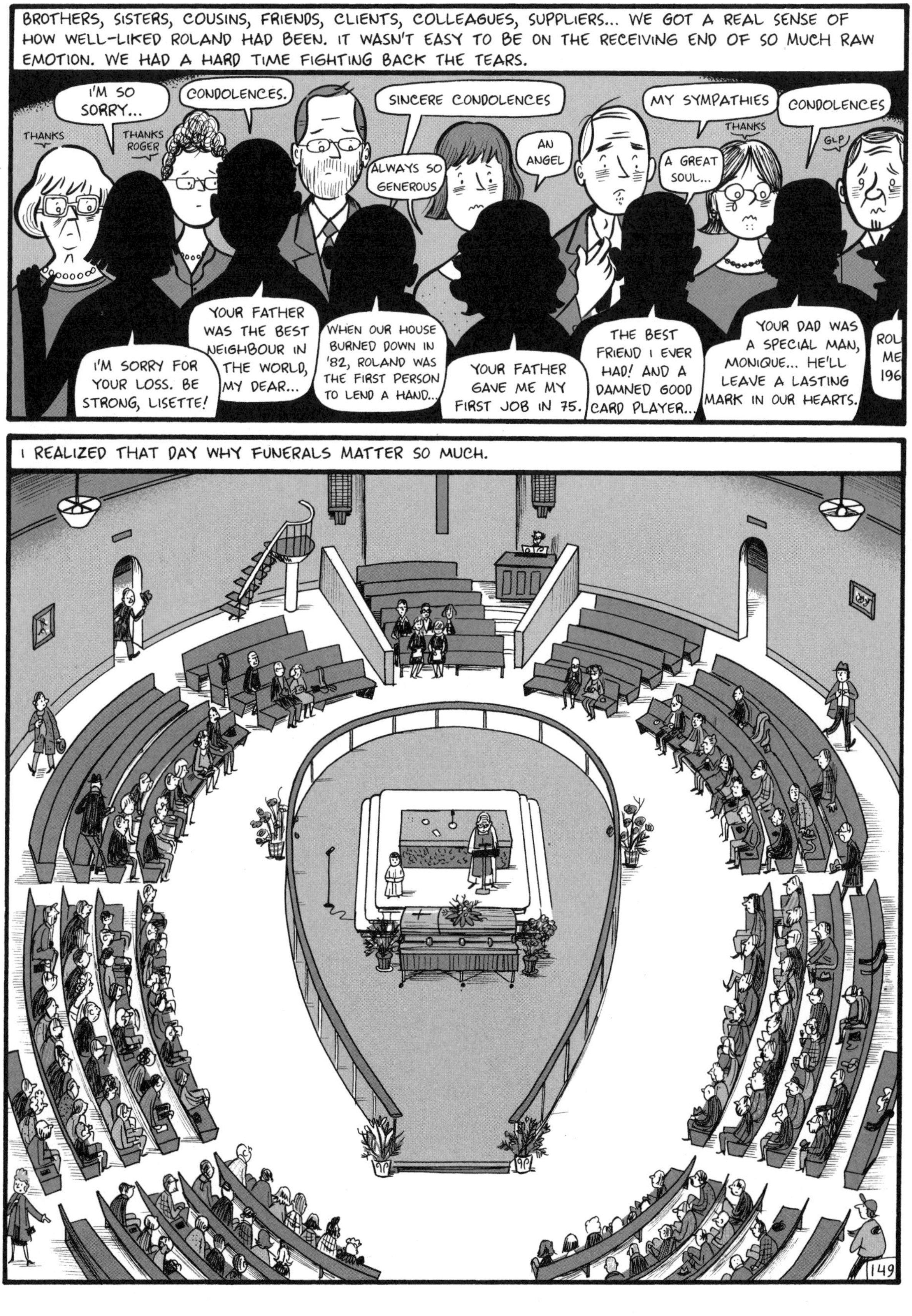
BROTHERS, SISTERS, COUSINS, FRIENDS, CLIENTS, COLLEAGUES, SUPPLIERS... WE GOT A REAL SENSE OF HOW WELL-LIKED ROLAND HAD BEEN. IT WASN'T EASY TO BE ON THE RECEIVING END OF SO MUCH RAW EMOTION. WE HAD A HARD TIME FIGHTING BACK THE TEARS.
THANKS
I'M SO SORRY...
THANKS ROGER
CONDOLENCES.
SINCERE CONDOLENCES
ALWAYS SO GENEROUS
AN ANGEL
MY SYMPATHIES
A GREAT SOUL...
THANKS
CONDOLENCES
GLP
I'M SORRY FOR YOUR LOSS. BE STRONG, LISETTE!
YOUR FATHER WAS THE BEST NEIGHBOUR IN THE WORLD, MY DEAR...
WHEN OUR HOUSE BURNED DOWN IN '82, ROLAND WAS THE FIRST PERSON TO LEND A HAND...
YOUR FATHER GAVE ME MY FIRST JOB IN 75.
THE BEST FRIEND I EVER HAD! AND A DAMNED GOOD CARD PLAYER...
YOUR DAD WAS A SPECIAL MAN, MONIQUE... HE'LL LEAVE A LASTING MARK IN OUR HEARTS.
I REALIZED THAT DAY WHY FUNERALS MATTER SO MUCH.
149

THE PRIEST BEGAN HIS MASS. UNFORTUNATELY, HE HADN'T NOTED THE DECEASED'S NAME PROPERLY...

YES...YOUR LOVED ONES ARE HERE FOR YOU, RONALD...

ROLAND!

...AND NOW, IF YOU WOULD JOIN ME IN LISTENING TO A FEW SONGS INTERPRETED BY OUR CHOIR FOR RONALD...

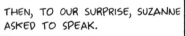

In paradisum deducant angeli in tuo adventu suscipiant te martyres...

THEN, TO OUR SURPRISE, SUZANNE ASKED TO SPEAK.

SUZANNE PREPARED A TALK?

I DON'T KNOW...

SHE STEPPED UP TO THE LECTERN, VERY SIMPLY, WITH HER HANDS BEHIND HER BACK AND A SMILE ON HER FACE.

HELLO.

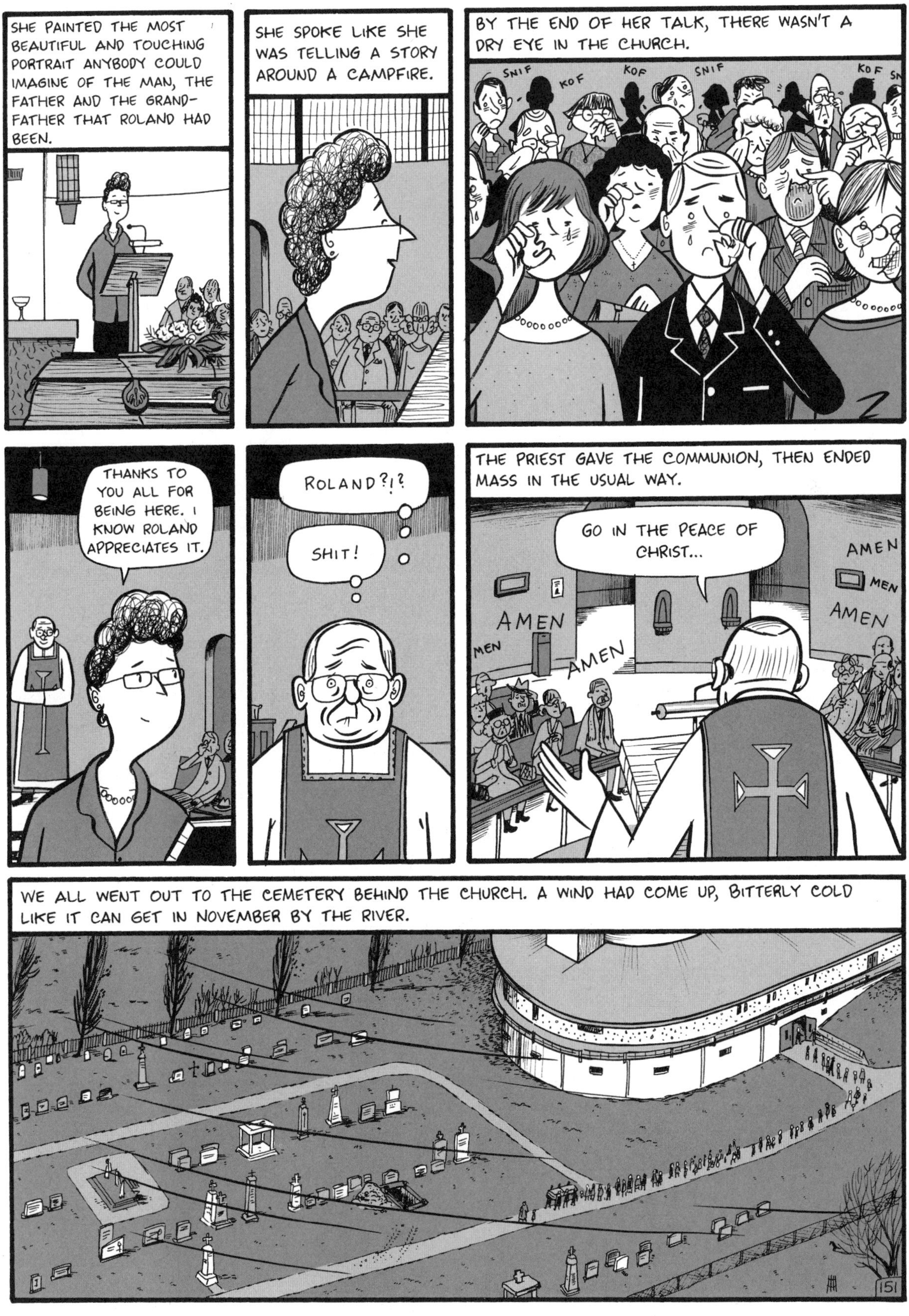
SHE PAINTED THE MOST BEAUTIFUL AND TOUCHING PORTRAIT ANYBODY COULD IMAGINE OF THE MAN, THE FATHER AND THE GRAND-FATHER THAT ROLAND HAD BEEN.
SHE SPOKE LIKE SHE WAS TELLING A STORY AROUND A CAMPFIRE.
BY THE END OF HER TALK, THERE WASN'T A DRY EYE IN THE CHURCH.
SNIF
KOF
KOF
SNIF
KOF
THANKS TO YOU ALL FOR BEING HERE. I KNOW ROLAND APPRECIATES IT.
ROLAND?!?
SHIT!
THE PRIEST GAVE THE COMMUNION, THEN ENDED MASS IN THE USUAL WAY.
GO IN THE PEACE OF CHRIST...
AMEN
MEN
AMEN
MEN
AMEN
AMEN
WE ALL WENT OUT TO THE CEMETERY BEHIND THE CHURCH. A WIND HAD COME UP, BITTERLY COLD LIKE IT CAN GET IN NOVEMBER BY THE RIVER.
151

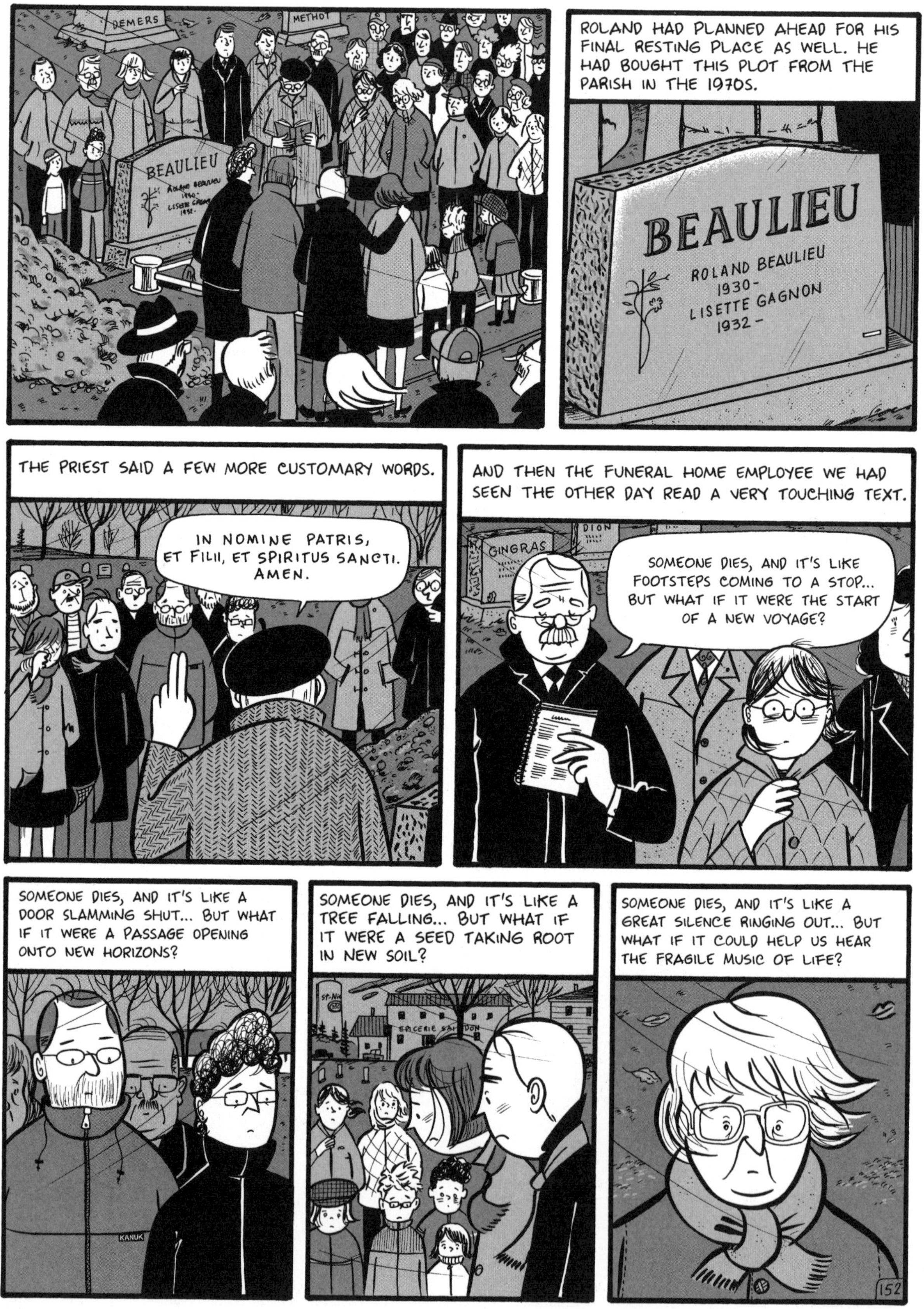
DEMERS
METHOT
BEAULIEU
ROLAND HAD PLANNED AHEAD FOR HIS FINAL RESTING PLACE AS WELL. HE HAD BOUGHT THIS PLOT FROM THE PARISH IN THE 1970S.
BEAULIEU
ROLAND BEAULIEU
1930-
LISETTE GAGNON
1932 -
THE PRIEST SAID A FEW MORE CUSTOMARY WORDS.
IN NOMINE PATRIS, ET FILII, ET SPIRITUS SANCTI. AMEN.
AND THEN THE FUNERAL HOME EMPLOYEE WE HAD SEEN THE OTHER DAY READ A VERY TOUCHING TEXT.
GINGRAS
DION
SOMEONE DIES, AND IT'S LIKE FOOTSTEPS COMING TO A STOP... BUT WHAT IF IT WERE THE START OF A NEW VOYAGE?
SOMEONE DIES, AND IT'S LIKE A DOOR SLAMMING SHUT... BUT WHAT IF IT WERE A PASSAGE OPENING ONTO NEW HORIZONS?
KANUK
SOMEONE DIES, AND IT'S LIKE A TREE FALLING... BUT WHAT IF IT WERE A SEED TAKING ROOT IN NEW SOIL?
SOMEONE DIES, AND IT'S LIKE A GREAT SILENCE RINGING OUT... BUT WHAT IF IT COULD HELP US HEAR THE FRAGILE MUSIC OF LIFE?
152

FRAC
FRAC
FROK
153

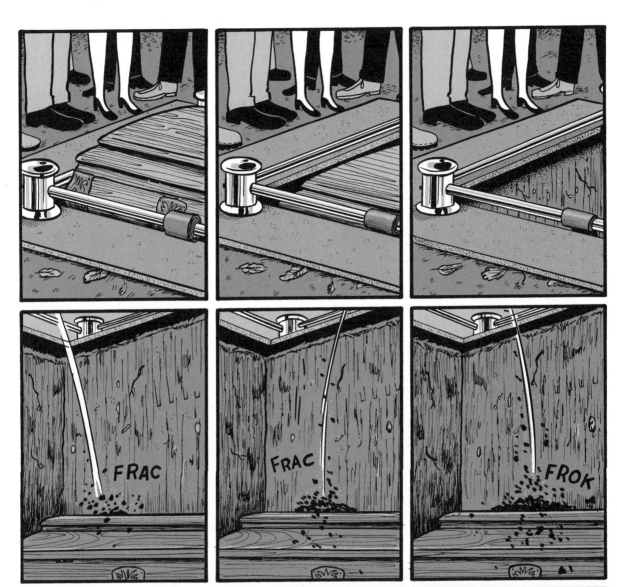

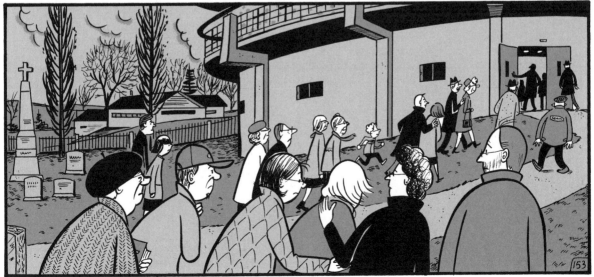

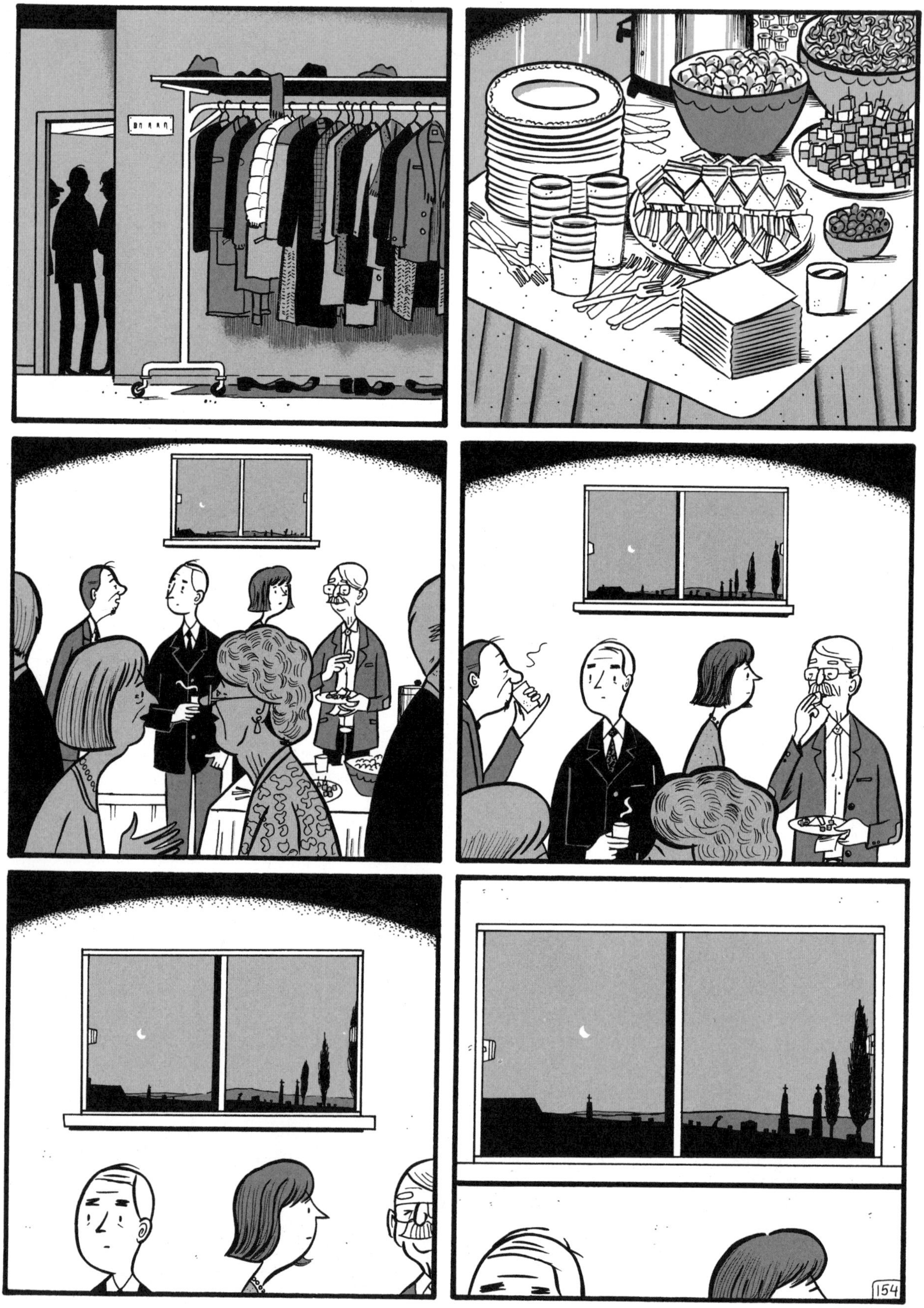
154

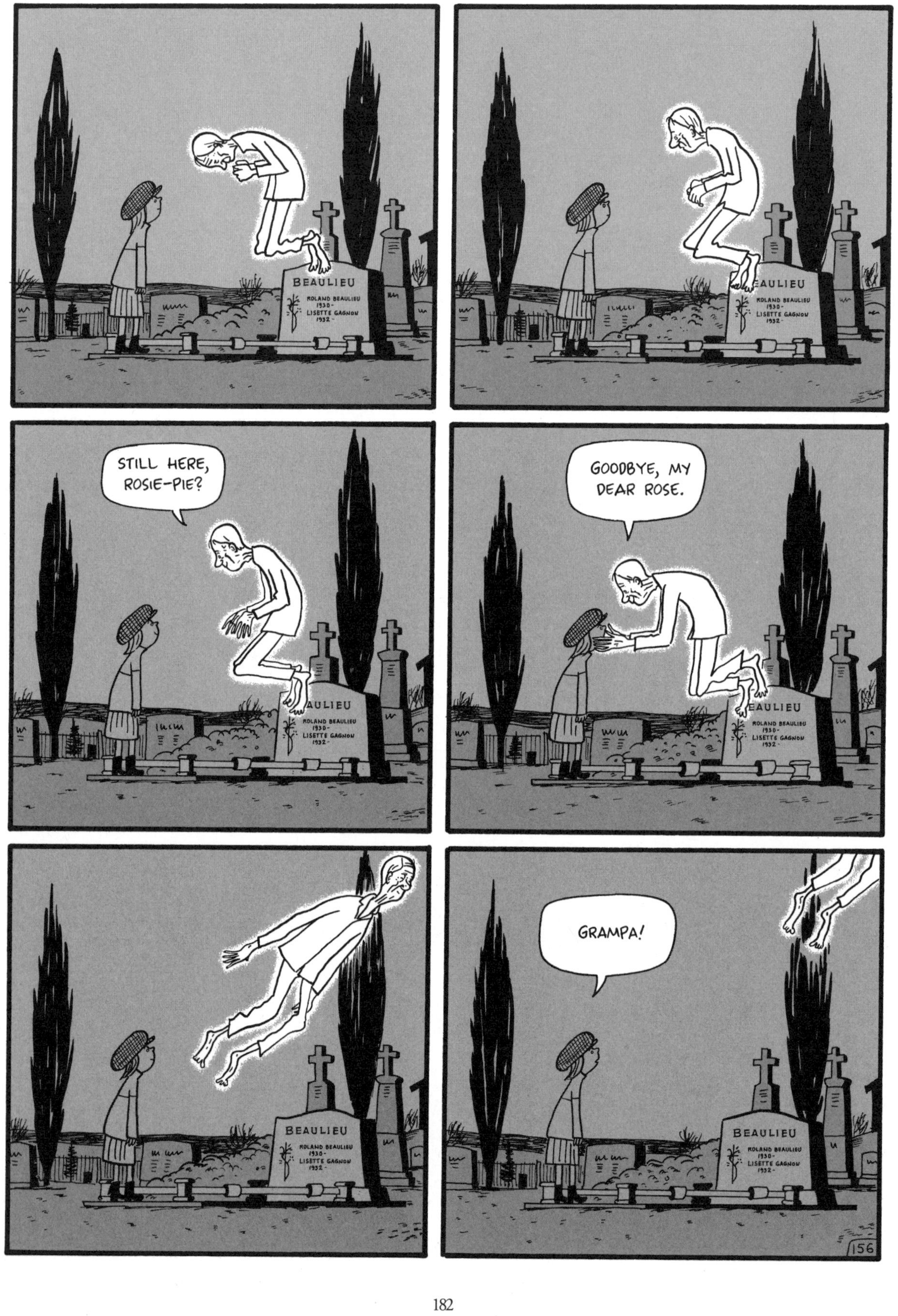
BEAULIEU
ROLAND BEAULIEU 1930-
LISETTE GAGNON 1932-
STILL HERE, ROSIE-PIE?
GOODBYE, MY DEAR ROSE.
GRAMPA!
156

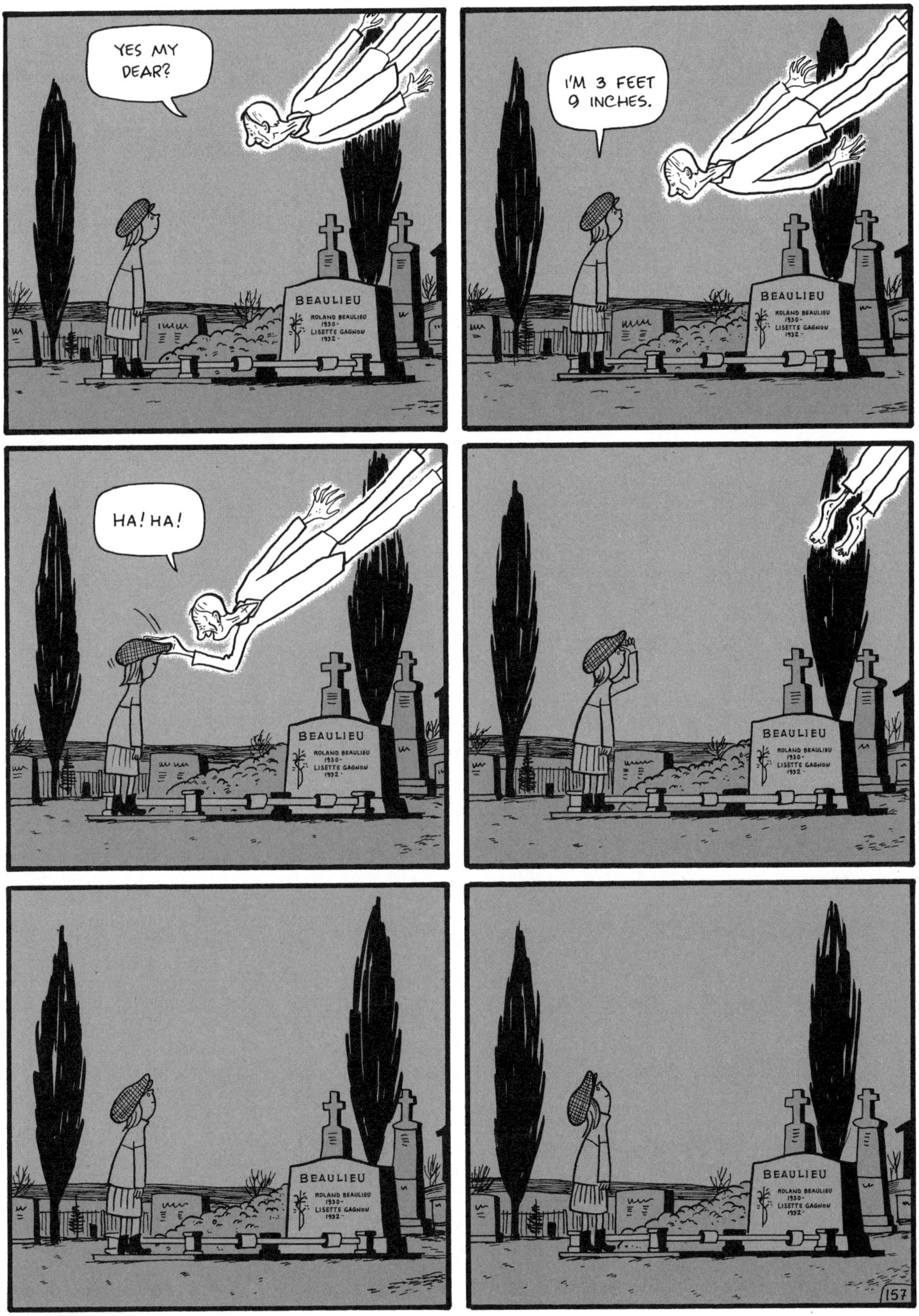
YES MY DEAR?
BEAULIEU
ROLAND BEAULIEU 1930-
LISETTE GAGNON 1932-
I'M 3 FEET 9 INCHES.
HA! HA!
157

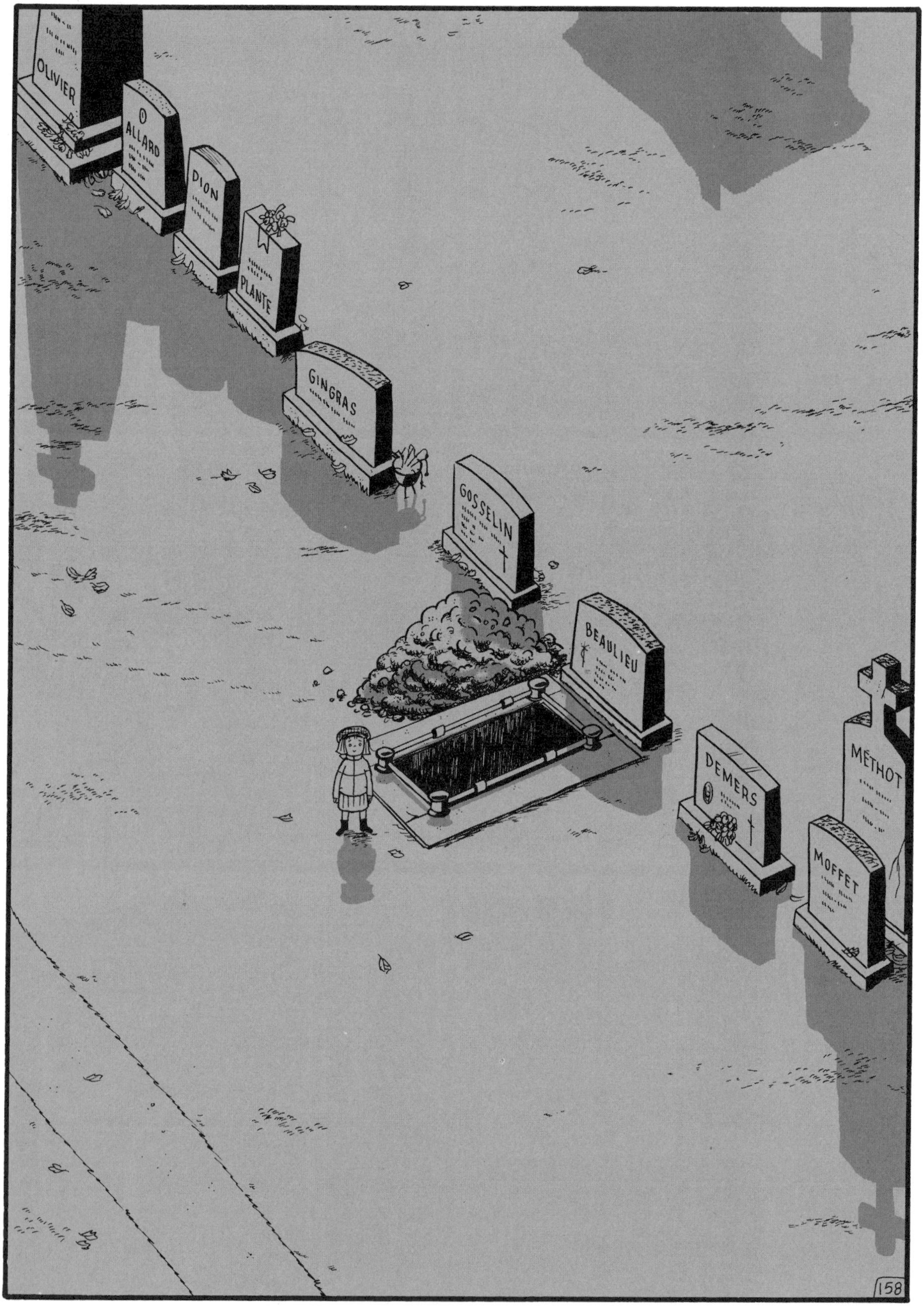
OLIVIER
ALLARD
DION
PLANTE
GINGRAS
GOSSELIN
BEAULIEU
DEMERS
MÉTHOT
MOFFET
158

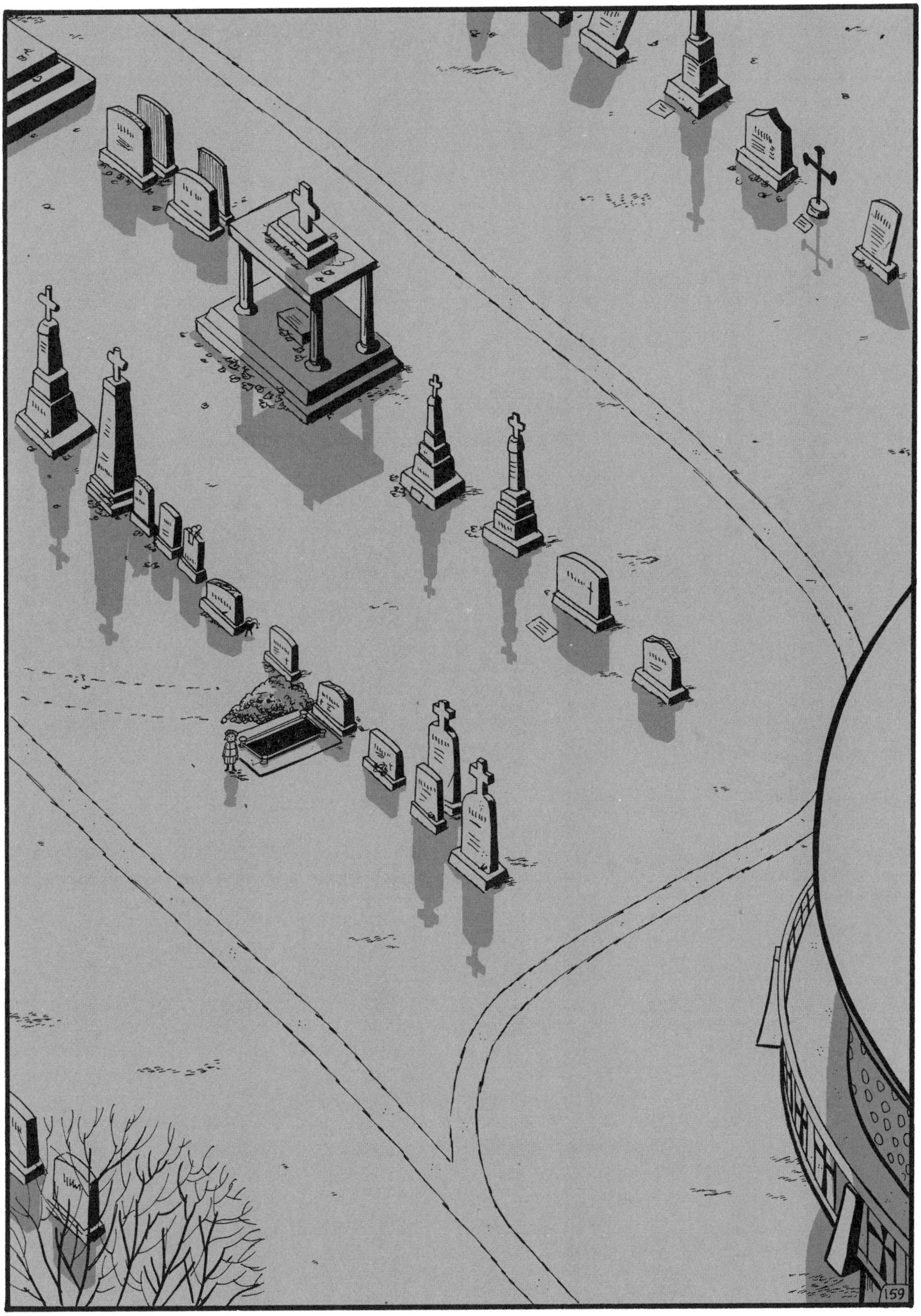
159

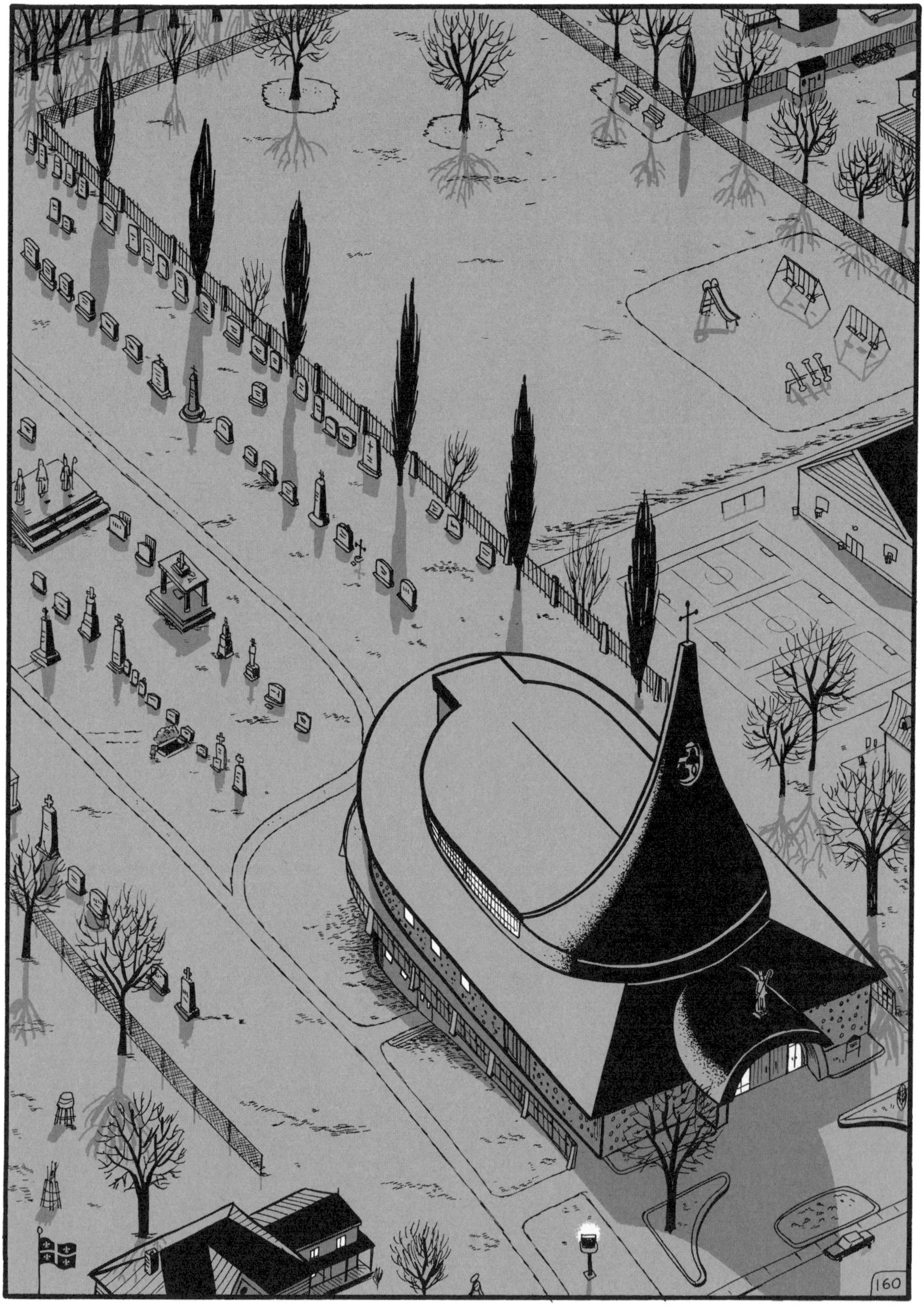
160

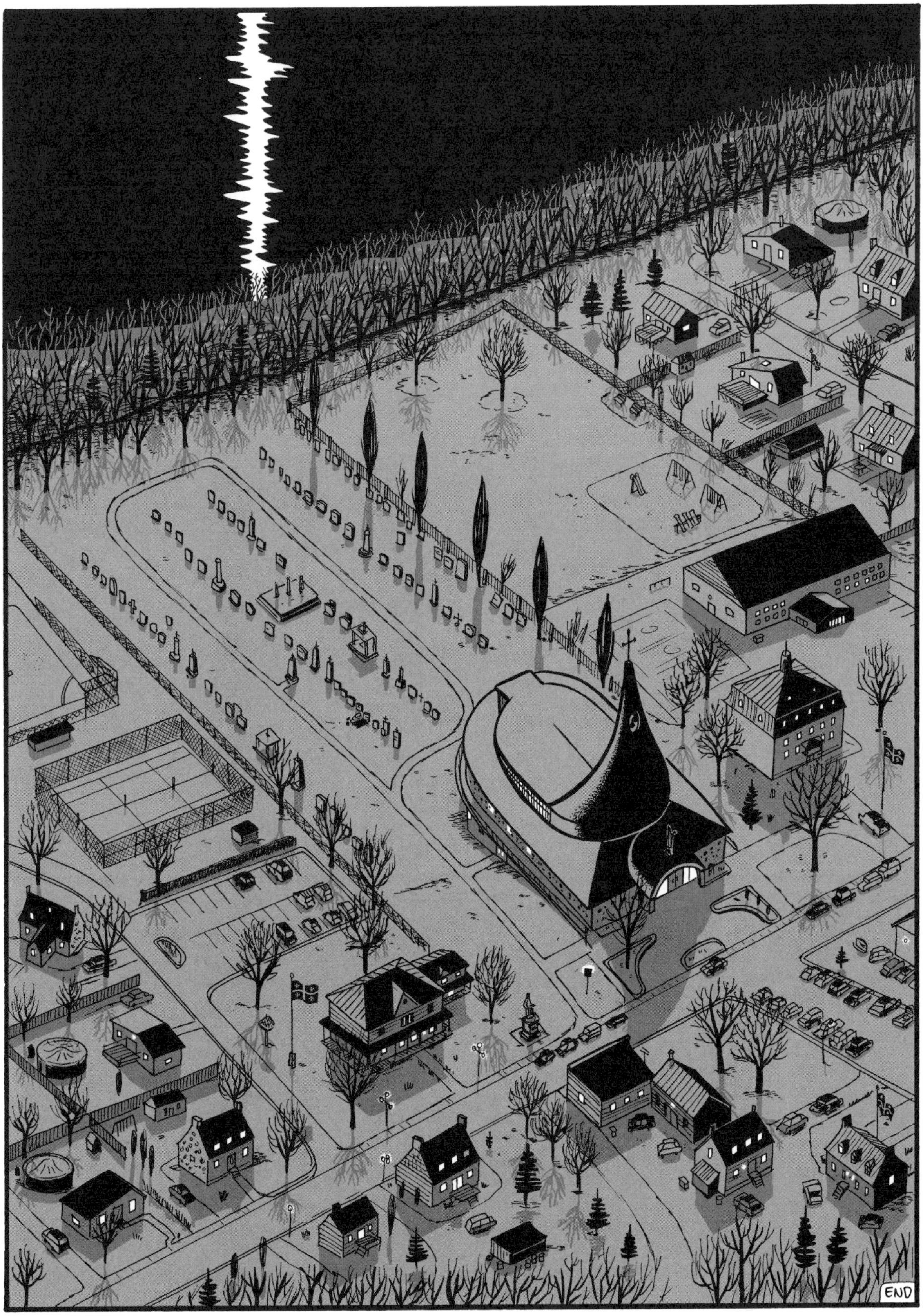
END

MICHEL RABAGLIATI - FEBRUARY 2009

Words and Music

Ave Maria
Franz Shubert, op. 52, no 6

Requiem, In Paradisum
Gabriel Fauré

L'arbre et la graine
Benoît Marchon

Just a Gigolo
1956 version recorded by Louis Prima

Nel blu dipinto di blu
[Volare]
Domenico Modugno and Franco Migliacci

Other titles in the BDANG Imprint from Conundrum Press

#1: *Hello, Me Pretty*
Line Gamache

#2: *My Life as a Foot*
Richard Suicide

#3: *Howie Action Comics*
Howard Chackowicz

#4: *Poof!*
Line Gamache

#6: *Ruts & Gullies: Nine Days in Saint Petersburg*
Philippe Girard

#7: *Suddenly Something Happened*
Jimmy Beaulieu

#8: *Killing Velazquez*
Philippe Girard

#9: *The Song of Roland*
Michel Rabagliati

#10: *Fanny & Romeo*
Yves Pelletier / Pascal Girard

BDANG

The Song of Roland

Conundrum
Greenwich, Nova Scotia, Canada
www.conundrumpress.com

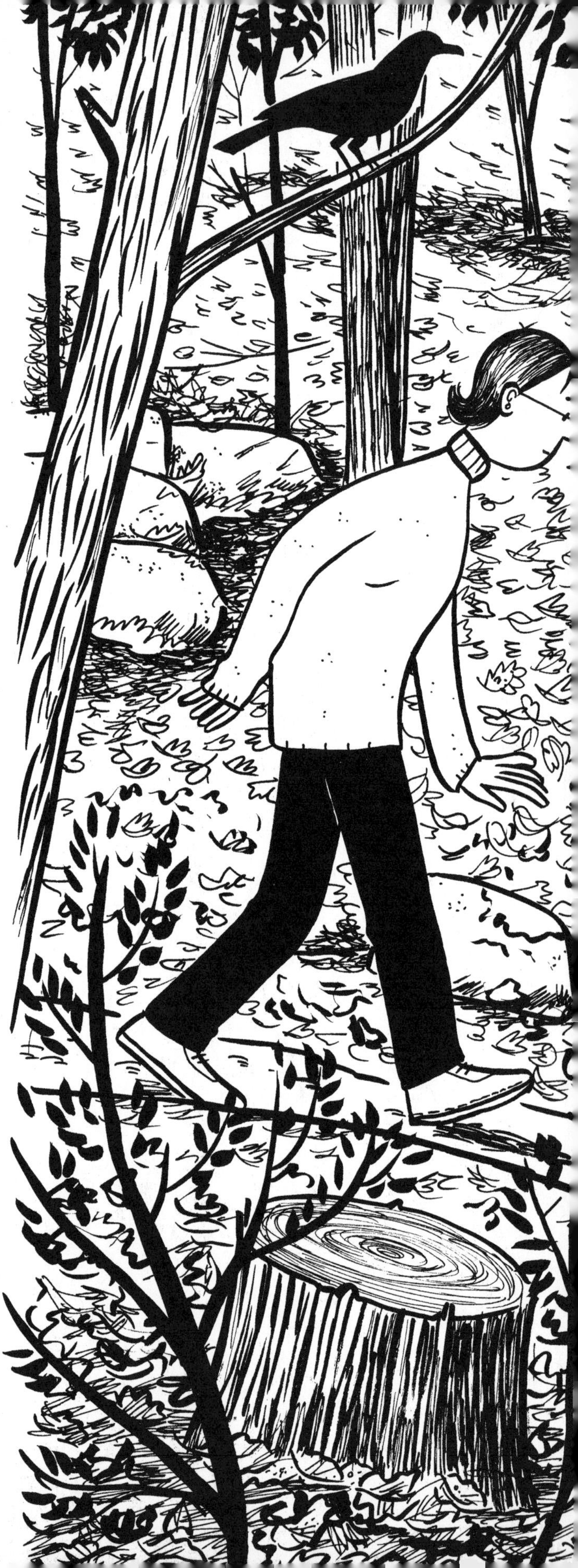